Business in a Global Economy

Les R. Dlabay
Lake Forest College

James Calvert Scott
Utah State University

SOUTH-WESTERN EDUCATIONAL PUBLISHING

Cover design by Jeff Davidson

Vice President/Editor-in-Chief:	Dennis Kokoruda
Developmental Editor II:	Nancy A. Long
Production Manager:	Carol Sturzenberger
Production Editor II:	Melanie A. Blair-Dillion
Senior Designer:	Elaine St. John-Lagenaur
Photo Editor:	Fred M. Middendorf
Marketing Manager:	Larry Qualls

Copyright © 1996

by

SOUTH-WESTERN EDUCATIONAL PUBLISHING
Cincinnati, Ohio

All Rights Reserved

ISBN: 0-538-71409-3

1 2 3 4 5 KI 99 98 97 96 95

Printed in the United States of America

I(T)P
International Thomson Publishing

South-Western Educational Publishing is an ITP Company. The ITP trademark is used under license.

Preface

Several events in the early 1990s increased the visibility of activities in our global economy. The Gulf War revealed the financial and political interdependence of nations all over the globe. Today, national boundaries and economic systems of nations in Eastern Europe continue to evolve. South Africa is pushing forward without the constraints of apartheid. The economic union of the nations of Western Europe attempts to take advantage of the strength in international unity. However, the struggles toward economic and political freedom all over the world also point out the many differences among societies, cultures, political beliefs, economic systems, and opportunities for personal growth. Companies and nations are learning to work together, while appreciating these differences.

On any given day, you can buy a book that was written, published, printed, bound, and distributed by the cooperative efforts of companies in several different countries. These companies employ hundreds of people who may speak different languages, belong to different religions, value different ideals, move at a different pace, and strive for different goals. However, global economic forces have brought them together to produce a book. The result is jobs, wages, food, clothing, housing, and health care around the world.

Business in a Global Economy is designed to help you develop the appreciation, knowledge, skills, and abilities needed to live and work in a global marketplace.

INTERNATIONAL BUSINESS COMPETENCIES

Every person has three roles in an economy: consumer, worker, and citizen. These roles involve making consumer choices, selecting a career, and making decisions that can affect the people of our world. As U.S.

companies increase international business activities, our roles as consumers, workers, and citizens expand. We need certain knowledge and skills to enhance our business education.

The content, features, and learning activities of *Business in a Global Economy* emphasize an awareness of the importance of history, geography, language, cultural studies, research skills, and continuing education. These abilities are necessary to remain up to date on changing international business situations.

CONTENT AND COVERAGE

The content and activities in *Business in a Global Economy* provide a foundation for becoming informed about international business and the global business environment. Unit 1 provides an introduction to international business activities and the economic, cultural, and political factors that affect international business. Unit 2 covers business structures, trade relations, international financial transactions, legal agreements, and global entrepreneurship.

Unit 3 presents the fundamental aspects of global business management, human resources, career planning, labor relations, and the challenges of managing global organizations. Unit 4 covers material on information systems, production activities, and computerized processes related to international business.

Unit 5 considers marketing activities and consumer behavior as they relate to developing, pricing, distributing, and promoting goods and services in a global economy. Unit 6 provides an understanding of global financial activities and managing risk for international businesses.

FEATURES OF *BUSINESS IN A GLOBAL ECONOMY*

To cover the many aspects of conducting business in our global economy, each chapter includes the following elements:

- Learning objectives provide an overview of the main topics in the chapter.
- An opening case presents a real-world situation as an introduction to chapter content.
- **Global Business Exercises** and **Global Business Examples** provide application activities and short essays that enhance and expand on the main text material.
- Figures and photos graphically portray major chapter ideas and business data.

- The **Global Highlight** is a brief insight into a particular country's culture, geography, history, or international business transactions.
- **Back to the Beginning** presents follow-up questions for the opening case.
- **Knowing Global Business Terms** reinforces your knowledge of international business terms.
- **Reviewing Your Reading** assesses your understanding of the main ideas of the chapter.
- **Expanding Your Horizons** suggests discussion questions that enrich your understanding of international business.
- **Building Research Skills** are critical-thinking activities that provide the opportunity to use research to build on relevant chapter material.
- The **Continuing Enrichment Project** presents an ongoing research assignment that can serve as a basis for portfolio assessment.

The text chapters provide the foundation for studying international business. However, *Business in a Global Economy* also offers several features that enhance the chapter content: regional profiles and appendices. Regional Profiles appear after the first chapter of each unit. These profiles explore the geography, culture, and history of the following regions of the world: North America, Asia and the Pacific Rim, Europe, Africa, Central and South America, and the Middle East.

Appendix A addresses methods for analyzing and evaluating international investment opportunities and provides some sources of investment information. Appendix B presents a series of world maps reflecting political boundaries, landforms, climates, population, time zones, and major trade organizations.

To supplement the main text, a *Student Workbook* has been developed. Each chapter in *Business in a Global Economy* has a corresponding chapter in the *Student Workbook* that includes the following:

- Chapter outline for notetaking,
- Vocabulary exercise,
- Content review exercise, and
- Student activities such as graph and map analyses, math exercises, writing activities, case problems, data charting, matching of examples and concepts, and library research.

WELCOME TO INTERNATIONAL BUSINESS

International business activities affect everyone. Consumers buy products made in countries around the world. Workers find changing employment opportunities due to international trade and global competition. And, companies everywhere compete with firms from other countries for the money spent by consumers.

Business in a Global Economy is a comprehensive textbook and instructional package that will help prepare consumers, workers, and citizens of the world for business activities, now and in the future.

Les R. Dlabay   *James Calvert Scott*
Lake Forest College   Utah State University

Contents

UNIT 3 • Managing in a Global Environment

The World of International Business

We Live in a Global Economy

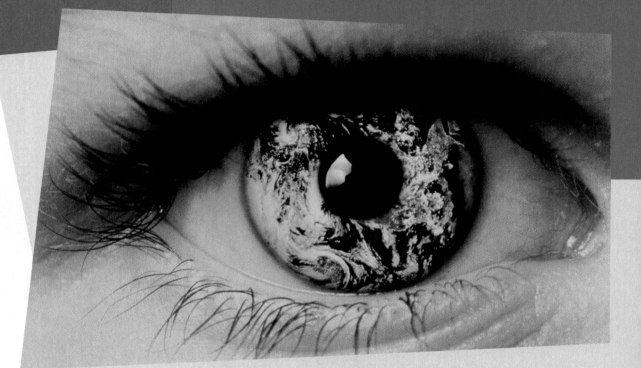

After studying this chapter and completing the end-of-chapter activities, you will be able to

- Define *international business.*
- Discuss the reasons why international business is important.
- Understand that international trade is not just a recent event.
- Describe basic international business activities.
- Explain the components of the international business environment.
- Name skills and abilities important for studying international business.
- Describe the importance of international business for workers, consumers, and citizens.

Golden Arches Around the World

If you have ever thought about having *saimin* for breakfast or a *Bolshoi Mac* for lunch, you were probably at a McDonald's restaurant in another country. Each day, millions of people eat at one of the 12,000 McDonald's restaurants around the world.

When the company started in 1955 with a limited menu (burger, fries, milk shake, and soft drinks), few people would have imagined that the organization would be serving meals in over 70 countries. When sales growth in the United States slowed, McDonald's management looked for new markets. This meant getting involved in international business.

In 1967, McDonald's opened its first restaurants outside of the United States in Canada and Puerto Rico. These were followed by openings in other nations. McDonald's, however, did not venture into Mexico until 1985. The delay was due to being unable to obtain the same quality meat as is used at its other restaurants.

McDonald's menu has been adapted to the tastes of various countries. For example, mixed spaghetti is served in the Philippines, and corn soup is available to McDonald's customers in Japan.

The company's success has not been without difficulties. In the late 1970s, political trouble in Iran resulted in the company closing its restaurants in that country. Then in early 1992, after only being open a few months, McDonald's shut down its 57 restaurants in Taiwan due to bombs exploding in or near a couple of its business locations. As McDonald's and many other companies have discovered, doing business in other countries can have its rewards and risks.

In the early days of our country, most families grew the food they ate and made the clothes they wore. As our population grew, production and distribution methods improved. People became dependent on others for goods and services. Today, we have a complex business system that makes a wide variety of items available for our use.

In many countries, however, people still labor independently to provide for their daily necessities. Most nations of the world do not have the extensive production and distribution facilities found in places like the United States, Canada, Japan, and Western Europe. While these highly developed countries have some level of economic independence, they are also dependent on other countries. For example, most of the coffee used in the United States comes from Brazil, and Japan is dependent on other countries for much of its oil.

WHAT IS INTERNATIONAL BUSINESS?

The majority of business activities occur within a country's own borders. The making, buying, and selling of goods and services within a country is called **domestic business.** Your purchase of a soft drink produced in the United States is an example of domestic business.

In contrast, if you purchase a shirt made in Thailand, you are now participating in our global economy. Even though you bought the shirt from a U.S. company, it was obtained from a foreign manufacturer. **International business** includes all of the business activities necessary for creating, shipping, and selling goods and services across national borders. International business is commonly called *foreign trade.*

WHY IS INTERNATIONAL BUSINESS IMPORTANT?

International business makes it possible for you to purchase many popular products; such as, video recorders, athletic shoes, and clothing. Without international business, you would probably have a different lifestyle. Also, people in other countries would not have goods and services created by companies in our country.

International business is important for many reasons. The following sections present the importance of international business as a source of raw materials, supplier of foreign products for resale, new market opportunity, investment opportunity, and path to improved political relations.

Source of Raw Materials and Parts

Products manufactured in this country often include raw materials and parts from throughout the world. Each year, the United States obtains oil, gas, iron, and steel from other nations for use in our factories. Also, many U.S.-made automobiles have engines, transmissions, and other parts that were manufactured in Japan, Germany, Mexico, Brazil, France, Korea, Italy, and England.

Demand for Foreign Products

A **global dependency** exists when many of the items consumers need and want are created in other countries. And, people do need and want goods and services produced in other countries. When the African country of Zimbabwe had very little rain, crops failed, farm animals died, and the nation had to buy 90 percent of its food from other countries.

New Markets for Businesses

As demonstrated in the opening case, companies sell to businesses and customers in other countries to expand business opportunities. Many businesses, large and small, increase sales and profits with foreign trade. These companies are involved with the buying and selling of products or services between countries.

Investment Opportunities

Many people invest money in businesses to earn additional funds. As companies expand their business activities in other countries, new investment opportunities are created. Investors, in hopes of earning money, also provide funds to foreign companies that are starting or growing enterprises.

Improved Political Relations

An old saying tells us that "countries that trade with one another do not have wars with one another." International business activities can help to improve mutual understanding, communication, and the level of respect among the people of different nations.

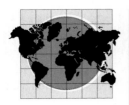

Global Business Example: The North American Free Trade Agreement

After intense debate, the United States House of Representatives passed the North American Free Trade Agreement (NAFTA). This pact unifies the United States with two of its major trading partners: Canada and Mexico. This treaty seeks long-term economic benefits associated with the formation of a free-trade zone. NAFTA eliminates taxes on goods traded among the three countries and eases the movement of goods.

NAFTA is designed to enlarge the markets and economic bases of the countries involved. Consumers should benefit by increased product variety and lower prices. Increased demand should create new employment opportunities. It is projected that the result of NAFTA could be the creation of 600,000 jobs in Mexico and several hundred thousand jobs in the United States and Canada. The benefits of the agreement are expected to outweigh the problems that might arise.

NAFTA creates a trading bloc comparable to those in other regions of the world. This economic link should help Canada, Mexico, and the United States compete effectively in the world marketplace.

We are all affected by international business. Even if business owners do not offer foreign products for sale or do not sell to companies in other countries, they are still affected. Every business competes against companies that are either foreign-owned or that sell foreign-made products. As a result, even when you may not realize it, international business is affecting your life.

WHEN DID INTERNATIONAL BUSINESS START?

As you know from your study of history, international business is not a new idea. Evidence suggests that countries such as China, India, and Japan were trading products throughout the world fifteen to twenty thousand years ago. There are also indications that people in Africa traded with people in South America several thousand years ago.

In the fifth century B.C., Greek and other middle eastern merchants were involved in foreign trade. The Roman Empire dominated international business from the second century B.C. until about the year A.D. 450. Although the next several hundred years witnessed limited international business activity, other events occurred. The Arab empire extended from Portugal and northern Africa all the way to China. The fall of this empire was followed by the rule of Charlemagne, who was crowned first Holy Roman Emperor. Norsemen and Viking explorers reached Iceland and Greenland.

The eleventh century saw renewed interest in global commercialism. European countries such as England, France, Spain, and Portugal were shipping products by water. By the fifteenth and sixteenth centuries, explorers like Columbus and Magellan sought a shorter water route to India. Instead of sailing around Africa, they ventured west. And the rest, as you might say, is history!

During the period between 1500 and 1800, several European countries established colonies in Africa, Asia, North America, and South America. These colonies provided European businesses with low-cost raw materials and new markets for selling products, often at the expense of the native inhabitants.

Most European countries maintained strong economic and political control over their colonies for years. Independence for these colonies was eventually achieved, but it took time. While the United States gained independence from England in 1776, the African country of Mozambique did not become independent from Portugal until 1975 (see Figure 1-1).

Figure 1-1
Many countries did not achieve independence until the last half of the twentieth century. Some countries are still struggling for independence.

SELECTED COUNTRIES AND THEIR COLONIAL HERITAGE

Country	Colonized by	Date of Independence
Australia	England	1901
Brazil	Portugal	1822
Cambodia	France	1953
Canada	France, England	1931
Chad	France	1960
Chile	Spain	1818
Cyprus	Greece	1960
El Salvador	Spain	1821
Iceland	Denmark	1918
Mexico	Spain	1821
Mozambique	Portugal	1975
Namibia	Germany, South Africa	1990
South Africa	England, The Netherlands	1961
United States	England	1776
Vietnam	France	1955

Various inventions created between the years 1769 and 1915 expanded interest in and opportunities for international business. Discoveries such as the cotton gin, steam engine, telephone, automobile, and airplane resulted in improved communication, distribution, and production methods and in new global industries.

Recent world events continue to point out the increasing importance of international business. Expanded trade among companies in different countries increases interdependence. World Wars I and II, the Korean War, the Vietnam War, and the Gulf War all demonstrated the need for political cooperation. However, these military conflicts limited global

Global Business Exercise: From Wisconsin to the World

In Dodgeville, Wisconsin (population 3,500), telephone operators take orders for swimsuits and sport shirts from customers in western Europe, Japan, Australia, Canada, and Mexico. The Lands' End Company sells a full line of clothing by mail, with shipments usually going out within 24 hours.

1. Why would a relatively small company (less than 1,000 employees) get involved in international business?

2. What technology made it possible for the company to be involved in international business?

3. What problems might the company encounter as a result of its international business activities?

business activities. A world at peace is important for countries to achieve economic benefits from international trade.

The economic association of western European countries, created in the early 1990s, is likely to change the way most countries do business with one another. And finally, political freedom for eastern European countries previously dominated by communism creates new global business opportunities to help emerging economies. The international business marketplace is evolving day by day.

THE FUNDAMENTALS OF INTERNATIONAL TRADE

Have you ever had lots of one item, such as sports trading cards or collectibles of some sort? A friend may have had something you wanted, so you decided to trade. You gave up some of what you had to obtain something else you wanted. That's what happens when companies in different countries trade goods or services.

These foreign *trades* usually are not an exchange of items for items. Instead, payments are usually made for the items bought or sold. For example, a manufacturing company in Korea sells radios to an electronics store in the United States. Or, a computer company in the United States sells its products to Russia.

These trade activities can be viewed from two sides—the buyer and the seller. Products bought by a company or government from businesses in other countries are called **imports.** In the previous examples, the imports are radios for the United States and computers for Russia.

From the point of view of the seller, **exports** are products sold to companies or governments in other countries. Using the same examples, Korea is exporting radios and the United States is exporting computers. Figure 1-2 on page 10 shows the flow of imports and exports for a country.

Although the process sounds simple, obstacles can arise. **Trade barriers** are restrictions that reduce free trade among countries. These barriers includes things such as import taxes that increase the cost of foreign products, restrictions on the number of imports, and laws that prevent certain products from coming into a country. Further discussion of importing and exporting activities is presented in Chapter 6, while trade barriers are covered in Chapter 4.

Global Business Example: U.S. Companies Face Trade Barriers

Japan does not allow foreign accounting firms to use their international names in advertising. Poland and Hungary impose high import taxes on products from other countries. These are some examples of trade barriers from the annual report of the U.S. Office of the Trade Representative. This federal government agency attempts to encourage other nations to reduce or eliminate trade barriers for U.S. exports. In exchange, restrictions on imports to the United States are lowered or removed. This ongoing discussion is aimed at creating a worldwide free trade environment.

Figure 1-2
Imports and exports are important factors in the health of the U.S. economy and the global economy.

IMPORTS AND EXPORTS OF THE UNITED STATES

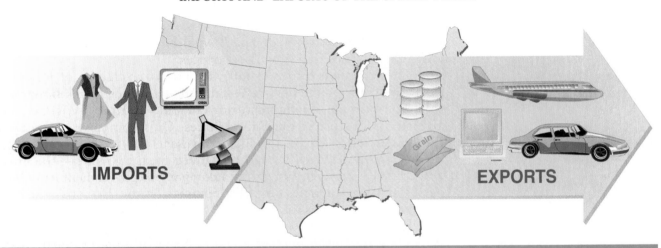

THE INTERNATIONAL BUSINESS ENVIRONMENT

The buying and selling of goods and services is rather similar in most parts of the world. Consumers try to satisfy their needs and wants at a fair price. Businesses try to sell their products at a price that covers costs and provides a fair profit. Why, therefore, is international business any different from local business?

In many parts of Iran, the exchange of goods and services takes place in an open market rather than in an air-conditioned store. Consumers in Japan buy food for their evening meal that non-Asians might not like to eat, such as raw fish. The government of England may require that television advertisements for toys costing over a certain amount include the price. In Cuba, office workers have been required to work several weeks in the farm fields to increase the supply of food.

These are examples of factors that make up the international business operating environment. As shown in Figure 1-3, the three major categories of the international business environment are cultural and social factors, political and legal factors, and economic conditions.

Cultural and Social Factors

In some societies, hugging is an appropriate business greeting. In other societies, a handshake is the custom. These differences represent different cultures. **Culture** is the accepted behaviors, customs, and values of a society. A society's culture has a strong influence on business activities. For example, many businesses are closed in the afternoon in Mexico while people enjoy lunch and a siesta (relaxing rest period).

The main cultural and social factors that affect international business are language, education, religion, values, customs, and social relationships. These relationships include interactions among families, labor unions, and other organizations. The topic of social and cultural influences on business is presented in Chapter 3.

Figure 1-3
Cultural, social, political, legal, and economic factors and conditions interact to create the international business environment.

THE INTERNATIONAL BUSINESS ENVIRONMENT

Cultural and Social Factors
- Language
- Education
- Religion
- Values and customs
- Social relationships

Political and Legal Factors
- Type of government
- Political stability
- Government policies toward business

Economic Conditions
- Type of economic system
- Natural resources
- Education level
- Types of industries
- Technology

Political and Legal Factors

Each day we encounter examples of government influence on business. Regulation of fair advertising, enforcement of contracts, and safety inspections of foods and medications are a few examples. In general, however, people in the United States have a great deal of freedom when it comes to business activities. This is not true in all countries of the world. In many places, the activities of consumers and business operators are restricted. The most common political and legal factors that affect international business activities include the type of government, the stability of the government, and government policies toward business.

Governmental and political influences on international business are discussed in greater detail in Chapter 4. Legal agreements are the topic of Chapter 8.

Economic Conditions

Every country and every individual face the problem of limited resources to satisfy needs and wants. This basic economic problem is present for all of us. We continually make decisions about the use of our time, money, and energy. In a similar way, every country plans the use of its land, natural resources, workers, and wealth to best serve the needs of its people.

Factors that influence the economic situation of a country include the type of economic system, the availability of natural resources, and the general education level of the country's population. Other economic factors include the types of industries and jobs in the country, the stability of the country's money supply, and the level of technology available for production and distribution of goods and services.

Countries with few natural resources must depend on imports. A country with well-trained workers and technology can use its resources to produce goods and services that create additional wealth. The basic concepts of international economics are presented in Chapter 2.

INTERNATIONAL BUSINESS SKILLS

By now, you might appreciate the importance of studying international business. This book will provide you with a basic knowledge of that area and help you to develop skills that you will be able to use in our global economy.

Global Highlight: Canada's Vast Natural Resources

Canada occupies more than 9.8 million square kilometers making it the second largest country in the world. With less than 2.7 people per square kilometer, compared to 26 per square kilometer in the United States, Canada is an immense haven of forests, lakes, rivers, and farmland. The country's economy is dependent on these abundant natural resources.

Canada's 3.4 million square kilometers of forests are a major source of wealth. More than 150 varieties of trees are native to Canada. Forestry-related products—such as paper, wood pulp, and timber—account for about 15 percent of the country's exports.

Commercial fishing has been a part of Canada's economy for 500 years. The Atlantic Ocean, Pacific Ocean, and the most extensive bodies of fresh water in the world make fishing an important industry. Common commercial species caught include cod, haddock, herring, salmon, lobster, scallops, and halibut.

Canada's fast-flowing rivers are also an important source of energy. The country is the world's second leading producer of hydroelectricity. Its coasts provide natural seaports in cities such as Vancouver, Halifax, and St. John. Water access through the St. Lawrence River earns Montréal, Toronto, and Québec City recognition as vital shipping ports.

Wheat—grown in the western prairie provinces of Alberta, Manitoba, and Saskatchewan—is Canada's primary farm product. Other agricultural commodities include barley, potatoes, corn, soybeans, and oats. Livestock such as beef cattle, poultry, dairy cows, hogs, sheep, and egg-laying hens are also major exports.

As a result of its natural beauty, over 40 million tourists visit Canada each year. Many of these travelers go to the cities; however, fishing, hunting, camping, and other outdoor activities are also major tourist attractions. Spending by visitors brings in over $3 billion a year to the Canadian economy.

Certain skills are needed in every type of job. For example, you must be able to read work manuals, do calculations, and write reports. These abilities will continue to be important as business activities among countries increase. Also important, however, will be skills that not everyone is emphasizing in their business education. These include the following:

- History. Your awareness of the past can help you better understand today's international business relations.
- Geography. Geography is more than names on a map. A knowledge of geography will help you appreciate how the climate and terrain of a country can affect transportation, housing, and other business activities.
- Foreign language. As countries increasingly participate in foreign trade activities, your ability to communicate effectively with people from other societies increases in importance.
- Cultural awareness skills. Understanding that cultures vary from nation to nation allows you to be more sensitive to customs and traditions of people in all societies.
- Study skills. Asking questions, taking notes, and doing library research are the tools necessary to keep up to date on changes in international business.

The text material, end-of-chapter activities, and workbook will help you improve your ability in these critical international business skills.

YOUR ROLE AS A CITIZEN, WORKER, AND CONSUMER

Earning an income, voting, and shopping represent three common roles of people in our society. As a worker, citizen, and consumer in the United States, you are involved in many business activities. These roles are expanded as our country becomes more involved in international business.

Consumer choices increase. Your choice of goods and services is no longer limited to items produced in this country. As a worker, career opportunities expand because of international business. As a business owner you are affected by international business when your competitors import or export products.

Finally as citizens, international business activities make it necessary to have an increased awareness of our world. The decisions you make are likely to affect many people in your community, state, country, and world.

THE ORGANIZATION OF THIS BOOK

As you study this book, you will build an awareness of important topics for working and living in our global economy. Each unit includes a Regional Profile, which will help to enhance your awareness of geography and social studies knowledge about the regions of the world.

Unit 1, "The World of International Business," provides an introduction to global business activities and the economic, cultural, and political factors that affect international business. In Unit 2, "Organizing for International Business," you will study business structures, trade relations, international financial transactions, legal agreements, and global entrepreneurship.

Unit 3, "Managing in a Global Environment," presents the fundamental aspects of management, human resources, career planning, labor relations, and the challenges of multinational companies. Unit 4, "Information and Production Systems for Global Business," covers material on data sources, data processing, production activities, and computerized business processes.

In Unit 5, "Marketing in a Global Economy," you will learn about marketing activities; consumer behavior; and, developing, pricing, distributing, and promoting goods for a global economy. Finally, Unit 6, "Global Financial Management," provides an understanding of financial activities and risk management in a global setting.

Back to the Beginning: Golden Arches Around the World

Reread the case at the beginning of this chapter and answer the following questions:

1. What factors prompted McDonald's to open restaurants outside the United States?

2. How have social and cultural factors affected the company's international business activities?

3. What risks has the company faced when opening restaurants in other countries?

4. What actions would you suggest for McDonald's to continue to be successful in international business?

KNOWING GLOBAL BUSINESS TERMS

The following terms should become part of your business vocabulary. For each numbered item find the term that has the same meaning.

- culture
- domestic business
- exports
- global dependency
- imports
- international business
- trade barriers

1. Products sold to companies or governments in other countries.
2. People need and want goods and services produced in other countries.
3. The business activities necessary for creating, shipping, and selling goods and services across national borders.
4. The making, buying, and selling of goods and services within a country.
5. Products bought by a company or government from businesses in other countries.
6. The accepted behaviors, customs, and values of a society.
7. Restrictions that reduce free trade among countries.

REVIEWING YOUR READING

Answer these questions to reinforce your knowledge of the main ideas of this chapter.

1. How does domestic business differ from international business?
2. Why is international business important?
3. What are some examples of international business activities that occurred before 1800?
4. What are imports and exports?
5. What is a trade barrier?
6. What are the three main parts of the international business environment?
7. How does culture affect international business activities?
8. What are the main factors that influence the economic conditions of a country?
9. What skills are important for someone who wants to be successful in an international business career?

10. How does international business affect you as a consumer, worker, and citizen?

You will not find the complete answers to the following questions in your textbook. You will need to use your critical-thinking skills. Think about these questions, gather information from other sources, analyze possible responses, and discuss them with others. Then, develop your own oral or written response as instructed by your teacher.

1. Explain how both domestic and international business activities create jobs.
2. What are some examples of our global dependency on other countries?
3. How do investments by a company in a foreign country help the economies of both nations?
4. What actions might a country take to encourage exporting of goods and services?
5. For what reasons might a country use trade barriers?
6. How might religious beliefs affect international business activities?
7. How could a country's type of government affect its business activities?
8. Why would a country with many natural resources have the potential for a strong economy?
9. What actions could you take to improve your history, geography, foreign language, cultural awareness, and study skills?

BUILDING RESEARCH SKILLS

The ability to find information from various sources is an important international business skill. The following activities will help you investigate various topics. You will also learn to apply class ideas to situations outside of the classroom.

1. Prepare a poster that shows examples of domestic business and examples of international business.
2. Conduct a survey of students and others about their knowledge of international business. Prepare a list of 8 or 10 questions on

the geography, culture, and economies of different countries. Ask 10 people to answer the questions. Determine the topics on which people are most informed and least informed, and write a one-page summary of your findings.

3. Do library research and prepare a short paper about how an event has affected international business. Suggested topics could include early Chinese trade with other areas of the world; business activities of merchants in ancient Greece; the European colonization of Africa, Asia, South America, and North America; the Industrial Revolution; World War I; World War II; the creation of the European Community; or, the political freedom of Eastern European countries.

4. Interview a local business person who imports or exports products. Obtain information on the procedures used to import or export merchandise.

5. Obtain an international economics article from the business section of a newspaper. Prepare a short written or oral summary of the information in the article.

6. *Global Career Activity.* Based on newspaper and magazine articles, advertisements, and product packages, prepare a list of international business job opportunities. What types of skills are needed for an international business career?

Continuing Enrichment Project: Creating an International Business Resource File

To help you learn about international business relationships, each chapter will conclude with a continuing activity. This instructional experience is designed to build knowledge and skills from chapter to chapter. The first activity involves the creation of an international business resource file that you will use and build on in future assignments.

Start a file of articles and information on (1) a country and (2) a company involved in international business. Obtain information related to the geography, history, culture, government, and economy of the country. For the international company file, include a list of products sold in different countries, examples of ways the company adapted to different societies, and other information about its foreign business activities.

Sources of information to create your file may include the following:

• reference books such as encyclopedias, almanacs, and atlases;

• current newspaper articles from the news, business, and travel sections;

- current news and business magazine articles including news stories, company profiles, and advertisements;
- materials from companies, airlines, travel bureaus, government agencies, and other organizations involved in international business; and,
- interviews with people who have lived in, worked in, or traveled to the country.

Present a short oral report (two or three minutes) about the country and company you selected. Tell the class about an example or situation involving international business. Plan to add to your file throughout the course, as these materials will be used for other chapter projects.

Regional Profile

North America

The year is 1392, 100 years before the arrival of Columbus. You are a 16-year-old Aztec woman, and it is your wedding day. Your city has a population of 100,000, and it sits on the site of present-day Mexico City. Your father is a merchant; your mother cares for the house and the younger children. Your older brother recently finished school, and he is training for a military career.

The houses in your neighborhood are adobe, and each has a courtyard containing a sauna that is surrounded by beautiful flowers. The man whom you are about to marry designs streets, canals, and irrigation systems for the city. This evening you will be carried on the back of an older woman to the groom's house while burning pine branches light the way. While sitting before the hearth, your partner's tunic will be tied to your blouse as a symbol of the union. After a festive meal, the two of you will spend four days alone in prayer.

The vast land that we now call North America was discovered and settled by people who probably migrated to Alaska from Asia. Over a period of 30,000 years, more groups arrived and gradually built a variety of civilizations in this Western Hemisphere. The foregoing Aztec example is just one Native American culture in which you could have been born. You could have lived among the Leni-Lenape of the eastern woodlands or on the plains with the Arapaho; or you might have raised a family in the great complexes built by the Anasazi in cliffs near the Grand Canyon. There were hundreds of cultural groups spread throughout the continent—each with its own unique language, religion, government, and customs. Which Native Americans once had communities where you live?

The Norwegians explored North America in the tenth and eleventh centuries; however, they had little effect on the native cultures. Explorers and settlers from Spain, Britain, France, Holland, and Sweden arrived in great numbers during the sixteenth and seventeenth centuries, bringing with them cultures that conflicted with those they met. The native population decreased quickly as a result of the battles and the diseases carried by the newcomers. And, so began a great cultural transformation—a destructive and creative process that continues today. Europeans came as soldiers, farmers, trappers, artisans, and merchants to help build colonies for their mother countries. Some came to escape religious or political persecution; conversely, others came to force their religion on the natives. Why do you think Columbus receives most of the credit for "discovering" North America?

Wars were fought to establish control over these valuable lands that held great resources. The Mexicans fought a war for independence from Spain. In 1810, Miguel Hidalgo y Costilla, a priest, set off the Mexican War of Independence among poor natives and mestizos (of mixed native and European ancestry). Although Miguel Hidalgo y Costilla soon died, José María Morelos y Pavón, also a priest, continued to lead the movement that declared independence in 1813. Morelos was captured and shot, but Mexico did form a republic in 1824.

The French lost control of Canada to the British in 1763; however, the French heritage is still very evident throughout Canada and most especially in the province of Québec. Over the next 100 years under the British Crown, the Canadian assemblies gradually won power without a war. In 1867 the Dominion of Canada was established and in 1931 Canada became a completely independent nation.

The United States won its independence from Britain through a treaty signed in 1783. Immigrants came to the new country from all over the world. Some stayed in the eastern cities and worked in the textile mills, while many others headed west with wagon trains hoping to build a new life in Kentucky, Ohio, California, and all the territories in between. How do you think the geographical features of the United States influenced the settlement of the West?

The economies of the West Indies and the southern United States depended on labor that was supplied by the violent importation of Africans to be used as slaves.

"The shrieks of the women and the groans of the dying rendered it a scene of horror almost inconceivable. . . . I began to hope that death would soon put an end to my miseries."[1] Olaudah, an Ibo man describing his trip to North America in 1756.

Some historians believe that the "New World" would not have developed without slavery, for it produced both labor and product. Colonial America thrived on this slave labor. After the United States outlawed the slave trade, it continued to flourish illegally to satisfy the demands of the cotton plantations. By 1860, the South was producing three quarters of the world's supply of cotton.

After the Civil War, Chinese, Japanese, Mexican, Irish, German, and Italian immigrants joined former slaves and Union and Confederate veterans to work in factories and fields. Together, they created the world's most powerful industrial economy.

Canada's earliest immigrants came from France, Britain, Ireland, and Scotland; but in the twentieth century, Russians, Ukrainians, and Germans were attracted to the western prairies. As occurs in the United States, more recent immigrants to Canada are Asian and Latin American.

Canada's 3.8 million square miles of territory is second in size only to Russia. Over 26 million people are concentrated near Canada's southern border with the United States.[2] The cold Northlands hold exquisite natural environments and few inhabitants. Canada's abundance of natural resources and manufacturing industries have produced a high standard of living for most of its people; however, its service industries create most new jobs. How do you think Canada has influenced the culture of the U.S. and vice versa?

Mexico is the largest Spanish-speaking country in the world. Its population is growing by 2 1/4 percent each year. Since 1950, land reform and a growing manufacturing base have increased incomes for a large number of Mexicans. Many, however, still live in extreme poverty. And, it is these people who often attempt to cross illegally into the United States with the hope of finding work.

Mexico's economic growth has centered on its silver, industrial minerals, and petroleum products. The country's white beaches and Aztec ruins attract tourists from all over the world.

All of the nations of continental North America and the West Indies have developed unique cultures that combine the diverse richness of Native Americans, Europeans, Africans, and Asians. Although conflicts still exist, the future of these societies depend upon the mutual appreciation of this diversity.

---

[1] *Newsweek,* Fall/Winter, 1991, p. 66.

[2] *Statistical Abstract of the United States, 1991,* Washington, DC, 1991.

Our Global Economy

After studying this chapter and completing the end-of-chapter activities, you will be able to

- Describe the basic economic problem.
- List the steps of the decision-making process.
- Explain the factors that affect price and cause inflation.
- Name the three main factors of production.
- Understand how different countries make economic decisions.
- Describe three levels of economic development.
- Discuss economic principles that explain the need for international trade.
- Identify various measures of economic progress and development.

A New Economic Direction for Mexico

In the early 1980s, Mexico had several economic difficulties. Its government created many barriers to international trade. This decision resulted in fewer foreign companies wanting to do business in Mexico, which, of course, meant fewer jobs for the people.

The government created programs to help those without jobs. This state assistance cost money, much of which the Mexican government had to borrow. As the years went by, the government was using more and more of its money to pay back the loans. Little money was left to spend on public services.

One problem lead to another until the country decided to take a new course of action. Mexico took the following steps toward economic reform:

- opened the trade system to allow foreign businesses to produce and sell goods and services in Mexico;

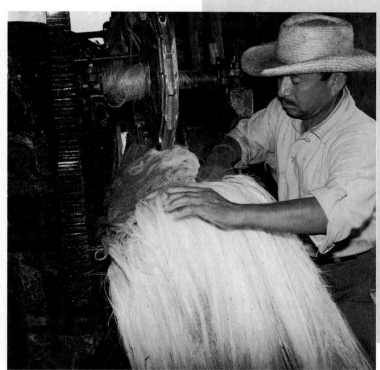

- reduced government spending and created programs that served only the neediest people in the country;
- sold several government-owned businesses that were operating at a loss and costing the taxpayers money; and
- worked out a new plan to reduce the amounts owed to other countries.

The Mexican government chose actions to help the country better compete in the global marketplace while also improving the economic situation of its citizens. In recent years, Mexico has experienced improved economic conditions. The prices of goods in the country have not increased as quickly as in the past. International business activities have expanded to create more jobs and higher incomes for Mexican workers.

Each day people throughout the world make economic decisions. For example, selecting what to have for lunch is an economic choice. Choosing whether to buy a shirt or a compact disc is an economic choice. As you make choices, you are probably not able to obtain everything you want. This is the basis of economics.

Chapter 2   Our Global Economy

23

THE BASIC ECONOMIC PROBLEM

We are all limited by the amount of time and money we have available to acquire the many things we would like to have. Countries as well as individuals are limited in the resources they have available. As a result, decisions are necessary to make the best use of resources.

Scarcity refers to the limited resources available to satisfy the unlimited needs and wants of people. As you well know, this is a situation faced by all people and all nations. A country must decide whether to grow its own food or to import agricultural products while workers produce other items. The choices made by an individual, a company, or a country are affected by many factors. The study of how people choose to use limited resources to satisfy their unlimited needs and wants is called **economics.**

Economics can be one of the most exciting topics you will ever study. A knowledge of economics can help you understand why some people earn more than others and why certain items cost more at different times of the year. Economic principles can explain why business managers select one choice over another.

MAKING ECONOMIC DECISIONS

People and countries cope with scarcity by making decisions. Every time you decide how to use your time, money, and energy, you are making an economic decision. Companies and nations also have to make choices.

The Decision-Making Process

One way to help you make economic choices is with the decision-making process. Using the steps shown in Figure 2-1 can help you make wiser decisions and get the best use of your resources. This process can help you make faster and better choices. Saving time when selecting the best choice is something most people want.

The steps of the decision-making process are as follows:

1. Define the problem—What do I need or want?
2. Identify the alternatives—What are the different ways my problem can be solved?
3. Evaluate the alternatives—What are the advantages and disadvantages of each of the different choices I have available?
4. Make a choice—Based on the advantages and disadvantages, which would be my best choice? Can I live with the consequences of that choice?
5. Take action on the choice—What needs to be done to put the decision into action? Do it.

Figure 2-1

The decision-making process helps individuals, companies, and nations make wiser economic decisions.

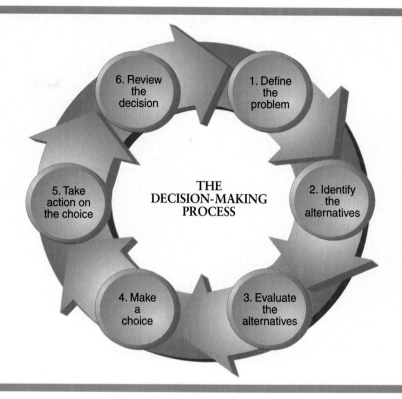

THE DECISION-MAKING PROCESS

1. Define the problem
2. Identify the alternatives
3. Evaluate the alternatives
4. Make a choice
5. Take action on the choice
6. Review the decision

6. Review the decision—Did your decision solve the problem? As time goes by, what different actions might be necessary? Were there consequences you did not predict when you evaluated the alternatives?

Decision Making in Action

How do companies use the decision-making process? An example of economic decision making for international business could involve a company in the United States that wants to increase the sales of its product. The problem is How can the Benson Electric Company continue to increase its sales over the next five years? At present, the company only sells its radios and other home audio products in the United States.

Possible alternatives for the Benson Company to solve this problem are

- increase advertising in the United States to attract more customers;
- reduce prices to attract more customers in the United States;
- sell products by mail to customers in other countries;
- ship products to other countries to sell in stores; and
- set up production plants to produce and sell products in other countries.

Each of these choices has benefits and costs. The process of evaluating these options involves comparing the risks and costs of each alternative. In addition, Benson must consider the expected increase in sales for each alternative. For example, reducing prices may increase the number of customers, but could reduce the total dollar sales. Or, the cost of building factories in another country may be greater than the money earned from additional radio sales. Once the Benson Company selects a course of action, it probably will not be able to choose other alternatives.

Every time a choice is made, something else is given up. **Opportunity cost** is what is given up when a choice is made. In your own life, a decision to go to college, for example, will mean you will not be able to use your time and money for something else. This decision to continue your education, however, is likely to benefit you throughout your life.

Finally, the Benson Company must put its choice into action. Then over the weeks, months, and years that follow, the company should continue to see if this decision needs to be changed or if other decisions need to be made. Remember, decision making is a continuing part of life.

Global Business Exercise: International Business Decisions

For each of the following international business situations, (1) describe the problem and (2) list two or three alternatives that the company could take to solve the problem:

a. A food company is having trouble selling its frozen products in other countries because it is very expensive to transport frozen foods.

b. A computer store is losing business to a competitor. The competitor is selling imported software at a very low price.

c. Buyers of a tool exported to Bermuda are not following the safety directions and some consumers are being injured.

PRICE AND THE CHANGING VALUE OF MONEY

Price is one of the most visible economic factors we encounter every day. The amount paid for goods and services results from economic decisions made by consumers, businesses, and governments. Daily economic decisions affect us in many ways. For example, if people rent many videos, more stores will make tapes available. In addition, more jobs will be available for people working in video stores. If consumers no longer want to purchase a certain movie on video, the availability or price of that item will decrease.

Price-Setting Activities

Have you ever noticed that when something has limited availability and many people want to buy it, the price increases? If many people want to buy tickets for a hockey game or jazz concert, for example, ticket prices are likely to go up. When freezing temperatures destroy the fruit blossoms and reduce the number of oranges available, prices also go up.

The opposite is true, too. If a musical group is no longer popular, the prices of its tapes, CDs, and T-shirts are likely to go down. The price system is a method of balancing unlimited needs and wants with limited resources.

Determining prices involves two main elements—supply and demand. **Supply** refers to the amount of a good or service that businesses are willing and able to make available at a certain price. The supply of an item tends to go up when producers see an opportunity to make money. For example, a few years ago only a couple of companies made baseball and other sports cards for collecting. As these cards became more popular, other companies got involved in the sports cards business.

Supply also works the other way. If companies can no longer make money producing an item, some will get out of that business. As video replaced film, most companies that made film projectors for schools and libraries went into other types of businesses. The supply of film projectors declined.

On the buyer's side is **demand,** which is the amount of a good or service that consumers are willing and able to purchase at a certain price. In general, as demand increases, the price of an item goes higher. As previously mentioned, demand for tickets to a sports event or concert will result in higher prices of admission to those events. Lower demand usually means lower prices. For example, near the end of the summer, swimsuits are usually at their lowest prices.

As shown in Figure 2-2 on page 28, as price declines, the demand for an item increases (note the downward sloping line marked *D*); this

Figure 2-2

The point where supply equals demand is known as the market price.

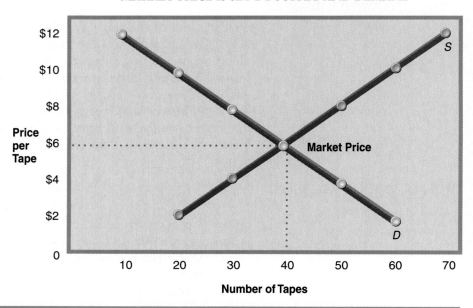

MARKET PRICE IS SET BY SUPPLY AND DEMAND

Price per Tape / Number of Tapes

is called *the law of demand*. For example, at a price of $12, 10 tapes are demanded; but if the price is $2, 60 tapes are demanded. On the supply side (the *S* line), higher prices mean a greater supply since businesses can make a larger profit. At a price of $2, 20 tapes are offered for sale; while at $8, 50 tapes are available.

The point at which supply and demand are equal is called the **market price**. Where is the market price in Figure 2-2? At a price of $6 sellers are willing to offer 40 tapes and consumers are willing to buy 40 tapes. The market price, therefore, is $6. This point is also known as the *equilibrium price*. While supply and demand in the real world do not work as neatly as on the graph shown, market forces do cause prices to rise and fall.

Changing Prices

As you probably know, prices are continually changing. The price of a gallon of gasoline over the past 25 years has gone from less than 50 cents to almost two dollars, depending on supply and demand. When the supply of oil (used to make gasoline) was threatened during the 1991 Gulf War, for example, gasoline prices went up. As hostilities lessened, prices dropped.

A common economic concern is continually rising prices. An increase in the average prices of goods and services in a country, known as **inflation,** means people cannot buy as many goods and services. Inflation is an indication of the buying power of a country's monetary unit—such as the U.S. dollar, the British pound, or the Japanese yen.

Inflation has two basic causes. First, when demand exceeds supply, prices go up. This is called *demand-pull inflation.* It can occur in countries when a government tries to solve economic problems by printing more money. The increased demand comes from the additional currency in circulation. A similar situation can occur if people increase borrowing for spending. Again, demand exceeds supply and prices tend to rise.

The other main type of inflation is *cost-push inflation.* This occurs when the expenses of a business (such as the cost of salaries or raw materials) increase. These operating costs result in a higher price charged by the company.

While the United States and Canada have had some periods of high inflation, other countries have experienced more extreme situations. Consumer prices in Peru, for example, increased by 400 percent in one month during the early 1990s. This means an item costing one Peruvian sol at the start of the month, would cost 400 sol by month's end—making the currency virtually worthless. The government had to take drastic action to solve the country's inflation problems.

Global Business Exercise: Supply and Demand in Action

For each of the following situations, tell (1) how supply or demand of the product would be affected and (2) if the price of the product item would go up or down as a result.

   a. New machinery allows faster production of automobiles.
   b. A medical report declares that certain foods are not as healthy as previously believed.
   c. Consumers want to buy products that bear the name and picture of a popular movie star.
   d. Rainstorms damage agricultural products to be used for food.

Every country makes economic decisions. These choices provide a basis for solving the basic economic problem—unlimited needs and wants but limited resources. The production of goods and services is a primary activity to satisfy the needs and wants of consumers.

You might have a business idea to produce a new food product that is healthful, tastes good, and is easy to pack in lunches. To start a company to make this product would require several elements. These elements are called the **factors of production,** and refer to the three types of resources used to produce goods and services. As shown in Figure 2-3, the factors of production include the following:

1. Natural resources (also called *land*). These are the raw materials that come from the earth, from the water, and from the air. Iron ore, gold, agricultural products, silver, rivers, and oxygen are examples of natural resources. These items are used in the production of goods and services used by individuals, businesses, and governments.

2. Human resources (also called *labor*). These are people who work to create goods and services. While technology has changed or eliminated certain tasks previously performed by people, new types of work are continually being created.

3. Capital resources (also called *capital*). These are buildings, money, equipment, and factories used in the production process. These items are expensive and are used over several years by business organizations.

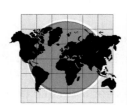

Global Business Example: Factors of Production for Fast-Food Companies

McDonald's and Kentucky Fried Chicken were joined by Burger King, Arby's, and Wendy's in selling their products to the consumers of Mexico. Each of the companies combined money, buildings, and equipment (capital resources) with beef, chicken, and wheat (natural resources) and hired local workers (human resources) to provide meals at their restaurants. Some of the most popular locations for the fast-food restaurants were Acapulco, Cancún, Tijuana, and suburban Mexico City.

Figure 2-3

The factors of production are used individually or in combination to produce the goods and services in any economy.

FACTORS OF PRODUCTION

Natural Resources

Human Resources

Capital Resources

TYPES OF ECONOMIC SYSTEMS

Every nation makes use of its factors of production to create goods and services for its people. The way in which these resources are used differs from country to country. The economic choices of a country relate to three basic questions:

1. What goods and services are to be produced?
2. How should the goods and services be produced?
3. For whom should the goods and services be produced?

Every country must decide how to use its productive resources to answer these three basic economic questions. An **economic system** is the method a country uses to answer the basic economic questions. Nations organize for production and distribution of goods and services based on customs, political factors, and religious beliefs.

Economic systems can be categorized based on ownership of resources and government involvement in business activities. The three common types of economic systems are command, market, and mixed economies.

Command Economies

Throughout history, many nations decided to answer the basic economic questions by using central planning. In a **command economy,** the government or a central-planning committee regulates the amount, distribution, and price of everything produced. The productive resources of the country are also owned by the government. Cuba is one of the few remaining countries that use a command system of economic decision making.

In some command economies, consumers have very few choices of products to buy. A government agency even decides what jobs people are to have. As of 1994, examples of such command economies included China and North Korea.

Market Economies

In contrast to command economies where all of the decisions are made by the government, market economies are based on the forces of supply and demand. **Market economies** are those in which individual companies and consumers make the decisions about what, how, and for whom items will be produced. This economic system, also called **capitalism,** has the following characteristics:

- Private property—Individuals have the right to buy and sell productive resources, including ownership of a business enterprise.
- Profit motive—Individuals are inspired by the opportunity to be rewarded for taking a business risk and for working hard.
- Free, competitive marketplace—Consumers have the power to use their choices to determine what is to be produced and to influence the prices to be charged.

Since market economies have minimal government involvement with business, they are commonly called *free enterprise systems* or *private enterprise economies*. Since every country has some governmental regulations affecting business activities, no perfect market economies exist. The United States, although not a pure market economy, is one of the best examples of this type of economic system. Despite strong government involvement in the country's business activities, the Japanese economy is also best labeled as a market economy.

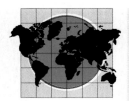

Global Business Example: Public Services Going Private

In recent years, many countries have decided to let private companies buy and operate various government-owned businesses. For example, the Mexican government sold control of the country's telephone company, airlines, and banks to private companies. This action helped to save the country tax dollars. The businesses also became more profitable. Privatization was also very popular in the countries of Eastern Europe in the 1990s as they changed from command to market economies.

Mixed Economies

Many economies are a blend between government involvement in business and private ownership. This is known as a **mixed economy.** For example, some countries have publicly-owned transportation companies, communication networks, or major industries. **Socialism** refers to economies with most basic industries owned and operated by government. However, individuals are usually free to engage in other business opportunities and free to make buying choices. In recent years, examples of socialist countries include Sweden and France.

In changing from a command economy to a market economy, a country may sell government-owned industries to private companies. This process of changing an industry from publicly owned to privately owned is called **privatization.** In recent years, local governments in the United States have hired private companies to provide services such as trash collection, landscaping, road repairs, and fire protection.

ECONOMIC DEVELOPMENT

In addition to type of economic system, countries can be categorized by their level of economic development. A country's level of economic development is influenced by the following:

- Literacy level—Countries with better education systems usually provide more and better goods and services for their citizens.
- Technology—Automated production, distribution, and communications systems allow companies to create and deliver goods, services, and ideas quickly.
- Agricultural dependency—An economy that is largely involved in agriculture does not have the manufacturing base to provide citizens with a great quantity and high quality of product.

Industrialized Countries

The nations with the greatest economic power are usually those with many large companies. An **industrialized country** is a country with strong business activity that is usually the result of advanced technology and a highly educated population. Such countries have attained a high level of industrialization with a high standard of living for their residents. Population is centered in large cities and suburbs rather than in rural areas.

Another factor that supports international trade in industrialized countries is infrastructure. **Infrastructure** refers to a nation's transportation and communications systems. A country such as Germany—with its efficient rail system, high-speed highways, and computers—is better prepared for international business activities than many other nations with a weaker infrastructure.

Industrialized countries are actively involved in international business and foreign trade. A portion of the wealth of these nations is the result of successful business activities throughout the world. Countries commonly described as industrialized include Canada, England, France, Germany, Italy, Japan, and the United States.

Less-Developed Countries

Many countries of the world have a very low standard of living. A **less-developed country (LDC)** is a country with little economic wealth and an emphasis on agriculture or mining. Most LDCs have an average annual income per person of less than $4,000. This compares to the United States with an average annual income per person of more than $20,000.[1]

As a result of low incomes in less-developed countries, citizens often cannot afford adequate housing, food, and health care. This situation results in a high death rate among newborns, a shorter life expectancy than in other countries, and potential for political instability. Examples of LDCs include countries such as Bangladesh, Bulgaria, Chad, Ecuador, Ethiopia, Hungary, Kenya, Liberia, Nepal, Nigeria, Pakistan, Peru, and the Philippines.

Future economic development for less-developed countries presents a challenge for all nations. Industrialized countries should consider assisting LDCs with the problems of poor health care, limited natural resources, low literacy rates, low levels of employment skills, shortage of investment capital, and uncertain political environments. As these obstacles are overcome, all countries will benefit.

Global Highlight: The Founder of Black History Month

Each February we celebrate the contributions of African Americans. Black History Month was the idea of Dr. Carter Godwin Woodson, the son of former slaves, who was born in 1875 in New Canton, Virginia. As a young boy, Woodson was only able to attend school a few months of each year. The rest of the year he worked in the coal fields of West Virginia. Despite this hardship, Woodson earned a bachelor's degree from Berea College and went on to earn a Ph.D. from Harvard in 1912.

Woodson's many contributions to education include serving as supervisor of a school in the Philippines; serving as a dean at Howard University and West Virginia State College; and teaching French, Spanish, English, and history in the District of Columbia. Despite this success, Woodson gave up his educational career in 1922 to devote his energies to developing materials and programs focusing on the experiences of African Americans. This effort resulted in the publication of 20 books—including *The Negro in Our History, The Negro Church,* and *The Miseducation of the Negro.* In 1926, Woodson started Negro History Week, which was later expanded and renamed Black History Month.

Dr. Carter G. Woodson made sure that everyone would know about the important role that Africans and African Americans have played in the history of the United States and in the history of the world.

---

[1] *World Development Report, 1991.* Oxford University Press for The World Bank, 1991.

Developing Countries

Between the extremes of economic development are the **developing countries** that are evolving from less developed to industrialized. These nations are characterized by improving educational systems, increasing technology, and expanding industries. These factors result in an increasing national income. Examples of developing countries include Brazil, India, Singapore, South Korea, Taiwan, and Thailand. Figure 2-4 summarizes the factors that affect a country's level of economic development.

THE ECONOMICS OF FOREIGN TRADE

In the past, economies were viewed solely in terms of national borders. With international trade expanding every day, these boundaries are no longer completely valid in defining economies. Countries are interdependent upon each other and so are their economies. Consumers have come to expect goods and services from around the world, not just from suppliers in their own country.

Buying and selling among companies in different countries is based on two economic principles. **Absolute advantage** exists when a country can produce a good or service at a lower cost than other countries. This situation usually occurs as a result of the natural resources or raw materials of a country. For example: South American countries have an

Figure 2-4
Nations vary in their levels of economic development.

LEVELS OF ECONOMIC DEVELOPMENT

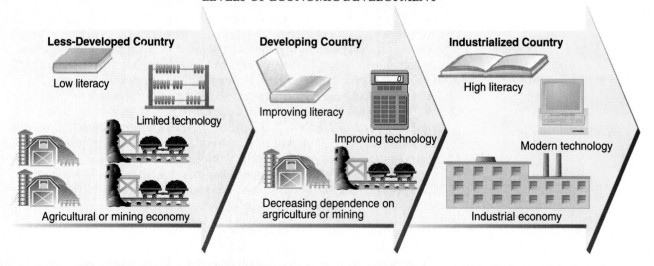

absolute advantage in coffee production; Canada, in lumber sales; and Saudi Arabia, in oil production.

A country may have an absolute advantage in more than one area. If so, it must decide how to maximize its economic wealth. A country, for example, may be able to produce both computers and clothing better than other countries. The world market for computers, however, might be stronger. This means the country would better serve its own interests by *producing* computers and *buying* clothing from other countries. This is an example of **comparative advantage,** a situation in which a country specializes in the production of a good or service at which it is relatively more efficient.

MEASURING ECONOMIC PROGRESS

As with sports, economics is concerned with the score of the game. Various business measures are used to evaluate and analyze the economic condition of a country.

Measure of Production

Gross national product (GNP) measures the total value of all goods and services produced by the resources of a country. GNP usually is reported on a yearly basis. It includes production in other countries using resources of the country whose GNP is being measured.

In recent years as international business has become more important, gross domestic product has become a more common measurement of economic activity. **Gross domestic product (GDP)** measures the output of a country within its borders, including items produced with foreign resources. For example, the GDP of the United States would include automobile manufacturing in the United States by foreign-owned companies.

Since all nations have different populations, comparing total GNP or GDP is not always meaningful. To help business people compare the economic progress of countries, they use a *per capita* comparison, which refers to an amount per person. The per capita GNP of the United States is total GNP divided by the number of people in our country. Figure 2-5 shows per capita GNP in U.S. dollars for selected countries.

International Trade Activity

An important measure of a country's international business activity is balance of trade. **Balance of trade** is the difference between a country's exports and imports. When a country exports (sells) more than it imports (buys), it has a favorable balance of trade. This is also called a *trade surplus*. However, if a country imports more than it exports, the nation has an unfavorable balance of trade or a *trade deficit* (see Figure 2-6).

Figure 2-5

Per capita GNP can be used to compare economic output among nations.

PER CAPITA GNP FOR SELECTED COUNTRIES

Country	Per Capita GNP in U.S. Dollars
Iceland	$24,031
Japan	23,730
United States	21,974
Canada	19,600
Italy	18,420
Sweden	15,700
France	14,600
New Zealand	12,555
Israel	11,296
Kuwait	10,500
Greece	5,605
Brazil	2,500
South Africa	2,380
Mexico	2,165
Thailand	1,160
India	400
China	320

Figure 2-6

In 1990, Canadian exports were greater than imports and the country enjoyed a favorable balance of trade (surplus). Mexico, however, experienced an unfavorable balance of trade (deficit) because it imported more than it exported.

BALANCE OF TRADE FOR CANADA AND MEXICO

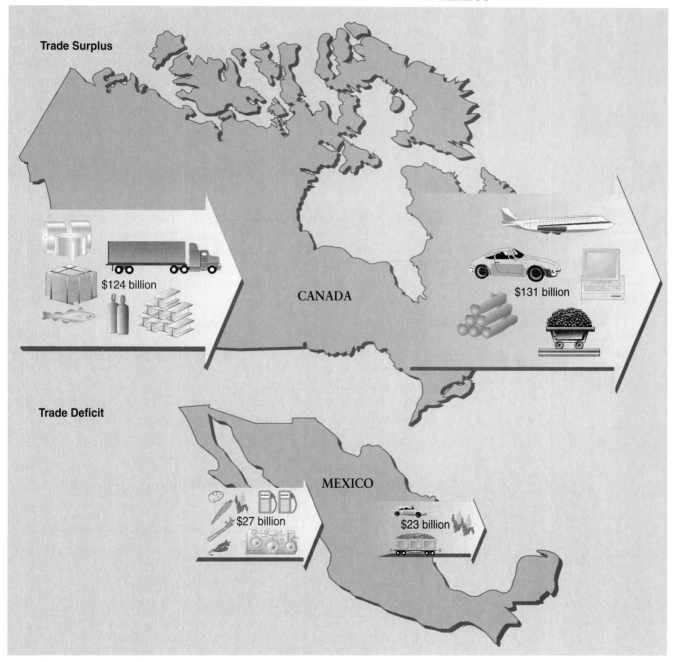

Source: *The World Almanac and Book of Facts 1992.* Scripps Howard Company, New York, 1991

In the process of doing international business, payments must be made among businesses in different countries. Since different nations have different monetary units, a comparison of the value of currencies is required. The **foreign exchange rate** is the value of one country's money in relation to the value of the money of another country. Each day in the business section of major newspapers, you can see the changing value of currencies for different countries. Balance of trade and foreign exchange will be discussed further in Chapters 6 and 7.

When you buy more than your current income allows, you go into debt. In the same way, when a country continually has an unfavorable balance of trade, it owes money to others. **Foreign debt** is the amount a country owes to other countries. While owing money to others will affect a country in several ways, the largest effect on the economy is that the nation must use future income to pay for current and past spending. This limits the funds available for improving a country's infrastructure and for providing services for its citizens in the future.

Other Economic Measurements

As previously discussed, inflation refers to general increases in prices in a country. In the United States, inflation is measured by the **consumer price index (CPI)**. The CPI is a federal government report published by the Bureau of Labor Statistics. Each month data are provided on price levels for various products and services in different regions of the country. This information can help consumers and business managers make buying decisions.

A final indicator of a country's economic situation is the unemployment rate. When people are not earning an income, they cannot purchase needed goods and services. This leads to other people losing their jobs. The result is a weaker economy. For any country to operate efficiently, a constant flow of money must be in circulation. When this monetary flow slows down, the economic potential of a nation is not realized.

Back to the Beginning: A New Economic Direction for Mexico

Reread the case at the beginning of this chapter and answer the following questions:
1. What factors created economic difficulties for Mexico?
2. Explain how the actions taken by the government helped the country's economy.
3. What future economic problems could occur in Mexico?

KNOWING GLOBAL BUSINESS TERMS

The following terms should become part of your business vocabulary. For each numbered item find the term that has the same meaning. (Not all terms are used.)

- absolute advantage
- balance of trade
- capitalism
- command economy
- comparative advantage
- consumer price index (CPI)
- demand
- developing countries
- economics
- economic system
- factors of production
- foreign exchange rate
- foreign debt
- gross domestic product (GDP)
- gross national product (GNP)
- industrialized country
- infrastructure
- inflation
- less-developed country (LDC)
- market economy
- market price
- mixed economy
- opportunity cost
- privatization
- scarcity
- socialism
- supply

1. The difference between a country's exports and imports.
2. A situation that exists when a country specializes in the production of a good or service at which it is relatively more efficient.
3. The study of how people choose to use limited resources to satisfy their unlimited needs and wants.
4. The amount of a good or service that businesses are willing and able to make available at a certain price.
5. The process of changing an industry from public to private ownership.
6. The limited resources available to satisfy the unlimited needs and wants of people.
7. The amount of a good or service that consumers are willing and able to purchase at a certain price.
8. The method a country uses to answer the basic questions of what to produce, how to produce it, and for whom to produce it.
9. A measure of the productive output of a country within its borders, including items produced with foreign resources.
10. The monthly federal government report on inflation.
11. The amount a country owes to other countries.
12. A measure of the total value of all goods and services produced by the resources of a country.

13. A nation's transportation and communications systems.

14. The three types of resources used to produce goods and services.

15. A country's ability to produce a good or service at a lower cost than other countries.

REVIEWING YOUR READING

Answer these questions to reinforce your knowledge of the main ideas of this chapter.

1. What is the basic economic problem?

2. What are the steps of the decision-making process?

3. Why does every decision have an opportunity cost?

4. What is supply? What factors affect the supply of a good or service?

5. How does consumer demand create inflation?

6. What is cost-push inflation?

7. What examples can you give of the three factors of production? List them.

8. What are the basic economic questions?

9. What are the three main types of economic systems? Describe them.

10. Why is infrastructure important to the economic development of a country?

11. What are the characteristics of industrialized countries?

12. What are some of the characteristics of less-developed countries?

13. What is the difference between absolute advantage and comparative advantage?

14. What does gross domestic product (GDP) measure?

15. How does a country's balance of trade affect its foreign debt?

EXPANDING YOUR HORIZONS

You will not find the complete answers to the following questions in your textbook. You will need to use your critical-thinking skills. Think about these questions, gather information from other sources, analyze possible responses, and discuss them with others. Then, develop your own oral or written response as instructed by your teacher.

1. Describe situations of people, companies, and nations facing the basic economic problem of scarcity.

2. Explain how a person goes through the decision-making process many times a day without thinking about the specific steps.

3. If the demand for a product in our society is high, what are some things that happen to reduce that demand?

4. Give examples of capital resources that are used by business organizations to produce goods and services.

5. If you were creating an economic system for a country, what traits would you want it to have? Explain your answer.

6. What problems may arise when a government decides to sell government-owned businesses to private companies?

7. How are people in all countries affected by poor economic conditions in less-developed countries?

8. Name a famous person who is able to do something better than anyone else. This is an absolute advantage. Now, for an example of comparative advantage, describe a person who does several things well but selects only one of these talents to make a living.

9. What actions could a country take to improve its balance of trade?

10. What factors could affect the value of a country's currency compared to the value of the currency of another country?

BUILDING RESEARCH SKILLS

The ability to find information from various sources is an important international business skill. The following activities will help you investigate various topics. You will also learn to apply class ideas to situations outside of the classroom.

1. Find an article that tells about changes in prices. Explain how supply and demand influence these prices.

2. Prepare a poster or display that shows how the factors of production are used to create a specific product.

3. Prepare a research report on a less-developed country. Describe ways in which that nation could improve its economic development and the quality of life for its citizens.

4. *Global Career Activity.* Find a recent news article that deals with a change in the economy as a result of international business. Describe how the events in the article could affect the supply and demand for certain international jobs.

Continuing Enrichment Project: Economic Conditions Around the World

Obtain data on GDP or GNP, per capita income, balance of trade, and unemployment for six countries for the past three years. Choose two less-developed countries, two developing countries, and two industrialized countries. (Include the country you chose in Chapter 1.) Use the *World Almanac, Statistical Abstract of the United States,* or other reference materials to obtain your data.

Find additional information about each country. Locate the countries on a world map or globe. Try to picture their climates, geography, and neighbors. What is it like to live in each of the countries? What natural resources are available? What type of economic system operates in each country: command, market, or mixed? What is the literacy rate in each country? Do most of the population live in an urban or a rural setting?

Prepare four graphs: one that compares GDP or GNP for the countries over the past three years, one that compares per capita income, one that compares balance of trade, and one that compares unemployment.

Prepare a written report that answers the following questions. Include your graphs as part of the report.

1. How has the level of economic development changed in recent years for less-developed countries? For developing countries? For industrialized countries?

2. What do these changes mean for countries involved in international business?

3. Are GDP (GNP), per capita income, balance of trade, and unemployment related to each other in any way? If so, how are they related?

4. How could a company involved in international business use this information to make better company decisions?

Cultural Influences on Business

After studying this chapter and completing the end-of-chapter activities, you will be able to

- Define *culture.*
- Explain how cultures and subcultures influence business.
- List six components of social organization and briefly explain each one.
- Explain which languages are most useful for international business.
- Identify and explain five major types of values that vary from culture to culture.
- Describe the two major reactions to cultural differences.

WALT DISNEY COMPANY ADJUSTS TO FRANCE

When the Walt Disney Company developed its Euro Disneyland in France, bridging cultures was a major goal. Many of the French disliked the introduction of popular U.S. culture into their country. They believed that this foreign culture present in Euro Disneyland would threaten French culture. Disney had not experienced this kind of opposition when it developed a theme park in Japan.

In response, Disney used a variety of strategies. It pointed out that Disney was of French descent: the name originally was D'Isigny. The company agreed to use French as the primary written language for theme park signs and designed several new attractions with French and other European cultural themes for Euro Disneyland. Disney also slightly relaxed its strict dress code for cast members (employees). Although males still are not allowed facial hair, females can wear redder nail polish than in the United States.

To maintain its U.S. traditional family image, Euro Disneyland initially refrained from selling liquor in the theme park. However after significant losses due to weak attendance, Euro Disneyland decided to sell champagne, beer, and wine at its upscale restaurants. These beverages are commonly sold at entertainment businesses throughout Europe, which has a different attitude about alcohol than does the United States.

In Chapter 1, you learned that a culture reflects the accepted behaviors, customs, and values of a society. In other words, it sets the boundaries of what you can and cannot do. In this chapter you will learn how culture affects business.

CULTURAL INFLUENCES ARE IMPORTANT

A **culture** is a system of learned, shared, unifying, and interrelated beliefs, values, and assumptions. *Beliefs* are statements about the nature of a person, thing, or concept. *Values* are the positive and negative ideals, customs, and institutions of a group. *Assumptions* are statements that are taken for granted as fact. Cultural beliefs, values, and assumptions are directly and indirectly acquired throughout a lifetime. They are accepted and valued by other members of the group. They cause group members to respond in similar and usually predictable ways. Put another way, culture is a mind-set or a way of thinking that is acquired over time. To members of a particular culture, their ways are logical and reasonable. To outsiders, their ways sometimes seem otherwise.

A culture is the sum of a group's way of life. Some—but not all—of the parts are discussed and recorded. Some parts of culture are taught in homes, in schools, in religious institutions, and at work. Still other parts are learned indirectly through experiences. Members of cultural groups often do not share their cultures willingly with outsiders.

A culture is like an iceberg; you can readily see only the tip. Most of the beliefs, values, and assumptions of a culture are hidden beneath the surface just as most of the iceberg is hidden beneath the water. You can easily see such objects of a culture as clothes, foods, and vehicles. You can read a culture's literature and hear its music. You can also observe the behaviors of its members. However, these items alone do not make a culture. Hidden away are unseen but important parts of culture. These include the supporting expectations, attitudes, values, beliefs, and perceptions of its members.

Global Business Exercise: Mirror, Mirror on the Wall

You are a member of a culture that has a system of learned, shared, unifying, and interrelated beliefs, values, and assumptions. You have been brought up to be what you are. Examine yourself in the mirror. Reflect on the cultural programming that has made you what you are.

1. Identify and explain one belief that shapes your behaviors.
2. Identify and explain one value that shapes your behaviors.
3. Identify and explain one assumption that shapes your behaviors.

CULTURES INCLUDE SUBCULTURES

A **subculture** is a subset or part of a larger culture that *may* have values, beliefs, and assumptions that are at variance with the larger culture of which it is a part. You are a member of many different subcultures. You are a member of the general U.S. culture, but you are also a member of some of its component groups. You are a member of the student subculture. You are also a member of the male or the female subculture. You are a member of an ethnic-based subculture. And, you may identify with various other subcultures, as well. However, you are not a member of some U.S. subcultures because you don't meet the requirements. For example, high school students are not members of the senior-citizen subculture because of their age.

Subcultures often choose from the allowable behaviors within their respective general cultures. For example, music is part of the general U.S. culture. However, not all U.S. subcultures choose to listen to the same music. The adolescent subculture generally prefers heavy metal, technopop, or rap music. The adult subculture generally prefers contemporary, jazz, or classical music.

Influences of Cultures and Subcultures

Cultures and subcultures are important because they influence the actions of their members. *Cultural baggage* is a term that describes the idea that you carry your beliefs, values, and assumptions with you at all times. Your cultural baggage influences how you respond to others. In business settings your cultural baggage influences what you say and do as you transact business. What are the personal beliefs, values, and assumptions that make up your cultural baggage?

Cultures and subcultures set the standards against which behaviors are judged. Consequently, people behave in ways that are acceptable to other members of their culture and subculture. You have learned through experience that, if you behave in unacceptable ways, members of your culture will let you know. If you are rude to your parents, for example, they may discipline you. If you insult your friends, they may not ask you to join them in future activities. If you steal a car, you may receive a jail sentence. The influences of cultures and subcultures on the behaviors of individuals are quite strong.

Subculture of U.S. Business

The *U.S. business subculture* is composed of the business-related part of the general U.S. culture. This business subculture has certain beliefs, values, and assumptions that differentiate it from the general U.S. culture. With some exceptions, business people share a core of common beliefs, values, and assumptions that shape their behaviors. These common behaviors allow U.S. business to be transacted in predictable ways.

Many of the important beliefs, values, and assumptions of the U.S. business subculture appear in common sayings. Such sayings are used by cultural groups to preserve and to transmit to others important guiding principles. Figure 3-1 lists several of the sayings of the U.S. business subculture. Can you think of some other common sayings with business-related meanings?

Variations in Business Subcultures Worldwide

Just as the U.S. business subculture has its own peculiar set of beliefs, values, and assumptions, so do other business subcultures. Consequently, no two business subcultures share *identical* sets of beliefs, values, and assumptions. However, when two general cultures are similar, their business subcultures are apt to be similar as well.

Why do you think the United States trades extensively with Canada and the United Kingdom? One reason is that the business subcultures of these countries are somewhat similar. These similarities cause U.S., Canadian, and British people to conduct business in somewhat similar ways. Less trade occurs between U.S. and Chinese or Kenyan businesses because their business subcultures are much different.

It is impossible for people to escape from the influences of business subcultures around the world. These subcultures are powerful; they shape the personal and professional behaviors of businesspersons

Figure 3-1
These common sayings reflect some widely held beliefs, values, and assumptions of the U.S. business subculture.

SOME GUIDING PRINCIPLES OF U.S. BUSINESS

Global Business Example: Let's Shake Hands

When Amy was transferred to the Montréal office of her employer, she was intrigued by some of the differences she observed. One was the way her Canadian colleagues shook hands. They did so somewhat differently than Amy and the other people from the U.S. did. When introduced to new people and when needing to be merely polite, the Canadians barely gave a handshake at all. When they wanted to be neutral, they shook hands firmly with a moderate grip and several pumps. When they wanted to suggest warmth or friendship, they shook hands more firmly with a stronger grip and a number of pumps. "Who would have thought that handshakes could communicate so much?" Amy thought to herself. "Are there other subtle differences between Canadians and U.S. citizens that I'm overlooking?" she wondered.

everywhere. Your behavior in the business world will be guided by the allowable behaviors of the U.S. business subculture. Other business subcultures will operate with different sets of beliefs, values, and assumptions. Becoming aware of these cultural differences is the first step toward understanding them and their influence.

CULTURAL INFLUENCES AFFECT SOCIAL ORGANIZATION

Cultures and subcultures influence the ways in which societies organize themselves. Social organization includes the relationships between the family unit and the culture's education, gender roles, family-work relationships, mobility, and class system. These components affect not only the entire society, but also its many institutions—including the business community.

Family Units

Most societies are at least partially organized around family units. A **nuclear family** consists of a parent or parents and unmarried children living at home. Most developed countries have societies organized around nuclear families. An **extended family** consists of the parents, children, and other relatives living together. Other relatives might include married children, grandchildren, the parents' parents, the brothers and sisters of the parents, and others. Many less-developed countries have societies organized around extended families.

Education

The family unit provides the early education of its younger members. It instructs the young in the ways of life of the culture. In advanced societies the family often shares responsibilities for providing later education with other cultural institutions. Religious groups often provide moral and spiritual education. Schools provide formal education, which prepares people to function productively as members of a society. Businesses sometimes provide specialized work-related education and training. This upgrades the job-related skills, knowledge, and attitudes of employees.

Families and their societies decide what types and amounts of education will be made available to members. In the United States, you have many opportunities to receive different types and amounts of education. One reason that U.S. business is so successful is that its workers are well educated and trained.

Gender Roles

In most cultures family members are assigned different roles to fulfill. Sometimes, these roles are assigned based upon gender. In some cultures only males or females are allowed to fill certain roles. In some societies females are the primary workers outside the household. In others, males are the primary workers away from home. In still other societies, both males and females are employed outside the home.

Viewpoints vary worldwide about the roles males and females may fill in business. Some business subcultures seem to favor males over females in the workplace. In the United States, women theoretically have equal workplace opportunities with men. In practice, however, women have sometimes had fewer opportunities for advancement. Today, U.S. women increasingly participate in international business as equals with men.

In Japan, native women have traditionally had very inferior workplace opportunities when compared to men. Japanese women rarely participate in the international business activities of Japanese companies except as translators and interpreters. In Libya, women have almost no workplace opportunities. They do not participate in international business activities.

Family-Work Relationships

Family ties to business are weak in some cultures and strong in others. In Canada, the United States, and most northern European countries, links between family and business are weak. Fairly often, there is no connection at all. However in most of the remainder of North and South America, much of southern Europe, most of Asia, northern Africa, and the Middle East, family ties to business are strong. Most often, employees of businesses—especially smaller ones—in these areas are family members. It is difficult to separate family from business. Figure 3-2 identifies some countries that have weak ties and some that have strong ties between family and business.

Figure 3-2

In certain parts of the world ties between family and business tend to be weak; whereas in other parts of the world, the ties are very strong.

TIES BETWEEN FAMILY AND BUSINESS

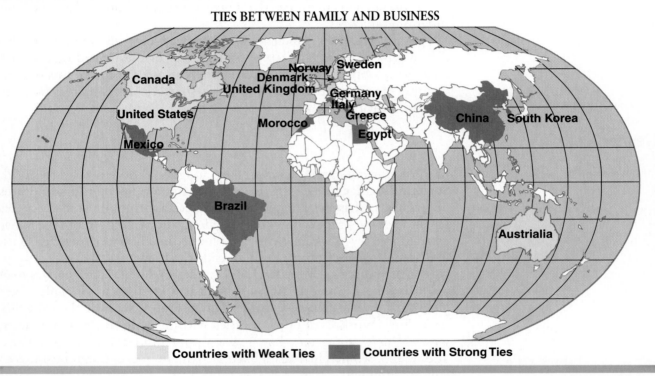

Mobility

Some cultures, such as the dominant one in the United States, have relatively little geographic attachment. In other words, the family members are not usually tied to their current location. They are mobile, willing to relocate for better employment opportunities. In some other cultures the ties to birthplace or region are much stronger. Members of these cultures would almost never consider moving away.

People from cultures who would not consider leaving their region permanently are sometimes temporarily willing to move elsewhere for better work opportunities. For example, guest workers from The Philippines are common in many countries of the Middle East. Guest workers bring their native culture with them. Sometimes their culture conflicts with that of the host country. Some host cultures do not make adjustments for guest workers. Other host cultures try to ensure that guest workers are treated similarly to native workers.

Class System

Cultures also organize their members beyond the family unit. A **class system** is a means of dividing the members of a cultural group into various levels. The levels can be based upon such factors as education, occupation, heritage, conferred or inherited status (e.g., nobility), or income. In some cultures you can move from one class to another. This is true to some extent, for example, in the United States, where the class system is weak. Sometimes, the levels are based upon your lineage. Then you are locked into your class. It is very difficult or impossible for you to change classes.

In the United Kingdom, for example, your bloodline still influences to a significant degree your class and occupational choices. If you are born into the British aristocracy, you belong to the highest class. If you work, you might oversee your family's property and fortune. However, you probably would not engage in trade. That would be considered beneath your privileged position. To the rest of British society, nobility is not a factor and people shift class levels to a lesser degree than in the United States.

Global Business Exercise: The Great Class Divide

Historically the United Kingdom of Great Britain and Northern Ireland has had a rigid class system dominated by the hereditary monarchy. Its royalty and other members of the aristocracy (nobility) have enjoyed special privileges not available to other citizens. In contrast, the United States, once a British colony, has no clearly delineated hereditary aristocracy—although family prominence is a factor in certain regions. Its flexible class system often allows individuals to shift from one class to another. All citizens are theoretically considered to be equal and entitled to the same privileges.

1. Why does the United States not have a reigning king or queen like the United Kingdom?
2. What fundamental principle in the United States requires that the class system be flexible, at least theoretically?
3. Why do you think that there are attempts in the United Kingdom to break down some of the barriers of its class system?

COMMUNICATION ACROSS CULTURES

All cultures and subcultures use languages to cross cultures. Languages facilitate the transaction of international business. Without languages, there would be no way to conduct business.

"Mr. Walter K. Flagg, Apex Corp., Detroit, Michigan, U.S.A. Dear Mr. Flagg: We are always very nice hearing from you. Your delighted letter which we receiving of you... pile it on thick. They really eat up this broken English..."

Language Differences

Many languages are used for business purposes. Nevertheless, English is widely considered to be the language of international business. More people use English to transact international business than any other language. However, it is not the language spoken by the most people in the world. That distinction belongs to Mandarin (a Chinese language). Figure 3-3 shows the numbers of native speakers of major world languages.

As a language for conducting business, English has some advantages over other languages. It contains many words drawn from other tongues, and ideas can be expressed in many ways. It also has a large number of business-related words. Further, English can be concise and precise. Often, it takes fewer words to send the same message in English than to send it in other major languages. For example, the French version of a message may be 20 percent longer than the English version. The Spanish may be 30 to 40 percent longer than the English. The Russian may be 35 percent to 50 percent longer than the English.

Figure 3-3

Most of the world's citizens are not native speakers of English, the accepted language of international business.

TWELVE MAJOR WORLD LANGUAGES

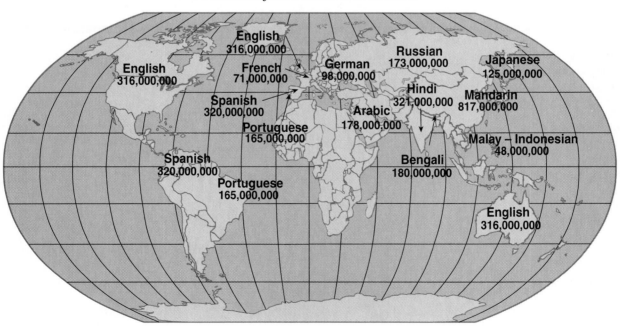

Source: *The World Almanac and Book of Facts,* 1993, s.v. "The Principal Languages of the World."

Learning a Second Language

Being a native speaker of English is both an advantage and a disadvantage. It is an advantage because you already know the major language of international business. It is a disadvantage because you may decide erroneously that there is little need to learn another language. Since people often prefer to transact business in their native language, you may wish to learn a second language.

You may be wondering which foreign language is most useful for business purposes. The answer is not easy; all languages have use in some business situations. Figure 3-4 shows the languages most frequently recommended to native U.S. English speakers by respondents from the 100 largest U.S. businesses.

Note that Japanese is the most frequently recommended language for U.S. businesspersons to learn. It is the language of one dominant trading nation. On the other hand, French, German, and Spanish, as well as most of the other languages, are used by several important trading nations.

Learning any language will help you to understand the culture of those who speak it. Some people say that a language represents the highest form of a group's culture. As you learn the language, you learn how things are done where the language is spoken. You learn the beliefs, values, and assumptions of that society.

Over time you may learn to think and to communicate like a native. This helps you transact business much as a member of that soci-

Figure 3-4
The languages most frequently spoken are not the same as those recommended for business purposes to U.S. native English speakers.

BUSINESS LANGUAGES USEFUL TO LEARN

Rank	Language
1	Japanese
2-3 (tie)	French and Spanish
4	German
5	Chinese
6	Russian
7	Arabic
8	Portuguese
9-10 (tie)	Italian and Korean

Source: Scott, James Calvert, and Diana J. Green. "Foreign Languages and International Business Correspondence: Perspectives from the Business Communities of Two English-Speaking Nations." In *Proceedings of the 1992 Delta Pi Epsilon National Research Conference,* edited by Robert B. Mitchell, 85–93. Little Rock: Delta Pi Epsilon, 1992.

Unit 1   The World of International Business

ety does. Being fluent in a second language for business purposes is a competitive advantage. It will help you succeed in the world of international business. Which language besides English will you choose to learn in order to get ahead in international business?

Direct and Indirect Communication

One important feature of communication is its ability to be direct or indirect. *Contexting* refers to how direct or indirect communication is. A low-context culture is one that communicates very directly. These cultures value words and interpret them literally. The general and business subcultures of both Germany and the United States are relatively low context. Members of these groups convey information fairly directly.

A high-context culture is one that communicates very indirectly. These cultures attach little value to the literal meanings of words and interpret them figuratively. The general and business subcultures of both Japan and Iraq are relatively high context. Members of these groups convey information indirectly.

The concept of *face-saving* or minimizing personal embarrassment is directly related to contexting. In low-context cultures, people are not too concerned about being personally embarrassed. In high-context cultures, however, personal embarrassment must be avoided at all costs. If you cause a Japanese business partner to lose face, you have blundered badly. You have jeopardized your personal and business relationship with that person.

Many international communication problems can be better understood if you understand contexting and face-saving. For example, you may have wondered why Saddam Hussein criticized the United States before, during, and after the Gulf War. Did he really mean what he said? Could he really deliver on all of his threats and promises? Probably not. Since the Iraqi culture is high context, President Hussein's words shouldn't be taken too literally. They should be interpreted figuratively. In Iraqi culture, intention is much more important than what is actually done. He lashed out at the United States to save face. During the conflict in the Persian Gulf, President Hussein endured considerable personal embarrassment. He was humiliated publicly. Consequently, he struck back verbally at the United States since he could not do so militarily in any major way.

Nonverbal Communication

Not all communication takes place with language. **Nonverbal communication** is communication that does not involve the use of words. You have probably heard the saying that actions speak louder than words. Actions are an example of nonverbal communication.

Body Language.   One type of nonverbal communication is called body language. **Body language** includes facial expressions, upper and lower body movements, and gestures. All cultures and subcultures use body language. However, they do not always attach the same meanings to body language. Put another way, the meaning of body language is not universal. When George Bush was president, he traveled to Australia to promote trade with U.S. businesses. He flashed a V-for-Victory hand gesture with his palm toward himself to the enthusiastic Australian crowd. Unknowingly, he insulted the crowd. The hand gesture he used meant something entirely different in Australia than in the United States. He gave the Australians the equivalent of the U.S. rude single-finger gesture.

Appearance.   In the international business world, your appearance counts. Your clothing has no voice, but it communicates, too. Although people dress much differently in various parts of the world, they dress similarly when conducting international business. For such purposes, you should dress in a conservative manner. You might, for instance, wear dark-colored suits and white shirts or blouses. As a male, you would choose color-coordinated ties that are not too bright. As a female, you might choose simple jewelry to complement your outfit. Of course, your clothing should be clean and well pressed. Your body should be carefully groomed, too. Your business associates will be favorably impressed if you always dress and behave in a professional manner. If you care about your appearance, you are likely to care about business matters, too.

Eye Contact.   Eye movements vary from culture to culture. They are another means of nonverbal communication. In the United States, you should have direct eye contact with the person to whom you are speaking. That is not the case, however, in South Korea. There you show respect for the person speaking by looking downward, away from the eyes of the speaker. This is also true in many other Asian cultures.

Touching.   Touching behaviors are another part of nonverbal communication. What touches are acceptable varies worldwide. In Arab countries, business associates hug and kiss each other when they meet. They may also hold hands as they discuss business matters. Such behaviors are considered inappropriate for business in the United States.

Personal Space.   Space is used differently for communication purposes by different cultural groups. Jordanians confer very close to each other; only a few inches separate them. People in the United States require more distance. They often confer at arm's length from each other. Japanese prefer even more distance between speakers than do people in the United States When businesspersons with different space requirements interact, they must remember to respect the space needs of others. If they don't, they may find themselves dancing around the room: as one moves forward, the other steps back.

Global Highlight: French Cuisine

Every country has foods for which it is well known. But which country has the most appealing foods overall? Perhaps the answer most often heard around the world is "France." The foods of France are recognized and highly regarded wherever you go. What makes French food so special? It is well known for the high-quality ingredients, the proven culinary techniques, and the recognition that time is an important factor in the preparation of outstanding food.

What might you eat at a simple, traditional French meal? For breakfast you might have a *café complet* (continental breakfast) of yeast rolls, *croissants, brioche* (cake-like buns of yeast dough), or other fresh breads with *confiture* (jam) or *marmelade.* You might drink hot chocolate or *café au lait* (hot coffee with hot milk in equal parts).

At luncheon, which is sometimes the main meal of the day, you might eat *hors d'œuvre* (side dishes or starters) of thinly sliced smoked meats and assorted vegetables marinated in oil, radishes with butter, and crusty bread (or, in Provence, homemade pizzas). This would be followed by a main course of fish, meat, poultry—or all three—or even an omelet with a starchy accompaniment—perhaps potatoes. Next you might have a separate vegetable course; it could be asparagus with hollandaise (a rich sauce made from egg yolks, butter, and lemon juice or vinegar). The next course, designed to cleanse your palate, would be a salad with vinegar and oil dressing that is mixed at the table. For dessert, you could eat a baked sweet such as *flan* (an open-faced pastry filled with custard and topped with other things, such as fruit) or, more likely, fresh fruit and cheese(s) with *creme gâteau* (cake).

For dinner the menu is similar to that for luncheon except that the hors d'œuvre are replaced by a soup course. A fish and a meat course are both definitely served. The dinner dessert course will likely be more elaborate than the one served at luncheon—perhaps a *mousse* (a sweetened mixture with a whipped-cream base sometimes stabilized with gelatin) or a sweet *soufflé* (a baked food made fluffy with beaten egg whites, egg yolks, and a thickening sauce).

The French enjoy leisurely meals with good talk accompanied by wine, beer, or cider. Black coffee, once the traditional finishing touch for a French meal, is often dispensed with today. After-dinner drinks, *liqueurs,* are often served.

Color.   Other forms of nonverbal communication exist. Color is one. For example, the U.S. culture values dental products that produce white teeth. However, in Southeast Asia, teeth blackened by chewing betel nuts are valued. This value could pose a problem for a U.S. company trying to sell its toothpaste in that area of the world.

Global Business Example: Saying No the Japanese Way

Carl Byrd, a U.S. businessperson, asked his Japanese trading partner, Masahiro Watanabe, for a lower price on the Japanese product he was purchasing. Mr. Watanabe smiled and replied, "I will do my best." Two weeks later Mr. Byrd discovered that the product was invoiced at the original price. Mr. Byrd appealed to Mr. Watanabe, asking that the price be decreased because of the size of the order. Mr. Watanabe replied, "That will be very difficult." Two weeks later Mr. Byrd received another invoice, and it showed the original price. Mr. Byrd felt letdown by Mr. Watanabe since he had not said "no" directly.

Several weeks later, in an international business seminar, Mr. Byrd learned that the Japanese culture is high context. Suddenly, things made sense to Mr. Byrd. Mr. Watanabe was not being deceptive after all; he was being very polite and indirect. Both "I will do my best" and "That will be very difficult" suggest an unlikely outcome. Mr. Watanabe had been consistently saying "no" in the correct Japanese manner, but Mr. Byrd was prepared to understand only "no" in the direct manner of U.S. businesspersons.

Numbers. Numbers also communicate. In the United Kingdom and continental Europe the first floor is the floor above the ground floor. The first floor in a building in the United States is customarily the ground floor. Numbers can confuse businesspersons since they sometimes carry different meanings in different cultures and subcultures.

Emblems. Emblems or other symbols communicate. A Canadian could wear a cross-shaped necklace in many countries. However, in a country that accepts only another religion, doing so would be culturally insensitive. In fact, it is illegal to display non-Islamic religious symbols in Saudi Arabia.

Smells. Smells are another means of nonverbal communication. Natural body odors are considered unacceptable in the United States. Selling such products as deodorants and colognes, therefore, is big business. In most African and Middle Eastern countries, body odors are acceptable as being natural and distinctive. People there do not try to hide them. Consequently, the market for deodorants and colognes in those regions is very small.

VALUES VARY FROM CULTURE TO CULTURE

Values vary from culture to culture, creating often great differences among cultures. Some of the more important fundamental values involve individualism versus collectivism; technology; leadership, power, and authority; religion; and time.

Individualism and Collectivism

Individualism is the belief in the individual and her or his ability to function relatively independently. Self-reliance, independence, and freedom are closely related to individualism in the United States. However, many other cultures see individualism as undesirable. They do not approve of the negative aspects of self-centeredness and selfishness. Instead, they prefer **collectivism,** the belief that the group is more important than the individual.

The Japanese culture has a strong collective orientation. It has a saying that translates: "The nail that stands out is soon pounded down." This saying means that individuals should not stand out from the group.

If they do, the group will force these individuals to conform to the expectations of the group. Japanese businesspersons tend to function collectively. Consequently, they do not make decisions without getting consensus or group agreement. Group harmony is more important to them than individual gain. In contrast, U.S. businesspersons tend to function individually. They often make decisions without consulting fellow employees. Individual gain is more important to them than group harmony.

No culture is based entirely on individualism or collectivism. All cultures have both, but most cultures lean toward one or the other. Cultures that lean toward individualism are apt to value the entrepreneurial spirit. That means they are willing to accept some risk for possible personal gain.

Technology

Fundamental beliefs about technology also vary from culture to culture. Some cultures embrace technology as a means of providing more and better material objects. Most developed countries have business subcultures that view improvements in ways of doing things positively. Often, less-developed countries have business subcultures that resist improvements in technology. Often they view technology negatively for cultural or religious reasons. For example, attitudes toward technological change are generally positive in France. In India, they are mixed. India tries to balance the use of technology so that it doesn't intrude on important spiritual beliefs and displace people from menial tasks. Technological change is viewed at best as neutral and often as negative in Iran. Technology is sometimes seen there as a threat to fundamental Iranian ways.

Leadership, Power, and Authority

Different cultures have different values relating to leadership, power, and authority. These three are shared among a number of different people and institutions in democratic societies. For example, in the United States the power to govern is divided among the legislative, judicial, and executive branches of government. That way no one individual or group has too much power. In authoritarian societies, leadership, power, and authority are granted to a few. There, much of the power seems to be in the chosen person and not in the institution.

In the People's Republic of China, for instance, the leadership, power, and authority are concentrated in the hands of a few older leaders, who govern without question. They make all of the major decisions, which are carried out by middle-aged bureaucrats. The younger generation has essentially no power. When they protested in Tiananmen Square in Beijing in 1989 for more freedom, hundreds were killed. The student-led democracy movement threatened the leadership, power, and authority of the ruling old guard. It also threatened the time-honored Chinese tradition of respect for the wisdom of age—a major cultural value.

Religion

Religious beliefs also regulate the behaviors of members of many cultural groups, including numerous businesspersons. Such beliefs influence how people view the world. Some cultural groups are dominated by one religion. This is the case in Iran, for example, which is strongly influenced by Islam. Businesspersons there must follow Islamic practices. Some countries, such as the United States, have several major religions. Businesspersons there must respect the value choices of various religious practices. In some countries, such as the United Kingdom, religion is not a major social force. The relationship between religions and business is controversial. Good arguments can be raised that various religions both encourage and discourage business activity.

Time

Time is another factor to which different cultural groups attach different meanings. In most developed countries time is often viewed in the clock or mechanical sense. There, time is seen as a scarce resource that must be carefully spent. It is viewed this way in both Canada and the United States. In most less-developed countries time is often viewed in a natural or fluid sense. Time relates to the unending cycles of day and night and the seasons. Time is viewed this way in Mexico and Spain.

Global Business Example: Saudi Arabia Protects Its Own Cultural Values

To work in Saudi Arabia, guest workers and their families must agree to respect and adapt to the Saudi culture. For example, they must live a lifestyle that is acceptable to Saudis. They must wear modest clothes that cover most parts of their bodies. They must not drink alcoholic beverages. Women may not drive and must have written permission from their husbands to travel beyond their neighborhoods. Then, they must be accompanied by male chaperons.

To reduce the influences of foreign cultures on Saudi culture, guest workers and their families typically live in certain locations. These are called compounds. Most of the goods and services needed by guest workers are available in or near their compounds. Consequently, they have little need to interact with most Saudis and have little opportunity to influence Saudi culture.

CULTURAL DIFFERENCES NECESSITATE ADJUSTMENTS

Individuals and businesses must make cultural adjustments. In other words, they must adapt to different cultural values. To show respect for other cultural groups, you may need to make adjustments when dealing with them. These changes will help to minimize the differences that separate the cultural groups. Businesses that operate in other countries also make cultural adjustments.

Ethnocentrism

Ethnocentrism is the belief that one's culture is better than other cultures. Ethnocentrism is a major obstacle to conducting international business. Worldwide cultures and subcultures are different. However, different does not mean that one is better than the other. Different simply means that the cultures are not alike.

When you engage in international business, you will frequently have to deal with other cultures. Interacting with a person from another culture is called a *cross-cultural experience*. As an international businessperson, you will have many cross-cultural experiences. With patience and practice, you can learn how to adapt to other cultures.

Reactions to Cultural Differences

When you enter another culture or subculture, you will experience culture shock. *Culture shock* is the reaction to all of the differences of another culture. When you experience culture shock, your reactions

Global Business Exercise: East Meets West

A possible business partner from Shanghai, Wang Jian-Jun, will meet with you next Monday to discuss a trading opportunity. Mr. Wang has never traveled to the United States before, and you have never traveled to China. Nonetheless, you know that your cultures are much different. How might you bridge the following cultural differences?

1. Mr. Wang may nod politely or bow slightly when he greets you.
2. Mr. Wang understands some spoken English but communicates primarily in the Wu (Shanghai) dialect of Chinese, which you do not understand.
3. Mr. Wang eats with chopsticks; you eat with a knife, fork, and spoon.

change from happiness to frustration to adaptation to acceptance. When you complete the culture shock process, you accept the new culture for what it is and enjoy it.

When you return to your native culture after having been gone for a while, you will experience reverse culture shock. *Reverse culture shock* is your reaction to becoming reacquainted with your own culture after having accepted another. Reverse culture shock is a normal reaction to the cultural readjustment process. The intensity of reverse culture shock is determined by two factors: the length of time spent abroad and the degree of isolation from your native culture.

A U.S. businessperson returning from England may notice the excesses of the U.S. culture. For example, room temperatures are carefully controlled. Most areas are brightly lit. People speak in harsher and louder tones. He or she may be initially overwhelmed by all of the choices. For instance, the grocery store has 50 different cereals from which to choose. She or he may become depressed. Later, that person may realize that he or she is homesick for the other culture. As the person readjusts to life at home, the symptoms of reverse culture shock decrease. Usually they disappear within a year after a long stay abroad.

To be a successful participant in the global economy, you must be culturally sensitive. You must understand the major role that culture plays in shaping human behavior. You must understand not only your own general culture and its business subculture, but also that of your international business partners. You must consider all of the various components of culture and how they affect your international business communication. You must be willing to make accommodations because of differences in your own and your international partners' cultures. Developing cultural sensitivity is one key for success in the global economy.

Back to the Beginning: Walt Disney Company Adjusts to France

Reread the case at the beginning of this chapter and answer the following questions:

1. In what country besides France and the United States does the Walt Disney Company have a theme park?
2. Why did many French people oppose Euro Disneyland?
3. What adaptations did the Walt Disney Company make to French culture?
4. Why do you think the Walt Disney Company initially chose not to sell alcoholic beverages in the theme park?

KNOWING GLOBAL BUSINESS TERMS

The following terms should become part of your business vocabulary. For each numbered item find the term that has the same meaning.

- body language
- class system
- collectivism
- culture
- ethnocentrism
- extended family
- individualism
- nonverbal communication
- nuclear family
- subculture

1. A system of learned, shared, unifying, and interrelated beliefs, values, and assumptions.
2. Nonverbal communication involving facial expressions, upper and lower body movements, and gestures.
3. Consists of parent(s), children, and other relatives.
4. Communication that does not involve the use of words.
5. The belief that the group is more important than the individual.
6. Consists of parent(s) and unmarried children living at home.
7. The belief in the individual and her or his ability to function relatively independently.
8. The belief that one's culture is better than other cultures.
9. A subset or part of a larger culture.
10. A means of dividing the members of a cultural group into various levels.

REVIEWING YOUR READING

Answer these questions to reinforce your knowledge of the main ideas of this chapter.

1. What is culture?
2. How is a subculture different from a culture?
3. How is the U.S. business subculture different from the general U.S. culture? the business subcultures of other countries?
4. How do cultures and subcultures influence the transaction of business?
5. Why should you study the cultures and subcultures of other countries?
6. How does social organization influence general cultures?
7. What language, if any, is most useful for international business purposes? Why?

8. How is nonverbal communication different from other forms of communication?

9. What are five important value categories that differ from culture to culture?

10. Why do people and businesses need to make adjustments for cultural differences?

EXPANDING YOUR HORIZONS

You will not find the complete answers to the following questions in your textbook. You will need to use your critical-thinking skills. Think about these questions, gather information from other sources, analyze possible responses, and discuss them with others. Then, develop your own oral or written response as instructed by your teacher.

1. How is culture like the programming in a microcomputer?

2. What evidence suggests that geographic attachment is weak in the general U.S. culture and in its subcultures?

3. Swahili is the Bantu language of the Swahili people in Africa. It is also a trade and governmental language among speakers of other languages in Tanzania, Kenya, and parts of Zaire. Do you think that this language has significant potential for international business purposes? Why or why not?

4. What do you think is the cultural relationship between the amount of space between business communicators and touching behaviors?

5. What are some other countries besides the People's Republic of China where leadership, power, and authority are concentrated in the hands of a few people?

6. A good friend recently said that she wouldn't even think of living temporarily in another country. Is her statement ethnocentric? How do you know?

BUILDING RESEARCH SKILLS

The ability to find information from various sources is an important international business skill. The following activities will help you investigate various topics. You will also learn to apply class ideas to situations outside of the classroom.

1. After interviewing a local businessperson, create a poster that depicts his or her cultural baggage.

2. Using library resources, uncover two similarities in the business subcultures of the United States and Mexico and two differences in the business subcultures of the United States and Canada.

3. Find out about the caste system in India, a highly structured class system, by interviewing a native of the country or by using library resources. Write a paper that explains the caste system and what the Indian government has done in an attempt to eliminate this system.

4. Select one primary color (red, yellow, or blue) and one secondary color (orange, green, or purple). Find out what these two colors represent in an Eastern and a Western culture of your choice.

5. Using library sources, investigate how the people of French-speaking Québec are trying to protect their French cultural heritage. What effects are their actions having on the people in other parts of Canada, who are primarily speakers of English? Do you think these differences will eventually lead to the breakup of Canada? Why or why not? Debate this matter with your classmates.

6. *Global Career Activity.* Interview someone who has worked in another country. What similarities and/or differences did he or she find in the job application process in the other country?

Continuing Enrichment Project: Creating a Cultural Iceberg Collage

Using library resources and the knowledge of people, investigate both the general culture and business subculture of a country of your choice. Find out about the country—including its topography, climate, history, government, economy, education, transportation, and communications systems. Also, investigate the people—including their general attitudes, appearance, population distribution, language(s), social interaction, religion(s), family life, food, work, and recreation. Further, find out as much about the business community as possible—including its size, business types, business practices, and the like.

Then, draw a large iceberg on a sheet of poster board with a pencil. Draw a waterline near the top of the iceberg so that about seven-eighths of its area is below water. Find pictures and other things that depict observable parts of the culture. Glue those items above the waterline on the iceberg, creating a collage in the process. Be sure to preserve the shape of the portion of the iceberg above the waterline as you create the collage.

Then, take a black marking pen and trace over the waterline and the outer edges of the portion of the iceberg below the water. In the space below the waterline, write the names of invisible elements that support the observable parts of the culture.

Government and Political Influences on Business

After studying this chapter and completing the end-of-chapter activities, you will be able to

- Distinguish between the various political systems around the world and their relationships to the way businesses operate.
- Discuss the impact political developments have on international business.
- Describe how governments can encourage and can discourage international business.
- Explain how political risks can disrupt selling and buying across borders.
- Identify the major types of taxes that governments place on individuals and businesses throughout the world.

U.S. Department of Agriculture Promotes the Export of U.S. Food Products

Do you want to export popcorn overseas? How about corn, apples, poultry, seafood, or even frozen convenience dinners? If so, the U.S. Department of Agriculture (USDA) can assist you. This U.S. government agency is responsible for promoting the export of U.S. agricultural, livestock, and processed food products and commodities worldwide.

The USDA provides various export marketing services for U.S. companies. The agency conducts international market research on the best foreign markets for U.S. food products. It also maintains a database on more than 18,000 foreign buyers of food and agricultural products. In addition, it distributes foreign trade leads to U.S. suppliers and promotes U.S. food and agricultural products in foreign trade shows in Europe, Asia, the Middle East, and Latin America.

The USDA also guarantees payment to U.S. banks who make loans to foreign governments that want to purchase U.S. agricultural products such as wheat, soybeans, and corn. The USDA maintains trade offices in 80 countries, all of which are major foreign markets for U.S. agricultural and food products.

POLITICAL SYSTEMS IN THE GLOBAL MARKETPLACE

A country's economy is usually a reflection of its political system. A **political system** is the means by which people in any society make the rules by which they live. Political systems vary around the world, ranging from democracy to totalitarianism.

Democracy

In a **democracy,** all citizens take part in making the rules that govern them. A democracy emphasizes the importance of the individual's needs and interests. In this political system, the people have equal rights, including the right to vote for political leaders. They also have many freedoms, including freedom of speech and freedom of religion.

A democracy's emphasis on individual rights and freedoms extends to its economy. In a democratic society, people have the freedom to own and operate private businesses. Democratic societies, therefore, usually have some form of a market economy. In a country with a market economy there is little or no government ownership or central planning of business and industry. Most businesses are run by individuals or groups of individuals. Companies, therefore, either succeed or fail based on their owners' abilities to compete effectively in a market. The United States is basically a market economy.

Totalitarianism

In a **totalitarian** system, most people are excluded from making the rules by which they live. Political control is instead held by one person or a small group of people. Examples of totalitarian systems include a military dictatorship, in which a general makes all the decisions; a pure monarchy, in which the right to absolute rule for life is based on heredity; or a system in which one political party holds all the power and prohibits others from participating. In a totalitarian system, people's rights and freedoms are restricted. People may not be allowed to travel freely outside the country or to practice the religion they choose.

Totalitarian systems tend not to have market economies, but command economies. In a command economy, the national government owns and controls almost all businesses. Individuals may be allowed to own a one-employee small business—using a somewhat mixed-economy approach. But, the government owns all larger businesses, industries, farms, utilities, transportation, and mining operations. Traditional communist countries, such as Cuba, are basically command economies.

Mixed Systems

In reality there is no pure form of either democracy or totalitarianism. Most political systems are considered mixed. That means that they have characteristics of both systems and fall somewhere in between. In the same way, economic systems of most countries are considered mixed systems. In most countries, the majority of businesses are privately owned, and some key industries are owned and run by the government. Key industries include steel production, mining, national airlines, and telephone and public utilities. Many European countries, for example, are mixed economies.

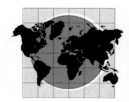

Global Business Example: The View from China

International businesspeople must be cautious when classifying the political system of a country. They must do their own research, because the classification claimed by the country, itself, can be misleading. For example, China's full name is The People's Republic of China. However, the people of China have very little representation in the actual governing body; and, the government is not responsible to elected representatives. In that sense, China is not a republic.

POLITICAL DEVELOPMENTS

International business has been dramatically affected by political developments in our rapidly changing world. Examples in the 1990s include the breakup of Yugoslavia, the peace initiative between Israel and the Arab countries of the Middle East, the reunification of Germany, and the breakup of the Soviet Union.

General Agreement on Tariffs and Trade (GATT)

A firm selling a product or service needs to understand how different types of political developments affect the business world. A major political development of the twentieth century that affected trade was the General Agreement on Tariffs and Trade, commonly known as GATT. After World War II, world leaders who wanted to promote peaceful international trade developed a set of ground rules—GATT—to guide the conduct of international trade. GATT was negotiated in 1947 and began operating in January 1948 when 23 countries signed the treaty agreement.

The goals of GATT are to promote world trade through negotiation and to make world trade secure. Working toward these goals helps to increase global economic growth and development. Today, GATT's membership has grown to more than 100 nations. It has sponsored nine rounds of negotiations to remove barriers to world trade in goods, services, and ideas. The most recent round was the Uruguay Round—which began in September, 1986.

Trends Toward Market Economies

The major political development of the early 1990s was the fall of communism in Eastern Europe and the former Soviet Union. These countries moved away from total government control and toward market economies.

One of the major changes occurring in these economies was privatization. **Privatization** is the selling of government-owned companies to private citizens. Often, government-owned companies are not run efficiently. Workers may have little motivation to help the company make a profit. Therefore, products made by government-owned companies may not be of the same quality as similar products made by privately owned companies. A privately owned company must produce quality goods to remain competitive and stay in business. A government-owned company has little or no competition; therefore, quality sometimes suffers.

Governments hope that through privatization, the former government-owned companies will become modernized, more efficient, and more competitive. Selling government-owned companies also raises revenue for the government. Privatization is the first step in the lengthy and complex move toward a market economy.

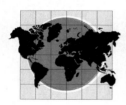

Global Business Example: Private Enterprise in Ukraine

As privatization evolves, opportunities for foreign involvement increase. Pursuing these markets poses new challenges and opportunities for the international businessperson. For example in 1992, New York-based Pepsi-Co, Inc., wanted to expand its sales in Ukraine (formerly a part of the U.S.S.R.). In conjunction with three Ukrainian companies, PepsiCo will build five Pepsi bottling plants and open 100 of its Pizza Hut chain restaurants.

GOVERNMENT ACTIVITIES INFLUENCE BUSINESS

Have you ever heard of "government red tape"? For centuries, business people have complained about government reports, licenses, permits, and forms they must obtain or complete. Every day, businesses throughout the world must comply with thousands of government laws and regulations. These laws directly affect how businesses operate.

Laws That Protect Workers and Consumers

Why do governments regulate businesses? Often, it is to protect the health and safety of workers. Many countries establish occupational protection laws to protect workers from dangerous conditions on the job. For example, in many countries, factory workers are required by law to wear safety equipment—such as protective eye goggles, hard hats, and earplugs. Other worker protection laws prohibit the use of children as agricultural laborers or factory workers. Today, there is even a growing interest in establishing new safety requirements for office employees who use computers all day.

In addition to occupational protection laws, governments establish consumer protection laws to ensure that products are safe to use. For example, most developed countries require that all food ingredients be listed on product labels. And, most developed countries have electrical safety standards to protect consumers from purchasing faulty electrical appliances, such as hair dryers and toasters. There are also laws to protect consumers from deceptive or false advertising practices, such as claiming a particular medicine can cure the common cold.

Complying with worker and consumer protection laws usually increases the cost of doing business for companies. These increased costs *may* make a product less competitive with products that are produced in countries that do not have occupational and consumer protection laws. In general, occupational and consumer protection laws are not as strict in poor, developing countries as they are in the major industrialized countries—such as the United States, Canada, Japan, and the countries of Western Europe. A product made in Canada will probably cost more than a similar product made in Mexico, even if both are marketed in Ireland.

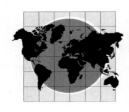

Global Business Example: Consumer Protection Laws Around the World

- In French-speaking Québec, Canada, the packages and labels of all consumer products must be printed in both French and English.
- The price of every retail product in Venezuela must be clearly marked, together with the date on which the price was marked.
- A law in Belgium limits how much noise the engine of a lawn mower may make.
- In Australia, children's nightclothes must be labeled to indicate the degree of fire hazard or inflammability.

Trade Barriers

Specific actions by governments can directly discourage or prevent the growth of international business. To protect local businesses from foreign competition, governments may establish trade barriers. Trade barriers are government actions or policies that make it difficult to trade across borders. Governments that establish such trade barriers are considered protectionist. **Protectionism** is a government policy of protecting local or domestic industries from foreign competition (see Figure 4-1).

Figure 4-1
Governments can discourage or prevent the growth of international business in many ways.

HOW GOVERNMENTS DISCOURAGE INTERNATIONAL BUSINESS

- Place quotas on the importation of certain products.

- Restrict or ban domestic companies from doing business with a particular country.

- Establish high customs duties to increase the price of imported products.

- Restrict or cancel import licenses.

Tariffs. A government can place a tariff or duty on imported products. A tariff or **duty** is a tax on products that are traded internationally. Duties raise the cost of the product to the importer, which discourages consumers from buying the imported products. Duties are the most common trade barriers.

Quotas. Governments also place quotas on certain imported products. A **quota** is a limit on the total number, quantity, or monetary amount of a product that can be imported from a given country. Once the quota has been met, no more of that product can be imported for the rest of a set period (often, a year). The quota creates a limited supply of the imported good. This protects domestic products from too much foreign competition. The textile, shoe, automobile, and steel industries are often protected by import quotas.

Boycotts. Sometimes a government issues an absolute restriction on the import of certain products from certain countries. This is called a **boycott.** For example, in India, the importation of most consumer goods is banned. This forces foreign companies that want to sell consumer goods in India to

invest in India and manufacture the products locally. In Japan, the government maintains a nearly complete ban on the import of rice. This is to protect Japanese rice farmers from foreign competition. And Norway protects its apple and pear producers by allowing imports only after the domestic crop has been sold.

Licensing Requirements.   Some governments control imports by requiring companies to have a government import license. The license grants permission to import a product. Such a license can be withdrawn at any time.

Encouraging International Business

Specific actions by governments can also directly encourage and promote international business. Governments around the world encourage domestic industries to export by providing export counseling and training, export insurance, and export subsidies and tax credits (see Figure 4-2). Exporting is viewed by governments as an effective way to create jobs and foster economic prosperity.

Free-Trade Zones.   To promote international business, governments often create free-trade zones in their countries. A **free-** or **foreign-trade zone** is a designated area, usually around a seaport or airport, where products can be imported duty-free and then stored, assembled, and/or used in manufacturing. Only when the product leaves the zone does the importer pay duty.

Figure 4-2
Governments can encourage or promote the growth of international business in many ways.

HOW GOVERNMENTS ENCOURAGE INTERNATIONAL BUSINESS

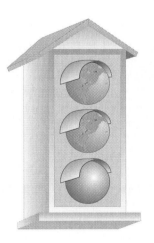

- Establish free-trade agreements.

- Provide export insurance to exporters to guarantee against foreign commercial and political risks.

- Provide free or subsidized export marketing assistance to exporters to help them research foreign markets, promote their products overseas, and find foreign buyers.

- Provide tax incentives for foreign companies to invest and locate manufacturing plants in their country.

- Reduce or eliminate trade barriers; such as tariffs, import licenses, or quotas.

- Grant most favored nation status.

- Establish free-trade zones.

Most Favored Nation.   A government can also encourage international trade by granting most favored nation status to other countries. Countries with **most favored nation (MFN) status** can export into the granting country under the lowest customs duty rates. Products imported from countries without MFN status are charged a higher rate.

Free-Trade Agreements.   A growing trend throughout the world is for countries to establish free-trade agreements with each other. Under a **free-trade agreement,** member countries agree to eliminate duties and trade barriers on products traded among themselves. This results in increased trade between the members. For example, the United States and Canada formed a free-trade agreement in January 1989. It will be fully implemented by January 1998. During this ten-year "phase-in period," duties on U.S. and Canadian products will be eliminated between the two countries. The result will be a duty-free zone between the two largest trading partners in the world.

Some countries join together in a common market to promote more trade among themselves. In a **common market,** members eliminate duties and other trade barriers, allow companies to invest freely in each member's country, and allow workers to move freely across borders. Common market members also have a common external duty on products being imported from nonmember countries.

A good example of a common market is the Latin American Integration Association (LAIA). Its members include Argentina, Bolivia, Brazil, Chile, Colombia, Ecuador, Mexico, Paraguay, Peru, Uruguay, and Venezuela. The goal of LAIA is to further trade between member states and promote regional integration (see Figure 4-3).

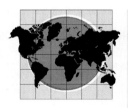

Global Business Example: Try Climbing Over This Trade Barrier!

Trying to export goods to Pakistan can be difficult. Pakistan's import customs duties range from 20 to 90 percent. All imports are also subject to a 5 percent education tax, a 6 percent import license fee, a 12.5 percent sales tax, and an import surcharge tax of 10 percent. A product costing $100 before entering Pakistan could cost $223.50 after clearing the Pakistani Customs Office!

POLITICAL RISKS IN INTERNATIONAL BUSINESS

There is always the possibility that government actions or political policies will *change* in such a way that foreign companies operating in those countries are adversely affected. This is called **political risk.** Major

Figure 4-3

The Latin American Integration Association took over from the Latin American Free Trade Association in 1981.

MEMBERS OF LAIA

political risks to international business include trade sanctions, expropriation, economic nationalism, and civil unrest or war. All of these actions can temporarily or permanently disrupt selling and buying across borders (see Figure 4-4 on page 80).

Trade Sanctions

Governments may impose various trade restrictions against another country to protest that country's behavior. This use of trade barriers as sanctions is usually the direct result of political disputes between countries.

Figure 4-4

Businesses must be aware of the various forms of international political risk.

TYPES OF INTERNATIONAL POLITICAL RISK

- Civil war, revolution, uprisings within the country
- War with other countries
- Trade sanctions due to foreign policy
- Expropriation
- Growth of economic nationalism

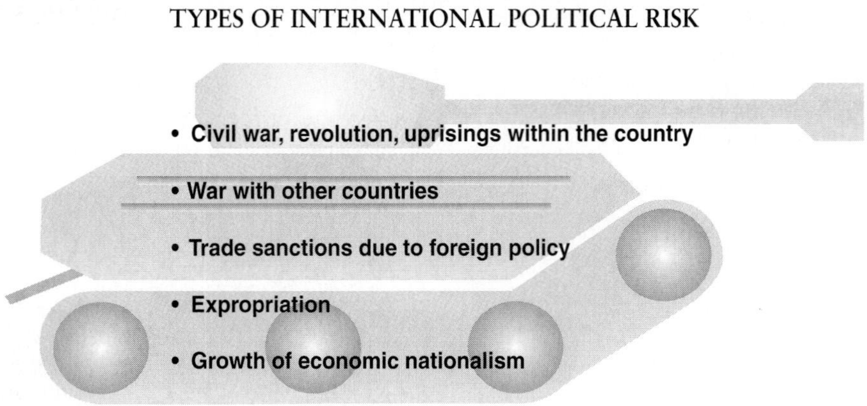

For example, in August 1993, the United States imposed a trade sanction that banned the sale of high technology equipment to China. The United States was protesting China's apparent sale of missile technology to Pakistan, which violated an international arms-control agreement.

Trade sanctions range from tariffs to boycotts. A country can impose a **trade embargo** against another country and stop *all* import-export trade with that country. In 1990, President George Bush issued a trade embargo against Iraq because the country repeatedly supported acts of international terrorism and invaded Kuwait. The Iraqi Sanctions Regulations banned the export of any goods, technology, or service from the United States to Iraq.

Expropriation

In extreme cases, the host government of a company could confiscate, or expropriate, the subsidiary. **Expropriation** is when a government takes control and ownership of foreign-owned assets and companies. This happened in 1990 as a result of the breakup of the Soviet Union. Some cities in the new republics took over property and assets of the ruling communist party of the former Soviet Union. Russian President Gorbachev moved to bar the expropriations.

Economic Nationalism

Economic nationalism is a political force that can also create political risk for companies conducting international trade. **Economic nationalism** refers to the trend of some countries to restrict foreign ownership of companies and to establish laws that protect against foreign imports. Economic nationalism is a form of protectionism. Protectionist governments may encourage their people to "buy domestic" instead of purchasing imported products.

80   *Unit 1   The World of International Business*

Civil Unrest or War

The presence of the following factors in a country are signals that the possibility of civil unrest exists:

1. Evidence of social disorder;
2. Evidence of extreme income unevenness, with a few very rich people and a massive number of poor people; and,
3. Evidence of frequent changes in the structure and activity of political parties.

Civil unrest interrupts production and sales. Transportation of goods may be hindered, and people may not be able to shop because of gunfire and riots. When unrest escalates to war, there is often massive destruction of property and goods.

Global Business Exercise: Where Is Yugoslavia?

In the early 1990s, former Yugoslavia was the sight of civil war and ethnic nationalism.

1. What is the current status of the republics that used to form Yugoslavia?
2. Use reference materials to find out if there were any signals to warn of the possibility of civil unrest prior to the eruption of hostilities in the region in 1991.
3. What can the new republics do to encourage international investments in their countries in the future?

TAXES AND INTERNATIONAL BUSINESS

Second to complaints about government "red tape," businesses worldwide complain that their governments tax them too much. Governments collect revenues to pay for welfare programs, build roads and bridges, provide health care insurance, and support military forces, among many other things. Revenue to pay for these programs comes from many types of taxes.

There are taxes on purchases, property, income, and wealth. The following sections briefly describe the major taxes imposed throughout the world.

Global Highlight: Protecting U.S. Businesses from International Risk

How can a company protect itself from international political risk? U.S. companies can protect their international sales and assets by using the services of two U.S. government agencies—The Export-Import Bank of the United States (EXIM) and the Overseas Private Investment Corporation (OPIC).

EXIM is the U.S. government agency that helps to finance the export sales of U.S. products. It provides export loans, export loan guarantees, and export credit insurance. An exporting company can purchase an export credit insurance policy from EXIM that will provide 100 percent political risk protection for international sales. This includes protection from foreign governments that refuse to convert local currency to dollars. It also covers damage or destruction of a shipment caused by wars, revolutions, and civil disorders. If these political actions occur, the exporter can then file a claim with EXIM for 100 percent reimbursement of all export sales losses.

The Overseas Private Investment Corporation (OPIC) provides investment insurance to U.S. companies that establish operations in developing countries. A U.S. company can protect its overseas investment by purchasing OPIC insurance. This shields the company from several types of political risk—including expropriation and damage or destruction caused by war, revolution, terrorism, and sabotage. If any of these political actions occur, the U.S. company can file a claim with OPIC to recover its losses.

Customs Duty

A customs duty, as discussed earlier, is a tax assessed on imported products. While sometimes used by governments as an import trade barrier, customs duties are also collected specifically to raise revenue to pay for government programs (see Figure 4-5).

Sales Tax

A *sales tax* is a tax on the sale of products. It is paid by the consumer at the time of purchase. Sales taxes are considered regressive taxes because the same rate of tax is charged to everyone, no matter what her or his income level. A sales tax takes a smaller amount, or proportion, of total income from a person with a high income than from a person with a low income. Some countries, such as Singapore and Canada, have taxes similar to sales taxes called consumption taxes or goods and services taxes.

Excise Tax

An *excise tax* is a tax levied on the sale or consumption of specific products or commodities—such as alcoholic beverages, tobacco, gasoline, and motor vehicles. For example, in the United States, gasoline excise

taxes are collected specifically for highway construction and repair. These taxes are often based on the "benefits received" principle, meaning that only automobile drivers, who would receive the most benefit from well-maintained highways, are assessed the tax.

Payroll-Related Tax

Payroll-related taxes are those taxes that are automatically deducted from an employee's pay. Typical payroll taxes in the United States include taxes to pay for Social Security, Medicare, and unemployment insurance—all matched by the employer.

Value-Added Tax (VAT)

A *value-added tax (VAT)* is a tax assessed on the increase in value of goods from each stage of production to final consumption. The tax on each stage is levied on the value that has been added before moving the product to the next stage. Value-added taxes are used in most European countries. VAT is similar to a national sales tax.

Figure 4-5
Governments assess customs duty rates as a method of raising revenue.

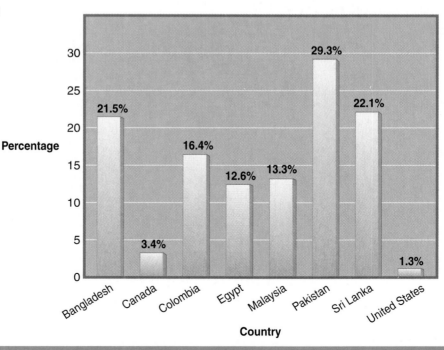

CUSTOMS DUTIES AS A PERCENTAGE OF NATIONAL GOVERNMENT REVENUE

Percentage

- Bangladesh 21.5%
- Canada 3.4%
- Colombia 16.4%
- Egypt 12.6%
- Malaysia 13.3%
- Pakistan 29.3%
- Sri Lanka 22.1%
- United States 1.3%

Country

Source: *The Journal of Commerce*, 4/27/93

Income Taxes

A tax on the amount of income a person or corporation earns, minus allowable deductions and credits, is an *income tax*. Income tax is usually a progressive tax because the percentage a person pays increases, or progresses, the more income a person makes. This tax is based on the "ability to pay" principle—the more income a person has, the more taxes that person is able to pay.

Corporations also pay income tax—which is based on corporate annual income, minus allowable business deductions or tax credits (see Figure 4-6). Governments may give companies various tax credits to enable them to purchase new equipment, invest in research and development, and employ new people. A corporate income tax is viewed as an *indirect* business tax on consumers. Corporations pass along the cost of the tax indirectly to the consumer via a higher price charged for the goods or services sold or produced by the company.

Tax Incentives

A basic practice of companies is to treat all business taxes as regular business costs. They recover those costs by increasing the price of the products they sell. The actual burden of tax payment, therefore, is usually shifted to the consumer in the form of higher prices.

Figure 4-6
Tax rates vary among countries.

COMPARISON OF INCOME TAX RATES BY COUNTRY

Country	Corporate Income Tax	Personal Income Tax
Chile	35%	5–50%
Denmark	34%	up to 68%
Germany	36%	19–53%
Ireland	40%	27–48%
Kenya	35%	10–40%
Mexico	35%	3–35%
Portugal	40%	15–40%
Russia	18%	12–40%
United Arab Emirates	*	None

*Most emirates have corporate income tax acts, but they have not been implemented except with respect to oil companies. Each ruler sets the corporate tax rate for oil companies within his own emirate. Rates vary among and, even, within emirates.

Source: *Individual Taxes: A Worldwide Summary,* Price Waterhouse World Firm Limited, 1993; and *Corporate Taxes: A Worldwide Summary,* Price Waterhouse World Firm Limited, 1993.

Unit 1 The World of International Business

In conducting international business, U.S. companies want to avoid being taxed twice on income they earn from their foreign operations. The U.S. government allows companies a corporate tax deduction on income earned by their foreign subsidiaries.

In addition, the U.S. government has double-taxation avoidance treaties with some countries. This provides relief from double taxation of U.S. multinational corporations. This is a tax incentive that foreign governments use to attract U.S. companies to invest in their countries and create local jobs. U.S. companies are more likely to invest in those countries with which the United States has such a treaty.

As a further tax incentive, many foreign governments provide a foreign company with a tax holiday. A **tax holiday** means the corporation does not pay corporate income taxes if it invests in their country. Typically, these tax holidays last for ten years.

Governments around the world influence—both directly and indirectly—the way businesses operate. These political influences can be negative or positive. Therefore, it is vital for business managers to be aware of these influences as they conduct business internationally.

Global Business Exercise: Investing in Saudi Arabia

Thinking about establishing a manufacturing plant somewhere in the world? If so, Saudi Arabia wants your business! The Kingdom of Saudi Arabia is actively encouraging foreign companies to invest in non-oil manufacturing operations. The goal is to diversify the Saudi economy so that it is less dependent on the oil industry.

Foreign companies that invest in Saudi Arabia will find few taxes, as well as several tax incentives. There is a corporate income tax rate of 25 to 45 percent on net income. However, new investors can receive a ten-year tax holiday. There is no personal income tax for foreigners and only a 2.5 percent wealth tax, called *zakat*, for Saudi nationals. Finally, there are no local, regional, property, or sales taxes.

Will you be exporting equipment and materials into Saudi Arabia for your factory? Don't worry, those products are exempt from Saudi customs duties. Do you need land, electricity, and water for your factory? The Saudi government will provide all three for a nominal fee.

And what do you do with all the profits you earn from this investment? Send the profits right back to the United States. The Saudi government has no foreign exchange controls and no restrictions on repatriation of earnings.

1. In addition to diversifying the economy, how else could Saudi Arabia benefit from foreign investment?
2. In spite of the tax incentives, what risks might there be in doing business in Saudi Arabia?
3. How could a U.S. company protect itself against those risks?

Source: *Doing Business in Saudi Arabia,* Price Waterhouse, 1991.

Back to the Beginning: U.S. Department of Agriculture Promotes the Export of U.S. Food Products

Reread the case at the beginning of this chapter and answer the following questions:

1. You are the manufacturer of Grandma's Original Jams and Jellies. In what ways could the USDA help you develop export markets for your products?

2. Why do you think the U.S. government spends tax dollars to promote the export of U.S. agricultural and food products?

3. Why would the USDA guarantee payment to U.S. banks that make loans to foreign governments that want to buy U.S. agricultural commodities?

4. The USDA also provides export subsidies or grants to U.S. farmers who export. How could this be viewed as an obstacle for a foreign farmer who doesn't receive export subsidies from his own government but is trying to export?

KNOWING GLOBAL BUSINESS TERMS

The following terms should become part of your business vocabulary. For each numbered item find the term that has the same meaning.

- boycott
- common market
- democracy
- duty
- economic nationalism
- expropriation
- free-trade agreement
- free- or foreign-trade zone
- most favored nation (MFN) status
- political risk
- political system
- privatization
- protectionism
- quota
- tax holiday
- totalitarian (system)
- trade embargo

1. A government system in which political control is held by one person or a small group of people.

2. A tax on imported products.

3. A limit on the amount of a product that can be imported from a given country.

4. Government policy used to protect local or domestic industries from foreign competition.

5. Designated area where products can be imported duty-free.

6. Designation given to certain countries that allow their products

to be imported into the granting country under the lowest customs duty rate.

7. An arrangement between countries that eliminates duties and trade barriers on products traded among themselves.

8. The selling of government-owned companies to private citizens.

9. A policy of restricting foreign ownership of local companies and hindering foreign imports.

10. Complete ban on any trade with a particular country.

11. Risk of government actions and changing political policies that will prevent companies from conducting international business.

12. A political system in which all people take part in making the rules that govern them.

13. An agreement among countries that eliminates trade barriers, encourages investment, and allows workers to move freely across borders.

14. Means by which people in a society make the rules by which they live.

15. Government takeover of a foreign-owned business.

16. Absolute restriction on the import of certain products from certain countries.

17. Tax incentive used by governments to attract foreign investment.

REVIEWING YOUR READING

Answer these questions to reinforce your knowledge of the main ideas of this chapter.

1. In what ways do governments discourage international business?

2. How can customs duties be used by governments as a trade barrier?

3. How can a government use import quotas as a trade barrier?

4. In what specific ways do governments encourage international business?

5. What are the advantages of free-trade agreements between countries?

6. What are three examples of political risk with respect to international business?

7. How do market economies differ from command economies?

8. Why do governments give tax incentives to encourage foreign companies to invest in their countries?

9. How do progressive taxes differ from regressive taxes? Which one takes a larger percentage of income from a lower income person? Why?

EXPANDING YOUR HORIZONS

You will not find the complete answers to the following questions in your textbook. You will need to use your critical-thinking skills. Think about these questions, gather information from other sources, analyze possible responses, and discuss them with others. Then, develop your own oral or written response as instructed by your teacher.

1. As a consumer, why might you object to your government creating import trade barriers, such as high customs duties or restrictive import quotas?

2. How could the study of international affairs and world current events help a company anticipate and evaluate potential political risks around the world?

3. How effective do you think trade embargoes are as a method of "punishing" another country for its actions?

4. What factors, other than tax incentives, should companies evaluate before deciding to invest in a particular country?

5. What services are provided by the U.S. government to help promote the export of nonagricultural or food products, such as manufactured products and consumer goods?

BUILDING RESEARCH SKILLS

The ability to find information from various sources is an important international business skill. The following activities will help you investigate various topics. You will also learn to apply class ideas to situations outside of the classroom.

1. Interview several small-business owners about the specific effect the government (local, state, and federal) has on their businesses. What ways has government made it more difficult to do business? What ways has government helped to start or promote their businesses?

2. Contact your state department of commerce to determine what specific kinds of assistance it provides to exporters in your state.

3. Spend two weeks reviewing newspaper and newsmagazine articles and television news reports. Record and report on all examples of potential and actual political risk to international companies.

4. Contact your local chamber of commerce or state department of commerce to find out what tax and financial incentives are available to attract foreign companies to invest in your state.

5. Interview a local company that exports. Ask about trade barriers to exporting that the company has faced. Also, ask if the company has ever experienced political risk in doing business internationally.

6. *Global Career Activity.* Conduct library research about government regulations of wages, employment opportunities, and occupational safety in another country.

Continuing Enrichment Project: Evaluating Canada and Mexico as Possible Investment Sites

Many U.S. companies are considering establishing manufacturing plants or subsidiaries in either Mexico or Canada. To help evaluate the advantages and disadvantages, as well as the risks of making such an expensive investment, companies collect specific information about the "investment climate" of these two countries. The more favorable the climate, the more likely it is that the company will profit from the investment.

Using your international business file and research skills, gather information on the investment climates in Mexico and Canada. Good sources of information include the U.S. Department of Commerce, the Mexican and Canadian embassies, international banks, major international accounting firms, international attorneys, local world trade associations, and the Mexican and Canadian chambers of commerce. Find information on the following topics:

1. political stability of each government/possible civil disruptions;
2. occupational safety laws;
3. number of trade barriers or investment restrictions;
4. restrictions on repatriating profits back to the parent company;
5. labor costs and labor laws;
6. tax and other investment incentives to foreign companies;
7. laws concerning establishing or restricting investment; and
8. other information you think important to making an investment decision.

Compare the investment climate in each country and determine which country is the better location for a manufacturing plant. Report your findings and analyses to the class.

Organizing for International Business

CHAPTER 5

Structures of International Business Organizations

After studying this chapter and completing the end-of-chapter activities, you will be able to

- Describe the three main forms of business organizations.

- Identify the advantages and disadvantages of the three types of business organizations.

- Describe the characteristics and activities of multinational companies.

- Explain different methods for getting involved in international business.

Mitsubishi: From Trading Company to Multinational Corporation

During the 20 years after it started as a trading company in 1870, Mitsubishi got involved in mining, banking, shipbuilding, and railroads. The company started as a *zaibatsu* (family-run conglomerate) and continued to expand into various types of business activities. In 1946, the organization divided into 139 separate entities. Twelve years later, Mitsubishi Trading established a division in the United States to export U.S. goods and raw materials to Japan.

As a result of growth and foreign investments, the company has expanded into many areas of service and production. Today, Mitsubishi is involved in banking, insurance, real estate, glass production, cable television, clothing fibers, chemicals, steel, plastics, electrical equipment, paper mills, motor vehicles, shipbuilding, power plants, aircraft production, and computers. In 1985, Chrysler and Mitsubishi formed a cooperative agreement to build automobiles in central Illinois.

The first four chapters of this book created a foundation for your international business knowledge. We now start using this information to expand your knowledge of the creation and operation of global companies. This process starts with a discussion of how companies are set up to do business.

Have you ever wondered how a business gets organized? Almost every company you can think of started small with the efforts of one or two people. Both Texas Instruments and Apple Computer started with two people who had an idea for a new business opportunity. As a business grows in size, the company is likely to expand its operations and increase the number of owners. Every business organizes as one of three types: sole proprietorship, partnership, or corporation.

The Sole Proprietorship

Most companies in the world are started and owned by one person. In fact, as shown in Figure 5-1, in the United States over 70 percent of all businesses are sole proprietorships. A **sole** or **single proprietorship** is a business owned by one person. Many of the stores, companies, and other businesses you see each day have a single owner, even though they employ many people.

For a person to start a sole proprietorship, three major items are needed. First, the new business owner must have a product or service to sell. Second, money for a building, equipment, and other start-up expenses will be required. Third, the owner must know how, or hire someone else who does know how, to manage the business activities of the company.

A person should consider the advantages and disadvantages of a single-owner business organization before a decision is made.

Figure 5-1
Most businesses in the United States are organized as sole proprietorships.

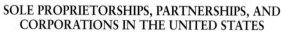
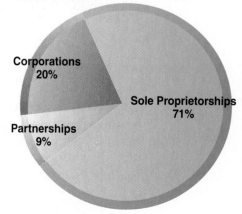

SOLE PROPRIETORSHIPS, PARTNERSHIPS, AND CORPORATIONS IN THE UNITED STATES

Corporations
20%

Sole Proprietorships
71%

Partnerships
9%

Source: *Statistical Abstract of the United States*

Advantages of a Sole Proprietorship. The major advantages of a business with a single owner include the following:

Ease of starting. Obtaining a business license and meeting other legal requirements are usually the only steps needed to start a sole proprietorship. Your idea, funds, and willingness to accept the risk associated with running a business are all you need to get started. Throughout the world each day, thousands of people start companies that serve their customers and create employment opportunities.

Freedom of making business decisions. As a single proprietor, all company decisions are your own. As owner, you can run things yourself or hire others.

The owner keeps all profits. The difference between money taken in and payments for expenses is called **net income** or **profit.** Since you are taking all of the risk, you receive all of the financial rewards.

Pride of ownership. As your own boss you have the chance to see the results of your efforts. Many people like to have their own company so that they do not have to work for someone else.

Disadvantages of a Sole Proprietorship. The major disadvantages of a sole proprietorship include the following:

Limited sources of funds. The ability to raise money for a sole proprietorship is limited to the owner's contribution plus loans. As a new business owner, lenders may see you as a risky borrower. Even if you get a loan, it is likely to have a high rate of interest resulting in higher costs for the business.

Potential of long hours and hard work. Since many new and small companies find it difficult to compete against established businesses, you will probably put in many long hours. When you own your own business, you cannot call in sick unless you have dedicated employees you trust.

Unlimited risks. In other forms of business organizations, several owners share the risks. As the sole owner, you are responsible for all aspects of the enterprise. The owner has unlimited liability. **Unlimited liability** means that the owner's personal assets also can be used to pay for any debts of the business.

Limited life of the business. If the owner dies or is unable to run the business, the enterprise will either cease to exist or be sold to someone else. When the business is sold, it becomes a different company with a new owner.

Global Business Example: A Sole Proprietorship Races into the Automobile Industry

Soichiro Honda opened his own auto repair shop in 1928. He repaired cars and also raced them. In 1936, after setting a Japanese speed record, Honda barely escaped injury in a finish-line crash.

One year later, Honda started a piston ring company. The Sino-Japanese War and World War II increased demand for his products. In 1945, after his factory was nearly destroyed by bombs and an earthquake, he sold it to Toyota.

Next, came Honda's venture into motorized bicycles using small engines left over from the war. The exporting of motorcycles started in the 1950s, followed by production plants in other countries. Then in 1973, the Honda Civic was introduced. Besides motorcycles and automobiles, today Honda manufactures lawn mowers, outboard motors, portable generators, snow blowers, tillers, and water pumps. Soichiro Honda died in 1991 at the age of 84, leaving a multinational firm with a reputation for excellence.

Partnership

Companies that need additional sources of operating funds or the combined talents of several people may organize as a partnership. A **partnership** is a business that is owned by two or more people, but is not incorporated. Each owner, or partner, usually shares in both the decision making for the company and the profits.

The partnership form of business ownership can be used for any type of business. Stores, manufacturing companies, and restaurants can be organized as partnerships. Law firms are common examples of partnerships. Many professional sports teams use this type of ownership format.

Advantages of a Partnership.   The main advantages of organizing a business as a partnership are

Ease of creation.   As with the single proprietorship, a partnership is fairly easy to start. A written partnership agreement should be created to communicate clearly the individuals' responsibilities and the method of dividing the profits among owners.

Additional sources of funds.   With more than one owner, a partnership has the ability to raise more capital, expand business activities, and create larger company profits.

Availability of different talents.   Many partnerships can take advantage of the different skills of people. One partner may be responsible for selling, another takes care of company records, while a third supervises employees.

Disadvantages of a Partnership.   The main disadvantages of a partnership are

Partners are liable for debts of the business.   As with the sole proprietorship, a partnership has unlimited liability. Any of the partners may be held personally responsible for the debts of the business.

Profits are shared among several owners.   The written partnership agreement determines the division of profits. Even if one of the partners works harder than expected, the net income is divided based on the original agreement.

Potential for disagreement among owners.   Differences in opinions are likely to occur in every work situation. Two or more people who work together closely may have disagreements. Some people suggest that you avoid going into business with friends or relatives to prevent possible personal conflicts.

Business can dissolve suddenly.   When one partner dies or cannot continue in the partnership, the business must stop. At this point a new company and partnership agreement must be created. This may not be easy since some of the company assets may have to be sold to buy the departing partner's share of the business.

Corporation

While sole proprietorships are the most common *type* of business in the United States, corporations account for 90 percent of the *sales* (see Figure 5-2). A **corporation** is a business that operates as a legal entity separate from any of the owners.

A corporation raises money for business activities through the sale of stock to individuals and organizations that wish to be part owners of the corporation. **Stock certificates** are the documents that represent ownership in a corporation. A sample stock certificate is shown in Figure 5-3.

The owners of a corporation are called **stockholders** or **shareholders**. Stockholders have two main rights: to earn dividends and to vote on company policies. Many people buy stock in corporations to earn **dividends,** which are a share of company profits.

Stockholders also indirectly control the management of the company. A stockholder has one vote for each share of stock owned. The stockholders vote to elect the board of directors of the company. The board of directors hires managers to run the company.

Unlike sole proprietorships and partnerships in which individual owners are responsible for any actions of the business, corporations act as a legal "person" on behalf of the owners.

Advantages of a Corporation.   When a group of people chooses to create a corporation, they have the advantages of

More sources of funds.   As a result of having many people interested in being part owners, corporations can raise funds more easily than can a sole proprietorship or partnership. This capital can be used for a company to purchase expensive equipment or to build large factories.

Figure 5-2
Corporations account for the major portion of sales in the U.S. economy.

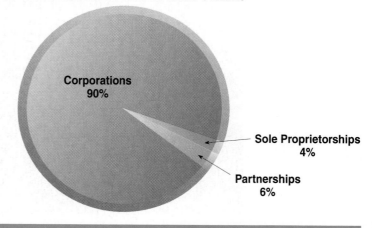

SALES OF SOLE PROPRIETORSHIPS, PARTNERSHIPS, AND CORPORATIONS IN THE UNITED STATES

Corporations
90%

Sole Proprietorships
4%

Partnerships
6%

Source: *Statistical Abstract of the United States*

Figure 5-3

A stock certificate certifies ownership in a corporation.

INCORPORATED UNDER THE LAWS OF THE STATE OF NEW HAMPSHIRE

The Corporation is authorized to issue 300 Shares Without Nominal or Par Value

This Certifies that _____ is the owner of _____ fully paid and non-assessable Shares of the above Corporation transferable only on the books of the Corporation by the holder hereof in person or by duly authorized Attorney upon surrender of this Certificate properly endorsed.

In Witness Whereof, the said Corporation has caused this Certificate to be signed by its duly authorized officers and to be sealed with the Seal of the Corporation.

Dated _____

SECRETARY-TREASURER   PRESIDENT

Fixed financial liability of owners. The business risk of a corporation is spread among many owners. A company such as General Motors or McDonald's has thousands of stockholders. Each person who buys a share of stock has **limited liability,** meaning that they are only responsible for the debts of the corporation up to the amount they invested. Unlike sole proprietors and partners, people who become part owners of a corporation can only lose the amount of money paid for the stock.

Availability of specialized management. Most corporations are large organizations that can afford to hire the most skilled people to run the company. The board of directors of the corporation hires the president and other administrative employees.

Unlimited life of the company. Unlike a sole proprietorship or partnership, a corporation is a continuing entity. When stockholders die or sell their stock, the company continues to exist. Ownership just transfers to other people.

Disadvantages of a Corporation. The organizers of a corporation have the disadvantages of

A difficult creation process. The organizers of a corporation must usually meet complex government requirements. A **charter** is the document granted by the state or federal government that allows a company to organize as a corporation.

Owners are usually limited in their control. Unless you own a large share of the stock, you are unable to influence the operations of a corporation. Small or family-held corporations may have only a few stockholders, but most large corporations are owned by thousands of individuals.

Double taxation on corporate earnings. Sole proprietors and partners pay individual income tax on their companies' earnings. In contrast, a corporation is first taxed as a separate entity; it pays corporate income tax. In addition, stockholders pay personal income tax on the dividends they receive. Therefore, corporate earnings are taxed twice.

Other Forms of Business Organizations

While most businesses are organized as one of the three mentioned so far, other types exist for special situations. A **municipal corporation** is an incorporated town or city organized to provide services for citizens rather than to make a profit.

    Nonprofit corporations are created to provide a service and are not concerned with making a profit. Included in this category are churches and synagogues, some hospitals, private colleges and universities, many charities, the American Red Cross, Boy Scouts of America, and the Salvation Army.

    A **cooperative** is a business owned by its members and operated for their benefit. Consumer cooperatives may be formed by a group of people in a community or at a place of worship. The group is organized to

purchase food or other goods and services at a lower cost than usual. Any profits are returned to the cooperative members. A credit union is a cooperative created to provide savings and loan services to its members.

Global Business Example: How Do You Spell *Inc.*?

In the United States you can tell that a business is a corporation if the abbreviation *Inc.* (meaning incorporated) follows the company name. In Canada, Japan, and England, *Ltd.* (for limited) is used, referring to the limited liability of the owners. The notation for a corporate form of business in other countries is

France, Belgium	.Sarl
Spain, Mexico, Portugal, and Brazil.	.S.A.
Germany, Switzerland	.GmbH
Netherlands	.N.V.
Italy	.Srl
Denmark	.A/S

THE MULTINATIONAL CORPORATION

In 1670, King Charles II of Britain granted a business charter to create a trading company named after English explorer Henry Hudson. The Hudson's Bay Company started as an international fur trading enterprise and today operates nearly 500 stores throughout Canada.

Just as the Hudson's Bay Company started as a global business, many firms today operate in several countries. A **multinational company** or **corporation (MNC)** is an organization that conducts business in several countries. MNCs are also called *global companies, transnational companies,* or *worldwide companies.* Figure 5-4 on page 102 shows an example of the global business operations that a multinational company might have.

MNCs usually consist of a parent company in a home country and divisions or separate companies in one or more host countries. For example, Mitsubishi of Japan (home country) consists of 160 companies doing business in several countries (host countries). IBM has business operations in over 100 countries.

Today, as a result of widespread international business activities, thousands of multinational corporations exist. Many of these companies are very large. Royal Dutch/Shell, Ford, Exxon, General Motors, IBM, and Toyota have annual sales that exceed the GDP of many countries in the world.

Figure 5-4

A multinational company has business operations in different countries.

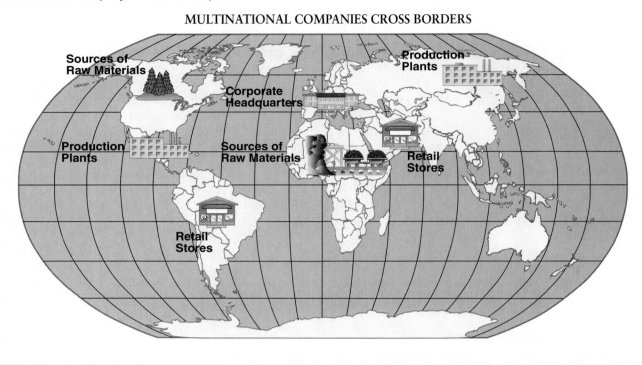

MULTINATIONAL COMPANIES CROSS BORDERS

Activities of Multinational Companies

Multinational companies get involved in global activities to take advantage of business opportunities in other geographic areas. The potential for MNCs to sell goods or services in other countries is the result of a competitive advantage held by a company. This edge can be the result of technology, lower costs, location, or availability of natural resources.

Another major activity of MNCs is the need to consider and adapt to different societies. As previously discussed, social and cultural influences and political and legal concerns must be continually monitored. For example, if a company is not aware of changes in a country's tax law, the result could be a decrease in profits.

Concerns About Multinational Companies

The presence of a multinational company can have many benefits for a host country—jobs, more products and services for consumers, and even improved roads created by the MNC. Two main concerns about MNCs, however, do exist.

As a foreign company becomes a major business, the economic power of the MNC can make a host country dependent. Workers will depend on the MNC for jobs. Consumers will be dependent on the company for needed goods and services. The MNC could become the main economic entity of a country.

When this occurs, another concern arises. The MNC could start to influence and even control the political power of the country. The company may require certain tax laws or regulations that only benefit the powerful MNC. The regulation and control of global companies is likely to be an issue for consideration for years to come.

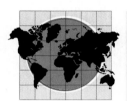

Global Business Example: South Korea's Samsung

Samsung started as a rice mill in 1938; however, nearly all of its factories were destroyed during the Korean War. Today, the company has 29 major divisions and is the fourteenth largest company in the world. Samsung is South Korea's largest *chaebol* (industrial group), manufacturing and selling electronics, ships, chemicals, food products, and heavy machinery.

METHODS FOR GETTING INVOLVED IN INTERNATIONAL BUSINESS

As shown in Figure 5-5 on page 104, there are eight main ways for a company to get involved in international business. As you move up the steps, the firm has more control over its foreign business activities. For example, indirect exporting has less risk associated with it than a joint venture. However, a company has more direct control over its business dealings with a joint venture than with indirect exporting.

Indirect Exporting

At first, a business organization may get involved with international business by finding a demand for its service or product without really trying. **Indirect exporting** occurs when a company sells its products in a foreign market without any special activity for that purpose.

During a sales meeting or other business encounter, for example, someone in a foreign company may show interest in your product. A buyer who represents several companies may tell a small manufacturing company about the need for its product in southeast Asia. Since the company was not looking for foreign business opportunities, indirect exporting is sometimes called *casual* or *accidental* exporting.

Figure 5-5

A company may choose from a variety of methods to get involved in international business.

METHODS FOR GETTING INVOLVED IN INTERNATIONAL BUSINESS

Wholly Owned Subsidiary

Foreign Direct Investment

Joint Venture

Franchising

Licensing

Management Contracting

Direct Exporting

Indirect Exporting

Indirect exporting makes use of agents and brokers who bring together sellers and buyers of products in different countries. This method of international business has minimum costs and risks. Many companies have started their foreign business activities using this method.

Direct Exporting

After sales increase and a company decides to get more involved in international business, the organization will probably create its own exporting department. **Direct exporting** occurs when a company actively seeks and conducts exporting. The company may still use agents or brokers from outside of the organization; however, a manager within the company plans, implements, and controls the exporting activities.

While direct exporting requires higher costs than indirect exporting, the company has more control over its foreign business activities. The exporting process is discussed in greater detail in the next chapter.

Management Contracting

Knowledge is a powerful tool in business. An ability to find business opportunities, coordinate resources, solve problems, and make productive decisions is a skill that will be in demand throughout your life. The abilities of managers to assist companies in developing countries are important exports for industrialized countries. A **management contract** is a situation in which a company sells only its management skills. This has a fairly low risk for a company since managers can usually leave a country quickly if the business environment becomes too risky.

An example of management contracting may involve an hotel company that agrees to help hotel owners in other countries. Additional discussion of management skills and activities are contained in Unit 3 of this book.

Licensing

To produce items in other countries without being actively involved, a company can allow a foreign company to use a procedure it owns. **Licensing** is selling the right to use some intangible property (production process, trademark, or brand name) for a fee or royalty. The Gerber Company started selling its baby food products in Japan using licensing. The use of cartoon characters or sports teams' emblems on hats, shirts, jackets, notebooks, luggage, and other products is also the result of licensing agreements.

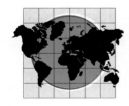

A licensing agreement provides a fee or royalty to the company granting the license. This payment is in return for the right to use the process, brand name, or trademark. The Disney Company, for example, receives a royalty from the amusement park it licensed in Japan. Licensing has a low monetary investment so the potential financial return is usually low. However, the risk for the company is also low.

Global Business Example: Businesses Expand to Malaysia

Since gaining independence in 1963, the political stability of Malaysia has made the country an attractive destination for many foreign investors. U.S. companies such as Colgate-Palmolive, General Electric, Goodyear, Motorola, and Texas Instruments have had a strong presence in the country. Malaysia's neighbors, however, are even larger investors. Taiwan and Japan have built and operate business facilities to produce manufacturing equipment, oil and gas equipment, computers, telecommunications equipment, chemicals, and electronics products.

Global Highlight: Australia's Importing of Convicts

Economic development in a geographic area can result from unusual circumstances. Consider Australia in the 1700s. At the start of the Industrial Revolution in Britain, food shortages, lost jobs, and strict laws contributed to an increase in crime. People were jailed for their inability to pay bills (there were no bankruptcy protections in those days). The British people wanted lawbreakers and debtors removed from their society. The newly independent United States no longer allowed British criminals to be sent there, so a new location was needed.

In 1787, Captain Arthur Philip of the Royal Fleet navigated 11 ships with 759 convicts to Port Jackson (now called Sydney) in Australia. One of the early governors of Australia was Captain William Bligh, who had gained notoriety when the crew of his ship, the H.M.S. Bounty, rebelled.

Australia continued to be used as a penal colony until 1840, when free settlers began to dominate the area. In total, about 160,000 convicts were sent to Australia over the years. The country gained its independence from Britain in 1901.

Franchising

Another method commonly used to expand into other countries is the **franchise**, which is the right to use a company name or business process in a specific way. Organizations contract with people in other countries to set up a business that looks and operates like the parent company. The company obtaining the franchise will usually adapt various business elements. Marketing elements such as the taste of food products, packaging, and advertising messages must meet cultural sensitivies and meet legal requirements.

Franchising and licensing are similar. Both involve a royalty payment for the right to use a process or famous company name. Licensing, however, usually involves a manufacturing process, while franchising involves selling a product.

Franchise agreements are popular with fast-food companies. McDonald's, Burger King, Wendy's, Kentucky Fried Chicken, Dominos Pizza, and Pizza Hut all have used franchising to expand into foreign markets.

Joint Ventures

As mentioned earlier in this chapter, the partnership can provide benefits to all owners. One type of international partnership is the **joint venture**, an agreement between two or more companies (from different countries) to share a business project (see Figure 5-6).

The main benefit of a joint venture is the sharing of raw materials, shipping facilities, management, or production facilities. Concerns of this business agreement are sharing of profits and less control since more than one company is involved.

Joint venture arrangements can share costs, risks, and profits equally or in any combination. One company may have only 10 percent ownership while the other has 90 percent. It all depends on the contributions and agreements that are reached.

Joint ventures can be used for just about any type of business activity. This arrangement is especially popular for manufacturing. Joint ventures between Japanese and U.S. automobile manufacturers have been common. For example, the Ford Motor Company entered a joint venture with Mazda Motor Corporation. Ford used Mazda-produced parts for several cars; Mazda set up assembly plants for Ford motor vehicles.

Figure 5-6

A joint venture allows companies in different countries to cooperate for a common business purpose.

A JOINT VENTURE IN ACTION

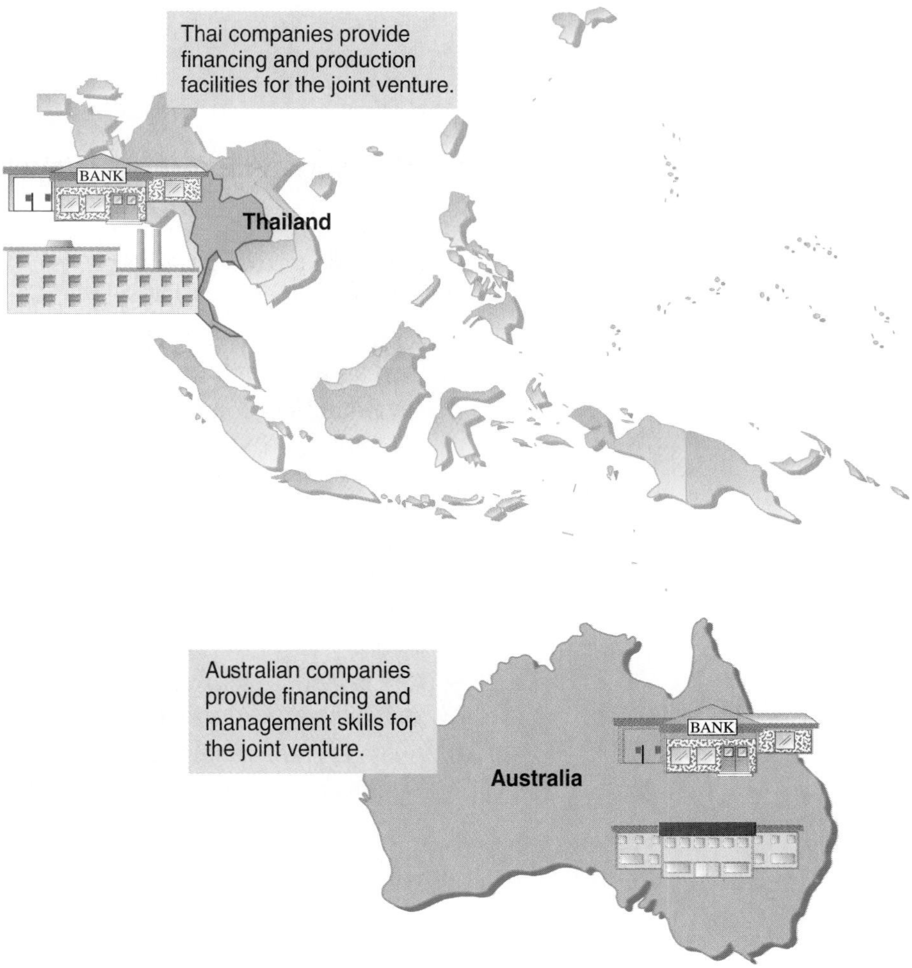

Thai companies provide financing and production facilities for the joint venture.

Thailand

Australian companies provide financing and management skills for the joint venture.

Australia

Foreign Direct Investment

As a company gets more involved in international business, it may use money to buy land or other resources in other countries. This is called a **foreign direct investment**. Common purchases with this method are real estate (such as office buildings, stores, and factories) and existing companies. As of the early 1990s, previously U.S.-owned businesses Burger King, Pillsbury, and Stouffers were owned by foreign companies.

Wholly Owned Subsidiary

A **wholly owned subsidiary** is an independent company owned by a parent company. Multinational companies frequently have wholly owned subsidiaries in various countries that are the result of foreign direct investment.

To prevent economic control of one country by another, a nation may restrict how much of its land or factories may be sold to foreign owners. For example, Mexico only allows a foreign investor to own 49 percent of a Mexican company.

Global Business Exercise: Ways to Do Foreign Business

For each of the following situations, tell what method the company is using for its global business activities.

1. A company from Singapore is working with businesses in Kenya to help organize and run hospitals.
2. A Vietnamese company decides to obtain assistance from an Israeli company to share the production costs and profits of a chemical manufacturing enterprise.
3. A British toy company allows a Japanese company to create clothing and school supplies with one of the British company's doll characters on the products.
4. A company in Egypt has purchased 51 percent of the stock of a company in Peru.
5. A small food-packaging firm cannot afford to sell in other countries, so it asks an export agent to obtain orders for the company.
6. An Italian restaurant is planning to allow a company in New Zealand to operate several restaurants using the same name and menu items.

Back to the Beginning: Mitsubishi: From Trading Company to Multinational Corporation

Reread the case at the beginning of this chapter and answer the following questions:

1. What economic and social factors may have contributed to the creation and expansion of Mitsubishi?
2. What are the benefits and potential problems of the company being involved in many types of products and services?
3. How might Mitsubishi expand its international business activities in the future?

KNOWING GLOBAL BUSINESS TERMS

The following terms should become part of your business vocabulary. For each numbered item find the term that has the same meaning.

- charter
- cooperative
- corporation
- direct exporting
- dividends
- foreign direct investment
- franchise
- indirect exporting
- joint venture
- licensing
- limited liability
- management contract
- multinational company or corporation (MNC)
- municipal corporation
- net income or profit
- nonprofit corporations
- partnership
- sole or single proprietorship
- stock certificate
- stockholders or shareholders
- unlimited liability
- wholly owned subsidiary

1. A business owned by its members and operated for their benefit.
2. The difference between money taken in and expenses.
3. The owners of a corporation.
4. Selling the right to use some intangible property for a fee or royalty.
5. A business owned by two or more people that is not incorporated.
6. The situation in which a business owner is only responsible for the debts of the business up to the amount invested.

7. The document granted by government allowing a company to organize as a corporation.

8. An incorporated town or city.

9. A share of ownership in a corporation.

10. The selling of a company's products in a foreign market without any special activity for that purpose.

11. An independent foreign company owned by a parent company.

12. The situation in which a business owner's personal assets can be used to pay any debts of the business that are unpaid.

13. A business that operates as a legal entity separate from any of the owners.

14. A situation in which a company sells only its management skills in another country.

15. A share of corporate earnings paid to stockholders.

16. A business owned by one person.

17. The right to use a company name or business process in a specific way.

18. An agreement between two or more companies to share a business project.

19. A company actively seeking and conducting exporting.

20. The purchase of land or other resources in a foreign country.

21. An organization that conducts business in several countries.

22. Organizations that are not concerned with making a profit.

REVIEWING YOUR READING

Answer these questions to reinforce your knowledge of the main ideas of this chapter.

1. Describe the three main types of business organizations.

2. What are the advantages and disadvantages of a single proprietorship?

3. What are the advantages and disadvantages of a partnership?

4. What is limited liability?

5. What are the advantages and disadvantages of organizing as a corporation?

6. What are some possible concerns about multinational corporations?

7. How does indirect exporting differ from direct exporting?

8. Why is management contracting a safe method for getting involved in international business?

9. What is the difference between licensing and franchising?

10. What is a wholly owned subsidiary?

EXPANDING YOUR HORIZONS

You will not find the complete answers to the following questions in your textbook. You will need to use your critical-thinking skills. Think about these questions, gather information from other sources, analyze possible responses, and discuss them with others. Then, develop your own oral or written responses as instructed by your teacher.

1. List reasons why most companies in the world start out and remain sole proprietorships. How does being a single proprietorship benefit or limit a company's ability to become involved in international business?

2. Describe a situation in which a partnership or sole proprietorship could raise capital to expand business activities more easily than a corporation.

3. Why do you think the government makes the creation of a corporation more difficult than the creation of other forms of business ownership?

4. Name goods and services that could be the basis for creating a consumer cooperative.

5. What are some ways a multinational company can have a competitive advantage over local businesses?

6. What types of restrictions might a foreign government put on a multinational corporation doing business in its country?

7. Describe actions a manager might take when (a) planning, (b) implementing, and (c) controlling a company's exporting activities.

8. What are some services companies could sell to other countries using management contracts?

9. How would a business that sells licenses and franchises control the image of the company name?

10. What are some concerns people might have about a company making many foreign investments in their country?

The ability to find information from various sources is an important international business skill. The following activities will help you investigate various topics. You will also learn to apply class ideas to situations outside of the classroom.

1. Collect advertisements, articles, and other information about businesses that buy or sell products made in other countries. Describe how these companies have gotten involved in international business.

2. Interview a local business owner about the form of business organization used by her or his company. Ask the owner how the company got started, and ask for suggestions he or she could give to people who want to start a business.

3. Conduct library research about a foreign company that conducts business in the United States. Obtain information on its history, type of organization, and the methods it uses for international business activities.

4. Create a poster or bulletin-board display of products that are produced and sold by multinational companies.

5. Conduct an opinion survey of students and others to determine their attitudes toward products and companies from other countries. Survey questions could include: Which countries make the best products? Do consumers benefits from being able to buy products from other countries? Should our government restrict products from other countries? Should foreign governments restrict U.S. products from entering their markets?

6. *Global Career Activity.* Talk to someone who owns a business. Obtain information about the types of jobs the person had before becoming an entrepreneur.

Continuing Enrichment Project: Planning and Organizing Global Business Operations

To complete this project either use the company you selected in Chapter 1, select another multinational company, or create a fictitious one. Make use of previously collected materials or do additional research to get the information you need.

1. Describe how your company might have started as a sole proprietorship or a partnership. Explain the factors that may have influenced the owners' decision to select this form of business organization.

2. If the company becomes a multinational corporation, what benefits and problems could result?

3. Describe appropriate international business opportunities for the company. What products and services would be most appropriate for different geographic regions? What economic, cultural, legal, or political influences must the company consider?

4. Which of the methods described in the final section of this chapter (see Figure 5-5) would be appropriate for the company to use for international business activities? Explain the possible use of two or more of these methods for getting involved in international business.

Prepare a written report that answers these questions. Or, if instructed by your teacher, create a poster or scrapbook with pictures and information obtained for these questions.

Regional Profile

Asia-Pacific Rim

Suppose you were born in the late twentieth century in the city of Djakarta on the island of Java in Indonesia. Indonesia is a 13,677-island archipelago located south of the Asian mainland. It was once known as the East Indies. Over 8 million people live in your city, speaking languages ranging from Bahasa Indonesian to Javanese. Although your relatives on Sumatra work on offshore oil rigs, you sell food to tourists.

Perhaps you would rather have been born in Japan. Here you might live in Toyota's company town, Toyota City, where you would attend a Toyota-owned school, live in a Toyota-built home, and eventually work in a Toyota facility. You would make an excellent salary, but you would live in a country that experiences 1,500 earthquakes per year.

Archaeologists believe that the earliest Asian civilization developed about 2,500 B.C. Its ruins lie in present day Pakistan and India in the Indus River Valley. This civilization is not as ancient as the oldest Egyptian kingdom; however, its achievements are interesting. These ancient Asian cities included well-planned streets, large public buildings, and multistory houses with indoor bathrooms.

Our knowledge of early Chinese civilization comes from the discovery of oracle bones that were used instead of paper. Priests in the Shang Dynasty (1700 to 1000 B.C.) scratched questions to their ancestors on animal bones before firing the bone, forcing it to crack. The priest would interpret the pattern of cracks as an answer to the question.

China has the oldest continuous civilization in the world. Mountain barriers, the Gobi Desert, and large bodies of water protected it from invasion and cultural influences for centuries. For added protection, The Great Wall in northern China was completed in about 200 B.C. By the 1800s A.D., a weak Chinese dynasty gave in to European demands for trading privileges, causing large sections of China to be claimed by Great Britain, France, Germany, Russia, and Japan. The communist government of the People's Republic of China (the ruling party from 1949 on) reacted to this western influence by isolating China. However, recent economic reforms have led to a more open policy.

The Japanese archipelago consists of four main islands and thousands of smaller ones. Together these islands make up the modern nation of Japan. Japan's history is rather brief when compared to that of India or China. By 500 A.D. it was ruled by emperors and powerful clans (noble families). The shoguns (great generals) took power in the twelfth century and created the shogunate (military government) that lasted until 1867.

Japan's cultural development borrowed heavily from the Chinese. In the sixth century, Prince Shotoku encouraged the Japanese to accept the Chinese political philosophy of Confucianism that stressed the importance of an orderly society with obedience to authority. The Chinese also brought Buddhism to Japan; it had been founded by the Indian philosopher Siddhārtha Gautama

(Buddha), who lived 563–483 B.C. He taught that suffering results from desire and that inner peace is achieved only by letting go of desire, doing good for others, respecting life, controlling your thoughts, and practicing meditation.

Like the Chinese, the Japanese wanted to protect the purity of their culture by preventing trade with the West. However, in 1853, the United States sent Commodore Matthew Perry and four warships to Japan in order to force an end to Japan's isolation. Instead of war, the shogun signed trade treaties with Britain, France, Holland, Russia, and the United States.

By the twentieth century Japan was competing actively in the global economy. With an expanding economy and population, Japan fought wars with Russia and China over control of Korea and Manchuria. By 1940, Japanese troops had taken the eastern part of China (beginning another war with that country) and Southeast Asia where they gained access to rich deposits of oil, rubber, and other essential natural resources. After the United States cut off exports to Japan in response to its occupation of China, the Japanese navy attacked the U.S. naval base at Pearl Harbor in Hawaii on December 7, 1941. This pushed the United States into World War II.

The atomic bombs dropped on Hiroshima and Nagasaki in August of 1945 killed about 100,000 people. Many thousands more were injured and Japan surrendered on September 2, 1945. Economic recovery began after the war and the manufacture of products for export has helped to drive an economy that provides one of the highest standards of living in the world.

The Southeast Asian Peninsula juts out of the Asian Continent south of China. Vietnam, a long narrow country, runs along the peninsula's east coast. Like other countries in the area, Vietnam contains lush tropical rain forests and fertile river valleys. And, like other countries in the area, Vietnam has a history of domination by stronger countries. China ruled Vietnam for about 1,000 years, and it was a French colony from the 1880s until it was lost to the Japanese in World War II.

The Vietnamese defeated the French, who had returned when the Japanese were forced out, in 1954 and negotiations divided the country into North and South Vietnam. The Cold War brought 500,000 U.S. soldiers to prevent the communist-ruled North from taking over the South. However, the U.S. troops were forced out in 1973 and a unified Communist Vietnam was formed in 1975. By the 1990s Vietnam's per capita income was just $125 per year. The Vietnamese look forward to loans from the International Monetary Fund and closer relations with the United States to build their economy.

Other nations in Southeast Asia—such as Myanmar (formerly Burma), the Philippines, and Thailand—face continuing political unrest. Vietnam's neighbor, Cambodia, suffered through years of repression and civil war. A communist government known as the Khmer Rouge killed between 1 and 2 million people in the late 1970s. As civil war continued in 1993, 90 percent of the country's registered voters turned out for the first free elections in Cambodian history.

Asia and the Pacific Rim is a region of contrasts. People living in Australia, Japan, and New Zealand enjoy a stable economy and a modern democratic society, while human suffering is the rule in Pakistan, Bangladesh, and Laos. Food shortages and political turmoil bring daily misery to millions. The region is faced with great challenges for the twenty-first century. Indians will seek relief from religious and ethnic violence, young Chinese reformers will battle political repression in China, and Koreans will struggle with reunification. Population and environmental problems will compete with the effort to build modern industrial states.

Importing, Exporting, and Trade Relations

After studying this chapter and completing the end-of-chapter activities, you will be able to

- Explain the importance of importing.
- Identify activities related to importing.
- Discuss the steps of the exporting process.
- Describe the economic effects of foreign trade.
- Differentiate between types of trade agreements.
- List factors that affect international business competition.
- Explain the types of competitive market situations.

The Scoop on Ice Cream Exports

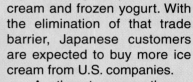

In recent years, annual U.S. ice cream exports were over $9 million. Many of these sales were in Pacific Rim locations such as Hong Kong, Singapore, and Taiwan. The growing economies in that region make it an attractive area for ice cream exports.

During the late 1980s, annual exports of U.S. ice cream to Japan were only $200,000. This was due to a Japanese import quota for ice cream and frozen yogurt. With the elimination of that trade barrier, Japanese customers are expected to buy more ice cream from U.S. companies.

Another strong growth area for ice cream exports is the Caribbean market. The hot climate and many tourists in that region create a strong demand for ice cream.

Imagine how life in the United States would be without international business. Most television sets, calculators, athletic shoes, and video recorders bought in the United States come from other countries. And, these products are only a few of the imported products in use each day. Importing provides a wide variety of products and services for U.S. consumers. Exporting creates jobs and expands business opportunities. Importing and exporting are primary international business activities.

THE IMPORTANCE OF IMPORTING

Imports are services or products bought by a company or government from businesses in other countries. Businesses can get involved in international trade by importing goods and services and selling them in their own country. The importing business can create new sales or expand sales with existing customers. A company usually gets involved in importing for the reasons described in the following sections.

Product Demand

Customers who want a unique item or a certain quality may desire to purchase a foreign-made product. Some goods and services may be available only from other countries. For example, clothing from Europe is often in demand among U.S. consumers.

Lower Costs

The prices of goods and services are constantly changing. An item from one country may be less expensive than the same item from another country. Electronic products manufactured in Taiwan are frequently less expensive than similar items produced elsewhere.

Production Inputs

Raw materials and component parts used for processing or assembly are regularly purchased from companies in other countries. For example, the radios, engines, transmissions, and windshield washer systems for many cars made in the United States come from companies in Canada, Mexico, Brazil, Japan, and Korea.

IMPORTING ACTIVITIES

What does a company have to do to become an importer? As shown in Figure 6-1, importing usually involves four main activities. The first activity is to determine if imported products will be purchased by consumers in this country. As with any business venture, risks exist. Many companies have imported goods to sell, only to have these items remain in a warehouse with no buyers.

The second importing activity is to contact foreign suppliers. Finding foreign companies that provide what you want, when you want it, may be difficult. By using the appropriate information sources, importers can identify the companies that will best serve their needs.

The third importing activity is to finalize the purchase agreement. The importing company must come to an agreement with the supplier

Figure 6-1

Importers go through several steps to find and purchase products that are in demand.

IMPORTING ACTIVITIES

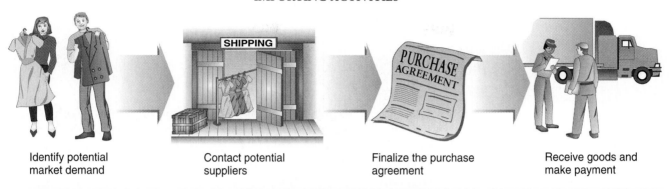

Identify potential market demand   Contact potential suppliers   Finalize the purchase agreement   Receive goods and make payment

on specific terms for the purchase. For example: Who will pay for shipping? When will items be delivered? How will payment be made? Will payment be made in advance, during shipping, or after the receipt of the goods? These are just some of the details that need to be described in the purchase agreement.

Finally, the fourth activity is to receive the goods and make payment (if not done in advance). This includes checking the order for accuracy or damage, paying for the order, and paying any import duties. A duty can be based on either the value of goods or other factors, such as quantity or weight.

These duties are paid to customs officials. **Customs officials** are government employees who are authorized to collect the duties levied on imports. The term *customs* also refers to the *procedures* involved in the collection of duties. You may have heard a person traveling to another country say "I have to go through customs." This means the traveler must report to customs officials the value of anything bought in the country they are leaving or anything they plan to sell in the country they are entering.

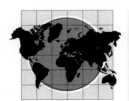

Global Business Example: An Importing Error

A U.S. retail company contracted with a foreign shirtmaker to manufacture men's shirts. The contract stated that the shirts must be made of 60 percent cotton and 40 percent polyester—and shirt labels were provided to that effect. The shirtmaker manufactured shirts that were 35 percent cotton and 65 percent polyester. Without verifying the material content, the U.S. company accepted the shirts and sold them with the incorrect information on the label. The company was fined by the Federal Trade Commission for deceptive labeling. How might this situation have been avoided?

THE EXPORTING PROCESS

A company can export its goods or services to companies in other countries. *Indirect* exporting occurs when a company sells its products in a foreign market without actively seeking out those opportunities. More often, however, a business will conduct *direct* exporting by actively seeking export opportunities.

Exporting activities are similar to importing, just viewed from the other side of the transaction. As exporters, however, businesses face different decisions. As shown in Figure 6-2, the exporting process involves five steps.

Figure 6-2
Successful exporting can help a nation expand its economic activities and create additional jobs.

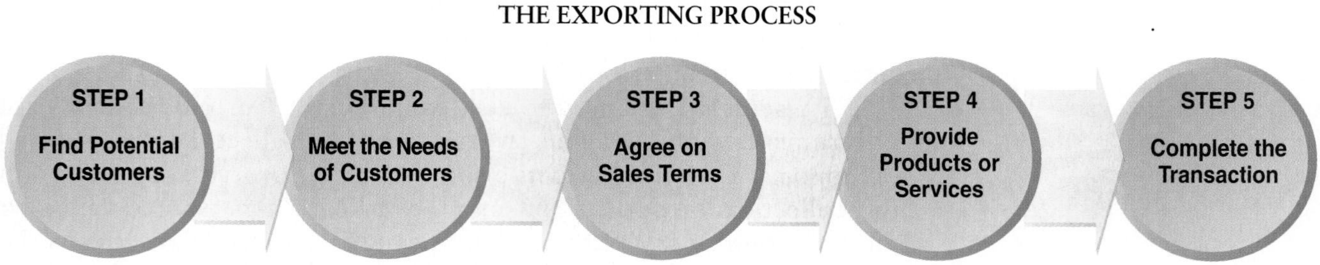

THE EXPORTING PROCESS

STEP 1	STEP 2	STEP 3	STEP 4	STEP 5
Find Potential Customers	Meet the Needs of Customers	Agree on Sales Terms	Provide Products or Services	Complete the Transaction

Step One–Find Potential Customers

Before you sell anything, you have to find buyers. Who are the people who want to buy your goods and services? Where are these people located? Are the potential customers willing and able to purchase your products?

Answers to these questions may be found partially through library research. Materials are available about the buying habits of people in different countries. Also, businesspeople familiar with foreign markets have experience helping companies that want to sell in other countries.

Step Two–Meet the Needs of Customers

Next, determine if your product or service can be used by people in other countries. Visits by company representatives to possible markets around the world are one way to make sure your product can be sold there. If visits are not possible, obtain reliable information from others.

Will your product be accepted by foreign customers exactly as it is or will it be necessary to adapt it? Product adaptation can be in the form of smaller packages, different ingredients, or revised label information to meet geographic, social, cultural, and legal needs.

Step Three–Agree on Sales Terms

Every business transaction involves shipping and payment terms. How will the product be shipped? Who will pay for shipping costs, the buyer or the seller? In what currency will the payment be made? What foreign exchange rate will be used? When is the payment due?

Shipping costs vary for different types of transportation. Air freight is more costly than water transportation; however, it is also much quicker. Items in high demand or perishable products might require the quickest available method of delivery.

Transportation costs can be a major portion of the cost of exporting. It is important to consider which party will pay transportation costs. Sometimes the seller pays for shipping; in other situations, the buyer pays. Certain terms are used to describe the shipping and payment methods. **Free on board (FOB)** means the selling price of the product includes the cost of loading the exported goods into transport vessels at the specified place.

FOB is just one way that buyers and sellers may agree to pay shipping costs. **Cost, insurance, and freight (CIF)** means that the cost of the goods, insurance, and freight are included in the price quoted. **Cost and freight (C&F)** indicates that the price includes the cost of the goods and freight, but the buyer must pay for insurance separately.

Banks and other financial institutions are commonly involved in export transactions. A company may have to borrow funds to finance the cost of manufacturing and shipping a product for which payment will not be received until a later date. Besides loans, international financial institutions offer other exporting services.

Step Four–Provide Products or Services

After agreement is reached on selling terms, the finished goods are shipped. Or if the exchange involves a service, the company must now perform the required tasks for its foreign customers.

Companies are available to help exporters with shipping. A **freight forwarder** arranges for the shipping of goods to customers in other countries. Like a travel agent for cargo, these companies take care of the reservations needed to get an exporter's merchandise to the required destination.

Often, a freight forwarder will accumulate several small export shipments and combine them into one larger shipment in order to get lower freight rates. Since these companies are actively involved in international trade, freight forwarders are excellent sources of information about export regulations, shipping costs, and foreign import regulations.

Various export documents are necessary for shipping merchandise to other countries. A **bill of lading** records the agreement between the exporter and the transportation company. This document serves as a receipt for the exported items. A **certificate of origin** states the name of the country in which the shipped goods were produced. This document may be used to determine the amount of any import tax.

Step Five–Complete the Transaction

If payment has not been received, it would be due at this time. Many times, payment involves exchanging one country's currency for another's. Financial institutions convert currency and are usually involved in the payment step.

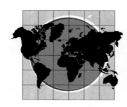

Global Business Example: Exporting Hurdles

The United States Department of Commerce estimates that thousands of small- and medium-sized businesses that do not export could easily get involved in international business. The following are common reasons that companies do not export:

- No company representatives in foreign countries.
- Products not appropriate for foreign consumers.
- Insufficient production facilities to manufacture enough goods for exporting.
- High costs of doing business in other countries.
- Difficulty understanding foreign business procedures.
- Difficulty obtaining payment from foreign customers.

Most of these barriers could be overcome if companies attempted to obtain assistance from government agencies or trade organizations.

THE ECONOMIC EFFECT OF FOREIGN TRADE

Every importing and exporting transaction has economic effects. The difference between a country's exports and imports is called its *balance of trade*. However, balance of trade does not include *all* international business transactions, just imports and exports. Another economic measure is needed to summarize the total economic effect of foreign trade.

Balance of payments measures the total flow of money coming into a country minus the total flow going out (see Figure 6-3). Included in this economic measurement are exports, imports, investments, tourist spending, and financial assistance. For example, in recent years, tourism has helped our nation's balance of payments because it has increased the flow of money entering the United States.

Figure 6-3

Balance of payments is the total flow of money coming into a country *minus* the total flow of money going out of a country.

BALANCE OF PAYMENTS

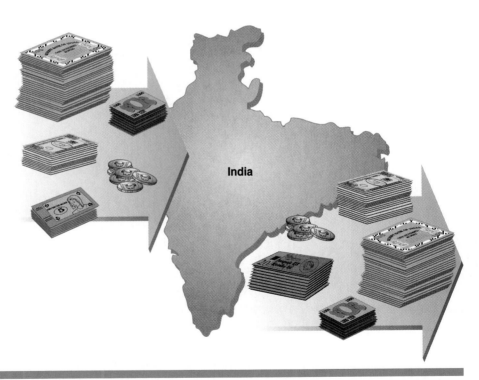

India

A country's balance of payments can either be positive or negative (see Figure 6-4 on page 124). A positive or favorable balance of payments occurs when a nation receives more money in a year than it pays out. A negative balance of payments is unfavorable. It is the result of a country sending more money out than it brings in.

Figure 6-4

When a nation receives more money from other nations than it pays out, that nation has a favorable balance of payments. When a nation pays out more money than it receives, that nation has an unfavorable balance of payments.

POSITIVE OR FAVORABLE BALANCE OF PAYMENTS

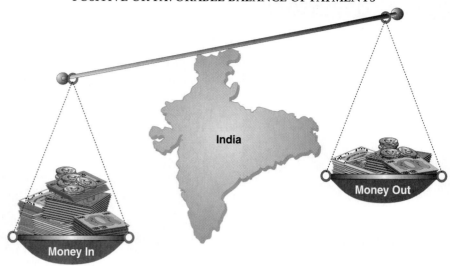

NEGATIVE OR UNFAVORABLE BALANCE OF PAYMENTS

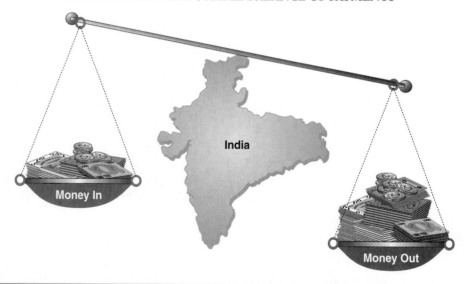

Some countries continually buy more foreign goods than they sell. The result is a **trade deficit,** which is the total amount a country owes to other countries as a result of importing more goods and services than are exported. The United States, despite being the largest exporter in the world, has had a trade deficit for many years. This situation can result in a country borrowing from other countries. Borrowing means the country must pay back money in the future, reducing the amount available for spending.

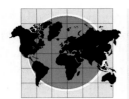

Global Business Example: Exporting U.S. Culture

The demand for U.S. clothing, soft drinks, fast food, candy, movies, music, television programs, and other entertainment is very strong throughout many parts of the world. Jeans, T-shirts, and athletic shoes are strong sell-

ers in many countries. People in some nations will wait in line for hours to pay a large amount for Coca-Cola or a McDonald's hamburger. Programs such as "I Love Lucy" and "Wheel of Fortune" are viewed by hundreds of millions of television viewers each day. What effect might U.S. culture have on the cultural environment in other countries?

TRADE AGREEMENTS

How can a country improve its trade situation? One answer is by negotiating trade agreements with other countries. As discussed in Chapter 4, the General Agreement on Tariffs and Trade (GATT) is a multicountry agreement intended to reduce trade barriers and to promote trade. GATT is continually changing as additional countries join the program and new agreements are reached.

Trade agreements also occur among countries that band together to promote economic development in a geographic region. Individual nations and companies may reach agreements that encourage international business activities.

Economic Communities

An **economic community** is an organization of countries that bond together to allow a free flow of products. The group acts as a single country for business activities with other regions of the world. An economic community is also called a *common market*.

Chapter 6 Importing, Exporting, and Trade Relations **125**

The European Economic Community, created in 1957 with six member countries, was designed to eliminate all tariff and trade barriers among these nations. As of the early 1990s, the European Community (EC), as it is now called, consisted of 12 countries with additional members expected. The group planned to eliminate all trade and financial restrictions among the member nations, including border controls and customs procedures.

As a common market, the EC has a strong economic position when trading with other regions of the world. The EC plans eventually to have a common currency, the same sales tax in all countries, and a free flow of all economic resources among the member countries.

The main benefits of an economic community are

- expanded trade with other regions of the world,
- reduced tariffs among the member countries,
- lower prices for consumers within the group, and
- expanded employment and investment opportunities.

Other examples of regional economic cooperation among countries include the Latin America Free Trade Association (LAFTA), the Association of Southeast Asian Nations (ASEAN), and the Economic Community of West African States (ECOWAS).

Barter Agreements

Most people have traded one item for another at one time or another. The exchange of goods and services between two parties with no money involved is **direct barter**. A company may use this method for international business transactions.

Since trading items of equal value is difficult, a different barter method is used. **Countertrade** is the exchange of products or services among companies in different countries; however, with countertrade some currency may be involved. PepsiCo, for example, sold soft drinks in China in exchange for mushrooms they used on their Pizza Hut pizzas. Figure 6-5 shows how countertrade can involve companies in several countries. Since countertrades are quite complex, they usually involve large companies. Smaller companies, however, can get involved in countertrade by working with large trading agents who bring together many buyers and sellers.

Companies use countertrade to avoid the risk of receiving payment in a monetary unit with limited value. Currencies from some nations are not in demand due to the weakness of those countries' economies. Countertrade also occurs when the government of an importing country requires the selling company to purchase products in return. This helps the importing country to avoid a trade deficit while stimulating economic growth.

Figure 6-5

Countertrade allows nations to participate in foreign trade with little or no exchange of currency.

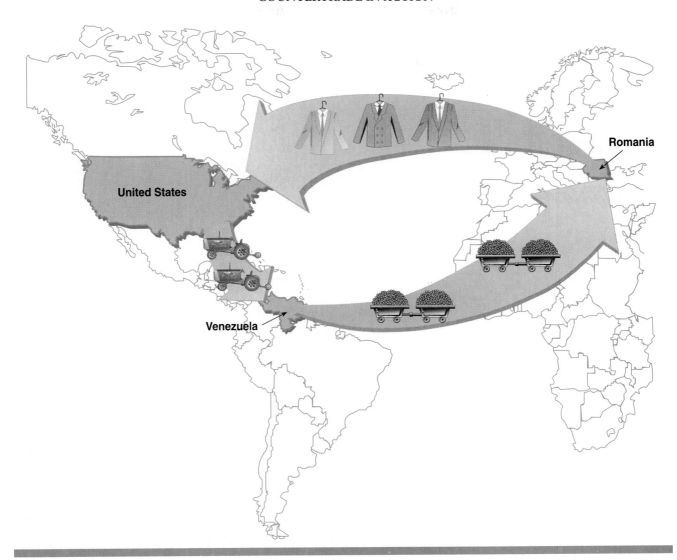

COUNTERTRADE IN ACTION

Free-Trade Zones

A **free-trade zone** is an area designated by a government for duty-free entry of nonprohibited goods. Free-trade zones are commonly located at a point of entry into a nation, such as a harbor or airport. Merchandise may be stored, displayed, or used without duties being paid. Duties are imposed on the goods only when the items pass from the free-trade zone into an area of the country subject to customs.

Global Business Example: The European Free-Trade Zone

The European Community (EC) and the European Free Trade Association have a free-trade zone consisting of 19 nations. The agreement of this association allows over 380 million consumers to purchase products from any of the countries without paying import or export taxes. This European Free Trade Zone includes the 12 EC member countries plus Austria, Finland, Iceland, Liechtenstein, Norway, Sweden, and Switzerland.

INTERNATIONAL BUSINESS COMPETITION

It is likely that you have participated in a sport or activity in which you attempted to do better than others or better than you had done previously. While winning may not always be the main goal, competition is an on-going activity for people, companies, and nations. In an effort to improve a country's economic situation, a strong competitive effort may be beneficial.

Companies compete in both domestic and international markets. The domestic market is made up of all the companies that sell similar products within the same country. In contrast, the international market is made up of companies that compete against companies in several countries.

For companies or countries to gain a competitive advantage they need to do something better, faster, or cheaper than others. While many people believe the best product is always successful, sometimes a company can also succeed through an effective delivery system. For example, Kodak film is available in almost every tourist location in the world. This distribution program makes it difficult for other film manufacturers to gain sales.

Companies can also compete by successfully doing one thing, and doing it well. For example, Japanese airplane companies have not been able to make aircraft that are in demand as much as planes made in the United States. Japanese companies, however, have specialized in producing parts used by U.S. aircraft manufacturers.

Factors Affecting Competition

Three major factors affect the degree of competition among businesses: the number of companies, business costs, and product differences. First, a product sold by many companies may appear to be very competitive. However if just a few large firms control the major portion of sales, competition is limited.

Second, the cost of doing business often affects competition. Expensive equipment or famous business names can prevent new companies from starting. If a business needs large amounts of capital and equipment to start operations, only a few companies are likely to enter the market. Or if a company has an established brand name, it will be very costly for new companies to make their name known.

The third factor that creates competition is product differences. Companies use advertising, brand names, packages, and ingredients to convince consumers that their products are different and better. The addition of flavoring to toothpaste or a pump on an athletic shoe are examples of attempts by companies to gain a competitive advantage. Companies use advertising messages to inform consumers about the benefits of their products and to persuade them to buy.

Benefits and Concerns of Competition

Competition can improve the economic situation and living conditions of a nation. Individual and company efforts to create better and faster goods and services have been a benefit for many nations. Some business competition, however, can result in major concerns. If a company becomes so large that it controls a geographic area or a portion of an economy, many people may suffer. Consumers will have to pay whatever the business charges. Workers will have to work for the amount the company wants to pay since other jobs may not be available. For these reasons, most countries have laws that limit the power of companies.

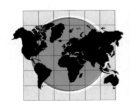

Global Business Example: Plane Competition

Japan's aerospace industry is very successful, but not because of aircraft manufacturing. Japanese manufacturers concentrate on components, such as fuselage parts, landing-gear doors, and on-board computers. These parts are used by companies such as Boeing and McDonnell Douglas.

Beside using successful planning and engineering methods, the airline parts companies are involved in hundreds of joint ventures and licensing agreements. These efforts increased Japanese aerospace exports 200 percent between 1987 and 1991.

Have you ever wondered why there are so many brands of breakfast cereal? Or why only a few stores sell a certain brand of shoes? These questions can be answered with an understanding of the competitive situations in an industry. An **industry** refers to companies in the same type of business. For example, Kellogg, General Mills, Kraft General Foods (Post), Quaker, and Ralston-Purina are the major companies in the cereal industry. Nike, Reebok, and adidas are in the athletic shoe industry. The competitive situation among companies is also called the *market structure* of an industry. Figure 6-6 illustrates four main competitive situations that can exist in an economy.

Pure Competition

Pure competition is a market situation with many sellers each offering the same product. For example when farmers sell their wheat or corn, there is little to differentiate one bushel from another. The forces of supply and demand determine the price. Rivalry among businesses is most free when many companies offer very similar products to buyers. Various factors in our economy and society, however, severely limit pure competition.

Monopolistic Competition

In order for companies to attract customers, they make their products slightly different. One hamburger company offers a special sauce, another adds bacon and cheese to its burger, while another serves the sandwich with a game or toy. **Monopolistic competition** refers to a market situation with many sellers who each have a slightly different product. The difference among products can be *actual*—such as ingredients—or *implied*—such as different advertisements, a brand name, or a package design.

Oligopoly

When a few large companies control an industry, an **oligopoly** exists. In this market situation the few sellers usually offer products that are slightly different. However, competition is mainly the result of large companies being able to advertise and sell their goods in many geographic areas. For example, only a few large companies make automobile tires; therefore, these large manufacturers are able to control the market. Another example: with only a few countries having oil as a natural resource, companies in these nations can influence the availability and price of oil.

Monopoly

When one company controls the supply of an item, no competition is present. A **monopoly** is a situation in which one seller controls the entire

Figure 6-6

The number of businesses and differences among products affect the amount of competition in a market.

COMPETITIVE MARKET SITUATIONS

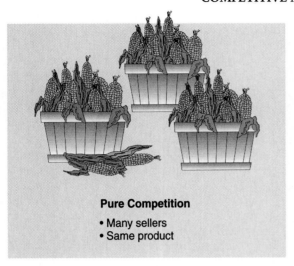

Pure Competition
- Many sellers
- Same product

Monopolistic Competition
- Many sellers
- Slightly different product

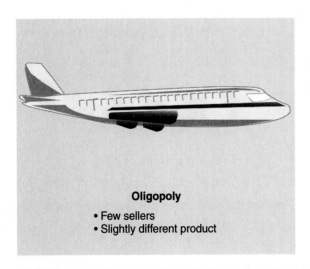

Oligopoly
- Few sellers
- Slightly different product

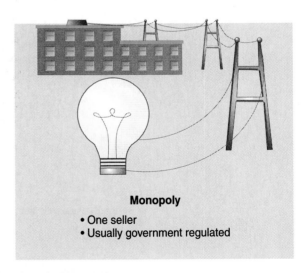

Monopoly
- One seller
- Usually government regulated

market for a product or service. It is very unusual for this to happen without actions by government or other businesses. Like pure competition, few examples of true monopolies exist. Situations that are almost monopolies include South Africa's diamond sellers and a small village or town served by only one store. Monopolies that exist in the United States, such as local telephone service and electricity generation, are government regulated.

Global Highlight: The Great Wall of China

While nations frequently take actions to communicate with others, sometimes a country wants to seclude itself. Imagine a structure about 2,400 kilometers (1,500 miles) long that varies in height between 5.5 and 9.1 meters (18 and 30 feet). Then, imagine that it is 4.6 to 9.1 meters (15 to 30 feet) wide at the base and tapers to about 3.7 meters (12 feet) wide at the top. The wall includes watchtowers about 12 meters (40 feet) high that are placed about every 180 meters (about 200 yards). Those are the dimensions of the Great Wall of China.

The Great Wall of China was built of earth and stone. The largest portion was constructed during the rule of Emperor Ch'in Shin Huang Ti, which ended about 204 B.C. The Great Wall was designed to protect the Chinese people from nomadic invaders. It runs along the northern and northwestern frontiers of the country.

During the Ming dynasty (1368–1644), the wall was expanded to its current length and received extensive repairs. The Great Wall continues to be a popular tourist attraction in China. The massive structure has the distinction of being visible from the moon by astronauts.

Back to the Beginning: The Scoop on Ice Cream Exports

Reread the case at the beginning of this chapter and answer the following questions:

1. What factors have increased the demand from overseas customers for ice cream?
2. What obstacles might an ice cream exporter encounter when doing business in other countries?
3. What actions might an ice cream company take to expand export activities?
4. How could foreign companies become more competitive in the global ice cream industry?

The following terms should become part of your business vocabulary. For each numbered item find the term that has the same meaning. (Not all terms will be used.)

- balance of payments
- bill of lading
- certificate of origin
- cost and freight (C&F)
- cost, insurance, and freight (CIF)
- countertrade
- customs officials
- direct barter
- economic community
- free on board (FOB)
- free-trade zone
- freight forwarder
- industry
- monopoly
- monopolistic competition
- oligopoly
- pure competition
- trade deficit

1. Government officials who collect duties levied by a country on imports.
2. A company that arranges for the shipping of goods to customers in other countries.
3. The direct exchange of products or services among companies in different countries with the possibility of limited currency exchange.
4. Control of an industry by a few large companies.
5. A document that records the agreement between the exporter and the transportation company.
6. The total flow of money coming into a country minus the total flow going out.
7. A market situation with many sellers who each have a slightly different product.
8. An organization of countries that acts as a single country to allow a free flow of products across borders.
9. Terms of sale that mean the price of the product includes the cost of loading the goods onto transport vessels at a specified place.
10. An area designated by a government for duty-free entry of nonprohibited goods.
11. A situation in which one seller controls the market for a product or service.
12. The exchange of goods and services between two parties with no money involved.
13. A group of companies in the same type of business.
14. A document that states the country in which goods being shipped were produced.

15. A market situation with many sellers each offering the same product.

16. The amount a country owes to other countries due to importing more than is exported.

REVIEWING YOUR READING

Answer these questions to reinforce your knowledge of the main ideas of this chapter.

1. What are the main reasons companies import goods?

2. What is the purpose of the customs department of a country's government?

3. How can exporting companies determine if their products can be sold in other countries?

4. How does a freight forwarder assist exporting businesses?

5. What two documents are commonly required when goods are shipped to other countries? Describe the documents.

6. How does a country's balance of payments differ from its balance of trade?

7. How can a trade deficit affect a country's economy?

8. What are the main benefits sought by nations when they create an economic community?

9. Why is countertrade used in international business?

10. What are the main factors that affect how much competition exists among companies?

11. How does pure competition differ from monopolistic competition?

12. Why are there few true monopolies in the United States?

EXPANDING YOUR HORIZONS

You will not find the complete answers to the following questions in your textbook. You will need to use your critical-thinking skills. Think about these questions, gather information from other sources, analyze possible responses, and discuss them with others. Then, develop your own oral or written response as instructed by your teacher.

1. Name some examples of imported products that the people in the United States need and want.

2. Why are taxes imposed on products imported into various countries?

3. List some resources you could use to determine the buying habits in different countries.

4. What factors would affect whether the buyer or the seller pays for the shipping costs in an international business transaction?

5. Why might a country's balance of payments be a better measurement of its international business activities than its balance of trade?

6. What problems might arise among nations when creating an economic community for international trade?

7. Describe some examples of countertrade involving products from different countries with which you are familiar.

BUILDING RESEARCH SKILLS

The ability to find information from various sources is an important international business skill. The following activities will help you investigate various topics. You will also learn to apply class ideas to situations outside of the classroom.

1. Prepare a poster or bulletin board display of products exported by businesses in your city or state.

2. Collect advertisements, packages, or other information about products made in another country and sold in the United States. Ask five friends or relatives to identify the country of origin for the product.

3. Investigate the duties and customs procedures of one of the following countries: Malaysia, Australia, Taiwan, China, India, South Korea, Singapore, or New Zealand.

4. Talk to someone who has shipped goods to another country. Prepare a short oral report about the procedures for transporting merchandise to a foreign country.

5. Some people believe products compete in our society based on very minor differences. Collect information on five different brands of soap, toothpaste, breakfast cereal, or shampoo. You can collect information from advertisements, packages, and periodicals. Based on your analysis and comments from others, list the similarities and differences of the brands selected. *Consumer Reports* is a good source of information for this activity.

6. Find the location of the free-trade zone closest to your city. Draw a map that includes your state, the location of the free-trade zone,

and all states in between. Then draw a line between your city and the free-trade zone. Mark the distance above the line. If the free-trade zone is in your city, draw a map of your city and identify the location of the free-trade zone.

7. *Global Career Activity.* Obtain information about the imports and exports of a country of your choice. What types of job opportunities would be created by these foreign business activities?

Continuing Enrichment Project: Creating an Exporting Plan

Select a product or service that your chosen company is actively exporting or that you believe has potential for sales in other countries. Then select a country in Asia that would provide a market opportunity for that product or service. Use information collected for Chapters 1–5 and additional research to prepare an exporting plan. Include the following components:

1. *Product description*
   - Describe the product or service in detail, including specific features.
   - Describe any changes in the product or service that may be necessary before exporting.

2. *Foreign business environment*
   - List cultural and social factors that may affect the sale of the product or service.
   - Discuss the geography of the country to which you have chosen to export this product or service.
   - Describe economic conditions that may affect exporting this product.
   - Report any political or legal factors that could affect the exporting activities.

3. *Market potential*
   - Describe the type of customer who is best suited for this product or service in the country you have chosen.
   - Identify methods that could be used to contact potential buyers in the country you have chosen.
   - Estimate sales for the product or service based on company size, market demand, and competition.

4. *Export transaction details*
   - Describe import taxes or other restrictions that may affect the exporting costs.
   - Discuss the type of shipping and documentation requirements for the country you have selected.
   - Identify the amount of time the exporting plan will take to execute.

Foreign Exchange and International Finance

After studying this chapter and completing the end-of-chapter activities, you will be able to

- Explain the role of money and currency systems in international business.

- Identify factors that affect the value of currency.

- Discuss foreign exchange activities.

- Calculate foreign exchange rates of various currencies.

- Name the main the activities of the World Bank and the International Monetary Fund.

- Discuss payment methods and financing sources for international business transactions.

- Describe various documents used in international trade.

An Unexpected New Currency for Ukraine

In the early 1990s, the Soviet Union divided into the separate countries that had been united for more than 70 years. When this occurred, the Russian ruble was no longer the monetary unit for these newly independent nations.

Ukraine was one of these nations. While the people of Ukraine were waiting to convert to a new currency, the need for money in circulation was critical. To prevent a financial crisis, the Ukrainian government issued coupons for use in buying the country's limited supplies of food and other products.

These coupons were not originally intended to be the new Ukrainian currency. However, as Ukraine's economy developed, these coupons became widely accepted as money. At first, Ukrainians were using both the coupons and the Russian ruble. As the new monetary system replaced the old one, rubles became less acceptable for purchases. The acceptance of the ration coupons made them the unofficial currency of Ukraine.

Each day billions of people buy goods and services using something called *money*. Have you ever thought about what makes money valuable? The metal and paper that make up coins and currency have very little actual value. So, why can you use these items to buy goods and services?

MONEY AND CURRENCY SYSTEMS

Most people take money for granted. If they have money and can buy what they need, they usually don't care how it works. However, an understanding of how money works can help people better understand international business transactions.

What Is Money?

Money is anything people will accept for the exchange of goods and services. Throughout history, many different things have served as money—including corn, cattle, tobacco, shells, and salt. As shown in Figure 7-1, money has five main qualities. The most important characteristic of

Figure 7-1

For something to be used as money, it must possess certain qualities.

CHARACTERISTICS OF MONEY

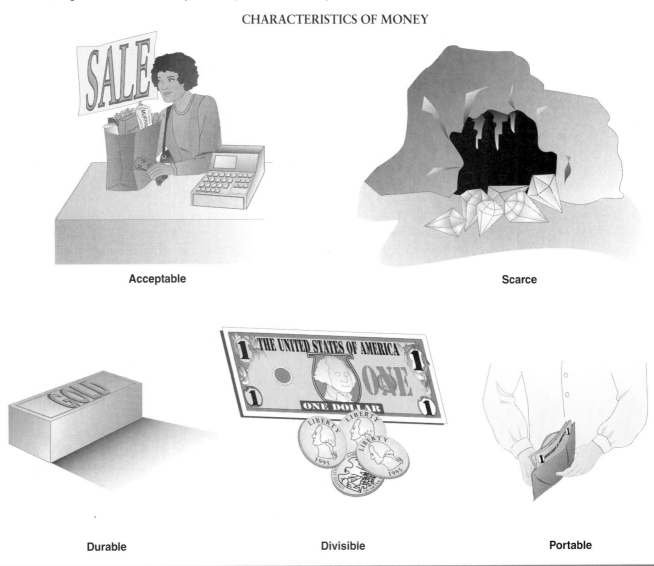

Acceptable

Scarce

Durable

Divisible

Portable

money is that it is *acceptable*. In other words, will people take an item in exchange for what they are selling?

For something to be used as money, it must also be *scarce*. If the item being used as money is very plentiful, it will not maintain its value. As items used for money become common they lose their buying power.

A problem with some items used as money in the past, such as farm products, is that they spoil or get damaged easily. Items used as money should be *durable*. Gold and silver, commonly used as money because of durability, were first made into coins in the seventh century B.C. in Greece.

For money to be useful, it should also be *divisible*. What would happen if someone wanted to buy something using a cow as payment? The item to be purchased would have to be of equal value to the cow since livestock is not easy to divide into smaller monetary units. Most nations have different units of money. In the United States, for example, we have the five dollar bill, the ten dollar bill, quarters, dimes, nickels, and pennies. In Mexico, the peso is divided into 100 centavos. In Japan, the yen is divided into 100 sen. And in Thailand, the baht is divided into 100 satang.

Some objects used as money in the past were not easily moved from one place to another. As people became more mobile, they demanded a money form that was *portable*. The earliest known paper currency was issued by banks in China in the eleventh century.

Why Is Money Used?

Money serves three main purposes—as a medium of exchange, as a measure of value, and as a store of value. *Barter* is the direct exchange of goods and services for other goods and services. However, you may not want what someone else is offering. Money allows you to put a value on something you have to sell and to use the money received to buy something else, later.

Medium of Exchange.   Money is useful only if people are willing to accept it in exchange for goods and services. As a medium of exchange, money makes business transactions easier. At a store, you know coins, currency, or checks will be accepted rather than having to trade a good or service.

Measure of Value.   Is your time worth a steak dinner or one pair of jeans for four hours work? Without money it would be difficult to put a value on things like food and clothing. As a measure of value, money allows us to put a value on various goods and services. Money makes it possible to compare prices for different items so that you can decide how to make the wisest spending decisions.

Store of Value.   You may not want to spend all of your money at the same time. As a store of value, money can be saved for future spending. However, the amount you can buy with your money in the future may be reduced because prices increase.

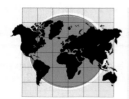

FOREIGN EXCHANGE

Business transactions between companies in different countries bring up money problems. Japanese companies want to receive payment in yen, while Mexican businesses expect to pay in pesos.

Since countries have different currency systems, a method of determining the value of one nation's money in terms of another's is needed. As companies in different countries exchange goods and services, payment must be made. A company usually wants its payment in the currency of its home country. As a result, the money of one country must be changed into the currency of another country. **Foreign exchange** is the process of converting the currency of one country into the currency of another country.

Exchange rate is the amount of currency of one country that can be traded for one unit of the currency of another country. Each day these values change. Figure 7-2 on page 142 shows the value of various currencies in relation to the U.S. dollar on a given day in 1994. For example, one deutsche mark was worth 64 cents in U.S. money, and you could exchange 1.55 deutsche marks for one U.S. dollar.

Figure 7-2

Currencies from various nations have different values compared to the U.S. dollar.

EXCHANGE RATES FOR SELECTED CURRENCIES (1994)

Currency	Country	Symbol	Value in U.S. Dollars	Units per U.S. Dollar
pound	Britain	£	$1.58	.63 pounds
dollar	Canada	$	.743	1.34 Canadian dollars
franc	France	Fr *or* F	.188	5.33 francs
deutsche mark	Germany	DM	.64	1.55 deutsche marks
rupee	India	Re	.032	30.98 rupees
yen	Japan	¥	.0104	99.60 yen
peso	Mexico	$	.294	3.4 pesos
riyal	Saudi Arabia	SR	.267	3.745 riyals
rand	South Africa	R	.273	3.663 rands
bolivar	Venezuela	B	.00588	170 bolivars

The value of a currency, like most things, is affected by supply and demand. If a country's money is believed to be a solid store of value, people will accept it as payment and its value will increase. However if a country is having financial difficulties, its currency is likely to lose value compared to the money of other countries.

Currency exchange rates among countries are affected by three main factors: the country's balance of payments, its economic conditions, and its political stability (see Figure 7-3).

Balance of Payments

The balance of payments, as discussed in Chapter 6, is a measure of the total flow of money coming into a country minus the total flow going out. When a country has a favorable balance of payments, the value of its currency is usually constant or rising. An increased demand for both the nation's products and for its currency is the cause of this situation.

However, when a nation has an unfavorable balance of payments, its currency usually declines in value. This results from lower demand for the monetary unit since fewer companies need to obtain the currency to make payments for goods and services purchased.

Economic Conditions

Every nation faces the economic conditions of inflation and changing interest rates. When prices increase and the buying power of the country's money declines, its currency will not be as attractive. Inflation reduces the buying power of a currency. High inflation in Brazil, for example, would reduce the demand for the cruzeiro.

The cost of borrowing money also affects the value of a currency. When individuals, businesses, and countries borrow money they incur a cost. The **interest rate** is the cost of using someone else's money. Higher interest rates mean more expensive products and lower demand among consumers. This, in turn, reduces the demand for a nation's currency, causing a decline in its value.

Figure 7-3
Currency exchange rates are affected by a nation's balance of payments, economic conditions, and political stability.

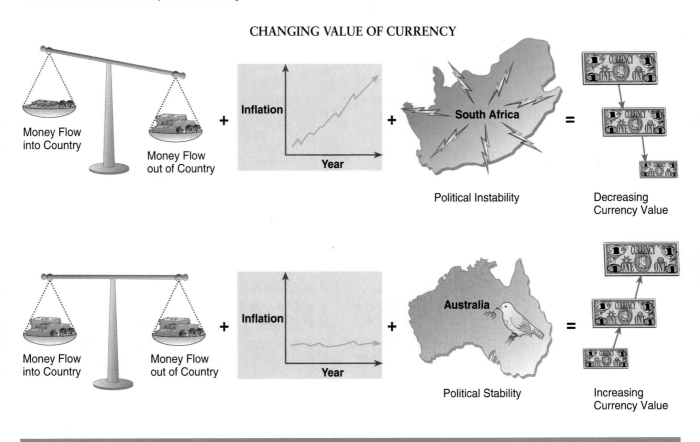

CHANGING VALUE OF CURRENCY

Interest rates are affected by three main factors:

Money supply and demand. When more people want to borrow than to save money, interest rates increase. In contrast, if money is available but few are borrowing, interest rates decline.

Inflation. As prices rise the buying power of money declines, so lenders charge a higher interest rate on loans. Lenders need to collect more money for a loan when inflation is present so that they are able to cover the lost buying power of the currency they receive.

Risk. The higher the risk associated with a loan, the higher the interest rate charged. The higher rates cover the business costs incurred when trying to collect a loan and to cover loans not repaid.

Political Stability

Companies and individuals want to avoid risk when doing business in different nations. If a government changes unexpectedly to create an unfriendly environment, a company may lose its building, equipment, or money on deposit in banks. Political instability may also occur when new laws and regulations are enacted. These rules may not allow foreign businesses to operate as freely.

Uncertainty in a country reduces the confidence business people have in its currency. In 1979, for example, when a revolution changed the government in Iran, many foreign companies were closed and several U.S. officials were taken hostage.

Global Business Exercise: Currency Calculations

For each of the following international business situations, calculate the number of monetary units that would be necessary to make payment. For example, a Greek company pays 108,000 drachmas for canned food from a Canadian producer. The Canadian company exchanges the drachmas for Canadian dollars. If the Canadian dollar is worth 160 drachmas, how much will the Canadian company collect? Solution: 108,000 drachmas ÷ 160 drachmas per Canadian dollar = 675 Canadian dollars.

1. A hamburger at a U.S. restaurant in Tokyo costs 400 yen. If one yen is worth $0.008 in U.S. money, how much would the burger cost in U.S. dollars?

2. A company in Thailand is buying computers that cost 68,000 baht each from a British company. One British pound is worth .025 baht. What is the price of each computer in British pounds?

3. A videotape made in the United States cost 85 markkaa in Finland. If each markka is worth $0.20 in U.S. funds, what is the cost of the videotape in U.S. dollars?

4. A U.S. citizen is renting a hotel room in Paris for $184.92 a night. If one franc equals $0.23 in U.S. funds, how many francs will the tourist need for each night's stay?

5. A U.S. tourist received a $A5 traffic ticket in Australia. If each Australian dollar is equal to $0.74 in U.S. money, what was the cost of this driving violation in U.S. dollars?

FOREIGN EXCHANGE ACTIVITIES

The value of a country's currency is important for success in international business. If a country's currency is not accepted by its trading partners, the country may have to make payment in another currency. A currency that is not easy to exchange for other currencies is called **soft currency**. While the currency is a medium of exchange in its home country, the monetary units have limited value in the world marketplace.

In contrast to soft currencies, money such as the Japanese yen, the Swiss franc, and the U.S. dollar are accepted for most global transactions. These monetary units are accepted by companies in most nations of the world. **Hard currency** is a monetary unit that is freely convertible into other currencies.

Changing Exchange Rates

In years past, the value of a country's currency was set by its government. More recently, most countries use a system of **floating exchange rates** in which currency values are based on supply and demand. When a country exports large amounts of goods and services, companies in that nation want payment in their own currency. To make these payments, buyers must purchase this monetary unit. As the demand for the currency increases, the value of that monetary unit also increases.

For most of the 1980s, Japan had a very favorable balance of payments as a result of high foreign demand for its automobiles, electronic products, and other goods. Since Japanese companies wanted payment in yen, importers in other countries had to buy yen in order to make their payments. This demand for Japanese currency resulted in its increased value. Figure 7-4 shows the changing value of the U.S. dollar compared to the Japanese yen in recent years.

Figure 7-4
The value of the U.S. dollar compared to the Japanese yen has changed repeatedly in recent years.

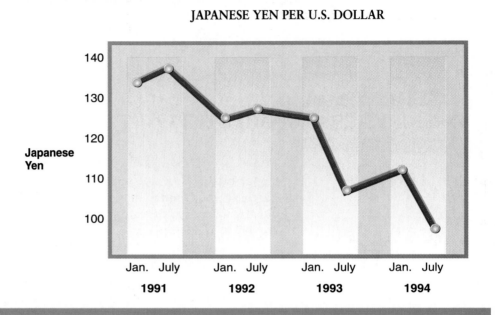

JAPANESE YEN PER U.S. DOLLAR

The Foreign Exchange Market

The process of exchanging one currency for another occurs in the foreign exchange market. The **foreign exchange market** consists of banks and other financial institutions that buy and sell different currencies. Most large banks are part of the foreign exchange market and may provide currency services for businesses and consumers. Before citizens travel outside of the United States, they can exchange dollars for the currencies of the countries they will visit. This exchange can be done at some large banks or companies that specialize in foreign currency services.

If a company knows it will need a certain currency in the future, it can enter into an agreement to buy that monetary unit later at a price agreed upon today. **Currency futures** are contracts to purchase for a fee a foreign currency at today's rate with payment and delivery at a later date. For example, suppose an Australian company needs 20 million yen in two months to pay for imports from a Japanese company. By buying a currency future contract, the importer will get the yen in two months at today's exchange rate. This protects the Australian importer from having to buy the currency later at a higher price. However, if yen are less expensive in two months, the importer does not have to exercise the option to buy the yen at the contract price. Instead, the currency may be purchased at the going market price. The importer will allow the option to expire, forfeiting the fee.

Foreign Exchange Controls

In an effort to maintain the value of its currency, a nation may place limits on the flow of money out of the country. **Exchange controls** are government restrictions to regulate the amount and value of a nation's currency. These controls can be in the form of either fixed exchange rates or limits on the amount and cost of currency. One common exchange control limits the amount of local currency a person can take out of a country. For example, in recent years, Australia, Bangladesh, France, Italy, Japan, Portugal, South Africa, Spain, and Sweden have all placed some restrictions on exporting local currency.

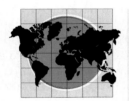

Global Business Example: Foreign Exchange and Tourism

Travelers to other countries usually have a choice of making payments with cash, traveler's checks, or credit cards. You would think the payment method would not affect the cost of a purchase. However, due to changing exchange rates and other factors, one payment method may be more costly than others. The foreign exchange on credit card purchases is not calculated until the charges reach the credit card office. If a foreign currency is declining in value, you would be charged less than if you had paid cash.

As the value of the dollar increases in relation to other currencies, the cost of traveling to other countries decreases. For example, in early September, 1992, a hotel room in London that cost £100 required about $200 U.S. Two weeks later the hotel room still cost £100; however, the exchange rate had changed and it cost $179 U.S.

INTERNATIONAL FINANCIAL AGENCIES

Exchange controls can help maintain the value of a nation's money supply by keeping an excess of currency out of the foreign exchange market. Two international agencies, the International Bank for Reconstruction and Development and the International Monetary Fund, work to maintain a stable system of foreign exchange.

Global Highlight: Vietnam: A Nation Divided

Political differences split Vietnam into communist North Vietnam and democratic South Vietnam in 1954. Then, for the next 21 years, military battles continued between the two areas. Between 1963 and 1975, 1.3 million Vietnamese, along with 56,000 U.S. soldiers, were killed. On April 30, 1975, the South surrendered and the country united.

Today, Vietnam is divided in another way. One part of the economy consists of traditional open markets with fish, farm products, and hand-made items. At stores just a few steps away, shoppers wearing NBA shirts are buying Coca-Cola, Huggies diapers, and Suave shampoo. Many Vietnamese live in single-room huts or on boats along one of the rivers that flow into the South China Sea, while others reside in modern apartments with video recorders and compact disk players.

Vietnamese companies have established business relationships with enterprises in Japan, Germany, Canada, and the United States. As Vietnam expands its trading partners, hopes are that economic development will improve living standards for most of the nation's people. As of late 1992 with exports rising faster than imports, the country had a small trade surplus.

Economic reform in Vietnam can also be viewed in other ways. As of the late 1980s, the nation's currency, the dong, had an annual inflation rate of 700 percent. More recently, cost of living increases are at 20 percent. Plans are also under way to start a stock exchange in Hanoi, building on the dong-U.S. dollar foreign currency exchange activities already in operation.

The World Bank

The International Bank for Reconstruction and Development, commonly called the **World Bank,** was created in 1944 to provide loans for rebuilding after World War II. Today, the bank's major function is to provide economic assistance to less developed countries. These funds build communications systems, transportation networks, and energy plants.

The World Bank, with over 150 member countries, has two main divisions: the International Development Association and the International Finance Corporation. The International Development Association (IDA) makes funds available to help developing countries. These loans can be paid back over many years (up to 50) and have very low interest rates.

The International Finance Corporation (IFC) provides capital and technical assistance to private businesses in nations with limited resources. The IFC encourages joint ventures between foreign companies and local companies to encourage capital investment within the developing nation.

The International Monetary Fund (IMF)

The **International Monetary Fund (IMF)** helps to promote economic cooperation by maintaining an orderly system of world trade and exchange rates. The IMF was established in 1946 when the economic interdependence among nations was escalating at a greater pace than ever before in history.

Before the International Monetary Fund, a country could frequently change the value of its currency to attract more foreign customers. As other countries lose business, they may impose trade restrictions or lower the value of their currency. As one nation tries to outdo another, a trade war may result. Today, cooperation among IMF nations makes trade wars less likely.

The IMF, with over 150 member nations, is a cooperative deposit bank that provides assistance to countries experiencing balance of payment difficulties. When a nation's debt continues to increase, its currency declines in value resulting in more debt. High debt payments mean less money is available for the country to improve its economic development. To prevent this situation, the International Monetary Fund has three main duties:

Analyze economic situations. In an attempt to help countries avoid economic problems, the IMF will monitor a country's trade, borrowing, and government spending.

Suggest economic policies. After analyzing the economic factors of a nation, the IMF will suggest actions to improve the situation. If a country imposes restrictions that limit foreign trade, for example, the IMF may recommend changes to encourage global business.

Provide loans. When a country has a high foreign debt, the IMF lends money to help avoid major economic difficulties. These low-interest loans can keep a country from an escalating trade deficit and a declining currency value.

Global Business Example: The Economic and Trade Problems of Ghana

Before taking a new course of action, Ghana, located on the west coast of Africa, had many economic problems. Inflation was 120 percent, exports had declined by 50 percent, and the nation had a crumbling infrastructure. An overvalued currency did not encourage extensive exporting of cocoa, Ghana's main export. Between 1983 and 1990, the cedi decreased in value from 2.75 per U.S. dollar to 350 per U.S. dollar.

Ghana obtained suggestions from the International Monetary Fund. To improve the trade situation, quotas, tariffs, and other import controls were used to limit products coming into the country. These actions, along with lower tax rates, helped to improve Ghana's balance of payments and stimulate economic growth for its economy.

FINANCING INTERNATIONAL BUSINESS TRANSACTIONS

When you go to a store to buy something, you must decide how to pay for the item. You may use cash. Other times, however, you may write a check or buy the item on credit. In a similar manner, global buyers must decide how to pay for an import purchase.

Foreign Trade Payment Methods

Three types of payment methods are commonly used for international business transactions: cash in advance, letter of credit, and sale on account.

Cash in Advance.   Making payment before the shipment of goods can be risky for the buyer. After paying in advance, you may not receive the items or you may have difficulty obtaining a refund for damaged or returned goods. Cash in advance is not often used. This method, however, may be required for first-time customers, small orders, or customers in high-risk countries. Since the payment was made before shipping, goods will usually be sent without delay.

Letter of Credit.   A **letter of credit** is a financial document issued by a bank (for an importer) in which the bank guarantees payment. A letter of credit is a method of payment in which the importer pays for goods before they are received, but after the goods are shipped. This agreement, issued by the importer's bank, promises to pay the exporter a set amount when certain documents are presented.

The letter of credit communicates to the exporter that it will receive payment once the goods are shipped. Before the payment is made, certain documents—usually including a bill of lading—must be presented as proof that the goods have been shipped.

Sale on Account.   Almost every business buys or sells on credit at one time or another. A very common practice in the United States is to sell on account. This means regular customers have a certain time period to make payment, such as 30 or 60 days. **Credit terms** describe time required for payment and other conditions of a sale on account.

When selling on account, a company wants to obtain its money as soon as possible. To encourage fast payment, a discount may be offered. In the United States, companies may sell on account with the following credit terms: 2/10, n/30. This means that customers may take a 2 percent discount if they pay within 10 days or pay the net (full) amount in 30 days.

Another example of the credit terms for a sale on account would be: 1/15, n/EOM. This means a 1 percent discount may be taken if paid in 15 days. The net amount is due by the end of the month (EOM). What would credit terms of 3/45, n/60 mean?

Sources of International Financing

Buying and selling on credit means that one party (an individual or company) uses the money of another party (an individual, company, or financial institution). This is commonly called financing. Financing may be viewed from the short-term perspective (one year or less) and the long-term perspective (more than one year).

Short-Term Financing.   A large portion of business transactions involve credit. A company may allow customers 30 days to make their payments. The same company probably buys store supplies, raw materials, and other items from suppliers on credit. The buying or selling on account is called **trade credit.** Trade credit comes in two forms: accounts receivable and accounts payable.

An **account receivable** is an amount owed by a customer to a company that sells on credit. Accounts receivable are the result of sales on account. A company that sells on credit allows its customers a certain time period to pay for purchases. An **account payable** is an amount owed to a supplier. Accounts payable exist when a person or company buys on account.

Accounts receivable and accounts payable may seem confusing. A helpful way to distinguish between them is that receivables are amounts to be received and payables are amounts to be paid.

Business loans, also called commercial loans, are another source of short-term financing. Business loans are commonly obtained from banks and other financial institutions.

Long-Term Financing.   Some business activities require financing for more than one year. Companies commonly need large sums of money for expensive business projects that will occur over several years. For example, a Japanese company may need funds to build an electronic manufacturing plant in the United States. Or, a German company may buy a food company in Mexico. An expensive, long-term financial activity is a **capital project.** Examples of capital projects include

- Introducing new products,
- Buying an existing company,
- Building a factory,
- Buying new equipment, and
- Opening a new office in another country.

Capital projects often require millions of dollars. To pay for capital projects, companies can do one of two things: borrow the necessary funds from a bank or other financial institution or issue bonds. A **bond** is a certificate representing money borrowed by a company over a long period of time, usually between 5 and 30 years. This document represents the company's promise to repay the money by a certain date with interest. Bonds are a type of financing commonly used by large companies.

Unit 2   Organizing for International Business

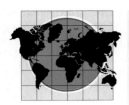

Global Business Example: Printing Money for the World

The United States Banknote Corporation prints money for many nations. Its main office is in New York and printing plants are in Philadelphia, Chicago, and Los Angeles. As bills wear out or new currency designs are needed, the company gets busy. After the revolution in Nicaragua in 1979, the picture on the 1,000-cordoba bank note was changed from General Somoza to General Sandino. Currency printing companies also meet special needs. Some of the shekels used in Israel have special bumps for reading by the blind.

OTHER PAYMENT METHODS AND FINANCIAL DOCUMENTS

With hundreds of nations and millions of companies in the world, many ways of doing business exist. Besides the import-export documents and payment methods already mentioned, several others are commonly used for global business.

The **promissory note** is a document that states a promise to pay a set amount by a certain date. Promissory notes are signed by buyers to confirm their intention to make payment. These documents communicate to both the buyer and the seller the amount of a purchase, the date by which it must be paid, and any interest charges.

A **bill of exchange** is a written order by an exporter to an importer to make payment. The instructions to the importer include the amount, the due date, and the location of the payment (usually a bank or other financial institution).

An **electronic funds transfer (EFT)** moves payments through banking computer systems. After an importer receives the ordered goods, a bank can be instructed to transfer the payment for the merchandise to the bank of the exporter. The main advantage of an EFT is prompt payment. Electronic funds transfer systems are commonly used by consumers to obtain cash, deposit money, and make payments.

A **commercial invoice**, prepared by the exporter, provides a description of the merchandise and the terms of the sale. As shown in Figure 7-5 on page 154, a commercial invoice includes details about the buyer, seller, merchandise, amounts, prices, shipping method, date of shipment, and terms of payment.

Proof of insurance is usually a part of import-export transactions. An **insurance certificate** explains the amount of insurance coverage for fire, theft, water, or other damage that may occur to goods in shipment. This document also lists the names of the insurance company and the exporter.

Figure 7-5

A commercial invoice gives the details of an international business transaction.

A COMMERCIAL INVOICE

ExIm EXPRESS
8612 Locust
Madeira, Ohio 45243
(513) 555-0835

SOLD TO:
Serendipity, Sarl
14 Siam
Bangkok, Thailand

SHIPPED TO:
Order of Shipper

CUSTOMER'S ORDER NUMBER AND DATE:
IMP 12
JAN 1, 1995

INVOICE NUMBER AND DATE:
EI/SS/01/95
JAN 10, 1995

DATE SHIPPED:
Jan. 15, 1995

VIA:
Ocean freight on CU WINGED SOUL

TERMS:
Sale: CIF Bangkok
Payment: Sight Draft

PACKAGE NO.	QUANTITY	OUR NO.	DESCRIPTION	PRICE PER UNIT	AMOUNT
1-40	100	10	Fire Extinguishers	US$ 40	US$ 4000
			Total shipment EX WORKS MADEIRA		US$ 4000
			Plus: Inland Freight to Port		US$ 200
			Total Boston Port		US$ 4200
			Plus: Ocean Freight		US$ 75
			Plus: Insurance		US$ 23
			Total CIF Bangkok Thailand		US$ 4298

We certify that this invoice is true and correct, and that the origin of these goods is the United States of America.

These goods licensed by the United States for ultimate destination Thailand.
Diversion contrary to U.S. law prohibited. LIC. G-DEST.

Jennifer Hamm

Jennifer Hamm, Export Manager
ExIm Express

Back to the Beginning: An Unexpected New Currency for Ukraine

Reread the case at the beginning of this chapter and answer the following questions:

1. What problems can occur in an economy that does not have enough money in circulation?
2. What made the ration coupons valuable in the Ukrainian economy?
3. What made the Russian ruble less acceptable among Ukrainians?
4. What actions might a government take to create and maintain an appropriate currency system?

KNOWING GLOBAL BUSINESS TERMS

The following terms should become part of your business vocabulary. For each numbered item find the term that has the same meaning. (Not all terms will be used.)

- account payable
- account receivable
- bill of exchange
- bond
- capital project
- commercial invoice
- credit terms
- currency futures
- electronic funds transfer (EFT)
- exchange controls
- exchange rate
- floating exchange rates
- foreign exchange
- foreign exchange market
- hard currency
- insurance certificate
- interest rate
- International Monetary Fund (IMF)
- letter of credit
- money
- promissory note
- soft currency
- trade credit
- World Bank

1. The network of banks and other financial institutions that buy and sell different currencies.
2. The amount of currency of one country that can be traded for one unit of the currency of another country.
3. The cost of using someone else's money.
4. Anything people will accept for the exchange of goods and services.
5. A currency that is not easy to exchange for other currencies.
6. A certificate representing money borrowed by a company over a long period of time.

Chapter 7   Foreign Exchange and International Finance

7. Buying or selling on account.

8. An expensive, long-term financial activity.

9. Contracts to purchase a foreign currency at today's rate with payment and delivery at a later date for a fee.

10. A financial document issued by a bank for an importer in which the bank guarantees payment.

11. Government restrictions to regulate the amount and value of a nation's currency.

12. A monetary unit that is freely convertible into other currencies.

13. A method of moving payments from country to country through banking computer systems.

14. A system in which currency values are based on supply and demand.

REVIEWING YOUR READING

Answer these questions to reinforce your knowledge of the main ideas of this chapter.

1. What are the five characteristics of money?

2. What are the three main purposes of money?

3. What is an exchange rate?

4. How does a country's balance of payments affect the value of its currency?

5. How does risk affect the cost of borrowing money?

6. How does political instability affect the value of a country's currency?

7. What is the difference between soft currency and hard currency?

8. What purpose do exchange controls serve?

9. What is the World Bank?

10. What are the main activities of the International Monetary Fund?

11. What are three common payment methods for international business transactions?

12. Why do capital projects usually require a company to borrow money?

EXPANDING YOUR HORIZONS

You will not find the complete answers to the following questions in your textbook. You will need to use your critical-thinking skills. Think about these questions, gather information from other sources, analyze

Unit 2 Organizing for International Business

possible responses, and discuss them with others. Then, develop your own oral or written response as instructed by your teacher.

1. Imagine we have no coins, paper money, checks, or credit cards in our economy. What could be used as money to serve the needs of business? Why?

2. What actions could a country take to make its currency more widely accepted around the world?

3. Some people believe that interest rates are one of the most important economic indicators. Name some ways in which people and businesses are affected by interest rates.

4. How might exchange controls affect the trade situation of a country?

5. Why do you think the letter of credit is the most popular payment method used for international business transactions?

6. What are the benefits of offering discounts to customers to pay within 10 or 15 days of a sale?

7. Name some examples of capital projects in your community. How do capital projects benefit the people of a community?

8. What are some concerns people might have about electronic banking?

BUILDING RESEARCH SKILLS

The ability to find information from various sources is an important international business skill. The following activities will help you investigate various topics. You will also learn to apply class ideas to situations outside of the classroom.

1. Using *The Wall Street Journal* or the business section of a daily newspaper, find an article or information about current interest rates. Describe to your class how changing interest rates affect business and consumer decisions.

2. Prepare a poster or bulletin board display on the changing value of the dollar in relation to other major currencies of the world.

3. Interview a person who has traveled to another country. Obtain information about how purchases were made and the exchange rate that was paid.

4. Do library research about the living costs for food, housing, medical care, and transportation in several Asian countries.

5. Interview a local business owner about buying and selling on credit. Ask the owner about the benefits and problems encountered when doing business on account.

6. *Global Career Activity.* Obtain information about the value of a nation's currency. Explain how changes in a country's exchange rate might affect the jobs in that nation.

Continuing Enrichment Project: Tracking the Changing Value of Currencies

Select a country and research its currency. Obtain information that will help you answer the following questions:

1. What is the main monetary unit used in the country? How is it divided into other units?

2. Over the past couple of years, what have been the economic conditions of the country (inflation, interest rates, unemployment)? How have these affected the value of the currency?

3. How has the country's balance of payments affected the value of its currency?

4. Have political factors affected the value of the currency?

5. Describe any exchange controls used by the country.

6. What factors might affect changes for this currency over the next few months?

7. Graph the recent value of the currency in relation to two other major currencies (e.g., U.S. dollar, Japanese yen, British pound, deutsche mark, Swiss franc).

Prepare a written report with a summary of this information and your graphs. Indicate on the graph any events that have caused a major increase or decrease in the value of the currency.

Legal Agreements Around the World

After studying this chapter and completing the end-of-chapter activities, you will be able to

- Identify and describe the legal systems upon which international law is primarily based.

- Explain some of the laws and international trade agreements that protect the property rights of businesses.

- Understand when an agreement has all of the components of a contract.

- Present several different ways to resolve international legal disputes.

- Describe the role that the International Court of Justice plays in international business.

NAFTA: Lifting Trade Barriers

In December of 1993 the North American Free Trade Agreement (NAFTA) was approved by the U.S. Congress. NAFTA was designed to allow more free movement of goods and capital among Canada, the United States, and Mexico, primarily by creating a freer economy in Mexico. With fewer governmental restrictions, U.S. and Canadian companies will have more incentives to make investments in Mexico, which will increase Mexico's economic growth. As Mexico becomes more prosperous, its standard of living will rise. This, in turn, will spur even greater demand for U.S. and Canadian exports to Mexico.

Before its approval, NAFTA was opposed by a number of groups in the United States. Much of the opposition was based on a concern that greater openness between the United States and Mexico would eliminate U.S. jobs and worsen pollution along the U.S.-Mexican border. NAFTA even faced a court challenge as environmental and consumer-activist groups brought suit to determine whether NAFTA must comply with the U.S. National Environmental Policy Act. While a U.S. district court judge ordered an environmental impact statement on NAFTA, the U.S. Court of Appeals overturned that decision. It ruled that the President of the United States has the power to negotiate and draft treaties to be submitted to Congress and that such treaties are not subject to judicial review.

To allay fears about U.S. jobs and the environment even before the court challenge, U.S. President Bill Clinton and Mexican President Carlos Salinas de Gortari negotiated side agreements to the treaty to deal with these two issues. Many people believe that free trade between the two countries will *not* have a negative effect on jobs. Because of lower labor wages and production costs, some U.S. companies that produce goods in Mexico will gain a competitive advantage, thus creating economic growth in the United States as well as in Mexico. NAFTA supporters believe that open trade between Mexico and the United States will benefit both countries economically and that a more prosperous Mexico will be better able to afford to clean up its environment.

Businesspeople of all nations must familiarize themselves with the laws of their own countries. They must make sure that they obey all laws affecting the ownership and operation of their companies. If they do not, they are subject to legal action, which may result in substantial losses to the companies.

When people conduct business in a country other than their own, they must observe the laws of the host country as well as the laws of their own country. They must first assess the internal political situation of the host country. Then they must decide whether the profits to be gained outweigh any risks—which may include political instability, a state of war, or hostilities between their native country and the host country. Once a country enters into business in or with a foreign country, business relationships are often guided by treaties and trade agreements.

The most comprehensive trade agreements in force today are those of the European Community. The European Community is guided by a set of principles that coordinate most aspects of its members' economies. Among European Community countries, there is free movement of goods, labor, services, and capital. There are no customs duties or restrictions on the quantity of goods flowing within the European Community.

There are four main branches of the European Community that coordinate and develop policies for member countries, as shown in Figure 8-1 on page 162. These branches are now working toward uniformity of the laws that govern business transactions among individual member countries.

People involved in international business are guided by the principles of international law as well as by trade agreements. Unlike the domestic laws of individual countries, there is no effective means of enforcing international law. Nevertheless, there is a growing body of international law, and many countries respect it.

LEGAL SYSTEMS

International law is largely based on the legal principles of Western civilization. This is a result of the continuous dominance in world affairs of the West since the time of the Roman Empire. In Western countries, there are two main systems of law: civil law, or code law, and common law.

Civil Law

Civil law, also called code law, is a complete set of rules that are enacted as a single, written system or code. When a government enacts a civil code, it attempts to write down all of the laws and rights that govern every aspect of its society.

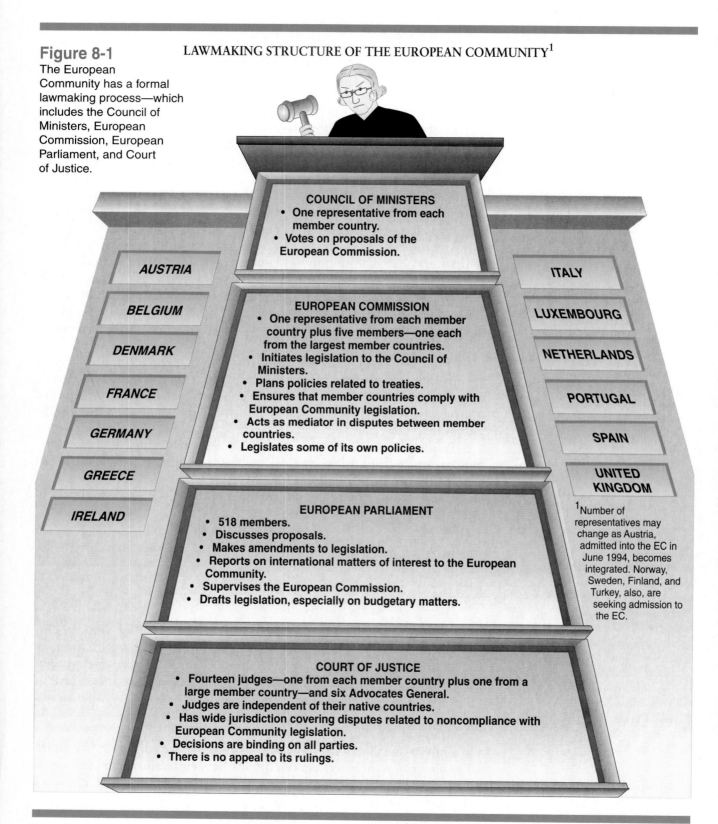

Figure 8-1

The European Community has a formal lawmaking process—which includes the Council of Ministers, European Commission, European Parliament, and Court of Justice.

LAWMAKING STRUCTURE OF THE EUROPEAN COMMUNITY[1]

COUNCIL OF MINISTERS
- One representative from each member country.
- Votes on proposals of the European Commission.

AUSTRIA

BELGIUM

DENMARK

FRANCE

GERMANY

GREECE

IRELAND

ITALY

LUXEMBOURG

NETHERLANDS

PORTUGAL

SPAIN

UNITED KINGDOM

EUROPEAN COMMISSION
- One representative from each member country plus five members—one each from the largest member countries.
- Initiates legislation to the Council of Ministers.
- Plans policies related to treaties.
- Ensures that member countries comply with European Community legislation.
- Acts as mediator in disputes between member countries.
- Legislates some of its own policies.

[1]Number of representatives may change as Austria, admitted into the EC in June 1994, becomes integrated. Norway, Sweden, Finland, and Turkey, also, are seeking admission to the EC.

EUROPEAN PARLIAMENT
- 518 members.
- Discusses proposals.
- Makes amendments to legislation.
- Reports on international matters of interest to the European Community.
- Supervises the European Commission.
- Drafts legislation, especially on budgetary matters.

COURT OF JUSTICE
- Fourteen judges—one from each member country plus one from a large member country—and six Advocates General.
- Judges are independent of their native countries.
- Has wide jurisdiction covering disputes related to noncompliance with European Community legislation.
- Decisions are binding on all parties.
- There is no appeal to its rulings.

The first civil laws were enacted in the seventeenth century B.C. by Hammurabi, a Babylonian king. Modern civil law is based on the Justinian Code and the Napoleonic Code. Justinian was Emperor during the period when Rome had conquered almost all of the world known to the West. To maintain an orderly administration of this empire, in 529 A.D. Justinian codified Roman law in a complete system of rules to govern the empire's citizens. The Justinian Code also described in detail the rights of Roman citizens, including rights to private property.

In 1804, Napoleon Bonaparte became emperor and established a civil code, based on the Roman model, for France. The Napoleonic Code established as law many of the changes that occurred in the aftermath of the French Revolution, including rights to a jury trial and civil equality. The majority of countries are governed by civil law, including many that were once a part of the Roman Empire, such as Italy, Spain, Germany, and France.

Common Law

England is the only western European country that did not develop a comprehensive set of rules at one time. Instead, England approached the establishment of law on a case-by-case basis. This approach came to be known as **common law,** which is the accumulation of decisions made in prior cases.

English common laws grew out of the deterioration of the feudal system. In medieval times, feudal lords were the supreme rulers of their castles, lands, and the serfs who lived within their territory. Disputes between lords were settled mainly in battle, and serfs had very few rights. Thus, there were few laws.

As serfs began to attain some rights as tenant farmers, disputes between them needed to be resolved. At first the feudal lords and (later) judges or magistrates, would simply listen to both sides of the dispute and then make a judgment. Since there was no law to guide these early magistrates in their decisions, they began to write down their decisions so that they and others could refer to them when similar cases arose.

After the conquest of England by Duke William of Normandy, "William the Conqueror," in 1066, English kings established a legal system alongside the developing common law. In this system, the king was the highest legal authority. Because most kings were not knowledgeable about common law, they based their decisions on common sense and the principle of fairness or equity. The king's courts were, therefore, referred to as the equity courts. Equity courts had exclusive jurisdiction over contracts. Gradually, the equity courts merged into the common law system.

England is still governed by common law, as is the United States. In modern common law, also referred to as case law, judges make their decisions guided by rulings in previous cases. The principle of equity or fairness is often cited. It retains particular influence in business law, where the concept of fairness is very important.

Statutory Law

Statutes are those laws that have been enacted by a body of lawmakers. The German Reichstag, the English Parliament, the Chinese National People's Congress, and the United States Congress, for example, were all formed to pass laws to govern their citizens. Statutes are most often enacted to add to or change existing laws and to define laws for new situations that arise. Figure 8-2 highlights the differences among civil law, common law, and statutory law.

PROPERTY RIGHTS AND RESPONSIBILITIES

Property includes everything that can be the subject of ownership—such as land, money, stocks and bonds, buildings, factories, and other goods. Land and whatever is built on or attached to land is considered to be *real property*. All other property, essentially property that does not have a permanent location, is called *personal property*. Property can also be intellectual in nature. Patented inventions; trademarks; and copyrights for literary, musical, and artistic works are all classified as *intellectual property*.

Property Law

All democratic countries recognize the individual's right to private property. These rights are protected by law. **Property rights** are the exclusive rights to possess and use property and its profits, to exclude everyone else from interfering with it, and to dispose of it in every legal way.

Figure 8-2

There are defining characteristics of civil law, common law, and statutory law that highlight their differences.

LEGAL SYSTEMS AROUND THE WORLD

Civil Law

An entire body of decisions is made, all at one time, by a government for all of its citizens.

Common Law

Individual decisions are made in various circumstances. As time goes on, the decision-makers refer to the decisions from previous situations and apply those decisions to other, similar situations. As new situations arise, new decisions are made. In time, a formal set of decisions, or rules, is developed to which decision-makers refer.

Statutory Law

Laws are made by a set of decision-makers whose specific purpose is to make laws. The decisions, or laws, made by this body often change or add to previous decisions.

A number of international agreements were designed to protect the rights of individuals and businesses to own property. These agreements were designed to ensure that individuals and corporations living or located in foreign countries are not deprived of their property except under due process of law or when just compensation has been made. For example, the 1883 Paris Convention for the Protection of Industrial Property, to which more than 95 countries are party, provides international protection for copyrights, patents, and trademarks.

At different times in history, some countries have rejected individuals' rights to own private property. For example, communist countries, especially when they were newly formed, subjected both domestic- and foreign-owned property to "controls" that amounted to a complete loss of property.

Developing countries, particularly those that are former colonies, sometimes expropriate, or confiscate, the property of foreigners. Often this expropriation is made in the name of nationalism or for the developing countries' best interests. As these countries enter into the mainstream of international relations, however, they tend to submit to international laws that recognize the rights of both individuals and businesses to private property. For example, the People's Republic of China, a communist country, adopted a new constitution in 1982 that includes assurances to foreigners engaged in business relationships with China that agreements and contracts will be honored and that violations by Chinese businesses will not be allowed. This new constitution was a direct result of leader Deng Xiaoping's far reaching changes to move China more broadly into international business.

Liability

Liability is a broad legal term referring to almost every kind of responsibility, duty, or obligation. In business law, these responsibilities can relate to debt, loss, or burden.

Liability for Debt, Loss, and Injury. Liability for debt generally includes such claims against a company as wages owed to employees, dividends owed to stockholders, taxes owed to government, and loans owed to banks. Business owners also are responsible for the condition and contents of their facilities and must ensure that their work procedures are safe for employees. Thus if an employee experiences any loss or burden as a result of unsafe conditions, the company could be declared negligent and, therefore, liable for that loss or injury.

Product Liability. **Product liability** is the specific responsibility that both manufacturers and sellers have for the safety of a product. A person can hold a company and its officers responsible for product defects that cause injury, damage, or death to buyers, users, or even bystanders. If a manufacturer does not use "due care" in designing and making a product, then it may be guilty of either intentional or negligent harmful action.

An intent to cause harm by a manufacturer or seller is rarely proven. **Negligence,** which is the failure to follow a generally accepted standard of care, also can be difficult to prove. Thus, modern law has developed the concept of strict liability to help consumers who have suffered loss from a product to prove the manufacturer's liability.

Strict liability imposes responsibility on a manufacturer or seller for intentionally or unintentionally causing injury to another. For a manufacturer to be held liable for damages under strict liability laws, all of the following six conditions must be met:

1. The product was sold in a defective condition.
2. The seller is in the business of routinely selling that product.
3. The product reached the user without having been substantially changed.
4. The product was unreasonably dangerous to the user.

5. The user of the product or a bystander has suffered harm or injury by the use of the product.
6. The defect was the primary cause of the injury.

Product liability laws vary from country to country. Many countries, such as the United States and members of the European Community, provide for strict liability of manufacturers, sellers, and importers of defective products. Figure 8-3 illustrates recent data about product liability cases in the United States. International law recognizes the general principle that a responsible party owes just compensation to the injured party.

Figure 8-3
Outcomes of recent lawsuits against corporations in the United States.

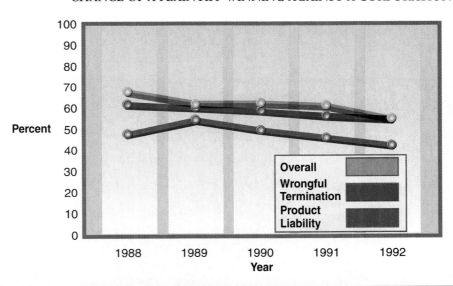

CHANCE OF A PLAINTIFF WINNING AGAINST A CORPORATION

Percent

Year

Overall
Wrongful Termination
Product Liability

Source: Adapted from *Business Week*, November 8, 1993, p. 101.

Global Business Exercise: You Be the Judge

Jean Claude Nallet, an eight-year old French boy, received a model fire engine as a present from his grandmother. The fire engine had been manufactured by and purchased from a French company. While playing with the toy, a sharp tip on the toy ladder punctured Jean Claude's finger, and he required medical treatment. Soon afterwards, Jean Claude's grandmother called his parents to tell them that the fire engine was defective and had been recalled by the manufacturer.

Review the section about product liability. Given that France is a member of the European Community, answer the following questions:

1. In your opinion, do Jean Claude's parents have a legitimate reason to file a product liability claim?

2. Under the guidelines of strict liability, which elements apply to Jean Claude's case?

3. If Jean Claude's grandmother had bought the fire engine secondhand at a yard sale and that model had never been recalled by the manufacturer, how would your answers to questions 1 and 2 be different?

Intellectual Property

Often, a business's greatest asset is its **intellectual property**, which consists of the technical knowledge or creative work that it has developed. This is true of computer software companies, clothing designers, film

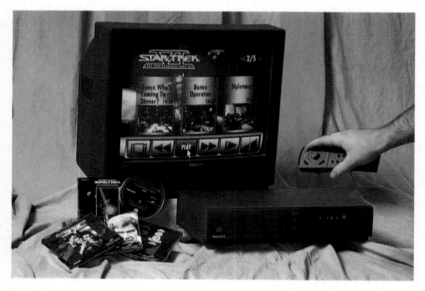

companies, and many others. When intellectual property rights are not protected by law, dishonest competitors can steal other companies' knowledge to make products similar to the original product to deceive consumers into buying them. The Counterfeit Intelligence Bureau of London estimates that counterfeit goods account for $60 billion annually in world trade. Such piracy is obviously of great concern to the honest companies that first developed these products. As trade becomes more and more international in character, the protection of intellectual rights continues to be a main focus in the development of international law.

Patents. A **patent** is the exclusive right of an inventor to make, sell, and use a product or process. To be protected, a product or process must be new and useful. Once a patent expires in the United States, it cannot be renewed unless a new improvement or design is incorporated into the idea or product.

Patent rights are limited by time, with the amount of time ranging from five to twenty years in different countries. Patent rights granted in one country do not necessarily extend to other countries. To be protected, a company must apply for patent rights in each country in which it

168   *Unit 2   Organizing for International Business*

plans to do business. There are, however, several international agreements that coordinate and streamline this process.

The Paris Convention for the Protection of Industrial Property provides minimum standards for the protection of patents in member countries. It sets forth the rights of fair treatment and the rights of priority, by which inventors have up to one year after filing in one country to file for protection in another country or countries. All of the industrial countries and all countries in both western and eastern Europe, except Albania, are parties to the Paris Convention. However, few developing countries are signatories.

The Patent Cooperation Treaty also makes the international patent process simpler and more efficient. More than 40 countries—including the United States, Japan, Russia, and members of the European Community—are parties to this treaty. A company can file a single patent application in which it names the countries in which it seeks patent coverage. The application will then be filed in each of those countries.

Other regional treaties provide similar coordination of patent rights. The Inter-American Convention serves the United States and Latin American countries, and the European Patent Organization coordinates protection among European Community members.

Trademarks.   A **trademark** is a distinctive name, symbol, word, picture, or combination of these that is used by a business to identify its services or products. Trademark protection was designed to protect the good reputation of businesses' services and goods. It prevents competitors from representing their products as being those of another business. Such a practice of misrepresenting is deceptive to the public and unfairly takes business away from reputable companies.

The symbol ® indicates that a name is a registered trademark in the United States. Most labels of brand-name products include the symbol identifying the name as a registered trademark. To remain protected, a trademark must be in continual use and must continue to be identified with the original business. Once a term becomes accepted to mean all things of that kind, it is no longer protected. For example, T-shirt and aspirin were once trademarks, but they are no longer protected by trademark because they have become everyday terms.

Trademark protection is covered by several international agreements. The Paris Convention of Industrial Property covers trademarks as well as patents. The Madrid Agreement of 1891 Concerning the International Registration of Marks enables businesses of its approximately 27 members to submit a single application for protection in all of its member countries. The European Community does not have its own comprehensive trademark agreement, but many of its members are signatories of the Madrid Agreement.

Copyrights.   A **copyright** protects the original works of authors, composers, playwrights, artists, and publishers. A copyright gives the originator exclusive rights to publish, sell, and exhibit his or her creative work for his or her lifetime plus 50 years. The copyright notice, ©, followed by the name of the copyright owner and the date of publication, must be prominently displayed on the publication. Anyone who uses work protected by copyright without the creator's permission can be subject to legal action.

The Berne Convention of 1986 established the International Union for the Protection of Literary and Artistic Works. More than 65 countries, including all members of the European Community, are signatories.

Global Highlight: Taiwan

Taiwan, officially called the Republic of China, is an island nation off the southeast coast of China between the East and South China seas. Mountains form the backbone of the country, but the western slopes are fertile and well cultivated. Most of Taiwan's people live in the lowlands on the western side of the island.

Chinese immigrants came to the island in the seventeenth century. After a brief period of Dutch rule (1620-1662), Taiwan experienced approximately 160 years of Chinese control. Japan ruled from 1895-1945, using the island for farming and military operations. After World War II, civil war between the Nationalist and Communist factions broke out in China. The leader of the Chinese Nationalist party, Chiang Kai-shek, fled to Taiwan. He proclaimed Taipei the provisional capital of China, renamed Taiwan as the Republic of China, and took control of the island. Since then, both the People's Republic of China and the Nationalist Chinese government in Taiwan have continued to declare Taiwan part of China.

The conflict regarding whether the Communist government—based on mainland China—or the Nationalist government—based in Taiwan—was the legitimate government of China was the source of bitterness, international tension, and armed clashes throughout the 1950s and 1960s. By the late 1980s, however, there had been a gradual decrease in the hostilities. In 1986, the mainland Chinese government announced that the principle of "one country, two systems" would be applied to Taiwan. This policy retains Taiwan's economic independence and army but submits it to China in matters of foreign policy.

After World War II, Taiwan enjoyed rapid industrial growth and now has one of the strongest economies in Asia. Its educational system is considered to be one of the biggest factors in Taiwan's economic success. Taiwan is one of the most literate countries in the world, with a literacy rate of 91.2. Most of its people work in industry or service jobs; only 15 percent work in agriculture. Taiwan particularly promotes high-tech industries such as those that produce computer and computer-related items.

Taiwan's economy is largely based on exports, which account for more than half of its gross national product. The Taiwanese government maintains some barriers to foreign investment and carefully selects the foreign companies that are allowed access to Taiwan's domestic market. In general, only companies that do not pose a competitive threat to local business or produce pollution are allowed entry into Taiwan's domestic market.

The Berne Union extends copyright protection in all member countries to its members as long as the first publication takes place in one of those countries. The International Copyright Convention of 1955 also provides international copyright protection, based on the agreement by its 65 members that each country will offer the same protection to foreign works that it does for domestic works.

CONTRACT LAW

A **contract** is a legally enforceable agreement between two or more persons either to do or not do a certain thing or things. A contract encourages competent parties to abide by an agreed-upon set of items. Contracts are the basis for almost all business arrangements.

Contracts can be either implied or express. An *implied contract* is one that is not explicitly agreed to by the parties, but is inferred either from the parties' conduct or from the law. An *express contract* is one whose terms are openly declared, either orally or in writing. Because it is wise for parties to an agreement to set forth very clearly what is expected of everyone, businesses nearly always enter into express contracts. However, both implied and express contracts are binding on both parties, and neither party can withdraw without the agreement of the other party.

Components of a Contract

For a contract to be considered *valid,* it must contain the following four essential components:

1. Capacity—All parties must be competent, of legal age, and mentally capable.
2. Mutual agreement—One party offers valid terms and the other party accepts.
3. Consideration—Something of value must be given by both parties.
4. Legal purpose—The terms of the contract must be in agreement with the law.

For a contract to be enforceable, the contract must be valid. That is, it must meet all four of the conditions. A valid contract can be enforced by either party. An unenforceable contract fails to meet one of those four requirements, and therefore, neither party can enforce it.

Businesspeople in the international arena frequently enter into contracts with representatives of companies from other countries and with the governments of other countries. Such agreements are most often made according to the rules of international law.

Treaties and Trade Agreements

Treaties and trade agreements between countries have a tremendous effect on the way in which companies do business in foreign countries. These agreements impose a degree of stability and uniformity in an international arena where members have widely different cultures and customs. Since contracts are the basis of business relationships, many trade agreements provide guidelines for the enforcement of contracts.

The most far-reaching international trade agreement in force today is the General Agreement on Tariffs and Trade (GATT). Negotiated in 1947, GATT is a series of trade agreements that define acceptable international business practices. It was designed to ensure open markets and fair competition among its 117 members. GATT encourages its members to expand multilateral trade and to establish tariffs that are favorable to other members. In its latest round of talks, GATT included guidelines for the protection of intellectual property rights, which is an area of great concern to many businesses. Approximately 30 countries have recently applied for membership in GATT, which currently covers more than 80 percent of world trade.

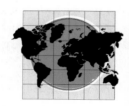

Global Business Example: Can South Korea Maintain Its Spectacular Economic Growth Rate?

Over the past three decades, South Korea has been a model of industrialization, rising from being one of the poorest countries in the world to one of the most economically successful. After the division of the Korean peninsula in

1945 and the war between North and South Korea, South Korea was left with widespread destruction, few industrial resources, and a largely unskilled labor force. The country's remarkable success in rebuilding its economy is to the credit of the industrious nature of its people. The economy was rebuilt by developing labor-intensive light industry and a large export market.

To accomplish this economic development, South Korea's governmental bureaucracy was given the power to decide which companies would develop which industries. A strong central bank controlled funding for these growth projects. The government was also given the power to regulate tightly foreign imports and foreign investments within the country.

While only a few years ago South Korea had the fastest growing economy in the world, the continuation of its success is uncertain in the 1990s. South Korean businesses are now struggling to break free of the bureaucracy's control. Although tight regulation helped to organize the country's economy during the developing years, such control is now restricting South Korea's international trade. Local businesses are being hurt by rising interest rates and wages, making their goods more expensive to produce and, therefore, less attractive to foreign importers.

RESOLVING LEGAL DIFFERENCES

Throughout the world, most legal disputes are resolved without the parties ever going to court. This is true of disputes between individuals, businesses, and nations.

There are many reasons why businesses, particularly those in the international arena, are willing to settle conflicts out of court. The time and expense involved in lawsuits, a need for a quick resolution, concern about bad publicity, uncertainty about outcomes, and a desire to maintain a good relationship with the other party all must be considered. Businesses may also fear that they will receive discriminatory treatment in a foreign court. Moreover, the complexity involved in determining which country's laws to use and the location of the trial contributes to companies' preference for dispute resolution outside of the courtroom. The two major means of alternate dispute settlement used by businesses in the international arena are mediation and arbitration.

Mediation

Mediation is an alternate dispute method that makes use of a neutral third party, or mediator. A mediator attempts to reconcile the disputing parties' viewpoints. A mediator is involved with the substance of the dispute, making suggestions and proposals, and therefore, is often an attorney or expert in the disputed matter. Mediators cannot make binding decisions; only when the disputing parties voluntarily agree to a mediator's decision is a settlement reached. Thus, mediation is most successful when both parties are willing to compromise.

Some cultures have a strong tradition in the use of mediation as a means of settling disputes. In Japan, for example, it is a point of honor for individuals and businesses to settle their disputes without having to go to court. In the People's Republic of China, approximately 90 percent of all civil disputes are settled by mediation. There are more than 800,000 Mediation Committees throughout China, each composed of a group of knowledgeable laypeople.

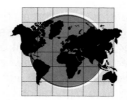

Global Business Example: Investment Opportunities in the Pacific Rim

The Pacific Rim has the world's fastest growing regional economy. As the countries in this region continue to experience rapid economic growth, their people's standard of living increases. As a result, they are able to afford more imported goods and services. To meet these demands, the governments of the countries in this region, such as South Korea, are beginning to ease their tight control over local markets. As Asian companies are allowed to develop business without the strict governmental control of the past, they are able to enter into more joint ventures and import agreements with foreign investors. Thus, many opportunities are opening for foreign companies to do business in the Pacific Rim countries.

Pacific Rim governments are also focusing on diversifying their largely export-oriented economies. They are beginning to venture into other areas of business and to put their resources into maintaining their infrastructures by repairing and rebuilding roads, bridges, dams, buildings, and airports.

When developing countries do not have the resources to complete these kinds of projects themselves, they can apply for funding from such sources as the World Bank, the Agency for International Development, or the Asian Development Bank. Once funding has been approved, companies from other countries can make bids on a contract to perform the work. Such development projects create many opportunities in the Pacific Rim for foreign companies.

The Asian Development Bank has sponsored many projects to upgrade the infrastructures of Pacific Rim countries, including the following:

- The Philippines—irrigation projects on the Tango River and rehabilitation of the North Harbor in Manila;
- Indonesia—consultation on the operation and maintenance of irrigation systems; and,
- Thailand—project preparation for 1,000 kilometers of secondary and rural roads.

Figure 8-4 shows some other infrastructure projects in the Pacific Rim.

Figure 8-4

Many major infrastructure projects are ongoing in Pacific Rim countries.

BUILDING AN INFRASTRUCTURE

Project	*Estimated cost (US$ million)*	*Project period*
Japan		
Trans-Tokyo Bay Highway	$8,900	1988–96
Taiwan		
Taipei mass rapid transit system	14,800	1989–99
Taichung coal-fired power plant	3,300	1990–95
Mingtan pumped-storage hydro project	1,850	1989–95
Tunnel expressway	1,500	1988–96
Hong Kong		
Kai Tak airport expansion, new airport and related facilities	7,600	1988–96
Major roads and rail extensions linking Kwun Tong and Junk Bay	2,170	mid-1990s
China		
Guangzhou-Shenzhen-Zhuhai superhighway	1,500	1988–93
Singapore		
10-year plan to expand ports, public utilities, and telecommunications	5,140	1990–2000

Source: *The Pacific Rim Almanac,* by Alexander Besher. New York: HarperPerennial.

Arbitration

Arbitration is a form of conflict resolution that uses a neutral third party to make a binding decision. Unlike a mediator, an arbitrator's decision is legal and binding on both parties. An arbitrator acts as a private judge in a place of the disputing parties' choice and establishes procedures and rules of evidence. The parties specify the issues to be decided by the arbitrator. In this way, they avoid receiving a decision based on legal technicalities or other reasons that are not central to the issue being decided.

Arbitration is particularly well suited to settling disputes involving international business. Such disputes normally do not involve serious or complicated legal issues; and, most businesses prefer to resolve disputes in a speedy, economical, and private way. Most often, a dispute comes to arbitration because a contract either requires it or allows a party to demand it. Such provisions are common in union contracts.

In the international business arena, the requirement of arbitration, as well as specific procedures to be followed, are frequently included in the original contract. An intermediary whom both parties agree to be impartial may also be provided for in the original contract. A representative from the international business community is often chosen to be an arbitrator. For example, a typical choice is an officer in a chamber of commerce or a trade association from a third country.

Litigation

When two parties are unable or unwilling to resolve their differences through mediation or arbitration, they may decide on litigation. **Litigation** is a lawsuit, or a contest in a court of law, to enforce a person's or an organization's rights or to seek a remedy to the violation of their rights. Litigation involves many complex procedural rules. These rules vary widely from country to country and even among courts within a given country. Most countries have a federal or national court; and, many also have state or provincial courts, as well as even more localized courts. Nearly all legal systems have separate rules for criminal and civil cases.

People living or doing business in a foreign country are subject to the laws of that country. Thus, if a dispute arises between a business and a citizen or between a business and the authorities of the host country, the matter must be settled in the host country's courts. When a conflict arises between two companies of different countries, the conflict may be settled either in the courts of the country in which the agreement was made or in the courts of the country in which the contract will be fulfilled. Figure 8-5 provides a brief outline of dispute settlement methods and options.

If a government violates the terms of a contract with a foreign company, the company is expected to pursue a remedy within that host country. If the company is unable to obtain a resolution by such means, it may present its claim to its own government, which may then press an international claim against the foreign country on behalf of the company. Many governments are unwilling to press such claims, however, for two reasons. First, the company is presumed to have had a clear conception of the risks involved in entering into such an agreement. Second, pressing such a claim may interfere with the sometimes delicate political balance that may exist between the two countries.

THE INTERNATIONAL COURT OF JUSTICE

The **International Court of Justice** was established in 1946 by the Charter of the United Nations. It sits in The Hague in the Netherlands. The International Court settles disputes between nations when both nations request that it do so. It also advises the United Nations on matters of international law. The decisions of the Court are binding for all parties.

Many of the procedures of the International Court of Justice are derived from Western civil law systems. For example, the International

Figure 8-5
Means of settling disputes between companies in different countries.

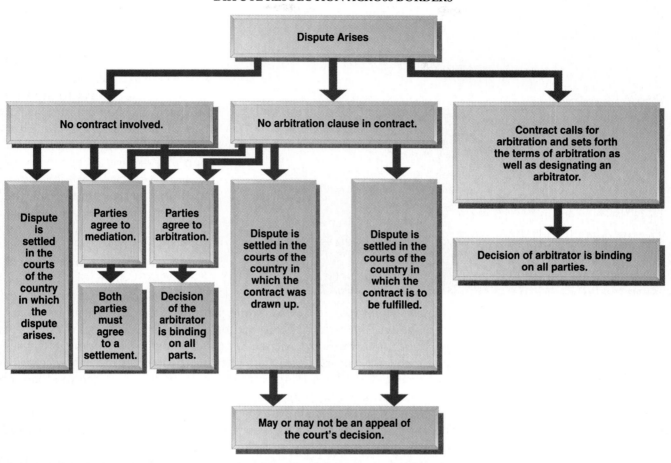

DISPUTE RESOLUTION ACROSS BORDERS

Dispute Arises

No contract involved.

No arbitration clause in contract.

Contract calls for arbitration and sets forth the terms of arbitration as well as designating an arbitrator.

Dispute is settled in the courts of the country in which the dispute arises.

Parties agree to mediation.

Parties agree to arbitration.

Both parties must agree to a settlement.

Decision of the arbitrator is binding on all parts.

Dispute is settled in the courts of the country in which the contract was drawn up.

Dispute is settled in the courts of the country in which the contract is to be fulfilled.

Decision of arbitrator is binding on all parties.

May or may not be an appeal of the court's decision.

Court primarily uses documentary evidence to decide a case. It also has the power to request additional evidence as it wishes. The International Court does not use procedures that are unique to common law. There is no jury; and, for that reason, oral testimony is rarely heard, evidence is rarely removed from the record, and perjured testimony and falsified documents are simply ignored rather than pursued.

While Western principles of law predominate in the International Court, some non-Western principles have been incorporated into international law. Islamic law has contributed to the division of law into primary and secondary sources. The primary source corresponds to the Islamic concept of certain or definite proof. The secondary source corresponds to the Islamic concept of reasoned proof. The great majority

of international rules of war, as well as many rules regarding treaties, are also based on Islamic law. The reliance of the International Court on negotiation and mediation as means of dispute settlement are derived primarily from Asian customs.

Because of the dominance of Western principles, some newly developed states have found that international law is in conflict with their interests. Communist and developing nations, for example, do not accept many of the legal principles of the older, developed states that form the basis of international law. Because of the past and continuing dominance of the West, these newer countries' effect on international law has been slight.

Since law must change to adapt to emerging situations, some principles that are not in harmony with Western ideas have been integrated into international law. As the world becomes more interdependent, the needs of developing countries tend to become more closely attached to the needs of the mainstream. As a result, these developing countries become more willing to abide by international law and offer new concepts to it.

It is important to note that only nations can be parties before the International Court of Justice. Individuals and organizations, including businesses, are specifically excluded. Thus, very few commercial cases are heard by the Court. Such cases are heard only when a government presses an international claim on behalf of one of its companies.

What, then, is the importance of the International Court of Justice to the world of international business? The answer is that it provides guidelines for acceptable ways of doing business for governments and citizens of all countries.

Predictability in the way that businesses will be treated in foreign environments is extremely important to the continuation and expansion of world trade. Businesspeople in all countries want to engage in profitable relationships. As long as international principles of law are observed—particularly property rights and responsibilities and enforcement of contracts—international business will bring countries of the world closer together.

Back to the Beginning: NAFTA: Lifting Trade Barriers

Reread the case at the beginning of this chapter and answer the following questions:

1. How might a joint venture between a company based in Mexico and a U.S.-based company benefit both companies?
2. How might the joint venture described in number 1 affect the Mexican economy? the U.S. economy?
3. What type of agreement or contract would the U.S.-based company and the Mexican company need to make to prevent legal difficulties in the future? Why?

KNOWING GLOBAL BUSINESS TERMS

The following terms should become part of your business vocabulary. For each numbered item find the term that has the same meaning. (Not all terms will be used.)

- arbitration
- civil law
- common law
- contract
- copyright
- intellectual property
- International Court of Justice
- liability
- litigation

- mediation
- negligence
- patent
- product liability
- property
- property rights
- statutes
- strict liability
- trademark

1. A legal system that relies on an accumulation of decisions made in prior cases.
2. A legal right that protects the original works of authors, musical composers, playwrights, artists, and publishers.
3. An agreement enforceable in a court of law.
4. Anything that can be owned.
5. The judicial branch of the United Nations.
6. The responsibility that manufacturers and sellers have for the safety of their products.
7. Laws passed by a body of lawmakers established specifically for the purpose of making laws.

8. The failure of a responsible party to follow standards of due care.

9. A distinctive name or symbol that identifies the product or services of a particular company.

10. A conflict resolution method that makes use of a neutral third party to bring about a mutually agreed-upon settlement.

11. The exclusive right of an inventor to make, sell, and use a product or process.

12. A method of conflict resolution that makes use of a neutral third party, who makes a binding decision between two parties.

REVIEWING YOUR READING

Answer these questions to reinforce your knowledge of the main ideas of this chapter.

1. The justice systems of the majority of countries in the world are based on what kind of law?

2. How did common law develop?

3. What are the three types of property? Define them.

4. Does negligence have to be proven in a successful strict liability case? Why or why not?

5. If you saw Pyrex® printed on a mixing bowl, what would the symbol following the name indicate?

6. What is the purpose of protecting a trademark?

7. For a contract to be valid, what four elements must it contain? Define each element.

8. What is the difference between mediation and arbitration?

9. What are some of the reasons why two businesses from different countries might prefer to resolve a dispute through mediation or arbitration rather than litigation?

10. What is the importance of international law to businesses engaged in international trade?

EXPANDING YOUR HORIZONS

You will not find the complete answers to this project in your textbook. You will need to use your critical-thinking skills. Think about this project, gather information from other sources, analyze possible responses, and discuss them with others before you finalize your written contract.

PROJECT: You and your parents decide to write a contract for the improvement of your school grades. Your parents offer to increase your allowance upon a satisfactory improvement in your grades, as evidenced by your report card.

Write a contract that includes all of the details of the agreement between you and your parents. Make sure your contract includes mutual agreement, consideration, contractual capacity, and legal purpose.

BUILDING RESEARCH SKILLS

The ability to find information from various sources is an important international business skill. The following activities will help you investigate various topics. You will also learn to apply class ideas to situations outside of the classroom.

1. Look for five examples of trademarks on products traded in international markets. Draw a picture of the trademark and describe why the company would seek a trademark for this word or symbol.

2. Research a patent on a product. Identify the inventor, the year the patent was granted, and the product's function. Develop a summary report of your findings.

3. Write a letter to a publishing company or a music/video production company requesting permission to copy an artist's work. Save a copy of your letter and summarize the response you receive in a short written report.

4. *Global Career Activity.* Find out what types of legal agreements a person would encounter when applying for a job with and working for a multinational company.

Continuing Enrichment Project: Laws Around the World

Work individually or in a group to research the legal system of another country. Choose a country with a legal system that is unlike the one in the United States. Focus your research on cultural issues that affect legal agreements in that country. Answer the following questions in your report:

1. What are some pressing issues that affect legal agreements in your chosen country?

2. How does the culture of the country affect its legal system?

3. What sort of out-of-court contract resolution process might work in your chosen country's legal system?

Global Entrepreneurship and Small Business Management

After studying this chapter and completing the end-of-chapter activities, you will be able to

- Explain the importance of entrepreneurs in the development of an economy.
- Differentiate the types of entrepreneurial businesses.
- Evaluate self-employment as a career option.
- Outline the process of financing a small business.
- Identify the major business activities of a small business manager.
- Describe telecommuting and the effect of technology on home-based businesses.

FinnTrade

Steve Siltanen did not want to use his education and business talents to make money for someone else. His technological knowledge, love of travel, and ability to speak Finnish combined to give him an idea. Steve and his wife, Eileen Spoth, started their own company.

FinnTrade, a high-tech trading company, started as a part-time small business. The company sells computers and related equipment to various European companies. FinnTrade also provides service and training to help customers effectively use what they buy.

Siltanen started his international business activities by attending a trade show in Helsinki, Finland. FinnTrade made its first sales at that time. Today, orders are received by fax. Using Finland as a base of operations, FinnTrade now sells computers and training in the countries of the former Soviet Union.

Source: Adapted from "Exporter Finds Big, Hungry Markets," *Home-Office Computing,* June, 1992, p. 56.

The world of business is constantly changing. No one knows this better than the 16 million small-business owners in the United States. Each day foreign competition increases. A store down the street now acquires items from manufacturers in Asia and Europe. Businesses of every type and size are adapting to the global marketplace.

THE ECONOMIC IMPORTANCE OF ENTREPRENEURS

Nations do not start out highly industrialized with international airports, super highways, and computer networks. In every country people get ideas and take action to make products better, faster, and more available. This inventive effort is the basis for economic development and improved quality of life.

Innovation and the Entrepreneurial Spirit

An **entrepreneur** is a risk taker who operates a business. Every business combines land, labor, and capital to sell a product or service. An entrepreneur is the person who brings together those resources for a company to get started and operate successfully.

Entrepreneurs may be people with a creative vision, such as Walt Disney who started the Disney Company, or Steve Jobs and Steve Wosniak who started Apple Computer. A common trait of entrepreneurs is they don't listen to people who say, "It can't be done!" These business innovators have an idea they believe in and dedicate their time, money, and effort to its success.

Economic and Social Benefits of Small Business

Most entrepreneurs start small. Some have started in a basement or garage. Small companies are an important part of every economy. A **small business** is an independently owned and operated business that does not dominate an industry.

Small businesses are commonly described by number of employees. The U.S. Small Business Administration defines a small business as one with fewer than 100 employees. About 95 percent of all businesses in the United States have fewer than 50 employees. These entrepreneurial efforts provide a nation with sources of new products, new jobs, and personal service.

Small businesses are major creators of new products. Entrepreneurs are willing to take risks and try ideas that may be rejected by larger companies. Entrepreneurs have invented products such as personal computers, ballpoint pens, video games, and fiberglass snow skis.

Small businesses are the major source of new jobs. Between 1980 and 1992, the 500 largest companies in the United States reduced their work forces by 4.4 million people. During that same period, small businesses hired over 20 million employees.

Small businesses often provide personal service. In that way, they compete successfully against larger companies to meet the individual needs of customers. A bank, for example, can grant loans to people in its community that may be denied funding by larger financial institutions. Small manufacturing companies can produce custom-made parts for foreign companies, an activity that large businesses might not find profitable.

Entrepreneurial businesses often turn to international business to expand their markets. Exporting is promoted by the Small Business Administration, World Trade Centers, and state departments of economic development. These agencies and organizations help entrepreneurs plan and execute international business activities.

Entrepreneurs may invent ways to adapt products and services to meet the economic, cultural, and legal needs of customers in other countries. Figure 9-1 shows common small business activities in Europe and Asia.

Figure 9-1

Entrepreneurial businesses are in operation all over the world.

COMMON ENTREPRENEURIAL BUSINESSES IN EUROPE AND ASIA

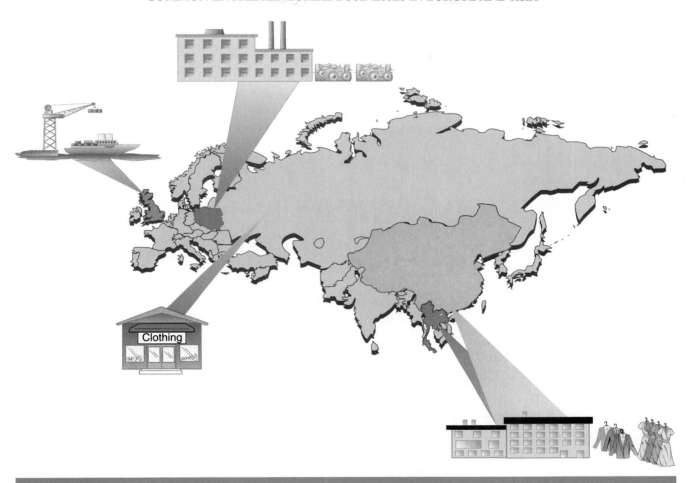

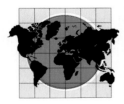

Global Business Example: Entrepreneurs in Modern Thailand

Thailand started as an agricultural society with a system of landlords and peasants. Chinese influence in the late 1800s helped change the economic emphasis of Thailand. By the 1970s over 30 major companies were based in the country. Entrepreneurial activities have stimulated economic development. Today, Thailand is one of the 30 largest economies in the world with an annual growth rate higher than most industrialized countries.

TYPES OF ENTREPRENEURIAL BUSINESSES

Types of entrepreneurial enterprises are as varied as types of large corporations. Entrepreneurial businesses can be grouped into five major categories: extracting companies, manufacturing companies, wholesalers, retailers, and service companies.

Extracting Companies

Diamond-mining companies in South Africa, oil companies in Saudi Arabia, and flower growers in California are examples of extractors. These enterprises take raw materials from nature or grow products. Extracting companies include businesses involved in agriculture, fishing, forestry, and mining.

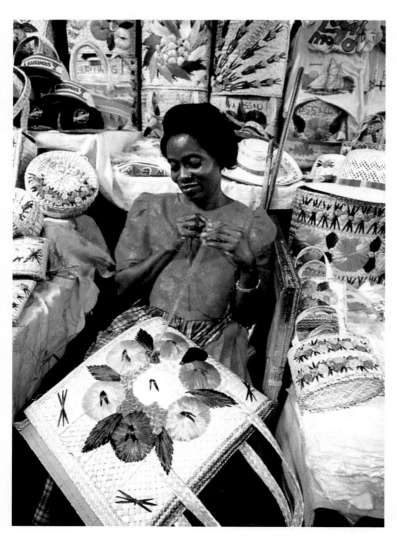

Manufacturing Companies

Manufacturing involves changing raw materials and parts into usable products. Entrepreneurs in this category range from computer manufacturers with many employees to basket weavers with just a few workers.

Wholesalers

Products must get from producers to consumers. If clothing manufactured in Taiwan is not shipped to appropriate selling locations, the garments have little value. A wholesaler is a business that buys from a manufacturer and sells to other businesses. Wholesalers are commonly called *intermediaries* because they are links between producers and final users of products.

Retailers

A retailer is a business that sells directly to consumers. In a typical week you probably go to several stores. You may also buy from mail order companies or vending machines. These are examples of retailing businesses.

Service Companies

How often does someone in your household have clothes cleaned, get the car washed, use a telephone, have film developed, or rent a product? These are all examples of services. Consumer services include businesses such as law offices, doctor's offices, dentist offices, hair salons, day-care centers, repair shops, travel agencies, and music schools. Business services are sold by one company to another company. Business services include advertising, data processing, custodial, security, and equipment rental. Each year, services become a larger portion of the U.S. economy.

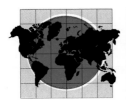

Global Business Example: Small-Business Growth Fields

Not only are 16 million workers in the United States self-employed, but another 2 million people have part-time businesses in addition to working for someone else. Government agencies and business experts project that in the next few years entrepreneurs involved in the following types of enterprises have the greatest potential for success:

- health care services;
- retailing and food service companies especially those using technology to interact with customers;
- environmental businesses that recycle and offer environment-friendly goods and services;
- training and education enterprises to help workers adapt to a changing workplace;
- personal services such as child care, financial planning, entertainment, and recreation; and,
- commercial services such as delivery, transportation, and information processing.

These businesses will be in demand both in the United States and in other countries.

SELF-EMPLOYMENT AS A CAREER

When you own your own business, the good news is that you don't have to listen to a boss anymore—because you are the boss. The bad news is that you can't call in sick unless someone else can be trusted to keep things going.

The Business Plan

Every trip, every team, and every company needs a plan to achieve its goal. A **business plan** is a guide used to start and operate a business. Every small business needs a plan to guide it to success. A business plan has two main uses. First, this document may be used to attract new investors or to convince a bank to lend money to the company. Second, the business plan provides a blueprint for company activities.

Figure 9-2 shows that a business plan includes seven main sections. The topics of business description, organizational structure, and marketing activities are presented in the following paragraphs. Financial planning, production activities, human resource activities, and information needs are given expanded coverage later in this chapter.

Figure 9-2
A business plan is designed to help a manager organize business activities.

THE PARTS OF A BUSINESS PLAN

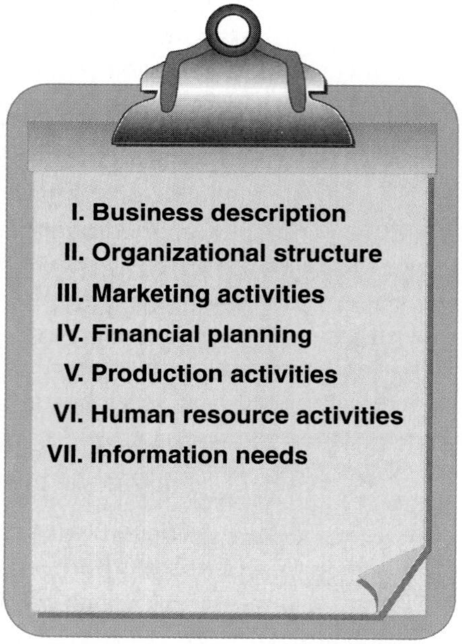

I. Business description
II. Organizational structure
III. Marketing activities
IV. Financial planning
V. Production activities
VI. Human resource activities
VII. Information needs

Business Description.   The introductory section of a business plan covers three topics. First, the legal name and location of the company is identified. Second, a brief description of the background and experience of the owners and main employees is given. Third, a description of the company's product or service, potential customers, and competition is presented.

Organizational Structure.   Most businesses are organized as sole proprietorships, partnerships, or corporations. A company's organizational structure, covered in the second section of the business plan, will be based on its size, number of owners, and method of financing.

Marketing Activities.   Communicating with and serving customers are important activities for every business; these are discussed in the third section of the business plan. **Marketing** involves activities necessary to get goods and services from the producer to the consumer. Marketing activities include product/service planning, risk management, marketing information management, promotion, pricing, financing, distribution, purchasing, and selling.

Many companies organize this phase of their business with a **marketing plan**. This document details marketing activities of an organization. A marketing plan should include information about customer needs, social and cultural factors, competition, target markets, economic trends, political and trade barriers, the marketing mix, and actions to be taken.

Advantages of Self-Employment

The two main advantages of owning a business are independence and pride of ownership. A small-business owner makes the company decisions and is at the center of action. Because of political and legal restrictions, however, this same independence is not available to entrepreneurs in all countries.

As entrepreneurs achieve success, they usually gain a feeling of accomplishment. They gain confidence in their ability to organize resources, make decisions, and manage business activities. Serving customers, employing workers, and contributing to the economic growth of a community or nation can also provide a sense of satisfaction for entrepreneurs.

Disadvantages of Self-Employment

Being the boss also has certain disadvantages. The drawbacks of self-employment are the time commitment, uncertain income, and possible loss of investment. Every small-business owner can tell you about the time involved. More than half of all small-business owners who sell their companies do so because of boredom or burnout.

As a business owner, income is uncertain. In the first few years of owning a business it is possible that the owner will not earn enough to get a salary. Business experts recommend that money be set aside for personal living expenses before starting a new business. Even after the business has been going for awhile, poor economic conditions can reduce sales and profits.

Each year more than 60,000 business failures occur in the United States, with owners and other investors losing millions of dollars. In that same time frame, however, more than 700,000 new businesses start in our country. Three out of four new companies are still operating after three years. Business failure is commonly caused by limited cash, poor management decisions, and a weak economy.

Qualities of Successful Entrepreneurs

What are successful entrepreneurs like? Most entrepreneurs have a desire for adventure. Risk takers are people willing to give up a secure job in exchange for the chance to own and operate a business. Global entrepreneurs must consider the added risk of potential cultural, social, political, and legal barriers.

Is there some activity you participate in and do well? Being self-confident is another quality of successful entrepreneurs. These people believe in themselves and believe that they can get others to get things done. Remember that it may mean getting things done in different ways in foreign markets.

Entrepreneurs spend almost all their time either on the job or thinking about their business. Hard working people have the potential for being the most successful. Are you someone who is willing to put in extra time and effort for your business?

Someone once said that if you don't know where you are going, you might end up somewhere else and not even know it. A goal-oriented person is someone who has a clear direction for the company in the business plan. Goals should be stated clearly and in a realistic manner. Goals should also have a time limit for achievement and should be measurable in some numeric way. For example, a business goal may be to have ten new customers in Greece in the next three months.

A new product idea or an old idea reformulated in a new way can both be paths for entrepreneurial success. Creativity is a key to entrepreneurial success. Think about ways existing products can be improved or create a business that can make the lives of busy people a little easier.

Finally, knowing about the world of business is important for success as an entrepreneur. Business knowledge refers to an understanding of economics, organizational structure, decision making, selling, advertising, finance, and technology. Business knowledge for the global entrepreneur should include information about exchange rates, shipping methods, product labeling, and more.

Global Business Exercise: Would You Like to Own Your Own Business?

To determine if you are a good candidate for running your own business, answer the following questions. If you answer "yes" to most of the questions, you would probably enjoy being a small business owner.

1. Do you feel comfortable making decisions even when others might not agree with you?
2. Do you have leadership ability? Are others willing to follow your instructions? Do others respect you as a leader?
3. Do you stay with a task until it is complete without becoming discouraged?
4. Are you able to see things from different views? Can you use creativity to solve problems?
5. Can you clearly communicate your ideas to others both orally and in writing?
6. Are you able to start a project without encouragement from others?
7. Are you able to plan effectively your use of time and money?
8. Do you learn from your mistakes? Are there situations in which a failure helped you to learn and improve?
9. Are you willing to do unpleasant tasks that are necessary?

This is not an exact test of your potential as a small-business manager; however, your answers will help you decide if owning your own business is something to investigate.

FINANCING THE SMALL BUSINESS

Money is needed for many purposes when starting and running a business. Funds are needed to buy advertising, to pay employees, to purchase supplies, and to acquire equipment. A **budget** is a financial tool that estimates a company's funds and its plan for spending those funds.

One of the most common causes of business failure is lack of money to pay company expenses. Small companies involved in international business have the additional problem of planning for changing exchange rates. The process of financing a business starts with calculating operating costs and determining how to acquire the funds to pay those costs.

Analyzing Costs

One of the most difficult tasks when starting a new business is determining how much money will be needed to get started and continue in operation. *Start-up costs* are those expenses that occur when a company is new. Start-up costs include equipment purchases, remodeling costs, legal fees, utility company deposits, and beginning inventory costs.

Continuing expenses are business operating costs that occur on an on-going basis. Continuing expenses include rent, utilities, insurance, salaries, advertising costs, employee training costs, taxes, and interest on loans.

Some business costs vary depending on the level of production; others do not. **Variable costs** are business expenses that change as the level of production changes. For example, the cost of materials and parts to make radios depends on the number of radios that are produced. If parts and materials cost $8 per radio, the variable costs for making 100 radios will be $800; whereas, the variable costs for making 10 radios will be $80.

Fixed costs are expenses that do not change as the level of production changes. For example, rent of $1,000 a month and a manager's salary of $3,200 a month will be the same whether the company makes 10 radios or 100 radios.

A comparison of variable and fixed costs with sales revenue will tell a company the amount of profit (or loss). The **breakeven point** is the production level at which profit is zero. Figure 9-3 illustrates the calculations for a breakeven point if a company has fixed costs of $44,000, variable costs of $8 per radio, and a selling price of $12 per radio. At the breakeven point of 11,000 units, costs are covered but no profit is earned.

Sources of Funds

Where do companies get the money to finance the start-up costs and continuing expenses? This funding can be secured in one of two ways: through equity or debt. **Equity funds** are business funds obtained from the owners of the business. Equity is the money the owners of a business have invested from their personal accounts.

Debt funds are business funds obtained by borrowing. The amounts owed by a business are called the debts of the company. Loans from financial institutions also help to finance companies and are debt funds.

Figure 9-3

A firm with fixed costs of $44,000, variable costs of $8 per item, and a selling price of $12 per item will break even at 11,000 units.

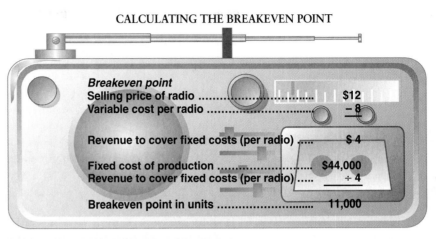

CALCULATING THE BREAKEVEN POINT

Breakeven point
Selling price of radio $12
Variable cost per radio .... − 8

Revenue to cover fixed costs (per radio) ..... $ 4

Fixed cost of production $44,000
Revenue to cover fixed costs (per radio) ..... ÷ 4

Breakeven point in units 11,000

Financial Records of Small Businesses

The financial records of a company are like the scoreboard for a sporting event. Financial record keeping helps a business keep track of its financial status. A **balance sheet** is the document that reports a company's assets (items of value), liabilities (amounts owed to others), and owner's equity (net worth). Assets include cash and anything that could be sold for cash, such as equipment, land, and inventory. The relationship among the items on a balance sheet is:

ASSETS - LIABILITIES = OWNER'S EQUITY (NET WORTH)

For example if a company has $4 million of assets and $1.5 million in liabilities, the company has a net worth of $2.5 million.

An **income statement** is the document that summarizes a company's revenue from sales and its expenses over a period of time, such as one year. If a company had sales revenue of $670,000 in one month with $430,000 in operating expenses, its profit would be $240,000. What would be the profit or loss of a business with $32,000 of sales revenue and $37,000 of expenses?

The continuing costs of a business are usually paid for with current cash flows. **Cash flow** is the inflow and outflow of cash. The major sources of cash inflows are cash sales and money owed on account that is collected from customers. Occasionally, a company will need additional cash inflows due to slow sales or a need to buy expensive equipment. When this happens additional investments from owners or borrowing could occur.

The main cash outflows of a business are for current operating expenses, new equipment, debt payments, and taxes. A cash flow statement reports the current sources and amounts of cash inflows and outflows. Weak cash inflows are a major cause of small business failure.

Global Business Example: Chinese Entrepreneurs Overcome Obstacles

In June, 1989, hundreds of Chinese student demonstrators were killed in Tiananmen Square. They were protesting for greater political and economic freedom. Months later, ten protesters were sentenced to prison. Despite these setbacks, economic freedoms are surfacing in China. Private enterprise now accounts for about 10 percent of the country's industrial output. Family-owned farms are most common; however, privately owned factories, stores, and restaurants are growing in number.

MANAGING THE SMALL BUSINESS

In a large company, a manager is usually responsible for only one area of the business, such as marketing or finance. In a small business, however, the owner may be responsible for several or all areas of management. Figure 9-4 presents the five major management areas of every business. Two of these, marketing and finance, were discussed earlier in the chapter. The three other areas—production, human resources, and information systems—are introduced in this section.

Figure 9-4
Every company has five major business activities.

MAJOR ACTIVITIES OF EVERY BUSINESS

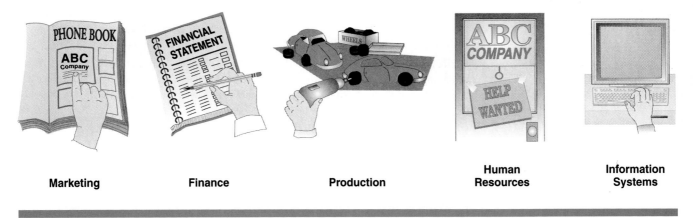

| Marketing | Finance | Production | Human Resources | Information Systems |

Production Management

The factors of production are combined to create goods and services. Every business must produce something to sell. Sometimes that something may not be too obvious. For example, what does a school produce? Or, what does a retail store produce?

The production department of a company may involve a factory with machinery or an office with computers. In both situations, production takes place. Production methods are influenced by the cultural and economic situation of a nation. A country with few machines will use more manual activities than automated methods.

Human Resource Management

Labor is probably the most important factor of production. Without people, highly automated equipment could not be built, operated, or repaired. Every business owner and manager must recognize this fact. Human resources are one of the most important components of every organization. Human resource management involves activities needed to obtain, train, and retain qualified employees.

First, a human resource manager must hire needed employees. A description that lists the qualifications for a job is advertised to prospective employees. Hiring involves screening applicants, interviewing candidates, and selecting the most qualified people for available positions.

A second major duty of human resource managers is training employees. Training does not occur only when a person starts a job; it is a continuous process. Technology, the economy, and legal rulings often have an effect on the job skills employees need to be productive. Continued training is important for all workers.

The final duty of human resource managers is to maintain employee satisfaction. Workers must be paid adequately so that they do not become discouraged or leave the company. Most businesses also provide employee benefits—such as paid holidays and vacations, medical insurance, rest areas, and discounts for company products. Human resource managers also motivate employees with awards; bonuses; and prizes for productivity, customer service, safety, and ideas that save the company money.

Information Management

Information is something companies have always needed but usually didn't think about too much. In recent years, computers have made information available easier, faster, and cheaper. Figure 9-5 shows the main areas of information needed by every business: financial, production and inventory, marketing, and human resources.

A management information system (MIS) is an organized method of processing and reporting data for business decisions. An MIS involves a plan for (1) identifying a company's information needs, (2) obtaining the information, (3) organizing the information in a useful manner, (4) distributing reports to those who make decisions, and (5) updating data files as needed.

Management information systems have resulted in expanded career opportunities for computer operators, software programmers, systems analysts, database managers, and computer service technicians.

Figure 9-5

Various types of business information are available to the business owner.

TYPES OF BUSINESS INFORMATION

Financial Information

includes budgets, sales reports, and financial statements.

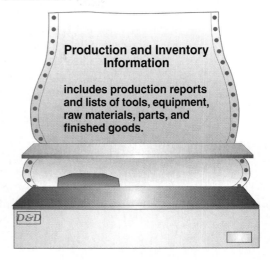

Production and Inventory Information

includes production reports and lists of tools, equipment, raw materials, parts, and finished goods.

Marketing Information

includes customer needs, competitors' actions, economic reports, and demographic trends.

Human Resources Information

includes employee evaluations, employee benefit reports, and salary data.

HOME-BASED BUSINESSES

Years ago most people worked from their homes as farmers, weavers, and toolmakers. This is still true in less-developed countries such as the Philippines, Nepal, Pakistan, Ethiopia, Chad, Nigeria,

Global Highlight: An Uncertain Future for the Wildlife of India

Their neighbors include crocodiles, leopards, rhinoceroses, tigers, and musk deer. The people in India share their land with more varieties of wildlife than does any other nation. The country has over 400 national parks and sanctuaries to preserve these natural wonders. Despite protected areas however, many species still face extinction.

Hunting and killing for food, animal skins, horns, and tusks result in vanishing breeds. Cutting down trees for firewood and using natural vegetation to feed livestock also threaten these endangered animals. Many species of wildlife no longer have the habitat necessary for survival. Currently the country has 140 animals on its endangered-species list.

As the second most populous nation in the world, India's diminishing resources are already stretched to an extreme. Tree planting and other conservation activities may help. Time will only tell if these efforts will allow for the survival of such animals as the jackal, Asiatic lion, and a tiny bird known as the Himalayan monal.

Source: "India's Wildlife Dilemma," *National Geographic,* May, 1992, pp. 2–29.

Liberia, Kenya, Ecuador, and Peru. In industrialized countries, however, most work moved to factories, stores, and offices during the industrialization process. Recently, technology is providing the opportunity for many workers to return to their homes to work. Millions of entrepreneurs and small business owners work out of their homes.

Telecommuting involves using a computer and other technology to work at home instead of in a company office or factory. Telecommuting is best suited to jobs that (1) do not require regular in-person contact with others and (2) may be done through computer networks and other telecommunications equipment. This employment arrangement is most commonly used with writers, editors, researchers, economists, accounting clerks, word-processing workers, database supervisors, and computer programmers.

Employers who use telecommuting report several benefits. First, businesses save money as they do not need as much office space. Next, companies are able to keep talented employees who may not want to work in a structured environment. Finally, telecommuting can save time and energy as workers do not travel to a place of employment. Many home-based entrepreneurs and telecommuters select working at home so that they can have more time with their families and save money on child care.

Global Business Example: Home-Based Entrepreneurs

Over 5 million people in the United States and nearly 2 million in Canada operate businesses from their homes. The most common businesses of these home-based entrepreneurs are

- sales—such as real estate, insurance, mail order, door-to-door, and agricultural;
- contracting, construction, mechanics, repair shops;
- personal service—such as hair stylists, pet groomers, child-care providers;
- arts and crafts;
- professional and technical services—such as lawyers, engineers, accountants, and consultants; and,
- clerical support—such as word processors, bookkeepers, and tax preparers.

People planning to work at home must consider the government regulations for these types of businesses. For example in Toronto, operation of a mail-order company from your basement is considered illegal.

Back to the Beginning: FinnTrade

Reread the case at the beginning of this chapter and answer the following questions:

1. What personal factors motivated Steve Siltanen to start FinnTrade?
2. In what ways did technology influence the starting and operation of FinnTrade?
3. What business decisions will FinnTrade face as it expands?

KNOWING GLOBAL BUSINESS TERMS

The following terms should become part of your business vocabulary. For each numbered item find the term that has the same meaning.

- balance sheet
- breakeven point
- budget
- business plan
- cash flow
- debt funds
- entrepreneur
- equity funds
- fixed costs
- income statement
- marketing
- marketing plan
- small business
- telecommuting
- variable costs

1. Business funds obtained by borrowing.
2. Business expenses that change in proportion to the level of production.
3. Business funds obtained from the owners of the business.
4. An independently owned and operated business that does not dominate an industry.
5. Activities necessary to get goods and services from the producer to the consumer.
6. A financial tool that estimates a company's funds and its plan for spending those funds.
7. A guide used to start and operate a business.
8. The document that reports a company's assets, liabilities, and owner's equity (net worth).
9. Expenses that do not vary with the level of production.
10. A risk taker who starts a new business.
11. The production level at which profit is zero.
12. The inflow and outflow of cash in a business.
13. Using a computer and other technology to work at home instead of in a company office or factory.
14. A document that details the marketing activities of an organization.
15. The document that summarizes a company's revenue from sales and its expenses.

Answer these questions to reinforce your knowledge of the main ideas of this chapter.

1. What are three benefits of small businesses in the development of an economy?
2. What are five common types of entrepreneurial businesses?
3. What are the advantages of owning your own business? What are the disadvantages?
4. What are common qualities of successful entrepreneurs?
5. What is the purpose of a business plan?
6. How do variable costs differ from fixed costs?
7. What is the difference between equity funds and debt funds?
8. What information is reported on a balance sheet?
9. What are common sources of cash inflows for a business?
10. What are the benefits of telecommuting to both the worker and the company?

EXPANDING YOUR HORIZONS

You will not find the complete answers to the following questions in your textbook. You will need to use your critical-thinking skills. Think about these questions, gather information from other sources, analyze possible responses, and discuss them with others. Then, develop your own oral or written response as instructed by your teacher.

1. What are some problems in the world that might be solved by new products or services created by entrepreneurs?
2. Name some ways that small businesses can provide personal service better than larger companies.
3. Why are wholesaling companies important to the business environment of a country?
4. For what reasons do people give up secure jobs and start their own businesses?
5. Explain how a budget helps a business.
6. A company sells shirts for $15. Each shirt has a variable cost of $9. The company has fixed costs of $7,200. What is the breakeven point for this business?
7. As a manager, how would you decide if you should let some employees do their work from their homes?

The ability to find information from various sources is an important international business skill. The following activities will help you investigate various topics. You will also learn to apply class ideas to situations outside of the classroom.

1. Interview the owner of a small local company about the influences of international business on the firm's activities. How has the company's competition changed due to global business? Are any local companies owned or controlled by foreign corporations?

2. Conduct library research about entrepreneurial activities in other countries. Locate articles and other information about new businesses, the type of products and services offered, and the problems encountered by new companies. Prepare a short written or oral report about the success of entrepreneurs in various countries.

3. Create a poster or bulletin board display with variable and fixed costs for different types of businesses. Use magazine photos or create drawings to show examples of these two types of business operating expenses.

4. Talk to someone who hires workers. What factors are most important when applying for a job and during an interview?

5. Conduct a survey of people who work at home. Obtain information about the type of work they do, the benefits of working at home, and the difficulties of this employment situation.

6. *Global Career Activity.* Interview the owner of a small business who exports or sells imported products. Ask the entrepreneur about the skills needed to be successful in that type of business. What are the most important things a person can learn in school to prepare for a career in entrepreneurship?

Continuing Enrichment Project: An International Business Plan

Create an international business plan for the company you have been using in this continuing project. Make use of previously collected information and do additional research. Your business plan should include the following components:

a. General description of the company—list the name, location, and major international business activities of the company.

b. Organizational structure—explain what type of organization (sole proprietorship, partnership, or corporation) the company uses.

c. Marketing activities—describe the company's customers, distribution systems, and advertising methods.

d. Financing activities—report on sources of cash inflows and costs and operating expenses for the company's global business activities.

e. Production activities—explain how the company obtains the products or services it sells.

f. Human resources activities—list the main types of jobs in the company and the general qualifications for employees in these positions.

g. Information needs—describe financial, production and inventory, marketing, and human resource information needed by managers to make appropriate international business decisions.

UNIT 3

Managing in a Global Environment

10

Management Principles in Action

After studying this chapter and completing the end-of-chapter activities, you will be able to

- Explain the characteristics of successful managers and how management styles vary.

- Understand the effects of cultural differences on a global workforce.

- Describe the basic components of the process of managing.

- Differentiate among organizational structures based on function, product, and geography.

- Discuss how the levels of management in an organization depend on the span of control, lines of authority, and delegation of authority and responsibility.

- Describe the four stages through which a business passes to reach global status.

- Explain several differences between management today and the way it is expected to be in the future.

Virtual Corporations—Here Today and Gone Tomorrow

The virtual corporation offers some promising approaches to the tough facts of life in the global marketplace. Most companies can't react fast enough to take advantage of changing opportunities. By the time managers of giant companies get the necessary people and other resources ready, those opportunities have vanished. The managers of smaller companies often lack the influence and resources to respond to opportunities that are here today and gone tomorrow.

Managers who want to form virtual corporations must first identify what their company does best. Then, they must form ties with other companies that represent "the best of the best." These fast-reacting, sharply focused, world-class competitors have the muscle and cutting-edge technology to pounce on short-term opportunities.

The U.S. film industry already functions in this way. Virtual corporations have replaced the old Hollywood studio system. Various industry talents temporarily link up for specific film projects before going their separate ways. Perhaps it's no small coincidence that the U.S. film industry has been very successful in the global marketplace—one of the biggest export successes for the country. Maybe Hollywood managers could teach managers worldwide a lesson or two!

MANAGERS IN ORGANIZATIONS

Managers are people in charge of organizations and their resources. They are men and women who assume responsibility for administering organizations. Managers work with and through people to attain organizational goals in an ever-changing environment. Managers oversee and control the people and things in their businesses. They try to use the available resources for maximum gain, just as you try to use your time and money to derive the most desirable benefits.

Whether you realize it or not, you already have some managerial experience. You are in charge of and responsible for yourself. You are also responsible for people and things. When you watch your younger siblings or other children, you are responsible for their welfare. You are also responsible for your textbooks, school supplies, and assigned homework. You may even be responsible for cleaning your room or for maintaining your own car. Consequently, managing is not a totally foreign concept to you.

Characteristics of Managers

Successful managers possess a wide variety of conceptual, technical, and interpersonal abilities. Supporting these abilities are certain skills and personal characteristics. One characteristic of managerial ability is leadership. Leadership is the ability to get others to follow. Another characteristic is the ability to communicate effectively. Managers must have strong communication and presentation skills.

The ability to plan and organize is important. Managers must be able to use resources to achieve goals. The ability to gather and analyze information is important, too. Managers must be able to acquire and use information to solve problems. The ability to make decisions is important. Managers must be able to take reasoned positions based on relevant information and to live with the consequences of those decisions.

The abilities to delegate and to control are also needed. Managers must be able to judge when they should be in charge and when others should be in charge. The ability to be objective is also useful. Managers need to know their strengths and weaknesses, as well as the strengths and weaknesses of others. The ability to be a change agent is required, too. Managers must be willing to lead others in new, untried directions. Do you possess a number of these important skills that influence managerial success?

Styles of Managers

One way to examine managers is to look at how they use power or authority. There are three distinct types of management styles: autocratic, participative, and free-rein. These three styles can be placed along a continuum that represents managerial power or authority as Figure 10-1 shows. Autocratic managers maximize their personal power or authority to control others. Free-rein managers minimize their personal power or authority to control others. Participative managers balance their personal power or authority to control others against the personal power or authority of others to control themselves.

Figure 10-1
Autocratic, participative, and free-rein managers use power or authority differently.

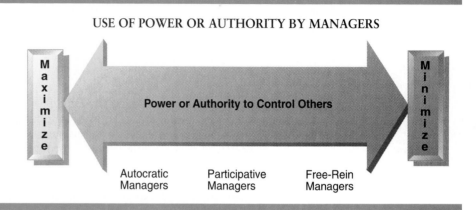

USE OF POWER OR AUTHORITY BY MANAGERS

Maximize

Power or Authority to Control Others

Minimize

Autocratic Managers   Participative Managers   Free-Rein Managers

Autocratic Management Style.   **Autocratic managers** centralize power and tell employees what to do. They are authoritarian and rule with a heavy hand. The autocrat takes full authority and assumes full responsibility. If an autocratic manager uses power negatively, then the employees feel uninformed, insecure, and afraid. If an autocratic manager uses power positively, then rewards are distributed to those who comply. Sometimes the term *benevolent autocrat* is used to refer to an autocratic manager who uses power positively.

Most people do not work well under autocratic managers, especially negative ones. In most circumstances, this old style of management should be replaced by a more participative management style.

Participative Management Style.   **Participative managers** decentralize power and share it with employees. The manager and employees work together to achieve goals. Participative managers keep employees informed and encourage them to share ideas and suggestions. The participative manager uses group forces rather than power or authority to keep the unit operating effectively. For most managerial situations the participative style is recommended.

Free-rein Management Style. **Free-rein managers** avoid the use of power. They let employees establish their own goals and monitor progress toward those goals. Employees develop themselves and supply their own motivation. Managers exist primarily as contact persons for outsiders. Since free-rein management can lead to chaos in many situations, it is recommended that managers use it in circumstances where employees are self-disciplined, self-motivated, and can make choices for themselves.

Global Business Exercise: Conversation with a British Manager

"I have been managing the Bristol office of a global corporation for seven years. The office has an international workforce drawn from 18 countries on four continents. Every employee is highly competent in his or her speciality. Consequently, I have learnt that I can rely on their judgements to a significant degree. I spend much of my time conferring with employees. Most decisions can be worked out by sharing our viewpoints, discussing the merits of those viewpoints, and selecting the best mutually agreeable viewpoints for implementation. It has been donkey's years since I have had to dictate the solutions to my employees."

1. Using a detailed map of the United Kingdom, England, or Europe as a guide, describe the location of Bristol, the city in which the British manager works.
2. What is the British manager's prevailing management style?
3. What facts from the narrative support your conclusion as to the management style?

INFLUENCES OF CULTURAL DIFFERENCES

Managers must remember that people's behaviors are shaped by their cultural backgrounds. Every culture and subculture has norms or standards for its members. However, certain members of cultural groups will deviate from those norms. Further, people from different cultural backgrounds are not alike although they may appear to be similar on the surface. They actually have significantly different beliefs, values, and assumptions. Consequently, managers must be very careful when managing people. Managers must be very sensitive to and respectful of cultural differences. They must also be aware that certain culturally based patterns of behavior exist and need to be considered.

For example, some cultural groups tend to want subordinates to be actively involved in decision making. This is generally true for natives of the United States. In contrast, natives of Venezuela may prefer little or no role in decision making.

In terms of hiring, different cultural groups value different selection criteria. For example, natives of the United States tend to value job-related qualifications. Natives of Greece tend to value family membership or friendship.

In terms of the permanence of employment, attitudes vary among members of different cultural groups. Natives of the United States generally accept less employment security than natives of Japan. U.S. workers are frequently laid off during economic downturns and receive minimal company compensation. The Japanese are less mobile and, until recently, expected lifetime employment from a company.

Labor-management relationships also vary by cultural groups. U.S. laborers tend to have confrontational attitudes with managers. They believe that confrontation brings about equitable work and reward relationships. By contrast, in Sweden many workers help to determine their work and reward relationships by serving on managerial boards.

In general, U.S. managers are shaped by a culture and subcultures that value personal freedom, independence, and self-respect. Employees from other cultural groups—especially European and Asian ones—tend to view these values as selfish and insensitive. Such opposing cultural perspectives can lead to conflicts between managers and employees in the culturally diverse business world unless those differences are sensitively addressed.

While it is useful for managers to be aware of prevailing cultural preferences, they must realize that not all individuals fit their cultural molds. Consequently, managers must temper their understandings about cultural preferences. They must also consider the values, beliefs, and assumptions of the individuals involved. Managers who fail to consider individual differences and cultural norms will be less successful in the culturally diverse global environment.

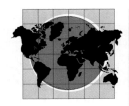

Global Business Example: The Managers Who Refused to Make Decisions

As the new plant manager, Terry Hopkins, a U.S. citizen, was shocked during his first encounters with his local Panamanian managers. Guillermo, Juan, and Diego refused to participate in decision making, politely deferring to Terry's judgments instead. When Terry made unilateral decisions for the managers in exasperation, he noticed that they made good-faith efforts to implement those decisions. Terry was puzzled by their reactions involving decision making. Was there something wrong with his managerial style? Did the Panamanian managers resent being supervised by a foreigner?

When Terry mentioned his uncooperative decision makers to another Panamanian plant manager, he was surprised by the explanation he received. Most Panamanians, like many Latin Americans, come from cultural backgrounds that place little value on acting independently or consultatively. A superior who seeks employees' opinions or encourages employees' decision making causes the employees to question the superior's decision-making abilities. When faced with the culturally unacceptable task of making decisions that they believed the plant manager should make, the Panamanian managers did not cooperate. To them, their participation in decision making undermined the role of the new plant manager.

Terry learned his lesson quickly. He tried to manage in a more culturally sensitive way. Rather than relying on participative U.S.-style management, he started making the decisions for his Panamanian supervisors. The employees were quite comfortable being told what to do. They carefully carried out Terry's decisions, and soon their working relationships with Terry became *muy simpatico*—very congenial.

PROCESS OF MANAGING

The process of managing includes such major components as planning and decision making; organizing, staffing, and communicating; motivating and leading; and controlling (see Figure 10-2). The exact mix of these components varies depending on the type of managerial job and the people and other resources involved. However, sooner or later managers will be involved with all managerial components.

Planning and Decision Making

Planning and decision making are important components of managing. Planning relates to setting goals or objectives to be attained. Planning is similar to deciding where you want to go. You have to know your destination before you can get there.

Once you decide the goal, then you can explore different options or routes that lead to the goal. At various points along the way, you have choices to make. You should weigh the advantages and disadvantages of each alternative and select the best alternative overall. In other words, you should make thoughtful decisions.

Organizing, Staffing, and Communicating

Organizing, staffing, and communicating are also important components of managing. Organizing involves structuring business operations in logical and meaningful ways. Sometimes organizing relates to how business activities or functions are put together. Sometimes organizing involves assembling the necessary resources in a manner that facilitates the accomplishment of goals.

Staffing is the process of acquiring employees with the necessary knowledge, skills, and attitudes to fill the various positions in the organization. Staffing is a component of human resource management discussed in Chapter 11.

Communicating is interacting with people through verbal and non-verbal means. Communicating is a vital managerial task. An organization cannot function cohesively and reach its goals unless all employees give, receive, and share information in a timely and effective manner.

Figure 10-2

The managerial process includes planning and decision making; organizing, staffing, and communicating; motivating and leading; and controlling.

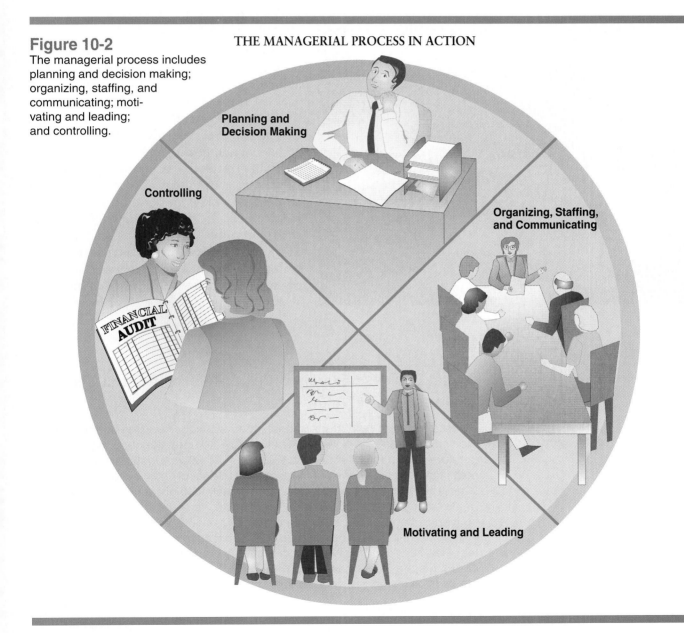

THE MANAGERIAL PROCESS IN ACTION

Planning and Decision Making

Controlling

Organizing, Staffing, and Communicating

Motivating and Leading

Motivating and Leading

Motivating is creating the desire to achieve. Managers realize that motivation comes from internal and external sources. *Internal motivation* comes from within the employee. The desire to perform work more efficiently is an example of internal motivation. *External motivation* comes from outside the employee. A salary increase is an example of external motivation.

Leading is getting employees to voluntarily pursue the goals of the organization. Managers who are effective leaders create a desire within employees to want to achieve what the organization sets out to achieve.

Controlling

Controlling is regulating the operations of a business. It involves taking both preventive and corrective actions to keep business activities on track. Controlling helps to ensure that business operations are both efficient and productive. Activities such as verifying, adjusting, and testing seek to maximize output while minimizing input. For example, businesses have the accounting records audited by outsiders periodically as a preventive measure. This verifies the accuracy and truthfulness of the financial records. Some businesses offer corrective programs such as substance abuse programs to afflicted employees. This helps troubled individuals return to productive status as workers.

Global Business Exercise: Alex Sainsbury, A Good Citizen

When events are held at the school in the evening, Alex Sainsbury opens the school snack shop. When Alex is unable to open the shop himself, he gets one of his reliable friends to do so. Alex selects the snacks that are sold in the shop. Every week Alex checks the supply of snacks and orders what is needed by telephoning the local snack-food distributor. Every week he also verifies the income and expense reports of the snack shop before delivering them to the school secretary. Alex and his friends receive no wages for their work. They donate their services to make the school a better place for students and other community members. Perhaps when Alex graduates, he will be rewarded with the scholarship that is funded by the profits from the school snack shop.

1. Is Alex Sainsbury a manager? Why?
2. What specific managerial skills, if any, is Alex developing through his volunteer work?
3. What snack foods that are global products are likely to be sold in the school snack shop?
4. Why do you think it might be good managerial strategy for Alex to offer some global products for sale in the school snack shop?

STRUCTURES OF ORGANIZATIONS

Businesses use various organizational structures to reach their goals. An **organizational chart** is a drawing that shows the structure of an organization. There are two types of positions: line and staff. *Line positions* are managerial. Individuals with line positions have authority and responsibility over people and resources. *Staff positions* are nonmanagerial. Individuals with staff positions assist or advise those in line positions.

An organization can be either tall or flat. A tall organization is one that has many levels of management. One manager generally supervises a small number of employees. This results in more levels of managers. A flat organization is one that has few levels of management.

Businesses are commonly organized in one of three ways: by function, by product, or by geography.

Organization by Function

When a business is organized by function, the departments are determined by what people *do*. For example, in a sportswear manufacturing company, the function of the manufacturing department is to produce sportswear. The function of the sales department is to sell sportswear, and the function of the accounting department is to keep accurate financial records. Other functional groups might be linked together and given relevant departmental names, too. Figure 10-3 on page 216 shows part of the organizational chart of a business organized by function.

Organization by Product

Another way to organize a business is by product. When a business organizes itself in this way, related products are grouped together to form departments. This type of organization is helpful when the product lines are very different. For example, a large manufacturing company that makes airplane parts and small consumer appliances may form two divisions. One division could be for the airplane parts; it might be

Figure 10-3
A simplified organizational chart
for a business organized by
function might look something
like this.

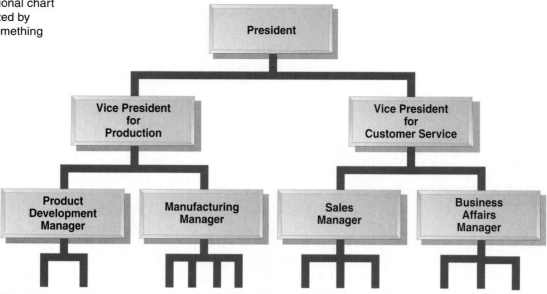

ORGANIZATION BY FUNCTION

called the aviation parts division. Another division could be for the
small consumer appliances; it might be called the consumer small appliance division. Figure 10-4 shows part of the organizational chart of a
business organized by product.

Figure 10-4
A simplified organizational chart
for a business organized by
product might look something
like this.

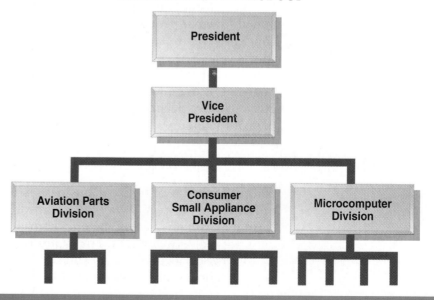

ORGANIZATION BY PRODUCT

Organization by Geography

Still another way to organize a business is by geography. When a business chooses this option, it organizes itself on some geographical basis. The geographical basis might be city, county, state, region, country, or continent. Companies that operate beyond the borders of one country often use geographic organization, as do some domestic companies. For example, a global corporation may have North American, South American, European, African, and Asian divisions. Each division would specialize in business operations in its designated territory. Figure 10-5 shows the organizational chart of a business organized by geography.

Figure 10-5
A simplified organizational chart for a business organized by geography might look something like this.

ORGANIZATION BY GEOGRAPHY

Global Business Exercise: What's the Basis for the Organization?

Barbara McCown owns an international agency that specializes in adapting advertisements to various ethnic groups. The head office of the company is in Los Angeles. There are branch offices in Berlin, Germany; Tokyo, Japan; and São Paulo, Brazil.

Barbara McCown is president and oversees the head-office staff. Each overseas office is headed by a senior manager. All company offices have middle managers who are in charge of newspaper advertisements, magazine advertisements, and multimedia advertisements. Depending on the amount of business transacted, each office subdivides each of the three broad advertising types into two or more specialized work units.

1. Is the international advertising agency organized by function, by product, or by geography?
2. What evidence supports your choice?

LEVELS OF MANAGEMENT

All businesses have managers in charge of operations. The number of managers a business needs, the lines of authority that are established, and the delegation of responsibility all depend on the size of the business and the complexity of its operations.

Span of Control

The **span of control** is the number of employees that a manager supervises. For example, a sole proprietorship is a business that has one owner-manager and may have limited operations. The owner-manager oversees and supervises all business activities.

When the volume of business, the complexity of business, or the number of employees grows, one person may no longer be able to manage the business. If a sole proprietor sells half of the business to a partner, then that partner could manage some of the operations. This would reduce the span of control of the original sole proprietor.

As a business continues to expand, more managers are needed. **Front-line managers** are needed to oversee the day-to-day operations in specific departments. The front-line managers may report to a middle manager. **Middle managers** oversee the work and departments of a number of front-line managers. A number of middle managers may report to a senior manager. **Senior managers** oversee the work and departments of a number of middle managers. In a large business senior managers report to the chief executive officer. The **chief executive officer (CEO)** is the highest manager within a company. Figure 10-6 shows the span of control of various levels of managers within a large organization.

Lines of Authority

Regardless of the organizational structure and the number of levels of management, a business must establish clear lines of authority. **Lines of authority** indicate who is responsible to whom and for what. The need for having clear lines of authority grows as the business expands. When a business starts, there may be one owner-manager, who is clearly in charge. The owner-manager has the authority or right to make all decisions. As the business expands and other managers are added, lines of authority must be clearly established. Otherwise, chaos results. Areas of responsibility for each manager must be clearly defined; so must the relationships among the managers. Who reports to whom must be known.

Delegation of Authority and Responsibility

One important decision that managers must make relates to how much authority and responsibility should be delegated, or transferred, to others. If managers retain too much authority and responsibility, they become autocratic. This may cause some employees to be rebellious because they feel powerless. If managers retain too little authority and responsibility, chaos develops. Employees who are not self-directed will have too much independence and more authority and responsibility than they can handle.

Figure 10-6

In this example, the president's span of control is five, the vice president of marketing's span of control is four, and the sales manager's span of control is three.

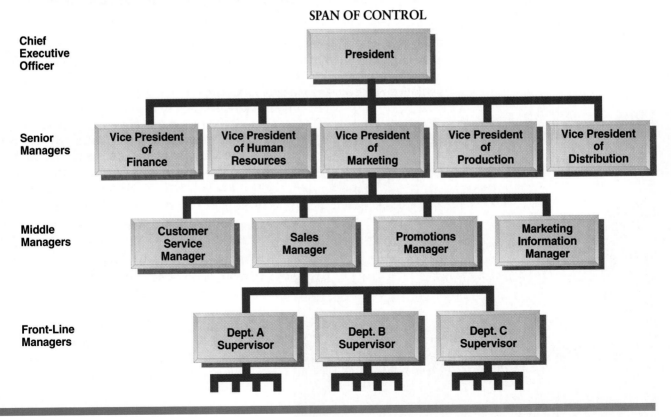

In most circumstances managers try to balance the authority and responsibility between themselves and their employees. Participative managers share authority and responsibility with employees. They give employees some degree of freedom to determine and achieve goals with a corresponding degree of accountability for achieving those goals.

The amount of authority and responsibility that is delegated to employees or to organizational units is a reflection of the **degree of centralization** within an organization. If the authority and responsibility are tightly held by the managers and organizational units, then a *centralized* style of management results throughout the organization. If the authority and responsibility are widely distributed among many employees and organizational units, then a *decentralized* style of management results. Centralization of authority and responsibility tends to make organizations more autocratic. Decentralization of power and responsibility tends to make organizations more participative. Global organizations must decide how much authority and responsibility to grant to each of their organizational units and managers.

Global Business Exercise: Managing the German Way

Franz Freund is a technician in a factory in Stuttgart. His fellow workers have selected him as one of their employee representatives. Franz is a member of the board that manages the factory. He and the other employee representatives present the viewpoints of workers whenever the board meets.

The views of factory managers are also represented on the board. Views from both perspectives are presented and discussed before the factory board makes decisions. Through their cooperative efforts, workers and managers find solutions to managerial problems that are generally acceptable to both groups.

1. In what country does Franz Freund work?

2. What term describes the type of managerial style used by the company that employs Franz Freund?

3. How do you think the relationship between labor and management in the company for which Franz Freund works is different from the typical relationship between labor and management in a U.S. company?

EVOLUTION OF ORGANIZATIONS AND MANAGEMENT

As a business evolves from a domestic company into a global corporation, unique challenges are encountered. The managerial process must be adapted to meet the particular challenges at each stage. Managing becomes more complex and demanding as the business evolves into a global organization. The following sections describe the stages in the evolutionary process and introduce related managerial dimensions.

Stage One: Domestic Company

The first stage on the way to becoming a global corporation is being a domestic company. A domestic company is one that operates completely within the country of origin. Such a company uses domestic sources to create and sell its products and services. In other words, it acquires and sells in the country of origin. A domestic company has no business dealings with anyone except natives of the country. Consequently, a domestic company is the easiest type to manage. The basic managerial process in the country of origin can be used to resolve most of the challenges of a domestic business.

Stage Two: Exporting Company

As a domestic company grows and becomes successful, it often begins to export or sell abroad. A company that sells in other countries is known as an exporting company. An exporting company typically relies on its domestic competitive advantages as it expands abroad. Often, the managers of an exporting company know little about the markets abroad. Consequently, an exporting company frequently uses independent agents or distributors, who understand the markets abroad. This arrangement simplifies the management of the business. Most of the export-related problems are handled by the independent agents or distributors. This lets managers focus their primary attention on domestic operations. This stage allows the company to take advantage of foreign markets while not having to accept full responsibility for operating abroad.

Stage Three: International Corporation

An international corporation, also known as a multinational corporation, creates and markets goods and services in both its country of origin and in other countries. The parent or founding company provides the international corporation with an organizational structure and operational strategy.

The local, national, or regional subsidiaries or companies of an international organization are usually responsible for decision making and customer service. They make decisions involving production, marketing strategy, sales and service, and the like. Often various subsidiaries of international corporations operate quite independently. An international corporation is like a group of interrelated companies operating in many countries.

The managerial skills needed in an international corporation vary widely. Those who manage from the parent company need broad managerial skills that cross countries. Managers at the local, national, or regional levels need more specialized skills adapted to their specific assignments.

Stage Four: Global Corporation

A global corporation is an outgrowth of an international corporation. A global corporation operates so that country boundaries are not an obstacle to operations. It searches for the most efficient combinations of goods and services on a worldwide basis. It markets those goods and services with little or no regard for national boundaries. A global corporation is like a domestic company except that it buys and sells worldwide rather than within the country of origin.

Global Highlight: Vatican City—Headquarters of a Worldwide Church

The world's smallest state, the State of Vatican City (Città del Vaticano), is the headquarters for one of the world's largest multinational organizations, the Roman Catholic Church. This independent state is completely surrounded by Rome, Italy. It consists of the Church of St. Peter, also known as the Vatican Basilica, the Vatican Apostolic Palace with its world-famous museums and library, various administrative and ecclesiastical buildings, apartments, and the Vatican Gardens. About 109 acres (44 hectares) in size, the State of Vatican City has a population of nearly 1,000 persons who perform special services for the Holy See (the realm, seat of power, authority, and jurisdiction of the pope).

The State of Vatican City has its own symbols of nationhood—constitution, coinage, postal system, seal, flag, and the like. It also has its own radio station, Radio Vatican, and its own daily newspaper, *L'Osservatore Romano.* It exchanges diplomatic representatives with other countries, but they are accredited to and from the Holy See, not the State of Vatican City.

Legislative, executive, and judicial power is vested in the pope within Vatican City, but actual internal administration is handled by a governor and other officials. Public order is maintained by a small force of *gendarmes* (or police-soldiers) assisted by the Swiss Guards, the pope's personal regiment of soldiers, when necessary. Judicial power is given to a local tribunal from which appeals go to the Sacra Romana Rota and, later, the Supreme Tribunal of the Apostolic Segnatura.

Those who manage in global corporations sometimes need broad managerial skills since they operate on a worldwide basis. Many decisions require local-, national-, and regional-specific knowledge along with specialized managerial skills.

Global Business Example: Dobriski Enterprises

Bogdan Dobriski, an immigrant from Poland, founded a small business in the United States that manufactures Polish-style foods. Five years ago the products were sold only in the Chicago metropolitan area. Bogdan and his family worked diligently at the business, and it has grown every year. Now Dobriski Enterprises exports food products to three countries. Within ten years Dobriski Enterprises hopes to manufacture and sell food products on five continents. Mr. Dobriski's children can then manage the subsidiaries abroad. Within twenty years Mr. Dobriski and his family hope to dominate the production and sales of Polish-style food products through worldwide operations. Then Bogdan Dobriski will have reached his entrepreneurial goal: to own and manage his own global corporation.

MANAGING NOW AND IN THE FUTURE

As business globalization expands, the role of the manager will change. The vision of the manager will shift from the domestic to the global marketplace. While today's managers predict the future based upon the past, tomorrow's managers will have insight into the future.

Managers of the future will not be content to be visionary; they will strive to facilitate the visionary development of others. Managers will shift from functioning alone to functioning as part of a team. While the managers of today enjoy the trust of boards and shareholders, the managers of tomorrow will need the trust of owners, customers, and employees. Managers increasingly will meet the needs of the diverse groups to whom they are responsible. Rather than being monolingual and monocultural as is the case today, tomorrow's managers will be multilingual and multicultural.

Successful global managers must develop and use global strategic skills. They must skillfully manage transition and change in a culturally diverse world. They must function effectively as team members while coping with changing organizational structures. They will need outstanding communication skills—listening, speaking, reading, and writing skills. They must be able to acquire and transfer knowledge throughout the organization. Successful global managers must quickly adapt to the changing environment. What is your potential to be a manager in the global marketplace?

Global Business Exercise: Molly McCoy: Choosing the Right Stuff

Molly McCoy is a student at your school. She is involved in pep club activities and maintains a B+ average. She aspires to a career in international business. Some day she would like to have an opportunity to manage a global corporation. Molly is taking as many business courses as she can sandwich into her college-prep schedule. She wonders what other types of courses and extracurricular activities would be good preparation for a career in management.

1. What other types of courses do you think would help Molly prepare for her career goal?
2. What types of extracurricular activities might complement the courses Molly selects?
3. What type of educational program do you think Molly should pursue after high school graduation and for how long?

Back to the Beginning: Virtual Corporations—Here Today and Gone Tomorrow

Reread the case at the beginning of this chapter and answer the following questions:

1. Why do virtual corporations exist?
2. What characteristic describes each component of a virtual corporation?
3. Why do you think the term *virtual corporation* was coined to describe these temporary "best of everything" businesses?

KNOWING GLOBAL BUSINESS TERMS

The following terms should become part of your business vocabulary. For each numbered item find the term that has the same meaning.

- autocratic manager
- chief executive officer (CEO)
- degree of centralization
- free-rein manager
- front-line managers
- lines of authority
- managers
- middle managers
- organizational chart
- participative manager
- senior managers
- span of control

1. A manager who shares power with employees.
2. People in charge of organizations and resources.
3. Supervisors who oversee the work of a number of front-line managers.
4. Amount of authority and responsibility that is delegated to employees within an organization.
5. Supervisors who oversee the day-to-day operations of a specific department.
6. A manager who is the top-ranking manager within the company.
7. A manager who centralizes power and tells the employees what to do.
8. A drawing that shows the structure of an organization.
9. The number of employees that a manager supervises.
10. Supervisors who oversee the work of a number of middle managers.
11. A manager who avoids the use of power to control others.
12. Indicates who is responsible to whom and for what.

REVIEWING YOUR READING

Answer these questions to reinforce your knowledge of the main ideas of this chapter.

1. List the personal characteristics that are often associated with being a successful manager.
2. Explain the differences between autocratic, participative, and free-rein managers.
3. What are four culturally influenced dimensions of behavior to which managers should be sensitive?
4. Briefly explain the components of the management process.
5. What are three ways in which businesses are commonly organized?
6. Differentiate the four common levels of managers.
7. What is the difference between a line and a staff position?

8. Explain how span of control and tall and flat organizations are related.

9. What is *degree of centralization* and how does it affect managerial styles?

10. What are the four stages through which a business passes on the way to global status?

11. How will management be different in the future than it is today?

EXPANDING YOUR HORIZONS

You will not find the complete answers to the following questions in your textbook. You will need to use your critical-thinking skills. Think about these questions, gather information from other sources, analyze possible responses, and discuss them with others. Then, develop your own oral or written response as instructed by your teacher.

1. Why is a participative manager likely to use autocratic and free-rein management on occasion?

2. This chapter suggested that a manager's planning and making decisions for a business is like your planning and problem solving for a trip. Suggesting that one thing is like another thing is using an analogy. Devise an analogy between another component of the management process and something that is familiar to you and your classmates.

3. Draw an organizational chart that depicts the business or social studies department of your school. What is the span of control for the head of the department?

4. What are some of the things that the managers of a domestic company may not know when that company decides to become an exporting company?

5. Managers in the global environment must become leaders as learners. What does the expression "leaders as learners" mean, and why is it necessary to be a leader as learner in the global marketplace?

BUILDING RESEARCH SKILLS

The ability to find information from various sources is an important international business skill. The following activities will help you investigate various topics. You will also learn to apply class ideas to situations outside of the classroom.

1. Pick a recent U.S. film of your choice. Through library research or through direct communication with the production and/or distribution company, investigate how the needed talents were brought together for the project. Determine whether or not the film project was the product of a virtual corporation.

2. Using library resources, investigate the culturally based patterns of behavior in a foreign business subculture of your choice. Identify and briefly explain two differences within that subculture that might be potentially troublesome for a manager from the U.S. business subculture.

3. Interview a manager of a business in your locality. Find out how he or she approaches the management of people and other resources. Then, prepare a paper that explains why you believe that person is primarily an autocratic, participative, or free-rein manager.

4. Using available resources, identify businesses that operate within your state that are organized by each of the following: function, product, and geography.

5. Identify and briefly describe one business that operates within your state that is a domestic company, one that is an exporting company, one that is an international (or multinational) corporation, and one that is a global corporation.

6. Your best friend aspires to manage an international business headquartered in Belgium. What advantages will she or he enjoy as an expatriate manager of this company if she or he can listen, speak, read, and write in French, Flemish, and German?

7. *Global Career Activity.* Talk to someone who has worked in another country or who is familiar with business activities in another country. How does the supervision of workers differ in that country from supervision of workers in the United States?

Continuing Enrichment Project: Developing a Five-Year Plan to Enhance Management Skills

Using people and library resources, create a comprehensive five-year plan to build and refine your managerial skills. The plan should list (1) the basic skills that constitute the management process, (2) appropriate activities with potential to build and refine those skills, and (3) appropriate means of assessing whether or not those skills have been built and refined during each of the five years. Remember that as you mature and graduate from high school, continue your education elsewhere, and/or enter the workforce, what constitutes appropriate activities and means of assessment will change.

Regional Profile

Europe

In 1962, the press was there to record Peter Fechter as he was shot and killed by East German border guards when he tried to climb the Berlin Wall to freedom. He was one of approximately 191 East Germans who lost their lives trying to escape to the West. But at midnight on November 9, 1989, an extraordinary event occurred: the gates opened, thousands of East Germans rushed around and over the Berlin Wall, and the guns remained silent. Border police, who had previously been ordered to shoot anyone going near the Wall, now lifted small children so that they could set foot on the other side. The Wall had stood for 28 years as a symbol of the Cold War that had divided Europe and simultaneously imprisoned Eastern Europe under the rule of the Soviet Union. Berliners from both sides were overwhelmed:

> "I don't feel like a prisoner anymore!" "This is the most marvelous moment of my entire life." "Everything we ever really wanted suddenly came true." "Knock it down."

And, so they did. Within days, souvenir pieces of the Wall were turning up all over the world.

The nearly half century of Soviet dominance over Eastern Europe was relatively brief when compared to some of the earlier periods of domination on the European continent. Two thousand years ago the Romans controlled a relatively peaceful Western and Southern Europe by subduing their neighbors with superior military forces. The Roman Empire forced people of different cultures to live together. It established local governments that took orders from Rome and created an economy that depended on roads, bridges, and public buildings. Do you think that a powerful nation should force people of different cultures to live peacefully together as one nation?

The Roman Emperor Constantine the Great gave Christians freedom of religion in the year 313. By 392, Christianity had become the official religion of the Roman Empire, and it continued to strengthen its influence in Europe by making alliances between popes and various kings who ruled the continent. On December 25, 800, Charlemagne—a Frankish king who had conquered nearly all the Germanic lands—was attending church services at St. Peter's in Rome when Pope Leo III placed a gold crown upon his head. The Pope proclaimed him Charles Augustus, "Emperor of the Romans." Charlemagne feigned surprise, but some evidence suggests that he and the Pope had planned this coronation after Charlemagne's armies had rescued the Pope from his enemies.

The newly crowned emperor expanded his empire until it stretched from the Danube River to the Atlantic, from Rome to the Baltic Sea. Those living within the empire—who were not already Christians or Jews—were forced to accept Christianity and all laws made at Charlemagne's capital at Aix-la-Chapelle (present day Aachen, Germany). These were diverse people, living great distances from one another and speaking many different languages. Do you know of any nations in existence today that base their authority on a particular religion?

The task of controlling the empire was too great for Charlemagne's successors. After his death the empire began to dissolve as local nobles regained power. This set the stage for a return to the political and economic system known as feudalism, which had preceded Charlemagne's empire.

At the same time that Charlemagne was building his empire, the Byzantines in Southeastern Europe were fighting to control land on both sides of the Mediterranean Sea. The Byzantine Empire had existed since 395, when it split from Rome. The empire was centered in Constantinople (present day Istanbul, Turkey) which was built on a point of land above the Bosporus Straits that separates Europe and Asia. Throughout history Persians, Arabs, Russians, Europeans, and Turks have fought over this strategic location because it links the trade routes between Europe, the Middle East, Asia, and Africa.

Later attempts to control the European Continent were short-lived. Napoléon I, like Charlemagne, wanted to be crowned by the Pope. Unlike Charlemagne, however, the French Emperor called the Pope to Paris, where he took the crown from the Pope and crowned himself. By 1812, Napoléon controlled most of Europe. Nevertheless, his dreams were soon destroyed when most of his empire rebelled against him after his disastrous invasion of Russia.

Hitler's attempt to control Europe precipitated World War II. His country house at Obersalzberg offered him a view of the Untersberg where, legend has it, Charlemagne sleeps and from where he will return in glory. Hitler said it was no accident that his residence sat opposite this great emperor. By 1941, Hitler's armies occupied most of Europe, threatened England, and marched into Russia. Hitler committed Napoleon's mistake by stranding his troops in the harsh Russian winter, and Soviet counterthrusts stopped the German advance.

The many ethnic groups of Eastern and Southeastern Europe have lived side-by-side within empires for centuries. Many conflicts have resulted from their nationalistic interests in self-determination. Bulgaria, Greece, Montenegro, and Serbia declared war on Turkey in 1912 to free members of their nationalities from Turkish rule. In 1914, a Serb assassinated the Austrian Archduke Ferdinand in support of Bosnian nationalism. This event helped precipitate World War I. When they sought greater freedom, the Hungarians (in 1956) and the Czechs (in 1968) were violently crushed by the Soviets, who predominated in the region after World War II.

As the might of the communist systems in the Soviet Union and Eastern Europe crumbled in the late 1980s and early 1990s, some nationalist forces peacefully formed new governments. Others, such as those in the former Yugoslavia, began killing each other over historical hatred or current jealousy.

Although the history of this continent is heavily marked by wars and political repression, its writers, explorers, philosophers, scientists, and artists have created a world that is known as Western Civilization. The entire planet has been enriched by the likes of Homer and Plato, Chaucer and Shakespeare, Michelangelo and Renoir, Pasteur and Einstein, and Bach and the Beatles.

Europeans have contributed many things to the world: self-government; the abolition of slavery; the first microscopes and telescopes; vital antiseptics and vaccines; theories of evolution and psychoanalysis; and initial discoveries in molecular physics, electricity, radioactivity, relativity, and rocketry.

Strong nationalistic values continue to separate Europeans, but another attempt to unify the continent is in process. The key players this time are not emperors and dictators with swords and tanks. Rather, they are economists armed with arguments about competition from the United States and Japan. The European Union has eliminated trade barriers between the member countries. Its plans also call for a European Central Bank and a common European currency before the end of the century. The Treaty of Maastricht provides for a common European citizenship and European passports.

Human Resource Management

After studying this chapter and completing the end-of-chapter activities, you will be able to

- Differentiate host-country nationals, home-country nationals, and third-country nationals.

- Define the four dominant human resource management approaches.

- Explain how staffing needs are determined, potential employees are recruited, and qualified applicants are selected for employment.

- Identify the common types of training and development for international managers.

- Understand that employee motivation is culturally based.

- Explain the common components of compensation packages for parent-country nationals.

- Appreciate the complexities of evaluating employee performance in an international setting.

- List strategies that help to minimize repatriation problems.

I Want to Go Home

"Sue, we've got to go home! I can't stand living here any longer."

Two months after her transfer to the British office of her employer, Sue Smith (a U.S. citizen) was shocked by the earnestness of her husband's appeal. She replied, "But, Doug, we've been here only a short while. Coming here was a big promotion for me. My career is on the line."

"My sanity is on the line. You go off to work, and I have to stay here and fight the Revolutionary War all over. Everything is a battle. Nothing

turns out as it should. Why did the contractor have to plaster over the existing telephone line when this apartment was remodeled? Why should it take four months to get a telephone installed?"

"But, Doug, . . ."

"I had to go to seven different shops to get the things for tonight's meal. Even if I had a car, there's no place to park! This tiny flat is four stories up in a building without an elevator. The refrigerator is so small it's like a toy. It takes two hours to launder four shirts in that washer-dryer. I'm not sure I made the right decision when I gave up my job in the United States. I've had it with this place."

Human resource management is somewhat different in the global environment than in the domestic environment. Several factors contribute to this. One factor is the differences in worldwide labor markets. Each country has a different mix of workers, labor costs, and companies. Companies can choose the mix of human resources that is best for them. Another factor is differences in worker mobility. Various obstacles make it difficult or impossible to move workers from one country to another. These include physical, economic, legal, and cultural barriers.

Still another factor is managerial practices. Different business subcultures choose to manage their resources, including people, in different ways. The more countries in which a company operates, the greater the problem of conflicting managerial practices. Yet another factor is the difference between national and global orientations. Companies aspire toward global approaches. However, getting workers to set aside their national approaches is challenging. A final factor is control. Managing diverse people in faraway places is more difficult than managing employees at home.

WHO MAKES UP THE LABOR MARKET?

Most companies obtain unskilled and semiskilled workers in local markets unless the supply is inadequate. **Locals** or **host-country nationals** are natives of the country in which they work. For skilled, technical, and managerial workers, companies have several options. They can sometimes hire these workers locally. In other cases, the companies must choose expatriates. **Expatriates** are people who live and work outside their native countries. Expatriates from the country where the company for whom they work is headquartered are called **parent-country nationals** or **home-country nationals**. Expatriates from other countries are called **third-country nationals**.

Each company must balance the advantages and disadvantages of hiring each type of worker. Locals are usually culturally sensitive and easy to find, but they may not have the knowledge and skills needed by the foreign company. Parent-country nationals often have the needed knowledge and skills and sometimes have the desired company orientation, but they often lack appropriate local language and cultural skills. Companies usually find parent-country nationals more costly to hire than other types of workers. Local laws could restrict employment of these nationals, too.

Third-country nationals could be more adaptable to local conditions than parent-country nationals. They may speak the local language and be able to make needed changes in culturally sensitive ways. In some cases, they could be more acceptable to locals than parent-country nationals. On the other hand, they may lack the desired company orientation. Regulations may make it difficult to hire them unless locals are unqualified. Selecting the best mix of employees from a variety of nationalities is challenging. Carrying out that mix in the global environment is even more challenging.

FOUR HUMAN RESOURCE MANAGEMENT APPROACHES

A company's approach to human resource management in the global environment is guided by its general company approach to human resource management. Most businesses in the global environment adopt one of four basic approaches to human resource management: ethnocentric, polycentric, regiocentric, or geocentric. The decision depends on several factors—such as governmental regulations and the company's size, structure, strategy, attitudes, and staffing.

Ethnocentric Approach

The **ethnocentric approach** uses natives of the parent country of a business to fill key positions at home and abroad. This approach can be useful when new technology is being introduced into another country. It is also useful when prior experience is important. Sometimes less-developed countries ask that companies transfer expertise and technology by using employees from the parent country to train and develop employees in the host country. The goal is to prepare the host country employees to manage the business.

The ethnocentric approach has drawbacks. For example, it deprives local workers of the opportunity to fill key managerial positions. This may lower the morale and lessen the productivity of local workers. Also, natives of the parent country might not be culturally sensitive enough to manage local workers well. These managers could make decisions that hurt the ability of the company to operate abroad. Figure 11-1 illustrates the ethnocentric approach to human resource management.

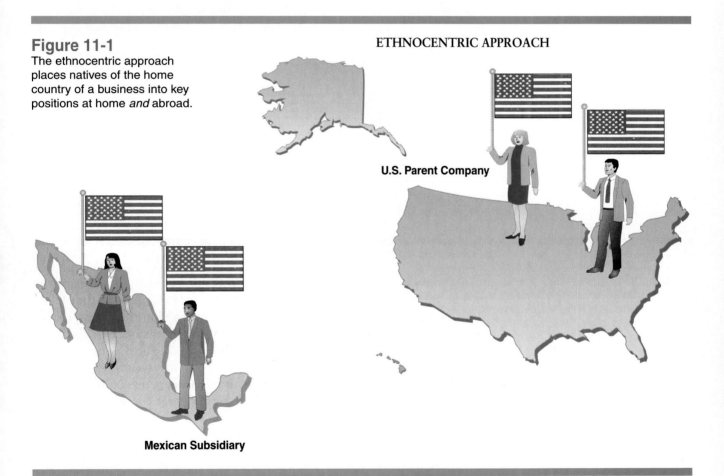

Figure 11-1
The ethnocentric approach places natives of the home country of a business into key positions at home *and* abroad.

ETHNOCENTRIC APPROACH

U.S. Parent Company

Mexican Subsidiary

Polycentric Approach

The **polycentric approach** uses natives of the host country of a business to manage operations within that country and natives of the parent country to manage at headquarters. In this situation, host country

Figure 11-2

The polycentric approach uses natives of the host country of a business in that country and natives of the parent country in the home office.

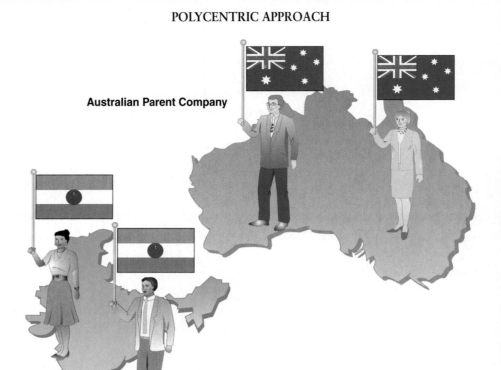

POLYCENTRIC APPROACH

Australian Parent Company

Indian Subsidiary

managers rarely advance to corporate headquarters since natives of the parent country are preferred by the company as managers at that level. This approach is advantageous since locals manage in the countries for which they are best prepared. It is also cheaper since locals, who require few, if any, incentives are readily available and generally less expensive to hire than others. The polycentric approach is helpful in politically sensitive situations because the managers are culturally sensitive locals, not foreigners. Further, the polycentric approach allows for continuity of management.

The polycentric approach has several disadvantages. One disadvantage is the cultural gap between the subsidiary managers and headquarters managers. If the gap is not bridged, then the subsidiaries may function too independently. Another disadvantage is limited opportunities for advancement. Natives of the host countries can only advance within their subsidiaries, and parent country natives can only advance within company headquarters. The result is that company decision makers at headquarters have little or no international experience. Nevertheless, their decisions have major effects on the subsidiaries. Figure 11-2 above illustrates the polycentric approach to human resource management.

Regiocentric Approach

The **regiocentric approach** uses managers from various countries within the geographic regions of a business. Although the managers operate relatively independently in the region, they are not normally moved to the company headquarters. The regiocentric approach is adaptable to fit the company and product strategies. When regional expertise is needed, natives of the region are hired. If product knowledge is crucial, then parent-country nationals who have ready access to corporate sources of information can be hired.

One shortcoming of the regiocentric approach is that managers from the region may not understand the headquarters view. Also, corporate headquarters may not employ enough managers with international experience. This could result in poor decisions. Figure 11-3 illustrates the regiocentric approach to human resource management.

Figure 11-3

The regiocentric approach places natives of the home country of a business into key positions at home and managers from various countries within the region of the subsidiary company into the host country.

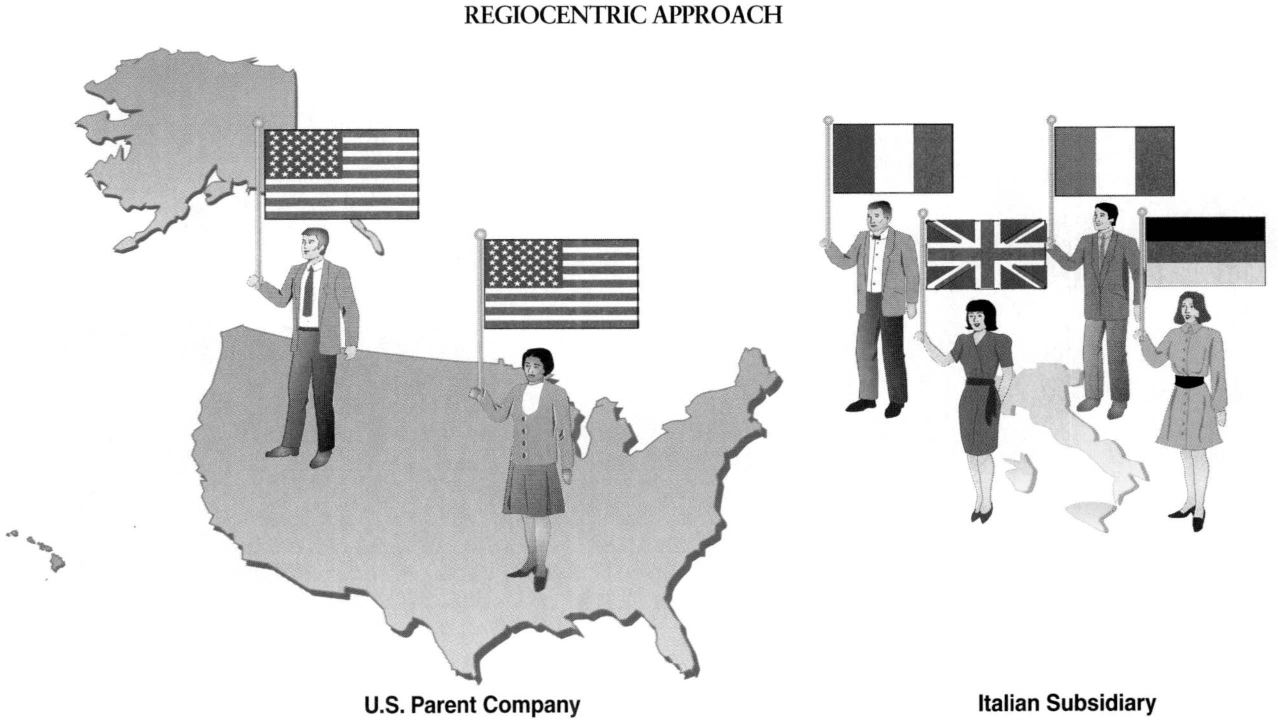

REGIOCENTRIC APPROACH

U.S. Parent Company

Italian Subsidiary

Geocentric Approach

The **geocentric approach** uses the best available managers for a business without regard for their country of origin. The geocentric company should have a worldwide strategy of business integration. The geocentric approach allows the development of international managers and reduces national biases.

On the other hand, the geocentric approach has to deal with the fact that most governments want businesses to hire employees from the host countries. Getting approval for nonnatives to work in some countries is difficult or impossible. Implementing the geocentric approach is expensive. It requires substantial training and employee development and more relocation costs. It also requires more centralization of human resource management and longer lead times before employees can be transferred because of the complexities of worldwide operations. Figure 11-4 illustrates the geocentric approach to human resource management.

Figure 11-4

The geocentric approach uses the best available managers for a business without regard for their country of origin.

GEOCENTRIC APPROACH

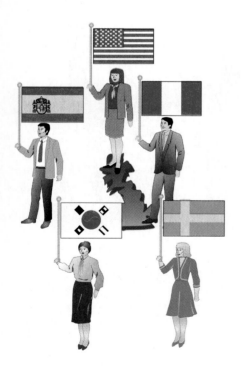

UK Parent Company

U.S. Subsidiary

Global Business Example: Procter and Gamble

Cincinnati-based Procter and Gamble is a global corporation that practices geocentric human resource management. Its global workforce is managed in a coordinated manner. International transfers in 53 countries develop the capabilities of employees and facilitate interaction that builds commitment to its operations worldwide.

DETERMINING STAFFING NEEDS

A company must assess its staffing needs to compete successfully in the international market. **Employment forecasting** is estimating in advance the types and numbers of employees needed. **Supply analysis** is determining if there are sufficient types and numbers of employees available. Through selection or hiring and reduction or terminating processes, companies balance the demand for and supply of employees.

Once a company assesses its overall staffing needs, managers begin to fill individual jobs. A number of factors must be considered. What will the new employee be assigned to do? What are the qualifications that the employee will need? What is the best combination of technical abilities, personality traits, environmental factors, and family situation to ensure success?

When these types of questions are answered, specific job data are gathered. This includes information about such things as assigned tasks; performance standards; responsibilities; and knowledge, skill, and experience requirements. From this information a job description is prepared. A **job description** is a document that includes the job identification, job statement, job duties and responsibilities, and job specifications and requirements.

Global Highlight: The Merchant-Venturers of Bristol

Bristol, England, 120 miles west of London, was once one of the world's major seaports. Yet Bristol is not on the coast. Medieval merchant-venturers from Bristol decided to build their docks and warehouses seven miles inland to protect them from pirates. To get to the port, early captains had to sail their ships up the treacherous Avon River—which rises and falls with nearly the highest tide in the world. Getting through the Severn estuary and up the river to Bristol was tricky business. One major risk for captains and merchant-venturers was getting their ships stuck in the mud during low tides. Even ships berthed at the Bristol docks were in danger of being broken up by tidal surges.

In the early eighteenth century this problem was solved when merchant-venturers had the Avon River channeled into a new location. This created a floating harbor with a constant water level. However, by then much of the important transatlantic trade had shifted to other more accessible ports.

Bristol actually became an important port city in the eleventh century when its merchant-venturers set out for fame and fortune. During the Middle Ages its merchant-venturers became well known for their trade in wines. During the fifteenth century the port of Bristol attracted adventuresome sailors bent on discovering new lands and better trading opportunities. For example, John Cabot—financed by a wealthy Bristol merchant—in 1497, became the first documented European explorer to reach the North American mainland. Later Bristol merchant-venturers helped to develop industry on the continent—growing rich in the process from trading profits from Virginia tobacco, West Indian sugar and rum, and other goods.

For their times the merchant-venturers of Bristol were very shrewd. They traded throughout the world known to their society, accepting significant risks in return for the possibility of lucrative profits. The merchant-venturers of Bristol were among the first anywhere to realize the value of training and developing their workers, not just exploiting their labor. Consequently, as early as medieval times they began to offer instruction that improved the capabilities of their workers. Bristol merchant-venturers also built and supported almshouses that cared for the poor.

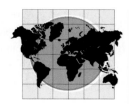

Global Business Example: Wanted: Student with International Business Interests

Job Description

Job Identification: Part-time student worker

Job Statement: This part-time job involves processing domestic and international orders and related communications for a growing local company.

Job Duties and Responsibilities:

1. Process domestic and international orders with a microcomputer.
2. Key business correspondence in English regularly and in French, German, and Spanish occasionally.
3. Answer telephones and provide routine responses to inquiries.

Job Specifications and Requirements:

1. Applicant must have some business knowledge and ideally is currently enrolled in business courses.
2. Applicant must be able to work for two to three hours weekday afternoons and weekends as needed.
3. Applicant must have keyboarding proficiency and be able to operate an IBM microcomputer using WordPerfect.
4. Applicant must have strong communication skills in English; the ability to communicate in basic French, German, or Spanish is desirable.

RECRUITING POTENTIAL EMPLOYEES

A company officially announces a job by circulating the job announcement and job description through appropriate channels. If the job will be filled by someone already working for the company, then internal channels will be used. The job information will be sent to all human resource offices within the company. These offices will post the information or notify company employees of the job availability in some other manner.

If the job will be filled by someone who currently does not work for the company, then different channels will be used. If a decision has been made to hire a parent-country national, then channels within the parent country will be used. If a host-country national will be hired, then channels in the host country will be selected. If a third-country national will be hired, then channels in other countries that could provide suitable employees will be used.

The specific types of outlets selected could be influenced by the type of employee needed. If an unskilled or semiskilled worker is needed, then local public outlets such as Job Service or its overseas equivalent might be used. If a skilled, technical, or managerial worker is needed, then public and private outlets might be used. For unusual or high-ranking managerial positions, the company might employ a specialized recruitment firm known as a headhunter. Such a firm, sometimes for a substantial fee, locates one or more qualified applicants for the position.

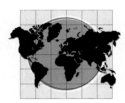

Global Business Example: IBM Uses Modern-Day Headhunters

International Business Machines (IBM) raised corporate eyebrows when it used two preeminent headhunters (job placement firms) to find a replacement for John F. Akers in 1993. The prize assignment went to headhunters Gerald R. Roche, chairman of Heidrick & Struggles, and Thomas J. Neff, president of Spencer Stuart & Associates. Both men have placed many chief executive officers in major companies. IBM purposely chose two headhunters so that they could hire each other's placements, broadening the field of candidates. Normally, corporate headhunters do not recruit employees they place and do not hire employees from a client company for two years after the search completion. For their services, Roche and Neff each received an estimated fee of between $400,000 and $500,000—one of the highest on record.

SELECTING QUALIFIED EMPLOYEES

Companies that operate in the global environment use a variety of methods to select the best applicant. The best applicant is the person with the highest potential to meet the job expectations. Most companies use a combination of several selection methods, including careful examination of the applicant's past accomplishments, relevant tests, and interviews. In the process of screening applicants, companies are usually concerned about three broad factors. These are competence, adaptability, and personal characteristics.

The factor of competence relates to the ability to perform. Competence has a number of dimensions. One important dimension is technical knowledge. Is the applicant competent in the desired specialty areas? Another dimension is experience. Has the applicant performed similar or related tasks well in the past? For managerial positions, leadership and managerial ability are important. Can the applicant work

with others to accomplish goals? For positions in other countries, cultural awareness and language skills are critical. Does the applicant understand the region or market for which he or she would be responsible? Is the applicant able to communicate fluently in the local language?

The factor of adaptability relates to the ability to adjust to different conditions. Possessing a serious interest in international business is necessary. Does the applicant really want to work abroad? The ability to relate to a wide variety of people is important, too. Does the applicant work effectively with diverse groups of people? The ability to empathize with others is needed. Can the applicant relate to the feelings, thoughts, and attitudes of those from other cultures? The appreciation of other managerial styles is also highly desirable. Can the applicant accept alternate managerial styles that are preferred by locals?

The appreciation of various environmental constraints is needed, too. Does the applicant understand the dynamics of the complex environment in which international business is conducted? The ability of the applicant's family to adjust to another location is particularly important for international assignments. Can the family members cope with the challenges of living abroad?

The factor of personal characteristics has many dimensions. The maturity of the employee is one dimension. Is the applicant mature enough, given the assignment and the culture in which the assignment will be undertaken? Another dimension is education. Does the applicant have a suitable educational level given the assignment and the location? In special circumstances gender is a concern. Will the applicant's gender contribute toward or interfere with the ability to be successful in the working environment? In Saudi Arabia, for example, women are not business associates. The social acceptability of the applicant should also be considered. What is the likelihood that the applicant will fit into the new work environment? Diplomacy is another trait to include. Is the applicant tactful in communicating, especially when unpleasant information is involved? General health is another consideration. Is the applicant healthy enough to withstand the rigors of the work assignment? Mental stability and maturity should not be overlooked. Does the applicant function on an even keel and in a responsible manner? The stability of the relationships within the family are important, too. Will the family be able to withstand the additional challenges of a new job—perhaps abroad?

As various applicants are screened, one fact usually stands out: no single applicant possesses the perfect combination of competence, adaptability, and personal characteristics. When this happens, the company will have to balance the strengths of the various applicants against their weaknesses. Overall, which applicant best matches the needs of the position? Which applicant has the greatest likelihood of being successful on the job? The answers to such questions result in the selection of the best-qualified individual to fill the job.

Homework ✓

Global Business Exercise: Whom Would You Select for the Milan Position?

Mark Evans and Harold Daw are the two finalists for a managerial position in Milan. While Mr. Evans has seven years of management experience at three different sites in one region of the United States, Mr. Daw has seven years of comparable management experience at two sites in different regions. Both Mr. Evans and Mr. Daw are adaptable individuals who want international managerial experience. Mr. Evans speaks fluent Swedish, and Mr. Daw speaks fluent French. Both have similar personal characteristics except that Mr. Evans is divorced and has no children and Mr. Daw has a wife and a teenager, who is a junior in high school. Mrs. Daw is currently employed and the company cannot guarantee that Mrs. Daw can find suitable employment in Italy should her husband be selected for the overseas assignment.

1. Which finalist is better qualified in terms of competence? Why?
2. Which finalist is better qualified in terms of adaptability? Why?
3. Which finalist is better qualified in terms of personal qualifications? Why?
4. Whom would you select for the overseas assignment? Why?

TRAINING AND DEVELOPMENT ARE CRITICAL

Employees make or break an international business, just as they do a domestic one. Their daily actions put the life of the company on the line. Consequently, companies need to be sure that all of their employees are well prepared for their work. This includes both lower-level and higher-level employees. Training and developing employees to work at their maximum potential are in the best interest of a company in the long run. Training and development are an investment in the future of the company. The better trained and developed the employees are, the greater the likelihood that the company will be successful.

Training and developing employees are major expenses for a company. Managers must decide what types of employees in which locations should receive specific types of training and development. These decisions are not easy. Because of limited resources, companies have to balance needs and potential benefits.

Historically speaking, many U.S.-based international companies have skimped on training and development. This has contributed to their difficulties abroad. Many of their employees have not been well prepared to compete in the global marketplace. Companies headquartered in other countries often invest extensively in training and development. In fact, some countries have laws that require companies to train and develop their employees. Such employees are often well prepared for work in the highly competitive global marketplace. U.S.-based international companies are now realizing the value of providing more extensive training and development.

Types of Training and Development

Managers working within international companies need a variety of training and development (see Figure 11-5 on page 244). Managers need training in job-related issues. For example, they need to be aware of the current economic, legal, and political environments. They need to be current on relevant governmental policies and regulations. Managers also need to be aware of managerial practices within their areas of responsibility. Current information about the company, its subsidiaries, and their operations is needed, too.

In addition, parent-country nationals and their families need training and development relating to relationships. At a minimum, they need to develop survival-skill knowledge in the local language before they are transferred abroad. Ideally, the manager will be fluent in the local language upon arrival or shortly thereafter.

Managers and their families also need cross-cultural training. They need to understand the various dimensions of the local culture that were discussed in Chapter 3. Also, managers need realistic training relating to life in the host country. For example, they need to know about the currency. They need to know what foods are available and their approximate costs. They need to understand housing options and prices, too.

Special counseling may be needed if the manager has a working spouse. Increasingly, both husbands and wives work, and career moves that are beneficial to one may not be beneficial to the other. If only one of the two benefits, is the job change worthwhile? Determining if the spouse can work in the host country is important in many employment decisions. Some governments prohibit the spouses of foreign workers from being employed. What realistic employment options, if any, exist for the spouse in the host country? If the spouse cannot work, can he or she adjust to that fact?

Providing training and development is costly. Nevertheless, companies cannot fail to provide it, especially for parent-country nationals. If parent-country nationals are unsuccessful abroad or if their families cannot adjust to life abroad, the company loses. In effect, a company that provides training and development is like a person who buys insurance: it helps to protect against the risks. Research suggests

Figure 11-5
International managers need job-related training, information on languages and relationships, and extensive training in the host country's culture.

TRAINING AND DEVELOPMENT

Figure 11-6

Training and development for work in Japan ranges in importance from essential to helpful.

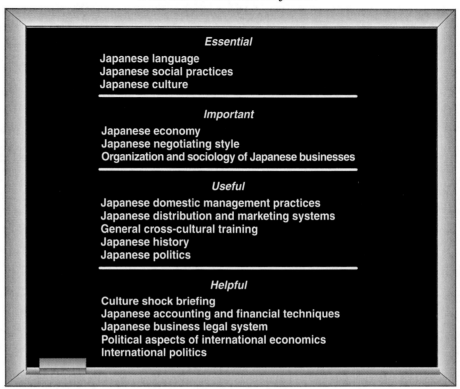

SUGGESTED AREAS OF TRAINING AND DEVELOPMENT
FOR EMPLOYMENT IN JAPAN

Essential
Japanese language
Japanese social practices
Japanese culture

Important
Japanese economy
Japanese negotiating style
Organization and sociology of Japanese businesses

Useful
Japanese domestic management practices
Japanese distribution and marketing systems
General cross-cultural training
Japanese history
Japanese politics

Helpful
Culture shock briefing
Japanese accounting and financial techniques
Japanese business legal system
Political aspects of international economics
International politics

Source: Adapted from John Frandenstein and Hassan Hosseini, "Advice From the Field: Essential Training for Japanese Duty." *Management Review* (July 1988): 40–43.

that relevant training and development does increase the likelihood of success abroad. Figure 11-6 shows the types of training and development recommended for people who are sent by their companies to work in Japan.

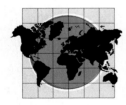

Global Business Example: Australian Employers Must Train Employees

Employers in Australia are required to provide training and development for their employees. They must spend 1.4 percent of their annual national payrolls to upgrade the skills of their employees. Companies can develop their own training programs, or they can contribute to educational institutions, industry skill centers, or industry training bodies. These units then provide the training and development experiences. Only employers with national payrolls of less than $200,000 and public charitable and religious institutions are exempt.

Training and Development Help to Prevent Failure

In spite of the efforts of many companies to provide parent-country nationals with relevant training and development, a number of them are unsuccessful abroad. These employees may return home early, angry and frustrated. They may muddle through the assignment abroad with little or no success. They may even leave the company during or at the end of the overseas assignment. The associated monetary and psychological costs of failure are high. Failure hurts both the company and the employee.

Why do parent-country nationals fail? One commonly cited reason is the inability of the employee to adjust to a different physical and cultural environment. Another is the spouse's inability to adjust to a different physical and cultural environment. Adjustment problems for other family members can also contribute toward failure. Characteristics of the employee's personality can cause parent-country nationals to fail. For example, the person's emotional maturity can be seriously strained by an overseas assignment. The person's inability to work productively can contribute to failure. The parent-country national may not accept the new responsibilities. He or she may lack the motivation to cope with the challenges of working abroad. She or he might even lack sufficient technical competence.

To reduce the chances of failure abroad, companies should select only successful and satisfied workers for overseas assignments. Companies should also provide extensive relevant training and

development before departure, throughout the assignment abroad, and after returning home. Companies should make the international assignment part of the long-term employee development process. This effort should benefit both the company and the employee in planned and purposeful ways.

The international assignment should be accompanied with adequate communication between the company and its employee. The company should know about the employee's overseas experiences. The employee should know about changes at company headquarters, too. When the employee returns home, the company should provide a job that uses the employee's international experience. The knowledge and skills acquired abroad should not be ignored. Company managers, especially those without international experience, should be trained to value international experience. The company should expect returning employees to experience reverse culture shock. However, a supportive training and development program should minimize the readjustment time.

Global Business Exercise: What Types of Training and Development Are Needed?

Lisa Alver, a successful manager, received extensive training and development before she was transferred to the European division of her employer. She anticipates that she will be transferred back to the United States within the next two years. Her employer typically sends managers abroad for three to five years. Lisa has already worked three years in Norway, the homeland of her ancestors.

1. What training and development should the company provide for Lisa in preparation for her return to the United States?
2. From what type(s) of training and development do you think Lisa might profit after she returns to the United States?

MOTIVATING EMPLOYEES IS CULTURALLY BASED

Managers around the world try to motivate their employees to perform to their fullest potential. While this ideal is commendable, the specific things that contribute to peak performance vary. What motivates a U.S. worker to perform well may have little or no effect elsewhere. Employee motivation is not universal. Instead, it is culturally based; that is, it varies from culture to culture.

For example, the U.S. culture values individualism. It also values material possessions. It values taking personal risks to gain personal rewards. Consequently, for most U.S. workers motivation relates to the personal desire to assume risk in order to gain material rewards.

For many in the U.S. money is a major motivator. It is a reward for accepting individual risks and performing well. The more personal responsibility a U.S. worker accepts and handles well, the more money he or she receives. The more money a U.S. worker has, the more material possessions she or he can acquire. Money motivates many in the U.S. to perform well. Of course, money is not the only motivator. As money allows U.S. workers to fulfill their needs and wants, money becomes less and less a motivator. The possibility of earning $3,000 more motivates a U.S. worker who earns the minimum wage. It will allow him or her to have more creature comforts. However, it does not motivate a U.S. millionaire very much. The millionaire has already used money to fulfill basic needs and wants.

Money cannot buy everything. Some desires must be fulfilled in other ways. Other factors, such as personal recognition and the sense of reaching full potential, motivate many U.S. workers when money can no longer do so.

Experiences worldwide suggest that U.S. models of motivation work best with U.S. workers in their native country. When U.S.-based international companies try to apply their domestic models of motivation in other countries, the models do not work as well. U.S. models fail to explain motivation elsewhere because what motivates people differs from culture to culture.

For example, publicly praising the individual achievements of a U.S. worker may motivate him or her toward higher achievement. Treating a Japanese employee in the same manner may not motivate her or him. Since the Japanese culture emphasizes group harmony, praising an individual may disrupt the group harmony. It can cause the person singled out to lose face or to suffer personal embarrassment. It can cause that person to behave in the future in a way that will not draw attention to himself or herself. In effect, praising a Japanese employee publicly can backfire. Consequently, international managers must use motivation strategies that are culturally acceptable to the employee.

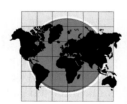

Global Business Example: The Company Picnic that Bombed

A U.S.-based international company decided it would hold a traditional company picnic at each of its sites worldwide since the event was very popular among the employees at headquarters. The first overseas company picnic was held near the location of the Madrid operations. While the U.S. picnic motivated employees and built teamwork at the company headquarters, the

Spanish version had the opposite effect. The local workers, Spaniards, were unaccustomed to socializing with those of other ranks. They also felt awkward being served by higher-ranking employees, several of whom were from the U.S. They perceived that their class and socialization standards were being violated. To make matters worse, they were coerced into playing the unfamiliar game of baseball, which further alienated them.

COMPENSATING EMPLOYEES

Employee compensation packages are influenced by the local culturally accepted standards. North American and European international companies generally reward employees based on the type of work performed and the skills required. In places like Singapore and Hong Kong, individual performance and skill influence compensation. In Japan such factors as age, seniority, and group or company performance determine compensation. In Latin America penalties for forcing older employees into early retirement are so high that most companies continue to pay these workers as much as younger workers. Since compensation standards vary around the world, companies should be guided by local laws, employment practices, and employer obligations as they design compensation packages.

Employees of international companies are motivated toward peak achievement by culturally sensitive compensation packages. These benefit packages include both cash and noncash items. The mix of employee benefits varies from country to country; however, the cash component is typically the largest. Some companies provide free or price-discounted products or services to their employees as noncash compensation. In European countries such items as lunches and transportation are often part of noncash executive compensation. In less-developed and developing countries, such basic foodstuff as rice and flour are sometimes part of noncash benefits.

Employee compensation packages for parent-country nationals usually are based on several factors. One factor is base salary. For the parent-country national, the base salary at least maintains the customary standard of living of the employee and the family while living abroad. Another factor is an expatriate bonus. Often a company must pay a premium to persuade an employee to work abroad. It provides compensation for adjustment problems and for hardship caused by living and working abroad.

Another factor is a cost-of-living adjustment. It compensates for the fact that basic living costs vary greatly around the world. Figure 11-7 shows the cost of living in selected locations around the world in comparison to the cost of living in Washington, D.C., U.S.A.

Figure 11-7

Compensation should take into account the vast differences in the cost of living in various cities around the world.

INDEX OF COST OF LIVING IN SELECTED LOCATIONS AROUND THE WORLD

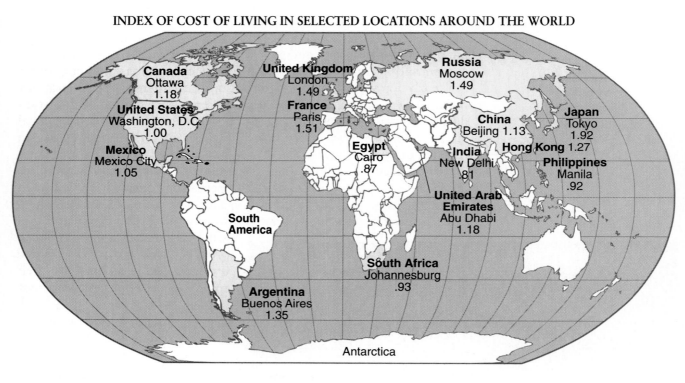

Source: Adapted from *U.S. Department of State Indexes of Living Costs Abroad, Quarters Allowances, and Hardship Differentials—October 1992* (Washington, D.C.: Department of State Publication 9994, Bureau of Administration, Office of Allowances.)

Finally, fringe benefits often are provided to compensate for the additional expenses of living abroad. They include compensation for having to pay various local taxes and contributions to government insurance programs. They also include relocation expenses, high-risk insurance premiums, extra educational expenses, and extra medical expenses.

Employee compensation packages for other types of workers vary worldwide. Typically, they include a base salary that reflects local living costs and some fringe benefits.

Global Business Exercise: Computing Cost-of-Living Allowances

Figure 11-7 is an index of the cost of living around the world compared to Washington, D.C., U.S.A. This index can be used by companies to compute cost-of-living allowances for employees who are living in cities where living costs exceed those in Washington, D.C.

For example, the index number for London is 1.49. The index number means that the cost of living in London is 1.49 times the cost of living in Washington, D.C. Consequently, an item that costs $100 in Washington, D.C., costs $149 in London.

The cost-of-living allowance can be computed by multiplying the appropriate index number for the foreign city by the employee's spendable income. Using data from Figure 11-7, fill in the blanks in the following cost-of-living allowances table. London has been completed as an example.

Location	Index	x	Spendable Income*	=	Cost-of-Living Allowance
Example: London	1.49	x	$25,000	=	$37,250.00
1. Mexico City	1.05	x	$35,000	=	_____
2. Ottawa	____	x	$20,000	=	_____
3. Paris	____	x	$30,000	=	$45,300.00
4. Tokyo	1.92	x	_____	=	$96,000.00

*Note: Spendable income excludes taxes, retirement deposits, insurance, savings and investments, charitable contributions, housing, and children's education.

EVALUATING EMPLOYEE PERFORMANCE

Companies that operate internationally must evaluate the performance of their employees. Employee performance, especially for parent-country nationals, is influenced by three factors: the environment, the task, and the individual's personality.

Business environments differ greatly around the world. Some offer better opportunities for success than others. Job tasks vary, too. Some jobs are more demanding than others. It is more difficult to perform jobs with many challenging tasks. Personality characteristics contribute to the likelihood of success, especially in international assignments. The match between personality types and job demands is important.

The human resource management approach used by the company determines who sets the employee performance standards. For example, with the ethnocentric approach, parent-country nationals primarily set and administer the standards. In contrast, with the polycentric approach, host-country nationals primarily set and administer the standards.

The nature of the employee performance standards vary from job to job. Different jobs require different combinations of competence, adaptability, and personal characteristics. Standards also vary from country to country since different cultures view employee performance in different ways.

Although many companies try to assess the performance of host-country nationals and third-country nationals much like parent-country nationals, it is difficult to do. Even if the evaluation forms are translated into the appropriate languages, misunderstandings can occur. If local evaluation forms are used, can the company headquarters interpret them correctly? Another problem is how employee performance evaluation is perceived in different parts of the world. In some locations it can be viewed as threatening. It can also be viewed as insulting or evidence of lack of trust. Finding ways of evaluating employee performance that are both culturally sensitive and meaningful is difficult. Balancing the needs of the employee and the company is indeed a challenge in the global business environment.

Global Business Exercise: The Evaluation of Bob Parker

Bob Parker, a U.S. national, was sent by his U.S.-based employer to The Netherlands to manage the European office in The Hague. He was evaluated by his immediate supervisor on the same form used to evaluate managers in U.S. offices of the company. The form focused on the environment in which he managed, his job tasks, and his personal characteristics.

1. Did the evaluation form focus attention on the relevant performance factors?

2. What do you think are possible disadvantages for using an evaluation form in a European country, when the form was designed for U.S. managers working in the United States?

Repatriation is the process a person goes through when returning home and getting settled after having worked abroad. The repatriation period often is a difficult one, filled with many adjustments. It is the challenging time when expatriates experience reverse culture shock. They have difficulty becoming reacquainted with their native culture. These major adjustments involve such things as work, finances, and social relationships.

Returning expatriates often experience a sense of isolation. They have grown in different directions while abroad. Because their extended families and friends have not had similar experiences, they seem like strangers.

To minimize the problems when returning home, expatriates need to plan ahead. It is not too early to start before ever leaving on an international assignment. With careful advanced planning, many of the problems of returning employees can be lessened. One should learn all about the host country and its way of life before going there. Once abroad, one must keep in frequent communication with former colleagues and friends. The expatriate should share new experiences with them and find out what is new in their lives. In addition, one can learn to enjoy the benefits of the host culture and its way of life whenever possible. One should also begin exploring new career options at least one year before the end of the international assignment. The soon-to-be repatriate should encourage the current employer to find a suitable job that makes use of international experience. Also, one can explore options abroad and at home with other companies. When returning home, the repatriate should be grateful for the adventures abroad. One can view one's native culture in another light: appreciate it more than ever before, having experienced firsthand another way of life.

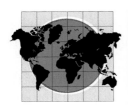

Global Business Example: I Wish I'd Given More Advance Thought to Repatriation!

Yvonne Wylie discovered the hard way how tough it is to repatriate. After having lived in culturally and professionally stimulating Vienna for only three years, she was sure that moving back to the United States for a position at company headquarters would be no problem.

Initially, Yvonne was excited to be back in the United States. However, she noticed that her relatives and friends seemed distant. She seemed to have little in common with them. At the company headquarters, her formerly friendly colleagues seemed surprised to see her. They showed little or no interest in what she had learned while managing the Vienna office. She was treated like a stranger. In fact, her recent international experiences were completely irrelevant to her new job assignment. Frustrated by the sense of isolation in her personal and professional life, she thought to herself, "I wish I'd given more thought to repatriation. I took it for granted, and I shouldn't have."

Back to the Beginning: I Want to Go Home

Reread the case at the beginning of this chapter and answer the following questions:

1. How long had the Smiths lived abroad?
2. Why did Doug want to return to the United States?
3. Recalling the discussion of culture shock in Chapter 3, at what stage of culture shock is Doug? How do you know?
4. What advice would you give to Sue and Doug?

KNOWING GLOBAL BUSINESS TERMS

The following terms should become part of your business vocabulary. For each numbered item find the term that has the same meaning.

- employment forecasting
- ethnocentric approach
- expatriates
- geocentric approach
- job description
- locals or host-country nationals
- parent-country nationals or home-country nationals
- polycentric approach
- regiocentric approach
- repatriation
- supply analysis
- third-country nationals

1. The human resources approach that uses the best available managers without regard for their countries of origin.
2. Expatriate employees from the country where the company for which they work is headquartered.
3. The human resources approach that uses natives of the parent country of a business to fill key positions at home and abroad.
4. The process of returning home and getting settled after having worked abroad.
5. Natives of the country in which they work.
6. Determining if there are sufficient types and numbers of employees available.
7. The human resources approach that uses managers from various countries within the geographic region of a business.
8. Employees from countries other than the home country of the company for which they work or from the host country.
9. People who live and work outside their native countries.

10. A document that includes the job identification, job statement, job duties and responsibilities, and job specifications and requirements.
11. Estimating in advance the types and numbers of employees needed.
12. The human resources approach that uses natives of the host country to manage operations within their country and parent-country natives to manage at headquarters.

REVIEWING YOUR READING

Answer these questions to reinforce your knowledge of the main ideas of this chapter.

1. Why is human resource management different in the global environment?
2. Briefly explain the four dominant approaches to human resource management.
3. What process is used to determine staffing needs, and how does a company maintain a balance between supply and demand?
4. How are potential employees recruited?
5. How do international companies go about selecting employees?
6. Briefly explain common types of training and development that international managers receive.
7. What factors often cause parent-country nationals to fail in their overseas assignments?
8. Why is the following statement true: Motivation is culturally based.
9. What things typically are included in the compensation packages of parent-country nationals?
10. What are some of the difficulties in evaluating employee performance in an international setting?
11. What actions can international employees take to minimize the problems associated with repatriation?

EXPANDING YOUR HORIZONS

You will not find the complete answers to the following questions in your textbook. You will need to use your critical-thinking skills. Think about these questions, gather information from other sources, analyze possible responses, and discuss them with others. Then, develop your own oral or written response as instructed by your teacher.

1. Why do you think that the human resource managerial approach of filling key positions at home and abroad with natives of the parent country is called the ethnocentric approach?

2. In what situations might staffing with third-country nationals be preferable to staffing with parent-country nationals?

3. What are several factors that would cause a German-based international company to pay its employees who live in Tokyo, Japan, more than its employees who live in your hometown?

4. If one of your parents accepted employment as a parent-country national in France, what are likely to be some of the adjustment problems that you would experience if you moved there?

5. Why do you think that all of the recommended training listed in the essential category in Figure 11-6 on page 245 relates to the general Japanese culture rather than to Japanese business practices?

6. Why might your best friend no longer seem to be your best friend when you return from a lengthy overseas assignment?

BUILDING RESEARCH SKILLS

The ability to find information from various sources is an important international business skill. The following activities will help you investigate various topics. You will also learn to apply class ideas to situations outside of the classroom.

1. Using people and library resources, determine if a U.S.-based multinational company should hold an annual company picnic and baseball game for the employees of its Portuguese subsidiary, 75 percent of whom are natives of Portugal. Justify your position.

2. Should a U.S.-based multinational company locate its European division human resource office in London, England, or in Paris, France, if the primary consideration is (1) the local cost of living, (2) the central location, (3) the ease of adjustment for parent-country nationals?

3. Using reference books in a library, identify a multinational company headquartered in a European country of your choice. Find out in which city the company is headquartered. Locate not only the country but also the headquarters city on a European map. Using the scale on the map, estimate the distance from the city in which the company is headquartered to Brussels, Belgium.

4. After locating and reading a magazine or journal article about living abroad, make a list of important points to remember.

5. If your family relocated in the United Kingdom and enrolled you in what the British call a private comprehensive secondary school, would your family be entitled to an educational adjustment as a part of your father's or mother's employee compensation package? Why or why not?

6. *Global Career Activity.* Your company has offices and stores in several countries. You need to interview applicants for a manager's job in another country. Prepare a list of questions you might ask an applicant.

Continuing Enrichment Project: Training and Development Practices

Write a letter to the human resource manager at the headquarters of your selected company. Ask for information about the types of training and development activities that the company routinely provides for upper-level, middle-level, and lower-level managers at its company headquarters. Also, ask for information about the training and development that are typically provided for the three levels of managers at one of its subsidiaries.

After studying this chapter and completing the end-of-chapter activities, you will be able to

- Describe the steps of the career planning process.

- Research sources of career planning information.

- Identify international business career opportunities based on personal factors and job availability.

- Create a personal data sheet and application letter.

- Exhibit successful interview techniques.

- Explain how careers can develop and change.

A Global Business Career

Jennifer Yoon is an administrative assistant in San Antonio, Texas, for a multinational company with offices in 16 countries. Her company recently posted a job opening for general manager of the company's new office in Austria. This position will require a knowledge of company operations, financial management, marketing, import-export laws, and Austrian business customs.

Jennifer has not worked full-time in any country other than the United States. However, she has traveled in nine other countries for meetings and short-term work assignments. During her years in school, Jennifer studied global marketing, economic geography, European history, and foreign political systems. While in college, she also participated in a work-study program at the Spanish trade office in Washington, D.C.

As Jennifer considers this job in another country, her thoughts go in two directions. "This is the opportunity I have been waiting and training for," she said to a friend. Then, Jennifer went on to say, "But, what if I can't adapt to the different culture and business activities?"

Some people jump out of bed in the morning and can't wait to get to work. Others go to work thinking only about the weekend or vacation. What is the difference between these two groups of people? Selection of your life's work could be the most important decision you make.

Work not only affects income, it also influences the amount of leisure time you have, the people with whom you will associate, and many other aspects of your life. Careful selection of work can result in a satisfying existence. In addition, career planning activities are likely to continue throughout your life. Changing personal, social, and economic factors affect job satisfaction and available employment positions.

THE CAREER PLANNING PROCESS

In every society, work is necessary. Work makes it possible for people to have food, clothing, housing, and transportation. Besides fulfilling physical needs, work has social and psychological benefits. Working allows people to gain personal satisfaction by interacting with others and being recognized for their performance.

The work a person selects can be viewed as either a job or a career. A **job** is an employment position obtained mainly for money. People may work in one or more jobs during their lives without planning for advancement.

In contrast, a **career** is a commitment to a profession that requires continued training and has a clear path for advancement. A person may select a career in health care, information systems, marketing, financial management, exporting, or other areas. Figure 12-1 shows the activities involved in career planning.

Determine Your Personal Goals and Abilities

As you plan for a career, start by evaluating your personal situation. Do you like to work with others, or would you rather work alone? Would you like to work outside or in an office? Do you enjoy working with words or numbers? Determining your personal goals and abilities will help you start the career planning process.

Evaluate the Job Market

Next, determine what types of jobs are available. You may want to work as a news reporter on television. However, few jobs may be available in that field. Look for career areas in which you can adapt your interests, skills, and knowledge.

Figure 12-1

Career decisions require careful planning to obtain a position that best suits your interests and abilities.

THE CAREER PLANNING PROCESS

Step 1
Determine your personal goals and abilities

Step 2
Evaluate the job market

Step 3
Identify and apply for specific job opportunities

Step 4
Accept the most desirable job offer

Step 5
Plan for personal career development

Identify and Apply for Specific Job Opportunities

The third step of the process involves presenting yourself on paper and in person. After finding organizations with available employment, you will need to communicate your abilities to those responsible for hiring. This communication comes in the form of a personal data sheet, application letter, and interview.

Accept the Most Desirable Job Offer

In this step, evaluate the positive and negative aspects of various companies. Compare salaries, employee benefits, work situations, and future opportunities in the organization. Remember, the highest paying job may not be the most enjoyable or offer advancement in the future.

Plan for Personal Career Development

Finally, workers should continually evaluate their future. As personal goals and employment opportunities change, you may want to obtain new training. Technology, economic conditions, or other factors may eliminate certain jobs and force a career change.

Most people work in jobs that are within one country. This is called the *domestic employment market*. Other work opportunities involve international business. For example, a company in Poland may make suits that are sold in Canada. Or, a Japanese bank may have an office in Egypt. As trade among nations expands, the number and types of global careers increase.

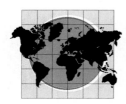

Global Business Example: What Is an Export-Related Job?

Over 10 million people in the United States have jobs related to the exporting of manufactured goods. In addition, more than 15 million people are employed in nonmanufacturing export industries—such as trading companies; business services, including insurance, delivery, information processing, and financial institutions; transportation; communication and utilities; and, mining and agriculture.

In the business services group, for example, a truck driver delivering finished goods from a factory to a port is considered an export-related worker. Other export-related jobs, as defined by the U.S. Department of Commerce, are in factories and offices that do not actually produce exported products. However, these business organizations furnish components, supplies, parts, and administrative services to manufacturing plants that *do* directly export products. For example, a steel worker who produces steel used in automobiles made for exporting has an export-related job.

Every business and personal decision can be improved by "doing your homework." Obtaining relevant information helps with all life's activities. Selecting and planning a career is no different. As Figure 12-2 shows, career information is available from four main sources.

Figure 12-2

Information about the availability of careers and how to obtain employment are available from many sources.

CAREER PLANNING INFORMATION SOURCES

Library Materials   **Personal and Business Contacts**

Media   **Community Organizations**

Library Materials

Your school or public library is an excellent starting point for career information. You can obtain books and other publications about selecting a career field, searching for a job, or planning for an interview.

One very helpful source is the *Occupational Outlook Handbook*, published by the Bureau of Labor Statistics (part of the U.S. Department of Labor). This reference book is revised every two years and provides detailed information about jobs in many career areas. Other helpful career resources include the *Dictionary of Occupational Titles* and the *Occupational Outlook Quarterly*.

Media

Most newspapers publish articles with job search hints and career trends. Television and radio reports about job planning and economic trends can be useful when studying careers. For example, news about a company expanding into other nations provides information about the availability of international jobs.

Personal and Business Contacts

Every person you meet can help you learn more about work and successful career planning. Friends, relatives, and people in your community all have worked at one time or another. Talking with them about their jobs can be very useful. An **informational interview** is a meeting with another person to gather information about a career or organization. In an informational interview, you can learn about required skills, job duties, and potential earnings for different careers. What are some questions you might ask a person who works for a multinational company?

Community Organizations

Most communities have business and civic organizations such as the Chamber of Commerce, Jay-Cees, and Rotary Club. Meetings held by these groups can be a source of current business trends. The Chamber of Commerce commonly publishes a directory of its member businesses, many of which may be involved in importing or exporting.

Global Business Example: Global Career Information Sources

At first, finding information about international business careers may seem difficult. However, the following sources may be consulted when planning a global business career:

- U. S. employers with foreign offices—contact the company's human resources department or public information office. Request information about the organization's business activities and career opportunities in other countries.

- Embassies of foreign countries—these official offices can supply information about work permit procedures, the culture of the country, and employment opportunities.
- U.S. federal government agencies—the Department of State and Department of Commerce have business representatives in over 200 countries.
- World Trade Centers Association (WTCA)—this organization has more than 200 member groups in over 60 countries. Created in 1968, WTCA promotes international trade and global business relationships. World Trade Centers are located in over 45 major U.S. cities.
- United Nations resources—UN publications and other materials provide background information on the economic, social, and political situation in member nations.

IDENTIFYING CAREER OPPORTUNITIES

Why do some people excel in their chosen career, while others never seem to find satisfying work? The answer to this question involves many things. As you start thinking about your life's work, consider your personal abilities and talents along with what jobs will be available. Trade among nations and technology eliminates some careers while others are created.

Factors Affecting Career Choice

Will your career be one that you enjoy? Will the work involve an activity that will be in demand in our global economy? Career choice is influenced by a variety of factors (see Figure 12-3 on page 266).

Personal Factors.   What do you like to do? What do you do well? Answers to these questions can be keys to successful career planning. In addition, when selecting a job, decide

- how much and what type of education you plan to obtain;
- what experience you have; and,
- what your personal goals are.

An evaluation of personal interests, experience, values, and goals is important for selecting the right career for you. A knowledge of global business activities, geography, foreign cultures, and another language provide a foundation for an international business career.

Chapter 12   International Career Planning

265

Figure 12-3
The career a person selects is affected by many factors.

FACTORS INFLUENCING CAREER SELECTION

Personal Factors – your interests. abilities, age, education, experience, and personal goals.

Demographic Trends – changes in population.

Geographic Influences – location of natural resources and industries.

Economic Conditions – consumer demand, inflation, and interest rates.

Industry Trends – global competition and changing uses of technology.

CAREER PLANNING

Demographic Trends.   As the population of a society changes, so do the jobs that are available. For example, an increase in the number of working parents in the United States increased the demand for food service and child-care workers. Also, as people live longer, employment in travel services, health care, and retirement facilities expand.

Geographic Influences.   The location of employment opportunities can change. As economic growth occurs in a geographic region, more jobs are available. However, when economic conditions decline fewer jobs will exist.
    The location of natural resources also influences employment. Areas with seaports and rivers commonly have shipbuilding and shipping industries. Fertile land usually is used for agricultural purposes. Rich mineral deposits lead to mining and related metal-product industries.

266

Unit 3   Managing in a Global Environment

Economic Conditions. Jobs, like goods and services, are affected by the basic economic principle of supply and demand. For example, as more people want and use home computers, employment in industries that make, program, and sell these computers increases. Consumer demand in the economy has a strong effect on the job market.

Changing prices affect available jobs. When inflation occurs, people usually reduce spending. Lower consumer demand, once again, causes a decline in the need for products and the workers who make the products.

As you know, changes in the value of a nation's currency will affect its balance of trade. As the demand for a country's goods and services increases, employment opportunities in that nation expand.

Interest rates affect employment opportunities, also. If companies must pay high rates to borrow for new equipment or to build a new factory, fewer businesses will make these capital purchases. As a result, people who would build this equipment and these factories will have fewer jobs available.

Industry Trends. Companies have always competed against each other. However, as global business activities expand, foreign competition changes the types of jobs available.

Another business trend affecting jobs is the increased use of technology. Computers in offices, stores, and factories require that employees be able to operate this equipment. In addition, many jobs previously done by people are now handled by computer systems.

Sources of Available Jobs

How does a person identify job opportunities? Advertisements are often a place to start looking. Classified ads provide information on some employment positions. Advertisements may help a person find work; however, most jobs are not advertised to the general public. For this reason, personal contacts are an important source of job information. Ask people you know about available jobs in their company. As previously mentioned, an informational interview can be helpful. The people you talk with may be able to tell you about what skills are needed, where jobs are located, and whom to contact.

Visit places where you would like to work. While most jobs are not advertised, work opportunities are sometimes posted at a place of business. The effort taken to go to the company can display a strong desire to work.

Employment agencies can sometimes be a helpful source of job information. However, be careful of organizations that charge a fee and give no guarantee of helping you find a job. State-funded employment services provide information on some available jobs.

People seeking work may also consider *job creation*. This involves communicating with possible employers about skills you have that could help their companies. For example, a person may be skilled at researching foreign locations. While an owner may have never considered exporting, a new job position could be created in the company.

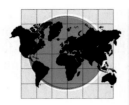

Global Business Example: Employment Trends in Industrialized Countries

Being prepared for jobs that will be in demand in the future is important for successful career planning. Between 1970 and 1990, employment growth was much faster in the United States, Canada, and Australia than in other industrialized countries. This was one finding of a study conducted by the Bureau of Labor Statistics of the U.S. Department of Labor. The research also involved Japan, France, Germany, Italy, the Netherlands, Sweden, and the United Kingdom.

Service jobs in the 10 countries grew faster than employment opportunities in agriculture and industrial companies. By 1982, all of the countries in the study reported that more than 50 percent of their jobs were in service industries. The largest increases were in information processing, global trade, health care, retail sales, finance, insurance, leisure, and personal services.

Source: Adapted from Godbout, Todd M. "Employment Change and Sectoral Distribution in 10 Countries, 1970-90," *Monthly Labor Review,* October, 1993, pp. 3–20.

THE JOB APPLICATION PROCESS

"Wanted: Stock clerk for import company. A knowledge of inventory methods and international business practices required." Someday you may encounter a job advertisement something like this. What actions are necessary for you to obtain this position?

Creating a Résumé

If you find a job in which you are interested, you must communicate your skills and abilities to your prospective employer. A **résumé** is a summary of a person's education, training, experience, and other job qualifications. Figure 12-4 shows a sample résumé, also called a *personal data sheet,* for a person just out of high school.

Personal Data Section.   A résumé starts with your name, address, and telephone number. A person's age (or birth date), marital status, gender, height, and weight should not be listed unless this information is related to specific job qualifications.

Career Objective Section.   Some personal information sheets may include the person's career goal. Many career counselors recommend that this section be omitted from the résumé. A career objective may best be communicated in the application letter.

Figure 12-4

A personal résumé informs employers of the skills and abilities you possess.

A SAMPLE RÉSUMÉ

Terry Connor
1654 Meadow Lane
Central City, Texas 76540-1654
(214) 555-4537

CAREER OBJECTIVE   An inventory clerk position with a business involved in importing or exporting.

EDUCATION   Browne High School
Graduated June, 1995

International Business Preparation:
• French I, II, III
• International Business I
• Global Marketing
• World Geography
• Economics
• Business Law

EXPERIENCE   Filing Clerk, Jefferson Furniture Co.,
Allentown, Texas, August, 1994—June, 1995

Volunteer, Kenton County Home for the Aged,
October, 1991—September, 1993

RELATED ACTIVITIES   Vice President, International Business Club

Secretary, Student Council

Foreign Missions Program, Student Assistant,
Central Baptist Church

HONORS AND AWARDS   Finalist, Martin Foundation Global
Business Scholarship

Community Service Award, Kenton County
Park District Recycling Program

REFERENCES   Furnished upon request.

Education Section. This section includes schools attended, dates of attendance, and fields of study. A listing of courses taken would be appropriate for classes that relate directly to the job for which you are applying.

Experience Section. This section should include organization names and responsibilities for past jobs, job-like community involvement, and the dates on which you did these things. Communicate skills that show you can work effectively.

Related Activities Section. School involvement, hobbies, and other interests that are directly related to your career can also help you get a job.

Honors and Awards Section. A listing of honors or awards can help communicate your ability to do high quality work.

References Section. **References** are people who can report to a prospective employer on your abilities and experiences. These individuals may be teachers, past employers, community leaders, or adult friends. Be sure to obtain permission from the people you plan to use as references. References are usually not included on the résumé. However, you will need to have this information ready when asked for it.

Developing an Application Letter

When applying for a job, your résumé should be sent with an application letter. An **application letter** communicates your interest in a specific employment position. This letter is designed to obtain an interview.

The opening paragraph of an application letter should get the reader's attention. Express your interest in the job. Communicate why the employer should consider you for the position.

The next paragraph (or two) highlights specific training and experiences that qualify you for the position. Remember, the employers don't care what you have done in the past. They want to know how your background will serve them in the future. You must communicate how your skills and training will contribute to the organization.

The final paragraph should ask for an opportunity to meet in person with your prospective employer. Tell where and when you can be reached to schedule an interview. You should conclude with one key reason that you should be considered for the job.

Remember, your application letter and personal data sheet (résumé) are your ticket to the interview. Be sure that they are neat, well organized, and properly addressed. Many job candidates are disqualified because of poorly presented résumés and cover (application) letters.

Completing an Application Form

Instead of or in addition to an application letter and résumé, a person may be required to complete an application form. This document will ask for information similar to the items listed on a personal data sheet. An application form should be filled out in a neat and complete manner. When preparing a job application, be sure you have the needed information available. An application form is likely to request your Social Security number; schools attended; work experience; and, the names, addresses, and telephone numbers of references. If it is allowed, you should take the form home with you and key the information before submitting it.

International Employment Documents

When traveling, studying, or working in another country, certain documents are usually required. A **passport** is a government document proving the bearer's citizenship in the country that issues it.

Global Highlight: The Bubonic Plague

Plagues are the result of widespread disease and poor health care. Between 1347 and 1351, about 75 million Europeans died from the bubonic plague. This reduced the population of Europe by about one-third.

Also known as the Black Death, the bubonic plague is a severe infection in humans and various species of rodents. The disease is spread by fleas that have fed on infected rodents and humans. Once infected, a person's body temperature rises to 40° C (104° F) within a few hours. Left untreated, death occurs for 60 to 90 percent of the victims within a few days. Today, certain antibiotics may be used to treat bubonic plague if used soon after the symptoms appear.

Plague pneumonia, spread by inhaling infected water droplets, is the most contagious form of the disease. Left untreated, death usually occurs in less than three days.

Today, improved sanitation has prevented outbreaks of the disease. And, the advent of modern drugs makes a cure possible. However, small epidemics of bubonic plague still occur throughout the world, including the United States.

Passports are issued to citizens of the United States by the Department of State and are valid for ten years. A passport application may be obtained from a post office, passport agency, or a federal or state court clerk.

A **visa** is a stamp of endorsement issued by a country that allows a passport holder to enter that country. A visa allows a person into a foreign nation for a specified purpose and period of time.

Most visas are issued for travel and personal business. People who plan to work in another country are usually required to obtain a work visa. A **work visa**, also called a **work permit**, allows a person into a foreign country for the purpose of employment.

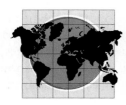

Global Business Example: Obtaining International Career Experiences

A common problem faced by beginning workers is a lack of experience. You are told, "You don't have enough experience." However, to get experience you need a job.

Work-related experiences can be obtained through part-time or summer jobs. Most schools offer cooperative education or internship programs. Volunteering for community organizations is another method of obtaining work experience. Participation may include working with a recycling project, assisting at a senior citizen center, or helping supervise youth activities.

To obtain international business career experience, a person can consider the following situations in other countries:

- temporary employment in child-care or elder-care facilities;
- agricultural jobs;
- teaching English in countries that do business with English-speaking countries;
- working as a sales clerk in small shops and other stores; or,
- summer work in a resort area.

Sources: Adapted from *Personal Finance,* Richard D. Irwin, Inc., 1994 and *International Careers,* Bob Adams, Inc., Publishers, 1990.

INTERVIEWING FOR A JOB

"Why should we hire you?" This is a common question that you will probably have to answer when applying for jobs. The process of interviewing for a job requires that you start getting ready well before the interview.

Before You Interview

Prepare for an interview by obtaining additional information about the company. News articles, annual reports, and current and past employees are sources of company information. Your knowledge of the organization will help you better answer questions about how you can contribute to the company.

Next, prepare questions to ask at the interview. Many interviewers are impressed by the questions a candidate asks. Common questions to ask in an interview include

- What are the main responsibilities of the job?
- What qualities do your most successful employees possess?
- What do people like best about working here?

Set up a practice interview. With the use of a video camera and someone asking you sample questions, you can improve your interview skills. Organize your thoughts before answering. Speak clearly and calmly. Show enthusiasm.

Finally, plan the proper clothing and grooming for the interview. Find out what employees wear to work. Regardless of the company's dress code, a business suit is usually appropriate for an interview. Avoid trendy and casual styles, and don't wear too much jewelry.

When You Interview

Arrive at the interview several minutes before your appointment time. While it may be difficult, RELAX! Remember, you will be asked questions about a topic on which you are the expert—you!!

You may first be required to have a **screening interview**, which is an initial meeting to select finalists from the applicant pool for an employment position. During the screening interview, you will be judged on your overall impression and answers to a few general questions.

Candidates who pass the screening interview are invited for a **selection interview** that involves a series of in-depth questions designed to select the best person for a job. Figure 12-5 on page 274 lists common questions that may be asked of someone just out of school in an interview.

After You Interview

While waiting to hear from a prospective employer, do two things. First, send a thank-you letter to follow up. You might include an item, such as a photograph or article, that presents the result of some activity discussed at the interview.

Second, evaluate your interview performance. Write down ways you can improve. List questions that you did not expect to be asked.

Figure 12-5

Planning answers to these questions can help you prepare for a job interview.

COMMON INTERVIEW QUESTIONS

What experience and training have prepared you for this job?

Besides going to school, how have you expanded your knowledge and interests?

What did you like best about school? What did you like least?

In what types of situations do you get frustrated?

What are your major strengths? major weaknesses? What have you done to overcome your weaknesses?

What do you believe makes a successful person?

Describe the work situation you would like to have five years from now.

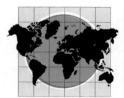

Global Business Example: Cross-Cultural Interviewing

International job interviews are often different from interviews for a job in your home country. In most cultures, certain topics should be avoided. For example, discussion of politics is usually not appropriate in Austria, France, Greece, the Netherlands, and Portugal.

Also, be aware of gestures and body language. While a head nod in most countries means "yes," in Bulgaria and Greece it means "no." In most Middle and Far Eastern countries, pointing with your index finger is considered impolite and vulgar.

Source: Adapted from *Do's and Taboos Around the World,* edited by Roger E. Axtell, A Benjamin Book, 1993.

A job is for today, but a career is for a lifetime. Every workday, employees have the opportunity to expand their abilities, knowledge, and career potential. Improving work habits may be achieved by watching others or creating better ways to do certain tasks.

Training Opportunities

Increased technology and changing work activities require employees to learn new skills. Each day on a job can result in new knowledge through informal and formal methods. Informal learning takes place every time people read current materials about their job or the industry in which they work. Talking with others within your company or at other organizations can also help you learn new economic and social trends affecting business.

Formal educational methods include company training programs, seminars, and college courses. Many companies encourage participation in continuing education by paying all or part of the tuition costs.

Career Advancement

As with every personal and business decision, choices might need to be revised as social and economic factors change. During the first stage of a career, workers are concerned with matching interests and abilities to a job. However, as a career develops, a person will seek new challenges, increased responsibility, and greater rewards.

Changing Careers

About 10 million people change careers each year. Most people will have five or more different jobs during their lives. The need to change jobs may come from within. Many people face mental stress or physical illness from their work. When this occurs, a career change is probably appropriate.

External influences can also cause a job change. As companies move or merge, a person's job may be eliminated. Technology may replace the need for certain jobs. For example, many bank tellers have been replaced by automated teller machines.

Numerous things may cause a person to change jobs. When this occurs in your life, review the information in this chapter to help you plan a revised career path.

Back to the Beginning: A Global Business Career

Reread the case at the beginning of this chapter and answer the following questions:

1. What educational and business experience prepared Jennifer for the position of general manager in another country?
2. What actions should Jennifer take to apply for the position?
3. What difficulties might Jennifer encounter if she is selected as manager of the new office in Austria?

KNOWING GLOBAL BUSINESS TERMS

The following terms should become part of your business vocabulary. For each numbered item find the term that has the same meaning.

- application letter
- career
- informational interview
- job
- passport
- references

- résumé
- screening interview
- selection interview
- visa
- work permit (work visa)

1. A stamp of endorsement issued by a country that allows a passport holder to enter that country.
2. A written summary of a person's education, training, experience, and other job qualifications.
3. A series of in-depth questions to select the best person for a job.
4. A commitment to a profession that requires continued training and has a clear path for advancement.
5. A document that allows a person into a foreign country for the purpose of employment.
6. A meeting with another person to gather information about a career or organization.
7. Correspondence that communicates your interest in a specific employment position.
8. An initial meeting with applicants to select finalists for an employment position.
9. An employment position obtained mainly for money.

10. A government document proving the bearer's citizenship in the country that issues it.

11. People who can report to a prospective employer on your abilities and experiences.

REVIEWING YOUR READING

Answer these questions to reinforce your knowledge of the main ideas of this chapter.

1. How does a job differ from a career?
2. What is the domestic job market?
3. What are four sources of career information?
4. What type of information can be obtained from an informational interview?
5. What personal factors affect career choice?
6. How can economic conditions affect the availability of jobs?
7. What are ways to identify jobs that are available?
8. What are the main sections of a résumé?
9. Name people who might serve as references.
10. What is the purpose of an application letter?
11. How does a passport differ from a visa?
12. What should a person do when preparing for a job interview?
13. How does a screening interview differ from a selection interview?
14. What training opportunities are commonly available to workers who want to improve and expand their skills?

EXPANDING YOUR HORIZONS

You will not find the complete answers to the following questions in your textbook. You will need to use your critical-thinking skills. Think about these questions, gather information from other sources, analyze possible responses, and discuss them with others. Then, develop your own oral or written response as instructed by your teacher.

1. List examples of domestic jobs and jobs in the international employment market.
2. Prepare questions to ask of a person working in international business during an informational interview.

3. Why would a person select a job that pays less money than another job that is available?

4. Describe international events that could affect the number and types of jobs in a country.

5. If nearly 90 percent of jobs are not advertised to the general public, how can a person find out about available employment positions?

6. Explain how a person can obtain work-related experience through class activities and participation in school organizations.

7. Why might a multinational company operating in Kenya hire a manager from Japan rather than a native Kenyan?

8. How should prospective employees answer an interview question about their weaknesses?

9. Describe situations in which technology has reduced the need for certain jobs.

BUILDING RESEARCH SKILLS

The ability to find information from various sources is an important international business skill. The following activities will help you investigate various topics. You will also learn to apply class ideas to situations outside of the classroom.

1. Prepare a poster or bulletin board that shows examples of international business careers.

2. Conduct library research about the educational background, training requirements, and other information for a specific international business career.

3. Collect examples of résumé formats from career planning books, counselors, and people who recently applied for and obtained a job. How do the formats of these personal data sheets differ? What format do you think is most effective?

4. Talk to people who conduct job interviews or who have participated in a job interview. Prepare a report about the common questions asked in an interview and common mistakes people make when being interviewed for a job.

5. *Global Career Activity.* Create a career planning portfolio for obtaining an international business job. List your employment skills and work experience, collect information about international careers and global companies, and describe additional information you need about applying for jobs.

Continuing Enrichment Project: Planning an International Career

Using the company researched in previous chapters or selecting a new company, obtain information to develop a career plan that includes answers to the following:

1. What types of international jobs are available within this multinational organization?

2. What training, skills, and experience are commonly required for an international business career?

3. How might social factors and economic conditions affect available jobs?

4. Create a fictitious résumé for someone applying for a job with this company.

5. List interview questions and tentative answers that might be a part of the application process.

CHAPTER 13

Organized Labor

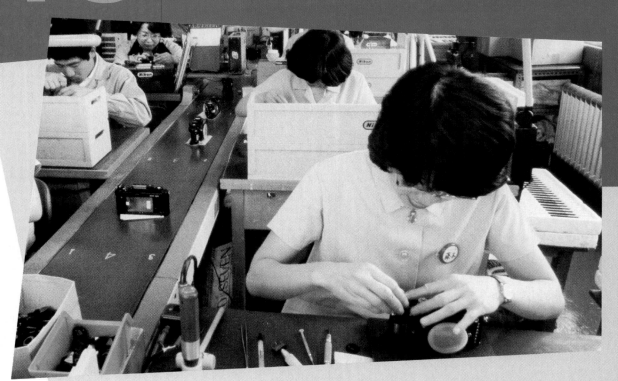

After studying this chapter and completing the end-of-chapter activities, you will be able to

- Understand the history of labor unions.
- Identify some key labor-relations laws.
- Outline the formation of the AFL-CIO.
- Discuss the effects and nature of international labor activities.
- Explain the decline in union membership.
- Describe the main purpose and activities of labor unions.

Solidarity in Poland

In the early 1980s, workers in the shipyards of Gdansk, Poland, desired greater economic opportunities and political freedom. The Solidarity labor movement, led by Lech Wałesa, organized a strike at the shipyards. This labor action spread to other industries, putting pressure on the country's communist government.

In December, 1981, in response to the union's activities, Solidarity was outlawed. Wałesa and others were jailed. For the next seven years, the union's activities moved underground. However, as governments in Eastern Europe began their move from communism to democracy, the Solidarity labor movement again became openly active. Its actions lead to the formation of a political party and in 1989, Solidarity candidates won a majority of the elected seats in Poland's parliament.

One year later, Lech Wałesa was elected the nation's president. Wałesa was awarded the Nobel Peace Prize in 1983 for his efforts that lead to changes in Poland and much of Eastern Europe.

This chapter looks at the issues that arise when employees in an organization are members of labor unions. The management of human resources is affected in important ways when a union exists in the workplace.

FORMATION OF LABOR UNIONS

A **labor union** is an organization of workers formed for the purpose of improving members' working conditions, wages, and benefits. The important principle behind unions is that there is strength in numbers. If one or two employees are unhappy with some aspect of their jobs, management can relatively easily ignore the complaints or replace the complaining workers. However, it is much more difficult to fire and replace a large, organized group of employees.

Labor Unions in the United States

The members of the early unions in the United States were skilled workers—such as shoemakers, printers, carpenters, and tailors. Their goal was to protect industry wage rates by preventing the employment of workers for lower wages.

The first large modern unions in the United States were formed during the nineteenth century as a result of the Industrial Revolution. Previously, goods had been made in small quantities and at a fairly slow pace by skilled workers. With the onset of the Industrial Revolution, more and more goods were produced cheaply and on a large scale with the help of machines in factories. Working conditions in factories consisted of long hours of work, unsafe machinery, low wages, the use of child labor, and few (if any) benefits. In an effort to improve these conditions, workers formed unions.

Establishing unions in the early years was not easy. U.S. employers formed their own associations to destroy the employees' efforts to organize unions. Management sought the help of the courts, which tended to sympathize with employers rather than with the employees. Unions were described as "criminal conspiracies" whose goal was to hurt trade and commerce. Union members were described as communists, anarchists, and outside agitators by the courts and management.

A common technique employers used to prevent union activity was to obtain an injunction. An **injunction** is a court order that immediately stops a party from carrying out a specific action until the court has heard both sides of the issue. Although injunctions often were lifted eventually, they stopped union activities and caused the unions to use their time and money to fight legal battles. Battles were not limited to those in the courtroom. Union and management conflicts led to violence and bloodshed. Still, as the U.S. economy continued to grow in the 1800s, more and more people joined the ranks of the industrial workers. Managements' efforts to keep unions in check were matched by the efforts of an ever-increasing union membership.

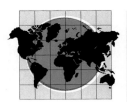

Global Business Example: The Knights of Labor

The Noble Order of the Knights of Labor was founded in 1869 as a secret organization by a group of tailors in Philadelphia. Its membership expanded to include both skilled and unskilled workers of all kinds from all over the country. The Knights of Labor supported a broad plan of reform including—the eight-hour workday, abolition of child labor, and public ownership of utilities and railways. The success of a large strike in 1885 against railroads boosted the union's membership significantly. By the late 1880s, membership had reached 800,000.

However, the Knights began losing strikes; and, other strikes were marked by violence and chaos. The very diversity of the union prevented a sense of solidarity among the members. Unable to manage the union's huge membership, leaders met with a steady stream of defeats and members began leaving the organization. By 1900 the Knights had virtually disappeared.

Labor Unions in Other Countries

In the United States, labor unions developed after laborers already had basic civil rights, such as the right to vote. Labor unions in the United States were mostly concerned with the right to bargain collectively about working conditions. European labor groups, however, were the vehicle through which workers gained freedom from feudalism, as well as various rights and powers through collective action. There is a strong sense of worker identity in these unions.

Unions in many European countries are major institutions that are often very active in national politics. For instance, in England, the Labour Party is very closely linked with labor unions. Unions provide funds to the party and help in national elections. Historically, when the Labour Party was in power, government policies were more favorable toward unions.

In Germany, unions are organized along industry lines. The unions tend to be quite wealthy and invest their money very carefully in businesses—such as banking, insurance, and housing. German unions are also actively involved in the management of businesses. By law, they have representatives on the board of directors of the companies. This policy of having union members serve on the board of directors is known as **codetermination.**

Japan suffered from great labor unrest in the late 1940s, and the 1950s brought so many strikes that industry was hampered. Today in Japan however, the relationship between unions and employers is usually cooperative in nature.

LABOR LAWS IN THE UNITED STATES

Today, U.S. workers have the legal right to join labor unions. The National Labor Relations Act (1935) gave most private sector workers the right to form unions, bargain with employers, and strike. **Collective**

bargaining is negotiation between union workers and their employers on issues of wages, benefits, and working conditions. Supervisors are considered to be agents of employers and do not have collective bargaining rights.

The use of injunctions in labor disputes has been limited since 1932. Congress has passed many laws to protect unions and to promote stable labor-management relations. State and local government employees are covered by the various state, county, and city laws. Federal government employees cannot go on strike or negotiate over wages or other money matters.

THE AFL-CIO

As mentioned earlier, labor unions were originally organized along craft lines. Workers with a particular skill formed a local or national union to represent their needs. The American Federation of Labor (AFL), formed in 1886, combined these craft unions to form a huge, national labor union—a union of labor unions, as it were.

In the 1900s, with the growth of large industries—such as automobile, rubber, and steel—some leaders of the AFL pushed to organize the ever-increasing number of mass-production workers. Indeed, workers had already begun to form unions not on the basis of their skills, but on the basis of the industry in which they worked. Thus, the workers in the automobile industry organized to form the United Auto Workers Union and steel industry workers formed the United Steel Workers Union.

Leaders of the AFL were divided on whether to allow these unskilled or semiskilled workers into the AFL. The division led to enormous tension in the country's single largest labor union. Some members of the AFL established the Committee for Industrial Organizations (CIO) in an effort to recruit members from the ranks of industrial workers. (Its name was later changed to the Congress of Industrial Organizations.) The CIO quickly gained millions of members, unionizing workers even where no unions had previously existed. In retaliation, the AFL expelled the unions and their leaders who had organized the CIO. The CIO, with its diverse union membership, became an organization completely separate from the AFL.

In 1955, the AFL and CIO merged to form the **AFL-CIO**. Today, most U.S. unions are members of this organization. Figure 13-1 on page 286 lists some of the major unions that are members of the AFL-CIO and the size of their memberships.

Unions that are strictly craft or strictly industrial are less common today. Most unions have both craft and industrial workers. In addition, unions today have a more diverse membership. Workers in a wide

Figure 13-1

Most U.S. labor unions are affiliated with the AFL-CIO.

MAJOR UNIONS AFFILIATED WITH THE AFL-CIO

Union	Membership (1991)
International Brotherhood of Teamsters	1,379,000
American Federation of State, County, & Municipal Employees (AFSCME)	1,191,000
United Food and Commercial Workers Union (UFCW)	997,000
Service Employees International Union(SEIU)	881,000
United Automobile, Aerospace, and Agriculture Workers (UAW)	840,000
International Brotherhood of Electrical Workers (IBEW)	730,000
American Federation of Teachers (AFT)	573,000
International Association of Machinists (IAM)	534,000
Carpenters Union	494,000
Communication Workers of America (CWA)	492,000
Steelworkers Union	459,000
Laborers Union	406,000

Source: *Statistical Abstract of the United States: 1992* (112th edition), U.S. Bureau of the Census, Washington, DC, 1992, p. 421.

variety of industries and occupations often belong to the same union. Teamsters Union members are an example. They range from truck drivers and chauffeurs to warehouse employees, from service station employees to workers in soft-drink plants, and from dairy workers to airline employees.

INTERNATIONAL LABOR ACTIVITIES

As mentioned earlier, unions are not confined to the United States. For example, the close economic relationship between the United States and Canada led to the formation of branches of many U.S. unions in Canada. Typically, these unions represent the workers of U.S. companies operating in Canada. Such unions call themselves international unions. In recent years, Canadian workers have begun to sever their ties with U.S. unions and to establish their own.

National unions realize that multinational companies can try to escape the unions by transferring production to other countries. Unions perceive this as a threat to the job security of their members. To prevent this, unions have tried to consult with unions in other countries and coordinate their responses to company actions.

Multinational labor activity may increase in the future as the global economy grows in complexity and interdependence. However, national labor unions are divided by differences of opinion. And, the influence of government and legislation varies significantly from country to country.

The level of economic development in a country has a strong effect on the strength and power of a union. The International Labor Organization is a specialized agency of the United Nations, with headquarters in Geneva, Switzerland. Its primary goal is to improve the conditions for workers all over the world. It has been active in establishing minimum standards of working conditions for member countries to meet.

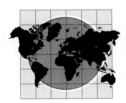

Global Business Example: Unions and Multinational Firms

In general, labor unions do not favor multinational firms. For example, if a U.S. multinational company sets up a factory in Mexico instead of in Indiana, the union views this as exporting U.S. jobs. Instead of creating jobs in the U.S., multinational firms often create jobs in other countries.

What about multinational businesses with headquarters in other countries that build factories in the United States? Unions may find it difficult to deal with these multinational firms because they are not sure where management decisions are made—in the United States or at the head office in the other country. Unions also know that striking against a foreign-based multinational company is not as effective as striking against a domestic one. A U.S.-owned company is much more likely to respond to a strike in the United States than to one staged in another country. The company probably has more invested in the U.S. plant; therefore, the local political consequences of the strike could be more damaging.

A foreign-owned company with a plant in the United States, on the other hand, could find it easier to shift production to another plant, rather than cater to striking U.S. workers. Finally, the general belief is that a firm's long-term business interests lie at home rather than abroad. The unions see this as a disadvantage to the U.S. workers in plants owned by multinationals based in other countries.

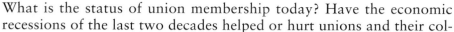
What is the status of union membership today? Have the economic recessions of the last two decades helped or hurt unions and their collective bargaining strength? What effect have the increasing strides in technology had on unionized industries?

Union membership in the United States is about 16 percent of the total workforce. In the early 1950s nearly 33 percent of the total workforce was unionized. There are many reasons for this decline in union membership. Manufacturing industries, which traditionally have been union strongholds, have become a smaller part of the economy. Today, more jobs are created in service industries—such as restaurants, banks, and hospitals—than in manufacturing. Unions have had less experience organizing in the service industries. The working conditions are much different than in factories.

The government has enacted laws that mandate minimum wage, overtime pay, safe working conditions, and equal employment opportunities for all. Therefore, there is less need to join a union today for collective bargaining with employers.

The decline in union membership is not confined to the United States. Most developed countries with economies and government policies similar to those of the United States have experienced a similar membership decline. However, compared to some countries, the level of unionization in the United States is quite low (see Figure 13-2).

ACTIVITIES OF ORGANIZED LABOR

The main purpose of a union is to improve the working conditions of its members. Before it can achieve this objective, however, it has to accomplish several steps. First, the union must win the right to represent the workers at a factory or an office.

Elections

Major unions send union organizers to workplaces to appeal to workers to become union members. Union organizers are trained and experienced in persuading workers to join a union. In other cases, workers in one location may decide they would like to join a union. In such a case, the workers themselves contact the union.

Figure 13-2

Compared to many other developed countries, the percentage of U.S. workers that belong to a union is quite small.

[1]Data are for 1989 and are adjusted to cover *employed* wage and salary union members only. Pensioners, the unemployed, and self-employed union members are excluded.

Source: Chang, Clara and Constance Sorrentino, "Union Membership Statistics in 12 Countries," *Monthly Labor Review,* December 1991, p. 50.

UNION MEMBERSHIP AS A PERCENTAGE OF THE LABOR FORCE IN 12 COUNTRIES[1]

Country	Percentage of Labor Force
Sweden	84
Denmark	75
Italy	47
United Kingdom	41
Australia	34
Germany	33
Canada	33
Netherlands	28
Switzerland	28
Japan	26
United States of America	16
France	11

Unions are always eager to organize workers to increase their membership base. Because union members pay membership dues, having more members means more resources for the union. This in turn allows the union to more effectively represent union workers and persuade new workers to join.

In most cases, the next step is to hold an election. A **representation election** is held to find out if the workers in a workplace really want to become union members. To win the right to represent workers, the union must get a simple majority of the votes cast. Once the union wins, the employer is required by law to refrain from making arrangements with individual workers. The employer must negotiate only with the union concerning issues such as workers' pay, work hours, benefits, handling of problems, and discipline.

The period before the election is often marked by intense campaigning by both the union and the employer. The union tries to persuade the workers to vote for the union. The employer tries to dissuade

Global Highlight: Unions in Great Britain

In Great Britain in 1978, a new government was formed under a new leader—Prime Minister Margaret Thatcher. She believed in a free market economy with as little government intervention, or involvement, as possible. She also thought that labor unions were preventing Great Britain from achieving economic success.

When Prime Minister Margaret Thatcher took office, more than half of the workforce were union members who were closely affiliated with a major political party, the Labour Party. In the dozen years that she governed, a series of laws designed to reduce the substantial power and influence of unions in British society were passed.

Many elements of the new laws in Britain were borrowed from the United States. Many types of strikes were outlawed, the role of union leaders was reduced, and workers were given the opportunity to stop having a union represent them or to change unions. As a result, union membership in Britain has fallen dramatically; and strikes, which were relatively commonplace, occur infrequently today.

the workers from doing so. To ensure that the election conditions are free and fair, various activities such as bribing or threatening workers are forbidden by law.

Representation

If the union wins the representation election, it obtains the right to represent *all* workers, not just those who voted for the union. However, some workers may not want to join; and, they cannot be forced to join. Because all workers will receive the benefits of union services, the union usually requires that they pay a certain fee in place of membership dues. This arrangement, in which all workers must pay either union dues or a fee, is called a **union shop.** It enables the union to obtain resources to perform its functions.

In a **closed shop,** workers are required to join a union before they are hired. Today, closed shops are generally illegal. The other extreme—an open shop—is also very rare. In an **open shop,** workers may choose to join the union or not. If not, they need not pay a fee of any kind. This arrangement is not in the best interest of the union since it may discourage workers from contributing to the union, while at the same time the union has the legal obligation to provide services to the nonmember workers.

Labor-Management Relations

Labor and management are required by law to bargain in good faith over the issues of wages, hours, and working conditions. However, they may also negotiate over any other issue, as long as it is not something illegal. For example, group health benefits or family leave allowances may be negotiated by the two parties. Collective bargaining negotiations are often complicated affairs, and it can take several months for employers and union representatives to reach an agreement.

The **grievance procedure** that is included in most collective bargaining contracts provides for a number of steps if an employee, the union, or the employer has a complaint. Discussion of complaints usually begins at the lowest level of employer management and union officials. If they are unable to settle the matter, the problem then moves up to higher levels until the two sides reach an agreement.

If the parties can't agree, an arbitrator is called in. An **arbitrator** is an unbiased third party who has no connections with either the employer or the union. The courts have agreed not to overturn or review an arbitrator's decision, so the decision of the arbitrator is generally final and binding.

While most arbitrators are usually lawyers or university professors, they may be anyone whom both the union and the employer mutually agree upon. Most arbitrators are members of the American Arbitration Association or the Federal Mediation and Conciliation Service (FMCS). The FMCS also provides services to break deadlocks or mediate disputes that arise when the union and the employer are involved in collective bargaining.

Strikes

When bargaining with employers, union leaders sometimes threaten strikes to force the employer to make the concessions union leaders want. A **strike** is a refusal by employees to work in order to force an employer to agree to certain demands. Part of the dues that members pay usually goes into a strike fund. The union then uses this money to pay striking workers, if the need arises.

Some grievance procedures include a no-strike clause, which makes it unlawful for workers to go on strike. This allows the company and the union to address a problem when it arises, but does *not* allow interruption of work. Agreeing to a no-strike clause is a big concession on the part of the union. Striking is the union's most powerful weapon against an employer. In turn, however, the employer agrees to a process to settle any complaints that arise.

Over the years, the number of strikes in the United States and the number of U.S. workers who strike have declined. Figure 13-3 shows that the number of strikes, the number of workers who actually go on strike, and the total number of workdays lost because workers are on strike have declined.

Figure 13-3

The number of strikes in the United States has declined during recent decades.

WORK STOPPAGES

Year	Strikes	Workers Involved	Days Involved	Percentage of Working Time Involved
1960	222	896,000	13,260,000	9
1965	268	999,000	15,140,000	10
1970	381	2,468,000	52,761,000	29
1975	235	965,000	17,563,000	9
1980	187	795,000	20,844,000	9
1985	54	324,000	7,079,000	3
1986	69	533,000	11,861,000	5
1987	46	174,000	4,469,000	2
1988	40	118,000	4,364,000	2
1989	51	452,000	16,996,000	7
1990	44	185,000	5,926,000	2
1991	40	392,000	4,584,000	2

Source: *Statistical Abstract of the United States: 1992* (112th edition), U.S. Bureau of the Census, Washington, D.C., 1992, p. 420.

Unit 3   Managing in a Global Environment

There are many reason for this decline in the occurrence of strikes. Some of the reasons are as follows:

- Union membership is lower.
- Strikes mean loss of income and benefits, which most workers are not willing to risk.
- Mediators help to resolve deadlocks before they turn into strikes.
- Employers have better prepared themselves for strikes by learning how to operate machines or by building up supplies in advance.
- Effectiveness of strikes has been reduced by increasing automation of the production process.
- Availability of workers who will defy the strike has increased.
- Workers' fears about losing permanent jobs as the result of a strike have increased.

Given the general decline in the effectiveness of the strike weapon, unions are resorting to techniques such as pickets, boycotts, and corporate campaigns to put pressure on employers.

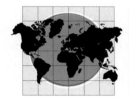

Global Business Example: International Strike Breakers

In August 1993, the workers at a brewery near Sydney, Australia, went on strike to demand job security. The brewery was owned by a New Zealand-based multinational company, Lion Nathan. Within hours of the beginning of the strike, Lion Nathan hired 50 New Zealanders and flew them to Sydney to take the jobs of the strikers. With unemployment at greater than 10 percent in New Zealand, there were many people willing to cross the Tasman Sea to work. Lion Nathan was able to hire New Zealanders and employ them in Australia with such ease because treaties between the two countries allow citizens of one country to work in the other.

Lion Nathan's conduct confirmed unions' worst fears about multinational firms. In New Zealand, itself, many people criticized the strikebreakers (that is, the 50 who went to Australia), pointing out that Australian firms in New Zealand could just as easily employ Australian strikebreakers if New Zealand workers went on strike.

Managers and Labor Unions

Generally speaking, managers would prefer to work without having to deal with labor unions. Labor unions reduce a manager's freedom to act and to make decisions. Managers must consult with the union on many issues. In addition, unions seek higher wages, better benefits, and improved working conditions for their members; therefore, the company's profits are reduced. At the same time, workers who feel secure in their jobs, who feel that their wages are fair, and who enjoy safe working conditions are more productive than workers who feel otherwise.

Employers use many techniques to keep unions out of the workplace. When wages and benefits are good and employees are treated fairly, the workers have no particular need for a union. Workers find unions attractive only when they believe they're being treated unfairly. Many employers resort to illegal activities, such as disciplining union sympathizers or threatening dismissal, to discourage workers from joining a union. In other situations, the employer may draw out the collective bargaining sessions in an attempt to discredit the union in the eyes of its members.

Employers have the right to a **lockout,** which is literally locking employees out of the workplace if they believe that the union's demands are unreasonable. A lockout is similar to the workers' right to strike.

Balancing the Needs of Workers and Business

Unions and employers have often viewed each other more as adversaries than as allies. In recent years however, there have been an increasing number of cases in which unions and employers have begun to cooperate not only to save jobs, but also to increase productivity. Employers are acknowledging that trained and experienced workers are an asset in that they can contribute to the efficient operation of the business. Unions, too, realize that their ability to demand better wages and improved working conditions depends on the overall success of the company.

Back to the Beginning: Solidarity in Poland

Reread the case at the beginning of this chapter and answer the following questions:

1. What caused the Polish workers to organize and strike?
2. What actions can workers take when they believe that their economic and political rights have been violated?
3. How did Solidarity contribute to changes in the political situation in Poland?

KNOWING GLOBAL BUSINESS TERMS

The following terms should become part of your business vocabulary. For each numbered item find the term that has the same meaning.

- AFL-CIO
- arbitrator
- closed shop
- codetermination
- collective bargaining
- grievance procedure
- injunction
- labor union
- lockout
- open shop
- representation election
- strike
- union shop

1. A neutral, third party called in to resolve problems; decision is usually final and binding.
2. A procedure in which workers vote to decide whether they want to allow a union in their workplace.
3. A court order that stops a party from continuing an activity.
4. A workplace in which nonunion members pay neither union dues nor any other fees.
5. Management situation in which union representatives are part of the board of directors of a company.
6. A series of steps included in a collective bargaining contract that are to be followed in case of disputes or complaints.
7. An association of workers whose goal is to improve their working conditions.
8. Workplace in which *only* union members can work.
9. The negotiation between an employer and a union over the terms and conditions of employment.
10. A refusal by employees to work in order to force an employer to agree to certain demands.
11. Workplace in which nonunion members must pay a fee in place of union dues.
12. The closing down of a workplace by an employer to force a union to agree to certain demands.
13. The huge labor federation of which most U.S. unions are members.

REVIEWING YOUR READING

Answer these questions to reinforce your knowledge of the main ideas of this chapter.

1. Explain how the Industrial Revolution created conditions that led to the rise of unions.
2. What is the significance of the National Labor Relations Act of 1935?

3. Why did the American Federation of Labor and the Congress of Industrial Organizations break apart?

4. Why do unions tend to prefer domestically owned and operated companies rather than multinational firms?

5. What are the differences among unions in Germany, Japan, and Great Britain?

6. Why do workers join unions?

7. What major factors are responsible for the recent decline in union membership?

8. What is the process for forming a union in a workplace?

9. What are the distinctions among union shops, closed shops, and open shops?

10. What role does the grievance procedure serve in a collective bargaining contract?

11. What are the reasons for the decline in strike activity?

12. Why is there a trend toward cooperation between employers and unions?

EXPANDING YOUR HORIZONS

You will not find the complete answers to the following questions in your textbook. You will need to use your critical-thinking skills. Think about these questions, gather information from other sources, analyze possible responses, and discuss them with others. Then, develop your own oral or written response as instructed by your teacher.

1. List reasons that workers in banking, financial services, and real estate are less likely to join a union. What do you think a union could offer that would attract these workers to join?

2. Why has it been very difficult for unions in different countries to cooperate with each other, apart from exchanging information?

3. Why are federal government and many other public employees (such as police officers and firefighters) not allowed to strike?

4. Under what conditions is a strike most likely to be successful?

5. What is the role of the AFL-CIO?

6. What reasons might a union use to persuade workers to support the union in a representation election?

7. What reasons might an employer use to persuade workers *not* to support a union in a representation election?

8. Why do you think that other developed countries have a greater percentage of workers who are union members than does the United States?

Unit 3 Managing in a Global Environment

9. What does an employer gain by having unionized workers?

10. Various U.S. laws govern labor-management relations. What government agencies administer these laws?

11. If a union and an employer fail to agree on a collective bargaining contract, what is likely to occur?

BUILDING RESEARCH SKILLS

The ability to find information from various sources is an important international business skill. The following activities will help you investigate various topics. You will also learn to apply class ideas to situations outside of the classroom.

1. Identify and contact a union member. Develop a list of questions to ask the person. In your interview, you may wish to ask how the person feels about the union and how the union affects her or his job and workplace.

2. Collect advertisements, pictures, articles, and other information used by unions to persuade consumers to buy union-made products or patronize unionized businesses. What reasons do the advertisements give for supporting those products and businesses?

3. Conduct library research about antiunion activities in the United States in the nineteenth and early twentieth centuries. Develop a list of the most common types of such activities. How do you think these activities affected the development of unions later in the twentieth century?

4. Create an opinion survey to give to your classmates. Develop five to ten questions to determine their attitudes toward unions. Would they join a union? Write a summary of the results of your survey.

5. Choose an industry (such as mining, farming, cloth weaving, or automobile manufacturing) and obtain information about its history of strikes in the United States as well as in other countries. Try to explain the differences among countries.

6. Contact a union in your community and obtain a copy of a collective bargaining agreement. Review the agreement and find out how the contract deals with grievances, union dues, seniority, leaves, and strikes. Summarize the information for your class.

7. *Global Career Activity.* Conduct library research about organized labor and union activities in another country. In what ways do labor unions benefit workers in that nation?

Continuing Enrichment Project: Planning and Preparing for Collective Bargaining Negotiations

To complete this project, refer to material in this chapter and carry out additional research to acquire the information you need. Imagine that you are the manager of a large, successful restaurant. Recently, your employees—servers, cashiers, chefs, and kitchen help—have formed a union. In two weeks you have a meeting with the union's leaders to negotiate a collective bargaining agreement. The agreement will cover wages, working conditions, and other terms of employment. Your goal is to obtain a contract that will keep the restaurant profitable and growing while meeting the demands of the employees.

You know that two of the union's terms are as follows:

- Minimum wage of $7 per hour for all employees.
- Two weeks of paid vacation for all employees (the union representatives feel that this is particularly important and have hinted that workers will strike if management does not agree to this term).

Consider your answers to the following questions. Then, prepare a summary that you might use to keep yourself on track in tomorrow's meeting.

1. Will you agree to the minimum wage? How could agreeing to a minimum wage affect your operation?
2. Might the union representatives be bluffing about striking? Can you afford to take the risk of finding out?
3. No agreement can anticipate every possible problem that may arise. What will be your suggestions for a grievance procedure?
4. If the union does not heed any of your suggestions or proposals, what options are available to you?

CHAPTER

14

Challenges to Managing Global Organizations

After studying this chapter and completing the end-of-chapter activities, you will be able to

- Identify the major groups to which multinational enterprises are accountable.

- List the five steps used to resolve issues involved in operating multinational enterprises.

- Describe three important issues that managers of multinational enterprises face.

Is the Price of Meeting U.S. Product-Approval Standards Too High?

Glaxton is a British-based multinational enterprise. It develops and markets pharmaceutical products around the world. Its scientists have recently developed a new treatment for acquired immunodeficiency syndrome (AIDS). Preliminary clinical trials of the drug in the United Kingdom and elsewhere suggest that the drug is very promising for patients with particular medical profiles who now face certain death.

Managers of Glaxton believe that all of the necessary clinical trials and paperwork for product approval in the United Kingdom and in most other countries can be completed in about two years. However, in the United States—a potential major market for the drug—the product-approval process is more complicated. The Food and Drug Administration (FDA) requires its own independent evaluation of the drug, which could take from four to seven years.

Managers of Glaxton are torn between two alternatives. One alternative is to market the potentially life-saving drug as quickly as possible, but not in the United States. The second alternative is to withhold distribution of the potentially life-saving drug until it has FDA approval and then market it aggressively throughout the world.

Who should set the standards against which the actions of multinational companies are judged, especially when those standards vary from country to country? What policies should guide the actions of multinational enterprises to ensure that they respond in a socially responsible manner? Answers to questions such as these are difficult. Multinational enterprises operate in many countries. What is appropriate, right, or legal in one country may not be appropriate, right, or legal in another. Occasionally, answers to questions about what multinational enterprises should and should not do are difficult. Managing a global organization is an ongoing challenge.

MULTINATIONAL ENTERPRISES HAVE MANY RESPONSIBILITIES

A **multinational enterprise** generally has responsibility to six groups: host countries, home country, employees, owners, customers, and society. Sometimes these responsibilities overlap. In addition, the importance of meeting those responsibilities is in the eye of the beholder. Different people believe that multinational enterprises have different degrees of responsibility to each group. Consequently, differences of opinion and conflicts can develop as multinational enterprises try to balance their responsibilities to various groups (see Figure 14-1).

Figure 14-1
Multinational enterprises try to balance their obligations to various groups.

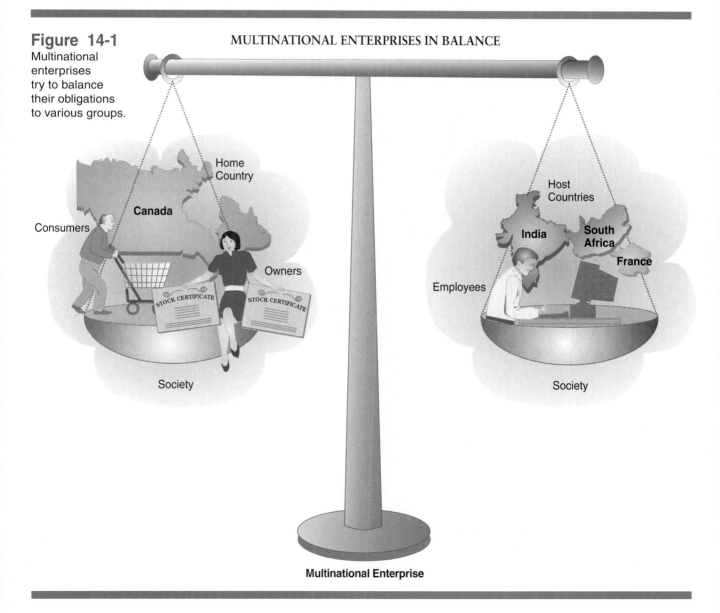

MULTINATIONAL ENTERPRISES IN BALANCE

You may have a different perception than your friend has about the degree of responsibility that a multinational enterprise has in a particular situation. However, that does not necessarily mean that one of you is right and the other is wrong. Sometimes there is no absolute answer.

Like individuals, multinational enterprises sometimes struggle when making decisions. Managers try to gather the relevant facts, weigh the evidence, and choose a course of action that is beneficial to the organization and responsible to the various groups the decision affects. Sometimes the decision satisfies all the groups; sometimes it does not. Occasionally, members of one or more groups challenge the decisions of multinational enterprises. In some instances the challenges take the form of protests and unfavorable publicity about the multinational enterprise. In more serious situations, unsatisfied group members use court cases or new regulations to counter the actions of multinational enterprises.

Multinational Enterprises Are Accountable to Their Host Countries

A **host country** is one in which a multinational enterprise is a guest. Multinational enterprises fulfill a number of positive roles in host countries while operating within existing economic, social, and legal constraints. Multinational enterprises stimulate economic activity. Whenever feasible, they purchase land, goods, and services locally. They provide employment for citizens of the host country. Often, they introduce more advanced technologies, which ultimately help the host country to develop.

Frequently, global companies train and develop natives of the host country—improving their capabilities and productivity in the process. Multinational enterprises are often responsible for creating new wealth in host countries. They do this by making more effective use of domestic and foreign resources. Thus, they help the host country to prosper, allowing residents to increase their standard of living.

In return, host countries expect multinational enterprises to comply with societal expectations and standards. They expect multinational enterprises to meet both the spirit and the letter of the laws of the land. **Social responsibility**—functioning as good citizens, sensitive to surroundings—is key to the success or failure of a multinational enterprise. For example, a multinational enterprise that pollutes the host-country's environment is not operating in a socially responsible manner. It is failing to meet societal expectations and standards regarding the environment. The multinational enterprise is harming the environment and its inhabitants.

By definition a multinational enterprise is a foreign enterprise in a host country. Its actions are often scrutinized more closely than those of domestic or local businesses. Multinational enterprises must be certain that their actions benefit the host country in acceptable ways; if that is not the case, then they can expect serious consequences. **Ethical standards** are rules that govern the acceptability of actions.

To have the right to operate within the host country, a multinational enterprise must substantially benefit the host country. The company must be able to document that it operates in full compliance with the local social and legal standards. If a multinational enterprise does not meet these conditions, then the host country may restrict or deny its right to transact business. In rare cases where the offensive actions are long-standing and serious, the host-country government might seize the assets of the multinational enterprise.

Multinational Enterprises Are Accountable to Their Home Countries

A **home country** is the one in which a multinational enterprise is headquartered. As a domestic corporation in its home country, a multinational enterprise is expected to comply fully with the home country's social, economic, and legal mandates.

The home country expects multinational enterprises based within its borders to demonstrate social responsibility. They must comply with societal expectations and standards and meet both the spirit and the letter of the laws of the home country.

Improper actions could jeopardize the right of the multinational enterprise to exist and to be headquartered in the home country. If the offensive actions are long-standing and serious, the home country could restrict or deny the multinational enterprise the rights to engage in business and to be headquartered within the country.

Multinational Enterprises Are Accountable to Their Employees

Multinational enterprises are ethically and legally bound to treat their employees in acceptable ways. The challenge is that acceptability differs from country to country. Each country has its own unique social and legal constraints. Multinational enterprises tend to have more demands from their employees in developed countries than in less-developed ones.

In general, multinational enterprises should offer as stable and as permanent employment to workers as economic conditions allow. Multinational enterprises should not take advantage of workers. They should provide employees with fair and reasonable wages. Multinational managers should regularly compensate their employees in culturally appropriate ways and provide safe working environments for employees. They should also promote the health and general welfare of employees.

If employees are not satisfied with the way they are treated by multinational enterprises, they may not be productive workers—which reduces the competitive position of the multinational enterprise. If the employees are very dissatisfied, they could participate in such disruptive activities as work slowdowns, strikes, or mass resignations. These further interfere with the ability of the multinational enterprise to operate efficiently. Thus, employees of multinational enterprises do have some power they can exercise when they believe that their employer treats them inappropriately.

Multinational Enterprises Are Accountable to Their Owners

Multinational enterprises must optimize their resources worldwide so that they provide the best possible returns to their owners. In exchange for accepting the risks of investing in multinational enterprises, the owners expect a reasonable rate of return from business activities. Most investor-owners of multinational enterprises expect them to be profitable on a consistent basis. Owners of multinational enterprises hope that the profits of the business grow year after year.

Some owners of multinational enterprises are concerned about the types of activities in which the business engages. Because they view the multinational enterprise as an extension of themselves, they are very concerned about its actions and reputation. Owners want to be sure that the multinational enterprise they own functions in an acceptable and responsible manner. They want to be proud and supportive of each action that the multinational enterprise takes. Some owner-investors choose to maintain investments only in those multinational enterprises whose actions they endorse, even though other investments might provide higher rates of return.

Owners who believe that the multinational enterprise has not fulfilled its obligations can exercise ownership rights. They can try to influence or even replace managers who have caused the multinational enterprise to act irresponsibly. In more serious situations, owner-investors can protest by selling their ownership rights. If many dissatisfied owners sell at the same time, this could depress the market value of the multinational enterprise. The image of the multinational enterprise could be tarnished in the process, and potential investor-owners might choose to invest elsewhere, depriving the multinational enterprise of needed capital. Thus, owners also have some ability to influence the actions of multinational enterprises.

Multinational Enterprises Are Accountable to Their Customers

Customers expect multinational enterprises to offer quality goods and services at competitive prices. Customers expect multinational enterprises to be stable sources of needed items. In other words, a company should not be in business one day and out the next.

Global Business Example: Paying the Price

Yolanda Griffin, an African American, strongly opposed the apartheid policies of South Africa. She believed that the long-standing racial segregation and discrimination against native Africans in South Africa was wrong, and she vowed not to support it in any way, shape, or form. Consequently, she refused to invest money in any multinational business that had operations in South Africa. She did not want to encourage or participate in what she perceived to be an exploitation of others of her same racial heritage.

Yolanda Griffin paid a price for her strong beliefs: she earned a lower rate of return on her investments. She bypassed South African investments with higher rates of return to avoid violating her principled stand against apartheid. Now that South Africa has abolished apartheid, she invests in multinational businesses that operate there. She earns a higher rate of return on her investments, and she thinks that her investments are helping to improve the lives of her brothers and sisters. Yolanda Griffin is an investor with a conscience.

Customers expect multinational enterprises to offer carefully designed goods and services that are not dangerous to the health and well-being of others. They also expect to be treated fairly and honestly on an ongoing basis. In general, customers expect multinational enterprises to operate in compliance with generally accepted business standards. They also expect multinational enterprises to meet the spirit and letter of relevant laws and otherwise to act in a socially responsible manner.

Customers who find the actions of multinational enterprises unacceptable usually respond by ending the business relationship. Often customers do not communicate the reasons for their dissatisfaction to the multinational enterprise unless they are asked to do so. Instead, they abruptly stop transacting business with the multinational enterprise.

Customers can usually end unsatisfactory business relationships if other sources of needed goods and services are available. Consequently, multinational enterprises must be very sensitive to their customers'

preferences and needs if they expect to be in business for a long time. They cannot afford to offend their customers. Once a multinational enterprise seriously offends a customer, it is difficult to restore the severed business relationship.

Multinational Enterprises Are Accountable to Their Society

The world community expects multinational enterprises to engage in legitimate business activities that benefit the groups to which the companies are accountable. By satisfying most or all of these groups, multinational enterprises can enhance the welfare of society at large.

Society prefers that multinational enterprises operate with high ethical and moral standards. It also prefers that multinational enterprises operate in full compliance with generally accepted business practices and standards. Society also prefers that multinational enterprises observe both the spirit and the letter of the laws in all of the countries in which they operate. Then, the actions of multinational enterprises are usually above question and reproach.

The high expectations of society place multinational enterprises in a difficult situation. Realistically it is very difficult—if not impossible—for businesses to operate in such a flawless fashion. Multinational enterprises are imperfect organizations operated by imperfect people in an imperfect world. These companies are involved in complex business activities in diverse countries throughout the world with different and sometimes conflicting rules of conduct. Furthermore, there is so much diversity and uncertainty that sometimes it is challenging—if not impossible—for society at large to agree on what constitutes acceptable and socially responsible behavior.

Two important issues for society at large are how multinational enterprises treat workers and the extent to which these enterprises affect the environment. Society is concerned that multinational enterprises not exploit or abuse workers. This is particularly true in less-developed countries where employment laws tend to be weak or nonexistent. For example, society is concerned that children be protected from unscrupulous employers who might subject them to unhealthy working conditions and deprive them of needed schooling.

Society is concerned that multinational enterprises not degrade the environment while conducting business. For example, the green or environmental movement, with its concern for the preservation and enhancement of natural resources—air, water, land, and wildlife—is particularly strong in several western European countries.

When society is dissatisfied with the actions of multinational enterprises, public opinion can bring pressure upon the offending enterprises. Consumers use such methods as unfavorable publicity and boycotts to cause the multinational enterprise to cease its offending actions. A **boycott** is a form of protest in which consumers regularly avoid the purchase of certain goods and/or services.

Individuals also pressure governmental units in the home or host countries to investigate or regulate the actions of the enterprise more closely. This could result in the refinement or enforcement of existing rules or in the development of new rules.

In response to the perception that multinational enterprises operate beyond the law, some governments have adopted policies that give countries more control over the operations of multinational enterprises. Some countries require citizens of the host country to have majority ownership in the multinational enterprise. Some place restrictions on the types of activities in which multinational enterprises can participate. The Foreign Corrupt Practices Act, for example, prohibits U.S.-based multinational companies from paying bribes abroad, even though they are expected and legal in certain countries. Other restrictions limit the use of **expatriate employees**—people who work and live outside of their native countries.

In extreme cases, governments have seized the assets of multinational enterprises that were perceived to be operating in ways that were not in the best interests of society. All of these responses are means that societies use to get some degree of control over multinational enterprises.

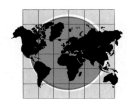

Global Business Example: Courts Help Multinational Enterprises Determine Acceptable Business Activities

A multinational enterprise is a legal entity that must behave in legitimate and socially responsible ways. It must comply with the social and legal constraints within the countries in which it operates. A multinational enterprise operating in the United States, for example, must comply with the country's antitrust laws, labor laws, pollution-control laws, and countless other legal requirements. Since provisions of these laws are occasionally vague and subject to individual interpretation, multinational enterprises sometimes find themselves involved in court cases. Courts help to clarify what multinational enterprises can and cannot do. Court rulings set legal precedents that serve as guidelines for acceptable behaviors by multinational enterprises.

For example, Sterling Winthrop, Inc., the U.S.-based manufacturer of BAYER® aspirin, sued the German-based Bayer AG for infringement on the former's BAYER® trademark and name. In 1994, the United States Court of Appeals for the Second District affirmed a lower court decision that Bayer AG had violated the trademark rights of Sterling Winthrop, Inc., and had breached its contracts with Sterling Winthrop, Inc., by placing advertisements in prominent magazines. The court ruling reaffirmed the right of Sterling Winthrop, Inc., to protect its valued BAYER® name, its goodwill, and its reputation from wrongful uses by Bayer AG.

MANAGERS OF MULTINATIONAL ENTERPRISES FACE MANY ISSUES

Issues are controversial matters for which there may be no final answers. Issues have two or more positions or viewpoints, and creditable evidence can be gathered to support each of the positions. In other words, issues are matters about which people may reasonably disagree.

Diversity in the Global Environment Creates Issues

Managers of multinational enterprises face many issues as they operate in the global marketplace. Because multinational enterprises are legal entities operating in culturally diverse countries, their managers are sometimes in a quandary. The managers have difficulty deciding what course of action is best for the multinational enterprise. Trying to please all of the groups to whom multinational enterprises are responsible is challenging—if not impossible. What one group perceives as beneficial may be perceived as detrimental by others. What is legal in one country of operation may not be legal in another. A major challenge facing managers of multinational enterprises is deciding how to balance their various and sometimes conflicting obligations.

Resolving Issues Using a Scientific Approach

Managers often can resolve the difficult issues they face if they apply a systematic problem-solving approach. That approach should be rooted in the five-step scientific method. Figure 14-2 identifies the major steps to follow to resolve an issue.

First, managers need to identify the issue. In the complex world of international business, defining the real issue can be challenging. Sometimes, it is overshadowed by other factors that confuse the matter. Or, it is so complex that it is difficult to identify. Further, the issue can be difficult to express concisely and precisely in words.

Second, managers need to gather the relevant facts. Determining which facts are relevant is easier if the issue is precisely defined. Managers must be careful to gather only necessary facts. They must screen out irrelevant facts. They must also be sure that they gather *only* facts. Inaccurate information and inferences, suppositions based on assumptions, sometimes masquerade as facts. Using such inappropriate information can result in poor decision making.

Third, managers need to determine possible alternatives. Given the relevant facts, managers should determine all possible courses of action. They should do so without prior ideas about how the issue should be resolved. This helps to ensure that all possible alternatives are given fair and equal consideration.

Fourth, managers need to analyze the possible alternatives. As managers carefully weigh the advantages and disadvantages of each alterna-

308   *Unit 3 Managing in a Global Environment*

Figure 14-2

Many issues can be resolved by using the five-step problem-solving approach.

PROBLEM-SOLVING APPROACH

1. Identify the issue
2. Gather the relevant facts
3. Determine the alternatives
4. Analyze the alternatives
5. Select the best alternative

tive, they need to do so in an unbiased manner. Managers should realize that they cannot please all of the groups to whom multinational enterprises have responsibilities all of the time. Nevertheless, they should try to satisfy as many groups as they can as they balance their obligations.

Fifth, managers need to select the best alternative and to implement it carefully. Managers must make difficult choices after careful analysis. In other words, they must make trade-offs by balancing one alternative against another. Companies must learn to live with the consequences of the choice that is made. Managers must also ensure that the chosen alternative is implemented in the best possible manner.

Managers of multinational enterprises must operate very carefully around the world. They must take actions that are carefully thought out, prudently implemented, and publicly explained. Managers of multinational enterprises need to realize the importance of communicating the reasons for their actions to those groups to which multinational enterprises have responsibilities.

Global Business Exercise: Resolving the European Fizz Biz

Part I

French wine companies blew their corks when they learned that Thorncroft Vineyards of the United Kingdom was marketing its sparkling

elderflower drink as "champagne." The French companies were concerned about maintaining the reputation of the distinctive French product from grapes grown in the Champagne region of France. Thorncroft uses the spelling "sham'pagne" on its non-alcoholic brew, making it the only non-French "champagne" marketed in Europe.

1. What is the issue?
2. What are some of the relevant facts from the British and French perspectives?
3. What are the alternative courses of action?
4. What are the arguments for and against each alternative?

Part II

French wine companies challenged the right of Thorncroft Vineyards to label its product as "champagne." The British High Court ruled that the use of the word *sham'pagne* on the nonalcoholic beverage caused little or no damage to the reputation of the alcoholic beverage named *champagne*.

1. Do you think that the managers of Thorncroft Vineyards made a good business decision when they used a play on words to name their elderflower product? Why or why not?
2. Do you think that Thorncroft Vineyards acted ethically when it named its elderflower product? Why or why not?

MANAGERS FACE COMPLEX ISSUES

Managers of multinational enterprises must address a wide variety of complex issues when transacting business in the global marketplace. They must accept the fact that practically anything they do can and will be questioned from one or more perspectives.

The remainder of this chapter describes several challenging issues that face managers of multinational enterprises. It briefly identifies selected, closely related issues facing managers of multinational enterprises; however, it does not attempt to resolve the issues. Instead, the reader must weigh the facts related to the possible alternatives and arrive at a personal position—much as managers must do in the real world. The reader should be ready, if necessary, to defend the chosen position to people who have come to a different conclusion.

What Roles Should Multinational Enterprises Fulfill Within a Country?

The roles that multinational enterprises should fulfill within a country are sometimes controversial. One concern is how dominant the multinational enterprise should be within a particular country. A multinational enterprise can be criticized, particularly by natives, because it is too influential. This is particularly true in developing countries, where other businesses are not so powerful.

Another concern is the extent of operations that the multinational enterprise conducts within the country. Should the multinational enterprise attempt to be an economic giant within the country? What basis does the multinational enterprise use to determine the extent of its investment in the country? Does the investment in that country

Global Highlight: The Rise and Fall of the Hanseatic League

The Hanseatic League was a medieval confederation of German cities and settlements located in northern Europe around and near the Baltic and North seas. This group was organized to protect the commercial interests of *hanse* or *hansa,* guilds or associations of merchants.

The Hanseatic League administered the common affairs of its members and established permanent trading posts. The trading posts had exclusive rights to sell products from the Baltic area. The Hanseatic League also regulated the foreign trade of its members. At its maturity the Hanseatic League brought about an integrated economic region that included northern and northwestern Europe. Such products as Polish grain, Russian timber, and Swedish copper traveled westward, while such products as Flemish and English cloth traveled eastward. Such products as Norwegian herring traveled southward, while such products as German salt traveled northward.

Since the Hanseatic League was a mercantile—not a political—organization, it had no written constitution, capital, or formal leader. When problems developed, a congress of representatives from some, but usually not all, of the involved cities met at whatever location was convenient. By excluding members from profitable monopolies, the Hanseatic League exerted control. It maintained and expanded its power by placing embargoes on uncooperative ports and by excluding them from Baltic trade. Through strict enforcement of trading privileges, the Hanseatic League grew in power and wealth.

From the fifteenth century onward, the Hanseatic League declined with the emergence of strong states along the Baltic Sea and the Atlantic Ocean and with the gradual shift of trade to the west and to the south. The European discovery of other continents and trade routes to the Orient further contributed to the demise of the Hanseatic League.

represent the best possible use of the owners' capital, the one that will yield the highest long-term rate of return?

A further concern is the extent to which the multinational enterprise should employ natives of the country. Should a multinational enterprise be a dominant source of employment within a country? If so, it can be criticized when employment must be reduced. The company can also be criticized if it employs too many foreigners and too few natives.

An additional concern involves the amount of education and training the multinational enterprise provides for natives of the country. Should it invest significant amounts of scarce capital in developing the local workforce? While training and development will enhance the capabilities and productivity of local employees, could the multinational enterprises invest those training-and-development resources elsewhere for a better return on investment?

Another aspect is the extent to which a multinational enterprise should be a change agent. Should a multinational enterprise, especially one headquartered in another country, be allowed to initiate economic and social change? If so, to what degree? What technologies should multinational enterprises be allowed to introduce? If a multinational enterprise uses labor-saving advanced technology, it might eliminate some jobs that would have been available had less advanced technology been used. If a multinational enterprise uses less-advanced methods, then it deprives workers and the country of modern technology.

What Products and Services Should Be Marketed?

Determining what products and services a multinational enterprise should market is sometimes controversial. Should universal or standardized products and services be offered? Because of economies of scale, most multinational enterprises try to standardize their products and services as much as possible.

Realistically speaking, it is not economically justifiable to adapt every good and service to every culture worldwide. From the perspective of a multinational enterprise, it is advantageous to market the closest thing possible to universal goods and services. Consumers, however, may prefer and sometimes will demand to purchase goods and services that are tailored to their specific culturally determined standards. How should a multinational enterprise balance the opposing preferences for standardized and unique goods and services with the need to produce universal products?

Another global business issue is deciding whose standard to follow when developing goods and services. Multinational enterprises find that for most goods and services no universal or even regional standards exist outside those of the European Union. Since local standards do not provide a market large enough to benefit from economies of scale, that leaves country standards. Should a multinational enterprise adopt the standards of the home country? the major host country? another country? How should the multinational enterprise respond if various country-specific standards are contradictory and irreconcilable?

For example, all major countries of the world except the United States use the metric system and metric product specifications. Multinational enterprises that refuse to accommodate the wishes of consumers in the United States risk losing a major market segment. Likewise, U.S.-based multinational enterprises risk losing international business if they do not accommodate consumers elsewhere who expect and demand the metric standard.

Who Should Regulate Multinational Enterprises and to What Degree?

Determining the scope and source of international business regulations is also controversial. People in general, and politicians in particular, are concerned that as trade becomes more internationalized and liberalized, they will lose their ability to control it. Political leaders are also beginning to realize that trade-related problems are very difficult to address in the global marketplace. Linkages and interdependencies among trading countries are often extensive. What benefits one country may jeopardize other countries. Countries may be affected economically, politically, militarily, and/or culturally. Sometimes, there are unanticipated consequences because of overlooked relationships.

For example, to protect U.S.-based multinational car manufacturers, the U.S. government could restrict or ban the import of cars made in other countries, such as Japan. However, Japanese cars can have components that are made in other countries, which would also be hurt by the restrictions. All of these countries could respond by restricting or banning some or all imports from the United States, straining at least economic and political relationships in the process.

Regulation of multinational enterprises is controversial. Should multinational enterprises be self-regulated? Can multinational enterprises be trusted to judge when their actions cross beyond the point of acceptability and to take necessary corrective action on their own? Whose standards would multinational enterprises use when assessing the need for corrective action? If outsiders should regulate multinational enterprises, which outsiders should do so? Should regulations on multinational enterprises be imposed by the host country? home country? employees? owners? society? some of the preceding groups? all of the preceding groups?

How should disputes between multinational enterprises and other groups be resolved? If multinational enterprises operate in key sectors of an economy, then there is the possibility that they can effectively counter governmental policies. For example, a dominant multinational enterprise may want to pay workers low wages, which could conflict with the desire of the government to improve the standard of living of its citizens. While a multinational enterprise seeks to optimize globally, the government of a country seeks to optimize locally. Who resolves such disputes, and whose standards are used?

Global Business Exercise: Caught in the Middle

Acme International, Ltd., a multinational enterprise, operates mining ventures in a number of less-developed countries. Operations in one of the countries have been very successful. Profits for the past five years amounted to the equivalent of $43.7 million, a sizable sum when compared to the gross national product of the country. The managers of Acme are torn between two options: transferring the accumulated profits out of the host country or investing the accumulated profits in the host country.

1. What charges might critics of Acme raise if it transfers the accumulated profits out of the host country?
2. What charges might critics of Acme raise if it invests the accumulated profits in the host country?
3. What course of action do you think Acme might take to minimize the criticism about how it disposes of the accumulated profits? Why?

Back to the Beginning: Is the Price of Meeting U.S. Product-Approval Standards Too High?

Reread the case at the beginning of this chapter and answer the following questions:

1. What is the home country of the multinational enterprise that developed the promising drug?
2. Does the home country or the United States have a more complicated drug-approval system?
3. Give some reasons why Glaxton might market the drug outside of the United States as soon as possible?

4. Give some reasons why Glaxton might withhold the drug until it can legally be sold in the United States.

5. If you were a manager of Glaxton, which of the two alternatives would you choose? Why?

KNOWING GLOBAL BUSINESS TERMS

The following terms should become part of your business vocabulary. For each numbered item find the term that has the same meaning.

- boycott
- ethical standards
- expatriate employees
- home country
- host country
- issues
- multinational enterprise
- social responsibility

1. Controversial matters for which there may be no final answers.
2. The country in which a multinational enterprise is headquartered.
3. Functioning as good citizens, sensitive to the surroundings.
4. The country in which a multinational enterprise is a guest.
5. Regularly avoiding the purchase of certain goods and/or services as a form of protest.
6. People who work and live outside of their native country.
7. A business that operates in multiple countries.
8. Rules that govern the acceptability of actions.

REVIEWING YOUR READING

Answer these questions to reinforce your knowledge of the main ideas of this chapter.

1. Identify and briefly define the groups to which multinational enterprises are accountable.
2. How is each of the groups to which multinational enterprises are accountable able to control the actions of multinational enterprises?
3. How can the courts help multinational enterprises?
4. What is an issue?
5. What are the five steps to resolving issues and what happens during each step?
6. What are major issues facing international enterprises?

Chapter 14   Challenges to Managing Global Organizations

EXPANDING YOUR HORIZONS

You will not find the complete answers to the following questions in your textbook. You will need to use your critical-thinking skills. Think about these questions, gather information from other sources, analyze possible responses, and discuss them with others. Then, develop your own oral or written response as instructed by your teacher.

1. If a pharmaceutical company sells the same medicine in a number of different countries, do you think the company should charge the same price in each country? Why or why not? Would you have a different opinion if you lived in Ethiopia? Why or why not?

2. If a country expropriates the assets of a multinational enterprise that does not demonstrate socially responsible behaviors on a continuing basis, how might this action hurt the country?

3. Should a government assess fines or penalties against a multinational company when it unintentionally pollutes the water because of a mechanical malfunction or human error? What are the arguments for and against fining unintentional polluters?

4. Should a multinational enterprise be able to cease its operations within the borders of one developing country and move elsewhere if another developing country can supply the needed resources at a lower price? What would be your response if you were

   (1) an owner of stock in the multinational enterprise?

   (2) a native employee in the country that supplies the needed resources at the higher cost?

   (3) a potential employee in the country that can supply the needed resources at the lower cost?

5. A foreign-based multinational enterprise offers you one free coach airplane ticket to any destination in the world if you buy $200 worth of its products within the next 30 days. Common sense tells you that the offer is too good to be true and that there must be some catch. What action, if any, should you take? Why?

6. Multinational enterprises are responsible to a variety of groups whose demands sometimes overlap. What does this statement mean? Give an example of overlapping groups.

BUILDING RESEARCH SKILLS

The ability to find information from various sources is an important international business skill. The following activities will help you investigate various topics. You will also learn to apply class ideas to situations outside of the classroom.

1. Using library resources, find an article that discusses the general topic of the social responsibilities of businesses. Prepare a one-page summary of the main ideas contained in the article. Then prepare a one-page critique of the article that points out its strengths and weaknesses. Do you agree or disagree with the ideas in the article? Why?

2. Using library resources, investigate the role of the Food and Drug Administration in the United States. Do you think that the Food and Drug Administration exercises too much control, about the right amount of control, or too little control over the business community in its attempt to safeguard the welfare of citizens?

3. Using historical and business library resources, uncover the facts surrounding the origin of the business-related word *boycott*. (Your search might begin with Charles C. Boycott, an English estate manager in Ireland in the 1800s.) Write a one-page report that summarizes the relevant information.

4. Using library resources, investigate the Sullivan Code for multinational enterprises operating in South Africa. Since conditions in South Africa have improved since the mid-1990s, this voluntary code is no longer in effect. Nevertheless, it illustrates one approach to regulating the actions of multinational enterprises. After studying the Sullivan Code and its effectiveness, debate the following matter with your classmates: Resolved that the actions of multinational enterprises can be sufficiently regulated by voluntary codes of conduct.

5. *Global Career Activity.* Prepare a short report about the career opportunities and potential difficulties that managers face when working for a multinational company.

Continuing Enrichment Project: A Code of Conduct for Multinational Enterprises

Assume that you are a manager of a U.S.-based multinational enterprise that has extensive operations throughout Europe. Develop a code of conduct to help guide the actions of your organization as it conducts business in various countries. The purpose of the code is to ensure that your organization meets its obligations to its host countries, home country, employees, owners, customers, and society at large. Present the code of conduct in the form of a listing of things to do and not to do.

Information and Production Systems for Global Business

Information Needs for Global Business Activities

After studying this chapter and completing the end-of-chapter activities, you will be able to

- Explain how a management information system (MIS) is used to improve decision making.

- Describe the uses of technology in providing information for global business activities.

- Identify three types of computer networks used for managing information.

- Describe the emerging technologies of artificial intelligence and expert systems.

- Provide sources of assistance for international business.

Thank Heaven for 7-Eleven—Japan!

In 1991, Japanese businesspeople bought into the Texas-based Southland Corporation and made 7-Eleven Japan an "informational miracle." At the center of a typical Japanese 7-Eleven store, which is about half the size of the U.S. version, is a powerful personal computer. Designed for 7-Eleven's needs, the computer is connected to each store's point-of-sale cash register. Data such as customer information, inventory, and time of sale are gathered with every purchase. For example, according to data collected at one 7-Eleven store, male customers who shop between 7 P.M. and 9 P.M. show a high demand for rice dishes. And school children deplete the potato chip stock every day after school.

The store uses these data to develop accurate customer profiles. These profiles enable the stores to tailor their inventory to customers' needs. The computer's automated inventory system allows clerks to order inventory items in a timely and efficient manner. The data collected are summarized in easy-to-read graphs that identify the items that should be ordered and when they should be ordered. The computer also controls the store's refrigerators and air-conditioning! All of this store information is available to corporate management via 7-Eleven's computer network.

To make ordering inventory items even easier, 7-Eleven Japan's vendors have access to 7-Eleven's computer system. Delica Ace, the company

that prepares the rice dishes for Tokyo's 7-Eleven stores, is one such vendor. The Delica Ace factory receives its rice dish order electronically each day at 10:30 A.M. Electronic ordering allows Delica Ace to prepare the right amount of fresh food at just the right time.

By automating information on sales, inventories, and customers, 7-Eleven Japan has increased daily sales by 30 percent over Family Mart, its closest competitor. The next step is to import 7-Eleven Japan's technology to the more than 5,000 stores in the United States.

Managers need organized, continuous, accessible, and timely information to make business decisions in the global market. In an age of information overload, the challenge is to gather information from reliable, current sources and to incorporate the powerful analytical capabilities of technology into the decision-making process.

MANAGEMENT INFORMATION SYSTEMS

Data are facts—expressed as numbers, symbols, or words—that are used as the basis for reasoning, discussion, or calculation. But data alone do not necessarily aid in decision making. **Information** is data that have been processed and organized into a usable format.

A **management information system (MIS)** is a computer-based system that delivers information to all levels of management in a company. The electronic systems automate gathering, processing, storing, and distributing information. The information that flows through an MIS should improve the company's productivity, as well as management's decision-making abilities.

As shown in the case of 7-Eleven Japan, the corporate-based computer electronically gathers the orders from each store. Those data are then stored, processed, and sent to the vendors who fill the individual orders. Data move efficiently through the system to bring about a productive response. For 7-Eleven, that response is putting products on store shelves to meet customer needs.

Figure 15-1 shows a typical management information system. For a management information system to be useful, data must be analyzed carefully and thoughtfully.

External Data Sources

The data processed in an MIS can originate from a variety of sources. Those sources outside an organization that provide input are called **external data sources**. Banks, consultants, industry associations, and customers are examples of external data sources.

Data that enter an MIS take many forms—including electronic bulletin boards, statistical reports, census figures, account balances, and rough-draft correspondence. In today's global business community, external sources of data and information include import and export regulations, telecommunications documents, business analysis reports, annual reports, demographics, and international news reports on current events and economic conditions.

Figure 15-1

A management information system (MIS) consists of set procedures to gather, analyze, store, and output information that will aid in management decision making.

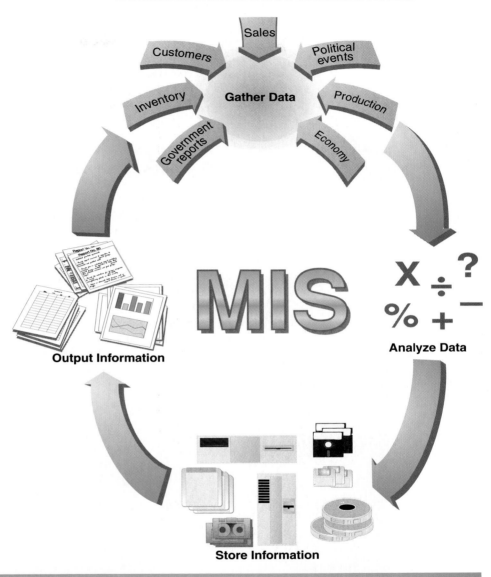

A TYPICAL MANAGEMENT INFORMATION SYSTEM

Internal Data Sources

Internal data sources are those sources that provide input from within an organization. Examples of internal data sources include market analyses, research reports, accounting records, customer orders, and company sales figures. Analyzing internal company information is essential for acquiring resources, providing services or products, and setting goals.

Decision Support Systems

Many MIS departments are beginning to include another level of decision-making analysis—decision support systems. A **decision support system,** or DSS, is a computer-based system that helps companies make decisions by summarizing and comparing data from internal and external sources. Managers can use a DSS to solve hypothetical problems and forecast sales. A DSS usually provides the following functions: statistical analysis, spreadsheets, graphics, and modeling.

Global Business Exercise: Blockbuster Entertainment

Renting movies on videotape is a commonplace activity for many people in the United States. Just ask any executive from Blockbuster Entertainment Corporation. Since 1986, this video rental company has grown steadily and it has about 1,000 stores thriving *outside of* the United States.

What makes Blockbuster so successful? One answer is the company's national inventory system. Another reason is its sophisticated information system. This system tracks each store's inventory and provides managers with customized purchasing data—information that helps them pinpoint the movies that will rent well in their own markets.

As Blockbuster expands its retail operations outside of the United States, it is extending its information system to a global operation. To date, Blockbuster has been successful in running its system in English, Spanish, and Japanese; French is next. One challenge has been to overcome the incompatible communications systems in different countries. For example, when Blockbuster expanded in Latin America, one of its biggest frustrations was the lack of sophisticated telephone systems. Moving information from stores to the information system proved to be very difficult.

In looking at its global marketing future, Blockbuster has determined that it will venture into combining music, video, and family entertainment. Trying to stay ahead of rapidly changing technology while diversifying will pose a challenge for the information system, as well as for management.

1. What internal data sources might Blockbuster executives use to help them diversify the video rental chain's services?
2. What external data sources might they use to help them diversify successfully?
3. How could Blockbuster benefit from a decision support system?

TECHNOLOGY IN THE GLOBAL INFORMATION SYSTEM

Reengineering is the process of tearing down and rebuilding old structures. This term refers to the organizational overhaul taking place in business worldwide. Corporate management structures are being reshaped and redefined. Vital to the reengineering of a global management system is advanced information technology.

Technology Is Constantly Changing

The new information technologies used in the reengineering process include items such as desktop computers, laptops, modems, wireless networks, handheld computers, remote and mobile computers, cellular telephones, car fax machines, electronic mail, and videoconferencing. Companies increase their productivity by billing vendors electronically through their telecommunications, for example. In return, the vendors may send payments electronically via modem.

Another step in the reengineering of management information is the decentralization of work. Many companies are "farming out," or subcontracting, routine work to facilitate production. For example: banks are sending out check-processing jobs to specialty firms; customer service phone calls are processed through an automated voice mail system. The next big step for financial institutions is to reduce the number of paper documents stored. By using image processing, companies can record documents digitally and save materials on disks or CDs.

Cultural and Social Norms Affect Technological Advances

A roadblock to technological advancement for international businesses is the effect of cultural and social norms. In Germany, for example, people who work in skilled trades, such as woodworking, take particular pride in their handiwork. Because craft workers have been schooled in the manual trades for generations, automated manufacturing causes a cultural problem. Additionally, the consumer is accustomed to the finer handwork.

In Italy, strong union membership has caused delays in the acceptance of technology. As auto, steel, and machine-tool makers begin to lose their jobs to automation, the fear and reality of unemployment emerges. Reengineering in this case means investing in training the displaced workers.

International businesses might also experience problems in communication because of differences between countries, such as languages and time zones. Companies wanting to establish international links may want to follow the example of the Seer Technology Company. Seer set up European sites called "solution centers" to handle European customer inquiries. European users of Seer's software are able to talk with a technical expert who speaks their language and who is located in their time zone. For most businesses, however, language and time zone differences still make international communication difficult.

The Pacific Rim countries face perhaps some of the biggest cultural and social changes related to technology. Reengineering in Japan requires changing basic aspects of the country's business environment and culture.[1] Japanese corporations belong to *keiretsus*. A *keiretsu* is a large corporation consisting of hundreds of separate companies that are interconnected in all their business dealings. The companies help each other stay competitive with foreign companies by sharing technology and assets. This type of corporation cannot exist in the United States because it violates U.S. antitrust laws. Because the Japanese *keiretsu* has long been a part of Japanese culture, reengineering of Japanese businesses, if it happens, will be a lengthy process.

---

[1] *Business Week,* "The Technology Payoff," June 14, 1993, p. 61.

Global Business Example: Communications Russian Style

The collapse of the Soviet Union's political, economic, and financial structures opened the door for many multinational enterprises. Companies such as AT&T, United Technologies, IBM, Hewlett-Packard, Corning, General Atomics, and Sun Microsystems have successfully developed facilities in the former Soviet Union.

Sun Microsystems had a large pool of jobless scientists, mathematicians, and computer programmers from which to choose when it first established labs in Russia. Sun tailored the projects it developed to the specific talents of the Russian employees. The company could, therefore, streamline its lab operations and produce efficiently. For example, because Russian computer scientists are experts at writing software that increases the speed with which the computer's hardware runs, Sun is concentrating its work in Russia on producing such software.

There *have* been some cross-cultural communication difficulties, however. Projects that involve exporting must be approved by the Coordinating Committee on Multilateral Export Controls (COCOM). Employees in Sun's California office cannot communicate with their Russian counterparts until they receive permission from the COCOM. Receiving permission can take up to two months!

Source: *The Wall Street Journal,* "Sun Microsystems to Fund Russians in Software Project," September 1, 1992.

COMPUTER NETWORKS

Computer networking is an important aspect of today's technology. Simply stated, a **computer network** is a collection of individual computers that are connected by communication channels, such as telephone lines, and that share data and information. There are three classifications of networks: local area networks, wide area networks, and storage access networks.

Local Area Networks (LANs)

A **local area network (LAN)** is designed for a limited area, such as an office, a building, or several departments within a company. A LAN connects a series of computers and peripheral equipment—printers and so on—with a continuous wire (see Figure 15-2 on page 328). Typically, at each end of the wire is a file server. A **file server** is a computer that houses the software and data that all computers on the LAN share.

Figure 15-2

A local area network is appropriate for a set of devices that can be wired together at one location.

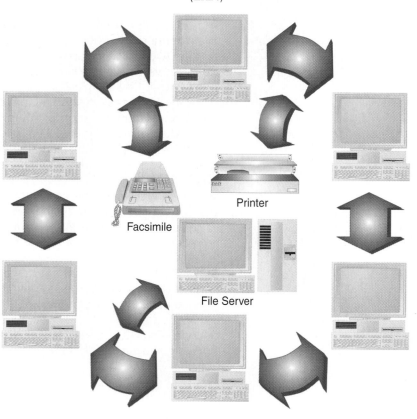

LOCAL AREA NETWORK
(LAN)

Printer

Facsimile

File Server

Wide Area Networks (WANs)

Wide area networks (WANs) are designed for businesses that communicate across a large geographic area such as a city, state, or country (see Figure 15-3). Communication channels used in WANs are telephone lines, satellites, microwaves, or a combination of carriers.

Storage Access Networks (SANs)

A **storage access network (SAN)** can work in connection with a LAN. The SAN does the read/write tasks for the file server and stores the data. SAN architecture is flexible and can work with a variety of drives, operating systems, and software.

Figure 15-3

A wide area network can connect computer systems at various geographic locations.

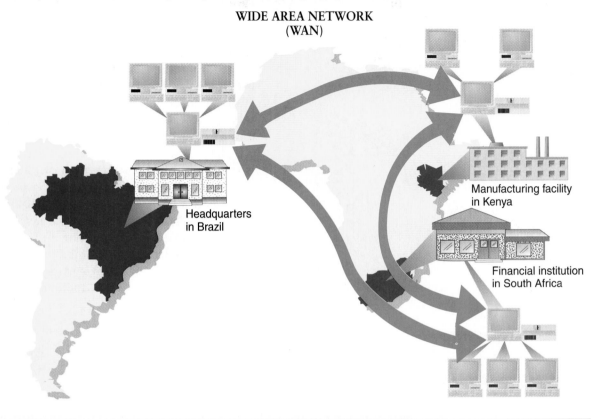

WIDE AREA NETWORK
(WAN)

Headquarters
in Brazil

Manufacturing facility
in Kenya

Financial institution
in South Africa

ARTIFICIAL INTELLIGENCE AND EXPERT SYSTEMS

Much research is being done in two new areas of information technology: artificial intelligence and expert systems. Business and industry are beginning to apply these technologies to the production of goods and services.

Artificial intelligence (AI) is a branch of computer science that deals with designing computer systems to perform tasks that seem to require human intelligence. These tasks include deduction and learning from past experience. Many interpret artificial intelligence as the computer's ability to "think." Computers with AI are programmed with software that gives them the capacity to analyze, compare and contrast, and make logical recommendations.

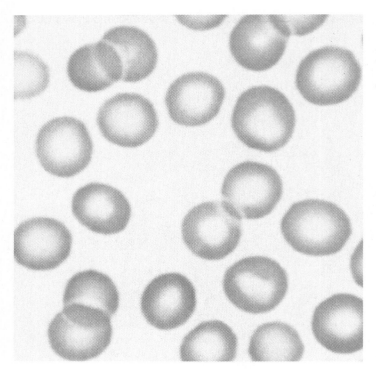

Some software systems using artificial intelligence are called expert systems. An **expert system** compares information from the past to information from a current situation. An expert system uses a knowledge base and inference rules as a basis for reaching conclusions. A **knowledge base** is the information on a specific subject that has been provided by human experts—the historical data on the subject. **Inference rules** are the processes of taking the knowledge base and comparing it to new circumstances.

One example of a rule-based expert system is the MYCIN program, which physicians may consult for advice on treatment of some bacterial infections of the blood. MYCIN deduces which type of infection a person has, based on rules derived from the field of medicine and a list of the patient's symptoms. Next, it recommends specific treatment—usually providing several alternatives for the doctor's review.

SOURCES OF ASSISTANCE FOR INTERNATIONAL BUSINESS

In addition to being aware of the latest advances in information technology, companies involved in global business must gather the information that will be input into the MIS. Information on international business procedures is available from several government and private sources.

Federal Government Agencies

The International Trade Administration (ITA), a division of the U.S. Department of Commerce, is the federal government's main agency for promoting exports. The activities of the ITA include programs and services to help companies start and expand export operations. The agency is also actively involved in creating the international trade policies of the United States.

Another federal agency that encourages export activities is the Small Business Administration (SBA). It provides smaller companies with loans to manufacture products for exporting as well as information on international business procedures.

The Export-Import Bank of the United States helps to finance exporting of goods and services produced by United States companies. Over the years, this federal government agency has used loans, loan guarantees, and insurance programs to promote more than $200 billion in exports.

The Foreign Agricultural Services (FAS) of the U.S. Department of Agriculture (USDA) offers global business assistance to the farm industry. Exportation of crops and food products is an important part of the U.S. economy, accounting for more than $40 billion a year in the early 1990s.

The main purpose of the U.S. Department of State is to promote positive political relations with other countries. This agency is, therefore, a source for social, cultural, and political information about other countries. The State Department publishes a series of reports on living standards, religious customs, and political trends in countries around the world.

International Trade Agencies

The United Nations (UN), an international organization that promotes cooperation among countries, is actively involved in global business. Economic development of less-developed countries is a major concern of the UN. The UN also assists businesses in obtaining loans, sets safety standards for products sold internationally, regulates international telecommunications, and promotes cooperation among postal services in different countries. Economic and political information about the nations of the world is also available from the United Nations.

The International Monetary Fund and the World Bank provide loans, financial advice, and other assistance to businesses in order to stimulate global business activities and create international economic stability.

Global Highlight: Croatia

Hostility has existed for many years between the Croats and the Serbs, the two main ethnic groups of the former Yugoslavian republic of Croatia. Croats, most of whom are Roman Catholic, make up 75 percent of Croatia's population. Serbs, who are members of the Serbian Orthodox Church, make up 12 percent of Croatia's population.

In June 1991, the hostility erupted into violence. Croats, complaining that the Yugoslavian federal government took too large a portion of their income, had been calling for complete independence for decades. They also believed that Serbia tried to control the whole country. The Serbian minority, dedicated to preserving a unified Yugoslavia, joined with the Yugoslav National Army to fight the Croats. By early 1992, the fighting ended. Croatia lost about one third of its territory, and about 40 percent of its industrial base was destroyed. Damage from the war is estimated at about $18 billion, which is almost twice Croatia's annual gross domestic product (GDP).

Croatians are now trying to rebuild. Before the violence erupted, their country's economy thrived on tourism, lumber, textiles, and petroleum industries. Now, Croatia is making an effort to assume a greater role in the international computer market. Croatian programmers are working to design specialty software to sell to U.S. and European software companies. Croatia is also developing new regulations to encourage foreign investment.

Foreign Government Agencies

A **consulate** is an office located in a foreign country that represents the home country and serves the interests and businesses of citizens of the country it represents. Many countries have consulates in large cities throughout the world.

Countries also establish trade offices in other nations to encourage international business. For example, the European Community has a trade office in Washington, D.C., to contact potential buyers and sellers in the United States.

International Business Organizations

The International Chamber of Commerce (ICC) is a private organization that serves companies involved in global business. The ICC has offices in more than 100 countries. It publishes materials to assist exporters with various international business procedures. ICC publications include information on terms of sale, shipping risks and costs, contracts, collection procedures, and transport documents.

The World Trade Center, located in New York City, has more than 200 branches in over 60 countries, including most large cities in the United States. This nonprofit organization works to bring together international buyers and sellers of goods and services. The World Trade Center in Chattanooga, for example, links exporting companies in Tennessee to potential customers throughout the world.

Back to the Beginning: Thank Heaven for 7-Eleven—Japan!

Reread the case at the beginning of this chapter and answer the following questions:

1. What information can store managers receive from their point-of-sale computers?

2. What are some advantages and disadvantages of using 7-Eleven's computer system for 7-Eleven suppliers?

3. If the Japanese model were adopted by 7-Eleven stores in the United States, what problems might be encountered?

The following terms should become part of your business vocabulary. For each numbered item find the term that has the same meaning.

- artificial intelligence (AI)
- computer network
- consulate
- data
- decision support system (DSS)
- expert system
- external data sources
- file server
- inference rules
- information
- internal data sources
- knowledge base
- local area network (LAN)
- management information system (MIS)
- storage access network (SAN)
- wide area network (WAN)

1. An office located in a foreign country that represents the home country and serves the interests of citizens of the country it represents.

2. A computer system designed for businesses in a large geographic area—in which communication channels used include telephone lines, satellites, microwaves, or a combination of carriers.

3. Facts expressed as numbers, symbols, or words.

4. A system that helps companies make decisions by summarizing and comparing data from internal and external sources.

5. Data that have been processed and organized into a usable format.

6. A branch of computer science that deals with designing computer systems to perform tasks that seem to require human intelligence.

7. A collection of individual computers that are connected by communication channels, such as telephone lines, and that share data and information.

8. Resources outside of an organization that originate data.

9. The processes of taking information from the knowledge base and comparing it to new circumstances.

10. Resources that provide data from within a company.

11. A computer that houses the software and data that all computers on a LAN share.

12. Information on a specific subject that has been provided by human experts; the historical data on the subject stored in a computer.

13. A communication network designed for a limited area.

14. A computer software system that uses a knowledge base and inference rules to make logical recommendations.

15. A computer system that performs the read/write tasks for the file server and stores the data.

16. A computer-based system that delivers information to all levels of management in a company.

REVIEWING YOUR READING

Answer these questions to reinforce your knowledge of the main ideas of this chapter.

1. What is the purpose of a management information system?
2. What is the difference between external and internal data sources as related to MIS?
3. What is reengineering and what role does reengineering play in overcoming barriers to success for international businesses? What barriers are especially difficult to break through? Give specific examples.
4. Describe the types of computer networks.
5. Give one example of an industry that uses artificial intelligence and expert systems.
6. Identify two sources of assistance to international businesses and explain what kinds of assistance they provide.

EXPANDING YOUR HORIZONS

You will not find the complete answers to the following questions in your textbook. You will need to use your critical-thinking skills. Think about these questions, gather information from other sources, analyze possible responses, and discuss them with others. Then, develop your own oral or written response as instructed by your teacher.

1. Explain how the future of telecommunications and networking will affect international business.
2. Choose a foreign country and describe how its societal and cultural norms may affect an international business's use of technology.
3. In what direction is MIS headed in the United States and in the international business arena?
4. Choose an existing business enterprise that uses artificial intelligence and expert systems. Describe how artificial intelligence and expert systems are incorporated into this enterprise to improve its ability to produce.
5. Choose a country and describe how its consulate, located in the United States, operates.

The ability to find information from various sources is an important international business skill. The following activities will help you investigate various topics. You will also learn to apply class ideas to situations outside of the classroom.

1. Gain access to an electronic bulletin board or a guide to periodical literature. Locate information about a company that is involved in international trade in Cameroon. Write a summary of the company's import and/or export trade.

2. A company wants to expand its business to Morocco. What recommendations would you make about using computer networks and management information systems in Morocco?

3. Create a fictitious case study about a company headquartered in Madagascar that wants to export to Mauritania. Identify the technological barriers the company faces.

4. *Global Career Activity.* A manager from the Ivory Coast was recently assigned to develop an MIS in Gabon. Prepare a list of things the manager would need to find out about before moving to Gabon.

Continuing Enrichment Project: Identifying International Business Information

Add to your international business resource file by completing the following activities. Update this file as you find more information throughout this course.

1. Summarize articles from current periodicals (such as magazines, newspapers, and electronic bulletin boards) related to the following topics: computer networks, telecommunications, telephones, videoconferences, artificial intelligence, CD-ROM, laser discs, facsimile machines.

2. Choose a country in Africa and read articles about that country or interview a businessperson from that country. Develop a profile of that country that includes information on several of these topics: population, cultural interests, language, religions, natural resources, industries, and trends in information technology.

3. Develop a brief summary of how the country you chose in question 2 could incorporate and use the technology you researched in question 1. Put that summary in your portfolio for reference at a later date.

Regional Profile

Africa

Francis Thuo is a successful businessperson, a member of the Lions Club, and chair of the Nairobi Stock Exchange. The view from his office in the International House includes not only the Hilton Hotel and the Parliament building, but also vast plains in the distance that are home to Kenya's antelope, zebra, and giraffe.

Thuo's view is symbolic of Africa's diverse cultural landscape that includes modern urban traffic jams, as well as nomadic cattle herders. African ethnic groups include Blacks, Arabs, Indians, Asians, Whites, and others. More than 1,000 languages are spoken and an uncounted number of religions are practiced.

Africa is over three times the size of the United States. The continent includes the great highlands in Kenya and Ethiopia and the Great Rift Valley. There are mountains in the north and southeast of Africa; however, the largest mountains are snowcapped and stand in the east—on the equator. Kilimanjaro is the tallest at 19,340 feet.

Much of the interior of Africa is a plateau consisting of rolling hills, deserts, savannas, and rain forests. The Nile, which is the longest river in the world, is in east Africa. The Sahara (desert in Arabic) covers one fourth of the African continent. The Sahara was once a fertile land that supported a thriving population. However about 4,000 B.C., the climate changed the Sahara region into a desert. Today, overfarming, overgrazing, and drought cause the Sahara to expand every year.

The earliest African civilizations grew along the Nile River and the Red Sea. Egyptian kingdoms date back to 3,100 B.C. To the west the kingdoms of Ghana and Mali ruled vast territories of sub-Saharan Africa from the fourth to sixteenth centuries A.D. Ghana's position—midway between the salt mines of north Africa and the gold deposits to the south—insured its hold on a trading empire that spread over 200,000 square miles. Caravans from north Africa carried salt, metal goods, and cloth across the Sahara to Ghana in return for gold, farm produce, and kola nuts.

By the thirteenth century, the kingdom of Mali had taken control of Ghana's empire and expanded it over an even wider area. Mali's city of Tombouctou (Timbuktu) was a center of learning that attracted scholars from Cairo and Makkah (Mecca).

Empires, kingdoms, and tribes continued to rule Africa until the late 1800s. Europeans had continued to arrive since the 1500s, but the opening of the Suez Canal in 1869 brought a new wave of immigrants. European traders were interested in gold, diamonds, ivory, and other natural resources. In 1885, fourteen nations agreed to partition the "prize" they would take from the native inhabitants. By 1914, France had conquered most of north and west Africa, Britain took control of Egypt, and (along with the Germans and the Italians), most of east Africa.

The southern part of the continent was divided among Britain, Portugal, and Germany. King Leopold II of Belgium took the Congo in central Africa as his own private colony. The people became his slaves; executions and torture killed thousands. In 1902, the British defeated the Dutch settlers (Afrikaners) in southern Africa; and in 1910, created the Union of South Africa, which excluded nonwhites from the political process. Ethiopia and Liberia were the only African nations to retain their independence.

Nationalist movements began to appear throughout the continent between the world wars; however, independence for most African nations was not achieved until the 1950s and 1960s. A few European nations relinquished control after mass protests and labor strikes; unfortunately, prolonged guerrilla warfare was usually the real force of liberation.

Today, greater mobility has led many to leave the home village, but family and tribal identity thrive. A renewed sense of pride in African culture was fostered with independence. Children are taught tribal and family history.

Islam has flourished, especially in the north, while European and U.S. churches and schools continue to promote Christianity. Ancient tribal religions are still important; often they are combined with Christianity. The indigenous African religions believe in one ultimate God along with lesser gods or ancestral spirits who act as channelers between God and mortals.

African arts are often associated with religion. Music, stories, dance, and carved wooden masks have roles in ceremonies that connect humans to the spiritual world. Art also entertains, educates, designs, and stimulates thought. African music is unique for its polyrhythmic structure, with as many as a dozen rhythms all played simultaneously. European painters have been influenced by African artists' expression of the essence of a human or animal subject through sharp angles and exaggerated features. African designs have found their way onto clothing made throughout the world.

The African landscape has often inspired the artist; however, it is a harsh land that at times punishes its people. Poor soils, drought, and wars have combined to starve millions of people in Chad, Ethiopia, Mozambique, Somalia, and Sudan during the 1980s and 1990s. The suffering in Ethiopia resulted in the famine relief concert Live-Aid, which raised funds for food for the hungry. In 1992, images on Western television of suffering helped to pressure the United States into sending a military force to protect relief workers in Somalia. Do you think that it was a good idea to send soldiers to Somalia?

South Africa's white minority used a government policy called *apartheid* to segregate and to discriminate politically and economically against non-European groups—which include Blacks, Indians, and Coloreds (of mixed race). However in 1990, under economic isolation from most of the world, President de Klerk began changing the system of white minority rule when he released Nelson Mandela from prison and lifted the ban on the African National Congress. In 1994, Nelson Mandela was elected president in peaceful elections. What is the situation in South Africa today?

Civil wars, military revolts, and political instability have prevented many African nations from making economic and social progress. Authoritarian systems are more common than democratic institutions; however, peaceful transfers of power have taken place in Kenya, Botswana, Senegal, and Cameroon.

During the 1980s the African elephant became an endangered species when the population was cut in half as a result of poaching (illegal hunting). In 1989, 112 nations agreed on a ban in ivory trade, and some countries began removing tusks to protect the animals. The program was successful, and by 1993, Botswana, Malawi, Namibia, South Africa, and Zimbabwe wanted to restore the trade on a limited basis. Do you think the ivory trade should be resumed? Should African nations be able to do as they wish with their elephants?

Technology in Global Business

After studying this chapter and completing the end-of-chapter activities, you will be able to

- Summarize the development of computer technology.

- Differentiate mainframe computers, minicomputers, and microcomputers.

- Identify the input, processing, and output components of a computer.

- Describe some common software applications that are used to facilitate international business operations.

- Explain how computers are an integral part of the automated global office.

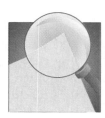

After the Storm

Operation Desert Storm, during the winter of 1991–1992, may be very real to you if it involved a family member or a friend. You may have memories of the news reports while the United Nations forces engaged in battle with Iraq. Can you imagine what it must have been like for the citizens of Kuwait to endure that war? The U.N. forces were able to free Kuwait from the control of Iraq. Now the Kuwaiti people are trying to reconstruct their businesses and homes.

A small group of construction-related U.S. businesses located in the state of Maryland saw an opportunity to develop an international business in postwar Kuwait. First, these businesses developed a partnership with a view toward helping to rebuild Kuwait. Second, the partnership assembled a computer database of the member companies and their resources. Specifically, the database includes the companies' names, addresses, and details about their areas of construction expertise. Finally, the partnership enlisted the help of the governor of Maryland, a state agency that promotes international business, and personnel from the Kuwaiti government. Together, this group is setting out to rebuild Kuwait.

The group is using the Port of Baltimore and the Baltimore-Washington airport to assemble all outbound goods. These staging areas allow for more efficient assembly, packing, and shipping of the building materials. The Kuwait government can look at a list of available materials and services. The Kuwaitis then can place their order for the construction materials they need. Once the U.S.-based partnership receives the order, the computer database of construction companies is scanned to see which companies can quickly and efficiently assemble the necessary materials for export. By using computers and software, two different governments and several businesses are working together to rebuild Kuwait and to help the Kuwaiti people resume normal lives.

Most of us take for granted the impact of technology on our daily lives. Programmable video cassette recorders, automated teller machines, bar code scanners at point-of-sale terminals, and debit card gasoline pumps are all examples of routine tasks that are now computerized. Thanks to the computer, the telephone, and the television, individuals and businesses are all rapidly becoming members of a global village. Computer technology has evolved into a *need* rather than a *want* for many people. Looking back at technology's development can make us appreciate the ideas that have become reality.

EARLY COMPUTER DEVELOPMENT

A **computer** is an electronic device that processes and stores data. Computers can manipulate many kinds of information, or data, and solve complicated problems at very high speeds. In the 1940s a single computer filled an entire room. The development of the transistor in 1947—a tiny device that controls electronic signals—resulted in the production of smaller computers that are also faster and much less expensive than earlier models.

During the 1960s and 1970s, researchers sought to make computers smaller and more efficient. They developed the integrated circuit, which combines electronic components into a single structure. This technology enabled engineers to design computers with much greater capacity than ever before.

The next great advance for computer technology came in 1971 when the first microprocessors were produced. A microprocessor is

called a large-scale integrated circuit because it contains so many transistors. A **microprocessor** is actually an arrangement of tens of thousands of transistors and other electronic parts on a silicon chip the size of a fingernail. The first microprocessors executed 50,000 to 100,000 tasks per second. Today, the devices carry out 5 million tasks per second.

Microprocessors allowed for the design and production of a new generation of computers that are compact and affordable. These small computers range in size from desktop models down to handheld models.

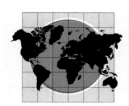

Global Business Example: India—Underdeveloped Country to Computer-Developed Nation

India—the second most densely populated country in the world—is considered an underdeveloped country. However, India does have a fine reputation for developing some of the world's brightest mathematicians, scientists, and computer programmers. For that reason, India is anxious to attract competitive computer businesses so these promising scholars will stay in India. Public schools in India stress computer programming education from the elementary levels (Logo programming) to the high school levels (BASIC and Pascal programming). With this educational emphasis on programming, Indians hope that this current generation of computer-literate students will create a great demand for computers. Until this student generation joins the Indian business community, however, there will be a tremendous need for foreign countries to develop technology-based industries.

As a result of many years of government restrictions, two-thirds of all software programs in India are used illegally. One company that is making an impact on the domestic software market is Tata Consultancy Services (TCS). In 1992, TCS, an Indian-developed software company, earned $44.7 million dollars in total export revenue. The goal of TCS is to become the top software producer in India and then to become a major exporter to other countries. TCS is making a commitment to use Indian knowledge and labor to change India from an underdeveloped country to a computer-developed country.

Source: Adapted from Ranade, J. "Report from India," *Byte,* March 1993 and "Software from India? Yes, It's for Real," *Business Week,* January 18, 1993, p. 77.

TYPES OF COMPUTERS

The most common type of computer is the digital computer. In fact, digital computers are so widely used that when we use the word *computer*, we almost always mean *digital computer*. In a digital computer, all data—including letters, numbers, and symbols—are represented by digits. The computer carries out its tasks, then, by comparing, counting, and rearranging digits.

Digital computers are categorized based on their size, speed, capabilities, and cost. The three categories of computer we will be studying are the mainframe computer, the minicomputer, and the microcomputer.

Mainframe Computers

A **mainframe computer** is a large, fast computer that can handle many tasks at once. It is capable of processing information at very high speeds. Mainframes often require a specialized environment. Temperature and humidity must be held constant to keep the machines operating efficiently. In addition, it takes people with special training to maintain the machines. Mainframes are expensive. For that reason, most mainframes are used by large organizations, such as government agencies and research and science institutions.

Minicomputers

The term **minicomputer** generally refers to a desktop-sized machine that has less capacity and operates more slowly than a mainframe computer. The minicomputer is slightly less powerful than the mainframe, but it can still store and process a large amount of data. Minicomputers take up less space than mainframes and do not require special environmental conditions. Minicomputers were designed for use by the engineering industry to perform complex mathematical calculations.

Microcomputers

The personal computer (PC), or microcomputer, is the most well-known, popular computer on the market. A **microcomputer** is a small computer designed to run software applications at home, in schools, and in small businesses. PCs are versatile enough to handle everything from household budgets to business correspondence to employee payroll records.

Microcomputers are much less expensive than mainframes and minicomputers; therefore, they are now the fastest-selling computers in business. They are quickly becoming a mainstay in many homes. The ability to link PCs via telephone lines into networks makes PCs even more valuable as information tools. Users can share information with each other, gather information from databases, or keep up with world events—all via their personal computers.

Two types of personal computers that are quickly gaining acceptance are laptop and notebook computers. Designed to be portable, both *notebook* and *laptop* computers usually weigh less than 7 pounds but have all the features of a desktop-sized PC. Notebook computers that are as small as a person's hand and weigh less than one pound are now available. Designed with the business traveler in mind, these smallest models fit easily into a briefcase or even into a pocket. They can communicate with desktop PCs, send and receive electronic mail, and store documents.

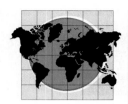

Golf clubs are shipped from the United States to Asia; BMWs from Germany to the United States; Seiko watches from Japan to Chile. Exporting has become the business gateway to the world! Today, exporting takes a leap into the future thanks to computers. By using software specifically designed for exporting, companies can automate manual functions. Exporting requires filling out forms, complying with government regulations, and communicating with people who speak other languages.

More than two dozen companies sell export-automation software. Most such programs help businesses include the legal phrases and financial data required by foreign banks. Some packages offer a "table-of-denial," which lists countries under embargo restrictions. This information keeps businesses from getting involved in illegal export activities. For example, shipping helicopter parts to Iraq from the United States is not permitted.

One innovation in export software is called electronic data interchange (EDI). By using a modem with EDI software, companies can send their export documents electronically—which saves mailing time and cost. However, EDI standards vary between countries and businesses. For example, you might need different electronic forms to import watches from Japan than to ship golf clubs from the United States. Currently, the U.S. Customs Service is working to improve the compatibility between countries and companies. To be an exporter in the world marketplace today, you should expect to invest in computers and export-automation software.

COMPONENTS OF A COMPUTER SYSTEM

A computer system consists of many different pieces of equipment. The word **hardware** refers to the physical parts—the electronic devices as well as the plastic housing—that make up a computer system (see Figure 16-1 on page 344). Advancements are made continually in both the number and capabilities of the various hardware components available for the computer.

Input Devices and Media

If you want to learn something, you use your senses to take in information. You read words with your eyes. You listen to a teacher's lecture with your ears. Your eyes and ears are human input devices. Computers work in a similar fashion. To input information into a computer, you can use a variety of devices.

Figure 16-1

A computer is made of various components that perform the functions of inputting, processing, and outputting data.

COMPONENTS OF A COMPUTER SYSTEM

Input Devices

- Keyboard
- Mouse
- Graphic input devices
- Voice recognition
- Scanners

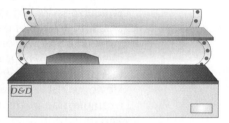

Central Processing Unit

- Processor
- Memory

Output Devices

- Monitor
- Disk
- Magnetic tape
- Microfilm
- Voice and music synthesizers
- Printer

Keyboard. Keyboards contain the alphabetic, numeric, symbol, and function keys necessary for inputting information. Some keyboards also have a numeric keypad, which is in a calculator format. Users are encouraged to input data by using touch keyboarding skills.

Mouse. A mouse is a device with a roller ball underneath that is moved across a flat surface to control the arrow or cursor movement on a computer screen. The mouse allows users to move rapidly through computer menus and applications.

The trackball is a variation on mouse technology. Rather than moving the mouse across a flat surface, you move the trackball around in a stationary device. With both the mouse and the trackball, cursor movement corresponds to the direction of the device's movement. If you move the mouse or trackball to the right, the cursor moves to the right on the screen.

Graphic Input Devices. Light pens, digitizers, and graphics tablets are all examples of graphic input devices. These devices are used to input graphic information, such as drawings and photos.

Light pens are handheld devices similar in appearance to ballpoint pens. By touching the pen to the computer screen, the user creates or modifies graphics. Digitizers translate points, lines, and curves from drawings into digital signals the computer understands.

Graphics tablets are typically used in manufacturing to give specific instructions to computer programs. A stylus, similar to a light pen, is used to touch sections on the graphics tablet and send instructions to the computer program. For example: to design an airplane, a graphics tablet and stylus could position predesigned airplane parts on the computer screen.

Voice Recognition. Voice recognition technology allows the user to speak directly to the computer. It is designed to take voice commands and digitize them into computer signals. The signals then tell the computer what commands to execute. Voice input can be used for language translation. The computer recognizes and translates words from one language into another. This allows people to interact even if neither knows the other's language. In international business, voice recognition will be a powerful tool for creating a more effective global workforce.

Scanners. Magnetic ink character recognition (MICR) was designed for the financial industry. These characters are the number code that appears on the bottoms of checks. By using an MICR reader, a computer can process the encoded data. Those data translate into bank numbers and account numbers for easy data tracking. Today, MICR is used most often by banks, telephone companies, and credit card companies.

An optical character reader (OCR) is a scanner that allows the computer to read typewritten, computer written, or handwritten characters. OCR standards are accepted worldwide and are commonly used in the European and

Japanese computer industries. Often, data are printed on invoices with a detachable stub to be returned with bill payment. The printed stub is then put through an OCR, which reads the code and quickly credits the appropriate account.

A similar product—a page scanner—is used in offices and printing businesses. A page scanner converts printed and graphical data into digitized images for reproduction in printed material. Page scanners are most often used in combination with desktop publishing activities.

Laser scanners are in use at most supermarkets and many other retail stores. The tabletop design includes a laser beam that reads the bar code printed on products. A computer program then translates the bar code into inventory and pricing information.

Central Processing Unit

Every computer contains a central processing unit. The **central processing unit (CPU)** is a hardware device in which electronic circuits process the data input to the computer. Data come into the CPU from input devices. Output from the processing operations is delivered to output devices.

The CPU establishes the power of a computer system, which is measured in terms of the *speed* of processing and the *size* of memory. In many respects, the CPU is the brain of the computer. The CPU has two components: the processor and the memory.

Processor.   The processor is made up of the control unit and the arithmetic/logic unit. The control unit controls the operations of all the hardware of the computer. The arithmetic/logic unit performs the calculations and makes comparisons between units of data.

Memory.   The computer's memory is the storage area for all data being processed, as well as the program that controls the processing. The size of a computer's memory is measured in terms of thousands or millions of bytes that can be stored at one time. A *byte* is the space required to store one letter, number, or character.

Main storage is often called random access memory. **Random access memory (RAM)** is easily accessible and stores several items: the operating system, applications programs, and the data. Because RAM is easily accessible and is designed to be changed, many software programs list a RAM requirement for the software to run. When purchasing hardware and software, RAM capacity should be a vital part of your decision.

Read only memory (ROM) is storage that is permanently installed in the computer's CPU at the time the computer is manufactured. Information in ROM can only be read and used, it cannot be changed.

Output Devices and Media

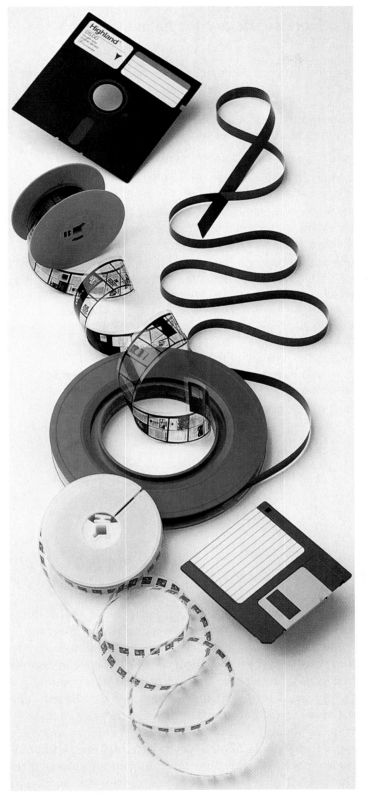

Once the CPU has processed the information, the output is given to the user. Information output from a computer comes in several forms. Output can be readily viewed on the computer monitor or display screen. This can be very useful in updating information and verifying the accuracy of the input.

Hard copy output is printed on paper. Many different kinds of printers are available. They can produce simple images by means of a dot matrix. More complex images—black and white as well as color—can be printed on laser and ink-jet printers. When output needs to be shared at a meeting or to be included in written correspondence, a printout is often the most appropriate output device to use.

Information that has been processed can also be output to storage devices, such as magnetic tape or disks. This makes retrieval and updating fairly easy. Tapes and disks also provide a backup for the files stored in a computer's memory.

Another output device is computer output microfilm (COM). COM is the result of a process that records output from a computer to a sheet of film called microfiche. Libraries and research groups use microfiche to store text from periodicals. Microfiche is inexpensive and easy to store.

Voice and music synthesizers are examples of output devices that are making great technological advances. As you already know, the voice can be used as an input device. Output from a computer may also be by "voice." Voice output is commonly used by telephone companies for automating information for services such as voice mail. Airline companies and even automobiles use voice output to provide information. Often voice output can be relayed in a number of languages.

Global Business Exercise: Make Mine Italian!

Your company is opening a branch office in Italy. You accept a transfer and become the new office manager. Your first assignment is to attend the Smau computer show—one of the world's biggest—which is held in Italy. Your task: visit the hardware vendors and decide what products they have that would meet your needs. This is what you learn:

- IBM and Olivetti have the largest sales in Italy.
- U.S. vendors, such as AST, Compaq, and Zenith, also command respectable market shares in Italy.
- Hantarex manufactures monitors in Florence and Milan and is well known in the international community. Many foreign businesses purchase their computer monitors from Hantarex.
- Olivetti is marketing a notebook computer as a "fashion accessory" rather than as production equipment. It seems Italians value style as much as function.

1. What questions do you need to ask yourself to determine your hardware needs?
2. What do you need to know about the equipment used at headquarters so that the hardware you purchase for the office in Italy will be compatible?
3. What benefits, if any, might there be in purchasing Italian-made equipment?

SOFTWARE APPLICATIONS

In order for the computer and the CPU to function, they must have instructions. The instructions are contained in a computer program or **software**. The computer follows the instructions given in the software to produce the desired result. By using an input device, users can change the data to suit their needs. Sometimes users may want to store data for later use, or they may want information printed in a document. The computer needs software to carry out either of these tasks.

Typical software applications about which you will learn more are word processing, spreadsheets, databases, desktop publishing, and communications. Software packages can be used independently or as integrated packages. Integrated software allows the user to work on two or more software programs at the same time. For example, one integrated package lets you create a letter in word processing and pull up a database list for the addresses.

Figure 16-2 lists some of the most widely used software programs for each application. There are many other programs available, with new software developed every day. You should carry out your own research to determine which program is right for you.

Figure 16-2
There are many popular software packages available that can be used in the global business environment.

POPULAR SOFTWARE PACKAGES

Application	Name of Program
Integrated software	Microsoft Works ClarisWorks
Word processing software	WordPerfect Microsoft Word Ami Pro
Spreadsheet software	Lotus 1,2,3 Excel
Database software	dBase III & IV Paradox
Desktop publishing software	PageMaker Ventura QuarkXPress
Communications	Prodigy CompuServe ProComm

Word Processing

One of the most common uses of the microcomputer is word processing. **Word processing** is a system of keying, changing, and deleting text in a document. The document may be a memo, letter, or report. Word processing packages differ in the options available to the user. Most packages, however, have the following basic functions: open, edit, print, save, merge, spell check, cut, copy, and format. The easier it is to use the various options, the more user-friendly the software is said to be.

Spreadsheets

A **spreadsheet** program allows the user to arrange and calculate numeric information in table form. The spreadsheet consists of a grid of columns and rows. Spreadsheets are useful whenever you need to calculate data. This is done by assigning a formula to a set of rows and columns. A user can enter known values—perhaps the number of hours worked and an hourly rate. The computer then carries out the multiplication to determine the amount of pay due. The computer could also calculate taxes and subtract them from the total. Some typical applications for spreadsheets are calculating sports statistics, grades, budgets, or product sales.

Databases

A **database** is a body of data, or information, stored in a systematic way. Users can manipulate, retrieve, and update information in a database. Planning a database is as important as entering the data accurately. A user should first determine how he or she wants to use the data. Then, depending on the software, information must be input in a certain format. Many businesses use a database to store client lists and sales records.

A sample database entry is shown in Figure 16-3. The user of this database could plan a marketing trip by identifying clients in a certain part of the state by sorting by ZIP Code. The clients also could be sorted by city or by phone number. The date of last contact can be used to make sure that all clients receive a regular call or visit. Other uses of databases include phone directories, club rosters, inventories, and mailing labels.

Figure 16-3

Information in a database can be sorted to allow businesses to identify clients by location, last contact, purchase amount, and any other way that is available in the database software.

SAMPLE DATABASE ENTRY

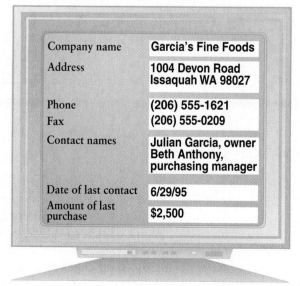

Company name	Garcia's Fine Foods
Address	1004 Devon Road Issaquah WA 98027
Phone	(206) 555-1621
Fax	(206) 555-0209
Contact names	Julian Garcia, owner Beth Anthony, purchasing manager
Date of last contact	6/29/95
Amount of last purchase	$2,500

Global Highlight: Africa's Largest Nation—Sudan

The country of Sudan is 966,757 square miles. That is one-fourth the size of the United States. Sudan is home to 27.2 million people—a population just smaller than that of California. Fifty-two percent of the population is Black, and 39 percent is Arab. Approximately 27 percent of the population is literate. The annual per capita income is less than $100.

The government of Sudan is a military republic and is led by General Omar Hassan al-Bashir. The government does not permit political groups, labor unions, or free-press newspapers. Fully 70 percent of the country follows the Sunni Muslim religion. Eighteen percent of the people are animists, who believe that all natural things have souls. The remaining population is Christian (5 percent) or other (7 percent).

In Sudan, a civil war is being waged between the Arab Muslim north and the Christian/animist south. Famine is widespread, estimated to be approaching the same desperate level as in Somalia. Sudan has a reputation for terrorist activities. The government has a strong connection with Iran and the radical Islamic group known as Hezbollah.

Source: Adapted from "Sudan: Africa's Largest Nation," *USA Today,* June 30, 1993.

Desktop Publishing

Desktop publishing refers to using the computer to produce documents containing text and graphics in an original layout. Desktop publishing combines both word processing and graphics arts techniques. Newsletters, bulletins, menus, brochures, and flyers are just a few of the uses of desktop publishing software.

Communications

Communicating with other computers or other networks is another application that is gaining in popularity and importance. Users can access or exchange information by connecting computers via telephone lines. However, software is necessary to make the communications system usable. For example, use of a modem to send files between computers via phone lines requires communications software.

On-line data services are available that link users with vast amounts of data. These services require specific software packages and usually charge a fee for on-line use.

COMPUTERS IN THE GLOBAL OFFICE

Every day computers are becoming more powerful, faster, and internally larger (possessing more storage capacity), while becoming smaller in physical size. Companies use computers in a number of different ways in addition to the common software applications. Salespeople can call all over the world and carry on a conversation through telephone lines using computers. Airlines use computer terminals for reserving seats, scheduling flights, and ticketing. Retail stores keep current inventories with "point-of-sale" programs. The medical field uses computers to help with disease diagnosis and treatment planning. Banks use computers to update account balances. Many medium- and large-sized companies use automated payroll systems to prepare paychecks. When we look at simple tasks done in the course of a day, it is easy to see the impact computers have made on society.

Offices around the world are changing as a result of the availability of computers, modems, and facsimile machines. Technology is helping to bridge business and cultural gaps. As standards for hardware, software, and communications become universal, integrated automated office procedures will increase. Let's take a look at the components of any electronic office. You will see how common the technology is to any country and any business.

Computers and Software Applications

Personal computers are sold worldwide. As you have learned, microprocessors are becoming smaller and faster. Alliances among hardware vendors—such as the one between IBM, Apple, and Motorola—will continue to bridge computer standards. Before long, a universal hardware standard for PCs could be a reality. As hardware becomes more interconnected, software will be developed to take advantage of the integrated activities. When that occurs, offices will easily be able to offer global services.

Electronic and Voice Mail

If an office has a computer, a telephone, and a modem, it can be connected in minutes with other networks and offices around the world. Communications software currently allows you to talk with businesses from across town or across continents. Thanks to a joint venture between Microsoft and various telephone companies, a standard is being written to link personal computers through telephone lines. Services such as PRODIGY, CompuServe, and Internet are opening the world of electronic mail to the business community.

Voice digitizing has entered the telephone market. When you leave a message on an answering machine you are leaving information on a tape. On a voice mail system, information is digitized onto a disk that the recipient can listen to later, replay, forward, respond to, or edit. Voice mail eliminates busy signals and unanswered phones.

Facsimile Machines

Sending documents over telephone lines can help close a business deal in a matter of minutes. Facsimile (often shortened to fax) machines are among the biggest selling office products of the 1990s. The **facsimile machine (fax)** digitizes the text and graphic images of a document and sends the digitized images over phone lines to a receiving facsimile machine. The receiving machine translates the digitized data back into the original image. A fax machine can transmit at any time to any place in the world that has phone lines and a receiving fax machine.

Teleconferencing

Teleconferencing or videoconferencing refers to the use of computers and television cameras to transmit images. Video and audio signals are sent over standard communications channels. In this manner, businesses can cut down on costly travel and accomplish as much as they could if they met with business associates in person.

Global Business Exercise: EuroDisney Meets Disney World

Monique and Julian, French citizens, were employed for two years at the French Pavilion in Disney World's Epcot Center. When EuroDisney was scheduled to open in France, they were asked to join the staff of that park. Because they were French and had knowledge of Disney's employment practices, company policies, and customer service, they were asked to assist with hiring personnel in France.

1. What training might Monique and Julian have received at Disney World that prepares them for their jobs in France?
2. What office equipment will the EuroDisney personnel office need in order to communicate with the Disney World personnel office?
3. What obstacles might Monique and Julian expect to encounter as they make the transition back to France to help launch this new theme park?

Back to the Beginning: After the Storm

Reread the case at the beginning of this chapter and answer the following questions:

1. What economic conditions existed in the United States that encouraged the Maryland businesses to export to Kuwait?
2. What governmental "roadblocks" might the partnership have encountered in trying to do business with Kuwait?
3. What benefits might the United States-based businesses enjoy from doing business with Kuwait?

KNOWING GLOBAL BUSINESS TERMS

The following terms should become part of your business vocabulary. For each numbered item find the term that has the same meaning.

- central processing unit (CPU)
- computer
- database
- desktop publishing

- facsimile machine (fax)
- hardware
- mainframe computer
- microcomputer
- microprocessor
- minicomputer
- random access memory (RAM)
- read only memory (ROM)
- software
- spreadsheet
- word processing

1. A software program that blends graphics and word processing in a page layout design package.
2. A type of computer that can range in size from desktop down to handheld.
3. A body of data, or information, that is stored in a systematic way so that users can manipulate, retrieve, and update the information.
4. A program that allows the user to arrange and calculate numeric information in table form.
5. Instructions contained in a computer program.
6. A computer program that allows the user to input text and create documents electronically.
7. A hardware component of the computer in which electronic circuits process and store data.
8. A desktop-sized machine with less capacity and slower operating speed than a mainframe computer.
9. An electronic device that processes and stores data.
10. The physical parts of a computer.
11. A very large, fast computer that can handle many tasks at once.
12. Computer storage that is easily accessible and stores the operating system, applications programs, and data.
13. A large-scale integrated circuit that runs a computer, and some can process millions of tasks per second.
14. Storage that is permanently installed in the computer's CPU at the time the computer is manufactured.
15. Machine that digitizes the text or graphic images of a document and sends the digitized images over phone lines.

REVIEWING YOUR READING

Answer these questions to reinforce your knowledge of the main ideas of this chapter.

1. What are three computer input devices and three computer output devices?

2. What are the three categories of computers? Give a brief description of each.

3. What are the most common software applications? Give an example of how each application could be used in international business.

4. If you were establishing an office in another country, what are some types of technology you would need to purchase?

EXPANDING YOUR HORIZONS

You will not find the complete answers to the following questions in your textbook. You will need to use your critical-thinking skills. Think about these questions, gather information from other sources, analyze possible responses, and discuss them with others. Then, develop your own oral or written response as instructed by your teacher.

1. Technological advances will affect all aspects of our lives. What predictions can you make about how technology could change the nature of international business during the next several decades?

2. How can a country use technology to improve its export/import trade?

3. How can a country's culture affect its technological advances?

BUILDING RESEARCH SKILLS

It takes time and research to make sound decisions when purchasing technology. The following activities will guide you through a research process that will help establish a foundation for good technology purchasing. Note: If you have a computer available, complete all written assignments using the computer.

1. Visit a computer store. Gather information about different computers, input devices, and output devices. Write a brief summary of the products you review. Be sure to compare at least two products for each of these equipment categories: computer, printer, modem, and mouse.

2. Interview an office manager or an international business person who uses technology on the job. Find out what hardware and software the manager needs at work. Prepare a report that summarizes your visit.

3. Review articles from newspapers and magazines on technology in international business. Write your own newsletter article identifying a technology currently used in the international marketplace.

4. *Global Career Activity.* Conduct library research to investigate the computer skills needed by airline reservationists in industrialized countries.

Continuing Enrichment Project: Creating an International Business Advertisement

Use a desktop publishing, word processing, graphics, or other software program to prepare an advertisement (magazine or newspaper) for an international business. Highlight the strong points of a product or service. Refer to the information you have gathered in previous chapters. Include the following items in your advertisement:

1. Name and address of the company (include the country).
2. Most convenient time to contact the business (include the time zone).
3. Features of the product or service offered.
4. The currency that is acceptable for sales transactions.

17

Production Systems for Global Business

After studying this chapter and completing the end-of-chapter activities, you will be able to

- Diagram the basic model for all production processes.
- Summarize the goals of operations management.
- Explain the reasons for different production methods.
- Identify two ways production output is measured.
- Differentiate producing products and creating services.
- Describe how technology continues to affect office practices.

Mauritania's Riches from the Sea

Have you ever tried an exotic seafood such as octopus or calamari (squid)? These foods—as well as fish, lobster, and shrimp—are important natural resources for Mauritania, a country on Africa's Atlantic coast. The fishing grounds off the coast of Mauritania are rich with lobster, octopus, and a variety of fish.

Although always important to its economy, fishing has recently become Mauritania's main source of foreign sales income. Production

increased when the Mauritanian government entered into joint ventures with companies from other countries—including Algeria, Iraq, and Romania. These nations also share the profits. Mauritania has benefited from the sophisticated fleets used by its partners, including large trawlers capable of freezing, processing, and transporting fish without entering a port.

Source: Adapted from Cronje, Suzanne. "Mauritania," *The Middle East Review*, 15th ed. Essex, UK: NTC Business Books, 1989, pp. 105–107 and Handloff, Robert E. "The Economy," *Mauritania: A Country Study*, 2d ed. Washington, D.C.: Library of Congress, 1990, pp. 77–117.

THE PRODUCTION PROCESS

The **production process** is the means by which a company changes raw materials into finished goods. The diamond miners of Angola find rough gems below ground. The stones are cut, polished, and set before they are finally sold as bracelets, necklaces, and rings to consumers around the world.

As the word *process* suggests, the production process is composed of a series of activities. The three major elements of the production process are resources, transformation, and goods and services—as illustrated in Figure 17-1 on page 360.

Figure 17-1

Organizations transform a combination of resources to produce goods and services that will meet consumer needs.

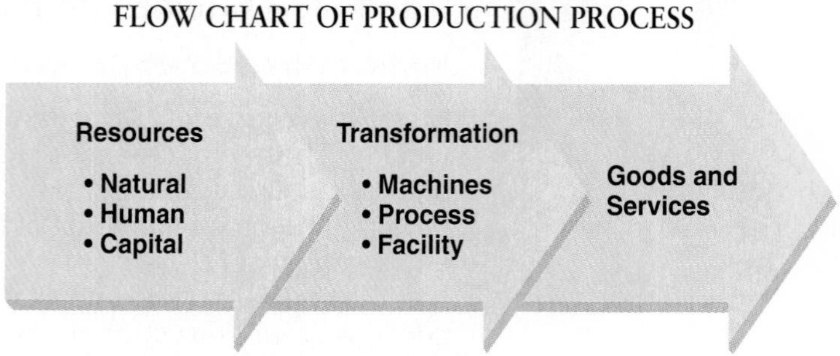

FLOW CHART OF PRODUCTION PROCESS

Resources
- Natural
- Human
- Capital

Transformation
- Machines
- Process
- Facility

Goods and Services

Resources

Resources are the people and things a company uses to produce a good or service. Resources fall into one of three categories: natural resources, human resources, and capital resources.

Natural Resources. **Natural resources** come from the air, water, or earth. These basic elements can be used to create goods. The fishing banks off the shores of Mauritania and the diamonds of Angola are examples of natural resources. Researching a country's natural resources is vital for companies choosing a new site for manufacturing. Many countries are concerned about the depletion of their natural resources; a loss of resources means a loss of economic vitality. Recycling is one way to renew natural resources.

Human Resources. The **human resources** of a country are its people and their physical and intellectual abilities. Culture (including traditions, gender roles, and religious beliefs), mobility, average age, and literacy rate are just a few of the characteristics of the available labor force a company must research. For example, India's numerous English-speaking workers with advanced degrees in mathematics make that country an important source of labor for the computer-programming industry.

Capital Resources. **Capital resources** are the funds and materials necessary to produce a good or service. In addition to financial investment, a country's monetary system, tax structure, economic conditions, and availability of materials contribute to the capital resources of a company.

Transformation

In the **transformation** stage of the production process, resources are used to create a good or service. A resource may be transformed by a machine (tractor, sewing machine, or computer), by a process (statistical analysis or teaching), or through a facility (colleges, restaurants, or health clinics). Resources are often transformed through the use of machines *and* processes. For example, cotton harvested along the lower Nile in Egypt must be cleaned and baled. Machines process the cotton and spin it into yarn and thread. Weaving machines turn the thread into cloth.

Goods and Services

The final stage of the production process is the output of the goods and services that have been created by the transformation activities. These goods and services are ready to enter the market as finished products for the consumer. A fish served at a restaurant is an example of output. Its production process began with a natural resource that was harvested, transported, and prepared (transformed) for a consumer's dining pleasure.

The production process does not end with the output of a product. Consumer response and changes in external factors (such as the economy) provide feedback in the process. The feedback affects input as the production cycle continues.

Global Business Example: South African Gold Production

South Africa leads the world in gold mining and production. Approximately 47 percent of the gold mined in the last 100 years has come from South Africa. This precious natural resource is found in the northeastern corner of the country. Most of the gold mines use workers rather than machines to extract the gold ore.

The gold is refined in South Africa and molded into bars. Banks and other institutions are the primary consumers of South African gold. The price is determined by the London bullion market. Some of the gold bars go to South African manufacturers to be transformed into other products.

OPERATIONS MANAGEMENT

Operations management is the process of designing and managing a production system. The goal of operations management is to produce a good or service at the lowest possible cost while maintaining the highest possible quality.

Operations managers use several methods to help them design efficient production systems. Forecasting is the method used to determine how much of a product to provide. Often, that decision is based on the company's previous sales. Adjustments are made for changes in consumer demand and the country's economic conditions.

Scheduling is the time frame for producing a good or service. Operations managers consider the availability of raw materials, human resources, and facilities needed for production when they create schedules.

Inventory control refers to monitoring the amount of raw materials and completed goods on hand. This count, or inventory, gives the operations manager an idea of how much to produce to meet consumer demands. One current method of inventory control is called just-in-time (JIT). **Just-in-time (JIT)** ties a manufacturer closely to a material supplier so that the raw materials are provided only when the production process needs them. This allows a company to respond quickly to changes in the marketplace while keeping only a small amount of inventory in stock. Warehouse costs are low, and the company is not left with unused goods at the end of the year. Goods are produced on an as-needed basis.

Production methods refer to the processes used during the transformation stage of production. Production methods can be categorized as manual production, automated production, and computerized production.

Manual Production Systems

The **manual production** method involves using human hands and bodies as the means of transforming resources into goods and services. Manual production was the earliest means of production and is still a primary method of production in many parts of the world. In some cases, as in the South African gold mines, workers perform the labor because machines are unable to do so. In other cases manual production is considered more valuable than another form. Handmade quilts, sweaters knitted by hand, or furniture handmade by a master carpenter are more rare and more costly than their machine-made counterparts. For many developing countries manual production is a necessity because of the initial cost of automation.

Automated Production Systems

In **automated production** systems, machines perform the work. Machines offer some advantages to production. They perform tasks quickly and precisely, and they do not get bored by repetition. Machines can do some tasks that people cannot do, such as refine oil or make plastic. In some areas of production, machines have replaced workers; cotton that once was spun by hand is now spun by machine. This shift in production has allowed workers to direct their attention to more complex tasks.

Computerized Production Systems

Computerized production systems use computers to control machines and perform work in the production process. From mainframes to personal computers, these highly efficient machines perform more tasks for us every day. In the information industry, for example, computers store information in high-density formats, such as CD-ROM (compact disc-read only memory). These discs store a great deal of information in a small space.

The automated factory, like the automated office, is designed to use the latest technology to increase productivity. Computer-controlled equipment reduces the number of people required for manual labor, but it increases the required number of trained technicians.

Computer-Assisted Manufacturing. **Computer-assisted manufacturing (CAM)** refers to the use of computers to run production equipment. Examples of CAM equipment are computerized assembly lines, drills, and milling machines. **Computer-aided design (CAD)** uses sophisticated computers that allow a designer to develop a very detailed design and key it to the CAM equipment specifications. CAD increases the creative potential of the designer. Figure 17-2 lists some of the more common computer-aided applications in use around the globe.

Figure 17-2
Computerized production methods are in use in both goods-producing industries and service industries.

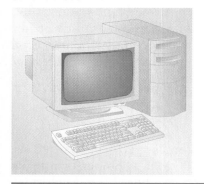

COMPUTER-AIDED MANUFACTURING APPLICATIONS

Type of Computer-Aided Application	Typical Business Use
Computer-aided design (CAD)	architectural design, interior decoration, drafting work
Computer-assisted manufacturing (CAM)	airplane manufacturing industry, nuclear plants, defense industry
Computer-aided engineering (CAE)	engineering, scientific research, highway and bridge construction
Computer-integrated manufacturing (CIM)	automobile production, prefabricated housing construction

Robotics. **Robotics** is the name for the technology connected with the design, construction, and operation of robots. **Robots** are simply computerized output devices that can perform difficult, repetitive, or dangerous work in industrial settings. The use of robotics has dramatically changed the appearance of many manufacturing plants. Robots carry out tasks that once posed risks for humans. Robots can also be programmed to deliver consistently precise work.

Automated Warehouses.   Similar to the automated factory, the automated warehouse relies on computers, software, and robotics to perform stock, inventory, order, and delivery tasks. Computers store large databases of inventory information. As robots disperse merchandise to trucks for delivery, they scan a bar code and the merchandise is automatically reordered. The repetitive nature of running a warehouse is handled by computers and robots rather than by people. Trained technicians and managers are still necessary to make sure that the warehouse stays in efficient working order.

Computer-Integrated Manufacturing.   In terms of evolving production systems, manufacturers will begin to incorporate computer-integrated manufacturing (CIM). In a **computer-integrated manufacturing (CIM)** production system, computers guide the entire manufacturing process. Production is completely controlled by computer integration—from product design through processing, assembly, testing, and packaging. Two elements of a CIM production system are minimum inventories and production based on consumer demand.

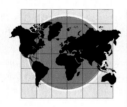

Global Business Example: *Linkage* to the Land Down Under

Klaus Jahn, a manager at Ford of Australia, needed to find a way to simplify automobile design, manufacturing, and assembly at his plant. Jahn knew there had to be a better way to prepare technical illustrations that were more efficient and cost-effective. The company was already using computer-aided programs at the Australian Ford plant. The challenge was how to develop manufacturing instructions to coordinate with the computer-aided designs.

After much searching, Jahn found his answer in a product called *Linkage*—a software toolkit for manufacturing process reengineering. *Linkage* is an internationally recognized software package created by a hardware/software company called Cimlinc, of Itasca, Illinois. After purchasing *Linkage,* the Ford plant in Melbourne, Australia, was able to restyle the Ford Capri convertible. The Capri was exported to the United States, where it became an instant hit! As a result of the positive effect on Ford of Australia, Cimlinc is expanding its markets in Japan, Korea, and China.

Global Highlight: An African-American Oil Entrepreneur

Jake Simmons, Jr., was born in 1901 in Oklahoma, the ninth child in an African- and Native-American family of cattle ranchers. Who could have guessed he would become an international tycoon, the most successful African-American in the history of the oil industry?

Two events helped young Simmons to find success. The first was being granted 160 acres of tribal land because of his birthright as a black Creek born prior to 1907. This land provided financial security. The second event was hearing Booker T. Washington speak in 1914. Simmons followed Washington to the Tuskegee Institute in Alabama where he studied for five years. Washington provided motivation for Simmons to take risks in his struggle to succeed.

When he returned to Oklahoma, Simmons began to broker (act as an agent in) oil leases for black landowners who had previously been cheated. Such work was risky; this was a time in U.S. history when racial segregation was enforced and lynchings were not uncommon. Simmons learned about the oil business from those real estate dealings.

In 1949, he formed the Simmons Royalty Company and began to drill for oil, himself. He became an important figure in state and local politics as well as a national figure in the administration of the A.M.E. church, the first Christian denomination created by African-Americans.

By 1952, Simmons was a rich man, respected in both his community and in the oil business. He expanded his interests into international business when he made his first trip to Africa. He visited Liberia, a country that had just begun to permit rights to its natural resources. Simmons proposed to pay for oil exploration rights by sharing the profits made from his company.

In 1963, he was part of a United States trade mission to East Africa; and, he became the first African-American to represent a major oil company abroad. As his peers recall, because he was an African-American, Simmons was able to interact with African leaders in a way that other oil executives could not. Contemporaries also describe him as a man of character.

In 1978, Jake Simmons was invited to Ghana as a special guest of the government to attend a *grand durbar*, or public celebration. He was seated in a place of honor, praised by his Ghanaian colleagues, and given the country's highest medal of honor. He died two years later. According to Jonathan Greenberg, Simmons' biographer, Simmons had become "a national hero, a bridge between two worlds and an example of international black synergy."

Source: Adapted from Greenberg, Jonathan, *Staking a Claim: Jake Simmons, Jr. and the Making of an African-American Oil Dynasty.* New York: Athenaeum, 1990.

MEASURING PRODUCTION OUTPUT

As mentioned earlier, the goal of operations management is to produce a good or service at the lowest cost while maintaining the highest quality. To evaluate the production process, operations managers measure production output. Production output is measured in terms of productivity and quality control.

Productivity

Productivity refers to the amount of work that is accomplished in a unit of time. Productivity can sometimes be increased by making a simple change in the work pattern, such as using all of your fingers to keyboard instead of just two. At other times an increase in productivity requires a cost investment, such as buying a personal computer to replace a typewriter. Operations managers want to increase productivity to get the most work possible for the cost of production investment.

One approach to productivity is the just-in-time (JIT) system of inventory control discussed in the operations management section of this chapter. Companies using JIT have a limited product inventory and little time delay in manufacturing.

Another approach to productivity, synchronized manufacturing, evolved from JIT. In **synchronized manufacturing,** the work flow is distributed as needed throughout the production cycle. The company distributes the work to all points of the manufacturing process according to output demands. The work flow may appear to be unbalanced in this approach. For example in a shirt factory using synchronized manufacturing, the fabric cutting department may work at 80 percent capacity due to an increase in orders. The packaging and distribution department in this scenario, on the other hand, may be working at only 40 percent capacity to meet current orders.

Quality Control

These two approaches to productivity depend on quality products. To evaluate the quality of their output, companies use a method called **quality control**—the process of measuring goods and services against a product standard. By using a standard for goods and services, companies can compare their products to similar products from all over the world. Many companies employ quality control inspectors to monitor the comparison between products and standards.

The Japanese created an approach to quality control called total quality control (TQC). **Total quality control (TQC)** requires every employee, not just the inspectors, to take responsibility for high-quality production. Many companies have reported an increase in their employees' work ethic as a result of TQC. Employees work harder because they see their value to the company's growth.

One method of improving output quality is the quality circle. A **quality circle** consists of a small group of employees who have different jobs within the same company but have the same goal: to produce a quality good or service. For example, a quality circle at a manufacturing plant might include the project supervisor, production-line workers, an employee from distribution, and an employee from accounting. This "circle" of employees meets on a regular basis to assess how well they are manufacturing. They brainstorm improvements to the production cycle or to the product itself. Because they are from all areas of the plant, together they can make informed decisions. Quality circles make use of a team management style.

Global Business Exercise: Trees into Tables

Finding a balance between trade and the protection of natural resources is important for all countries. In some African countries trade in tropical timber is restricted in order to save forests. Governments place heavy tariffs on exported finished-wood products, such as furniture. Yet, these countries are striving to develop their economies.

One Ugandan, Shada Islam, has suggested lifting the tariffs on finished-wood products. As a writer for the Ugandan publication *New Vision*, Islam suggests finished products, such as furniture, have a higher market value than raw timber. African countries could maintain their income levels while harvesting fewer trees.

1. What changes in input and transformation of the production process of timber does Shada Islam suggest?

2. Which production method (manual, automated, or computerized) would make Islam's suggestion most feasible?

3. Do you think Islam's suggestion would enable the African countries to increase their profits from tropical timber? Why or why not?

Source: Adapted from "Regional Report: Africa," *World Press Review,* Aug. 1993, p. 30.

CREATING AND DELIVERING SERVICES

Service industries perform tasks rather than provide goods for consumers. The private services industry accounted for 24.8 percent of the domestic industries for the U.S. national income in 1990, almost double the percentage it accounted for in 1960 (see Figure 17-3 on page 370). Service industries are growing. Some examples of service providers are telecommunications businesses, schools, hospitals, restaurants, hotels, and dry cleaners.

Meeting consumers' needs is essential in providing a service. Tailored logistics is a new strategy for meeting those needs. Companies using **tailored logistics** combine services with a product to better serve consumers. For example, the Coca-Cola Company has developed different varieties of Coca-Cola to meet customer demands: Diet Coke, Cherry Coke, Caffeine-Free Coke, and Coca-Cola Classic. By studying the cola consumers' demands, the company has tailored logistics to serve consumers and save production costs.

FIGURE 17-3

Service industries made up 24.8 percent of private U.S. industry in 1990.

U.S. NATIONAL INCOME FROM PRIVATE DOMESTIC INDUSTRIES (PDIs)

Private Domestic Industries	1960 (Billions of Dollars)	Percentage of Total PDIs	1990 (Billions of Dollars)	Percentage of Total PDIs
Agriculture, forestry, fisheries	$ 17.8	4.8%	$97.1	2.5%
Mining	5.6	1.5	38.1	1.0
Construction	22.5	6.1	234.4	6.1
Manufacturing	125.3	33.7	846.9	22.1
Transportation, public utilities	35.8	9.6	328.7	8.6
Wholesale trade	25.0	6.7	263.6	6.9
Retail trade	41.3	11.1	392.1	10.2
Finance, insurance, real estate	51.3	13.9	679.8	17.8
Services	46.9	12.6	948.3	24.8
Total	**$371.5**	**100.0%**	**$3,829.0**	**100.0%**

Global Business Example: Photo Safaris in Kenya

Hunting big game in Africa used to be the pastime of the rich and glamorous on safari. In an age of endangered species, hunting big game has fallen out of fashion. Game reserves in Kenya have responded with a way of maintaining the tourist trade and encouraging ecological awareness: photo safaris (where the only "shooting" done is with a camera). Guidebooks provide information on choosing a safari and a tour operator as well as descriptions of the parks—such as Aberdare National Park, former site of the annual elephant migration route.

OFFICE PRODUCTION

Technology causes constant change in the productivity of the office environment. Words that describe current trends in office productivity include *smaller, faster, complete,* and *connected.* Office machines are becoming smaller as computer technology moves from desktop to laptop and beyond. With the introduction of such advanced technology as the Pentium microprocessor, computers will easily be able to process information at rates we now consider to be extremely fast.

In addition, technological design is focusing on complete, one-solution-for-all systems. Recently, Macintosh computers introduced a personal computer integrated with an audio system, a television, and a CD-ROM drive—a way to bridge the entertainment and education markets. Telecommunications satellites enable us to connect our homes and offices to businesses across continents. We are quickly becoming a global information community.

Office workers once had telephones, typewriters, and paper and pencil. The 1990s offer these options: desktop computers, laptop computers, personal digital assistants (palmtop computers), laser printers, scanners, facsimile modems, pagers, cordless wrist telephones, and CD-ROMs. With these tools, offices have become more self-sufficient and are able to provide more and more services to consumers.

Back to the Beginning: Mauritania's Riches from the Sea

Reread the case at the beginning of this chapter and answer the following questions:

1. In the joint fishing ventures between Mauritania and its partners, which resources are contributed by Mauritania and which are provided by the partners?

2. Which production system(s) may be used in Mauritania's production of seafood? How could a change in production systems increase Mauritania's seafood production?

3. How have changes in technology contributed to Mauritania's success in the fishing industry?

KNOWING GLOBAL BUSINESS TERMS

The following terms should become part of your business vocabulary. For each numbered item find the term that has the same meaning. (Not all terms are used.)

- automated production
- capital resources
- computer-aided design (CAD)
- computer-assisted manufacturing (CAM)
- computer-integrated manufacturing (CIM)
- computerized production
- human resources
- inventory control
- just-in-time (JIT)
- manual production
- natural resources
- operations management
- production process
- productivity
- quality circle
- quality control
- robotics
- robots
- synchronized manufacturing
- tailored logistics
- total quality control (TQC)
- transformation

1. The means by which a company changes raw materials into finished goods.
2. Raw materials from the air, water, or earth.
3. A production system in which machines perform the work.
4. The stage of the production process in which resources are used to create goods or services.
5. The task of designing and managing a production system with the goal of producing a good or service at the lowest possible cost while maintaining the highest possible quality.
6. A company's labor force and their physical and intellectual abilities.
7. A measurement of production output referring to the amount of work that is accomplished in a unit of time.
8. A method of inventory control that ties a manufacturer closely to a material supplier so that the raw materials are provided only when the production process needs them.
9. A method of production using computers to control machines and perform work.
10. The process of measuring goods and services against a product standard.
11. A method of monitoring the amount of raw materials and completed goods on hand, which gives the operations manager an idea of how much to produce to meet consumer demand.
12. The means of production that involves using only peoples' hands and bodies.
13. A production system in which computers guide the entire manufacturing process, from product design through processing, assembly, testing, and packaging.
14. The method of monitoring products and production in which every employee, not just the inspector, is responsible for quality.

Answer these questions to reinforce your knowledge of the main ideas of this chapter.

1. What are the three main stages of the production process?
2. What are the three categories of resources used in production? Provide an example of each.
3. What is the goal of operations management?
4. What are the methods that operations managers use to design efficient production operations?
5. What are the three production methods?
6. How can production output be measured?
7. What are just-in-time systems and synchronized manufacturing?
8. What are two methods employers can use to involve workers in quality control?
9. How do service industries differ from manufacturing industries in their production processes?
10. How is office productivity changing?

EXPANDING YOUR HORIZONS

You will not find the complete answers to the following questions in your textbook. You will need to use your critical-thinking skills. Think about these questions, gather information from other sources, analyze possible responses, and discuss them with others. Then, develop your own oral or written response as instructed by your teacher.

1. A region's production opportunities are often determined by its natural resources. Which of your state's natural resources have been used to encourage business in your state? Are any of the natural resources unique to your state? If so, what has that meant for production in your state?
2. As a consumer of a particular product, how would you suggest tailoring the product to better serve consumer demands?
3. What effects do you think robotics and computer-integrated manufacturing (CIM) will have on U.S. business during the next two decades?
4. What methods of production do you use to accomplish daily tasks at home, school, or work? List examples for each method used.

The ability to find information from various sources is an important international business skill. The following activities will help you investigate various topics. You will also learn to apply class ideas to situations outside of the classroom.

1. Identify five companies that contribute significantly to your local economy. Are they part of the manufacturing or service industries? Which of your area's resources (natural, human, and capital) do you think have attracted these companies to this area?

2. Choose a company in your community. Read newspaper articles and annual reports or interview an employee of the company to gather information. Then, create a flow chart of the production process of this company. Include the resources used in input, the activities involved in transformation, and the goods and services produced as output.

3. Interview an employee at a local manufacturing company about measuring production output. How is productivity monitored? How is quality control maintained? Does the company use any of the following approaches to productivity and quality control: just-in-time (JIT) systems, synchronized manufacturing, total quality control (TQC), quality circles?

4. Contact your local chamber of commerce or city administration to find out whether your community has a "sister city" in another country. If so, is there an exchange of goods between the communities? What goods does your community send to its sister city, and what goods does it receive?

5. *Global Career Activity.* Conduct library research about the technology used in different countries. Prepare a list of computer and technology skills that office workers and other employees should possess for career success.

Continuing Enrichment Project: Evaluating Joint Ventures in South Africa

Many U.S. and European companies are considering joint ventures in South Africa now that apartheid is ended. Before they become partners with the South African government or with South African businesses, Western companies will gather information about the advantages and disadvantages of sharing resources with business concerns in South Africa.

Using your international business file and research skills, compile information on South African companies that might be a good match for a joint ventures with your firm. Focus on one industry—such as mining, transportation, telecommunications, or tourism. Find information on the following:

1. natural resources
2. human resources
3. capital resources
4. trade barriers
5. labor laws
6. methods of production used in the industry
7. any other information useful in making a decision.

Compile a list of the advantages and disadvantages of entering into a joint venture in South Africa and make a final recommendation. Report your findings and analysis to the class.

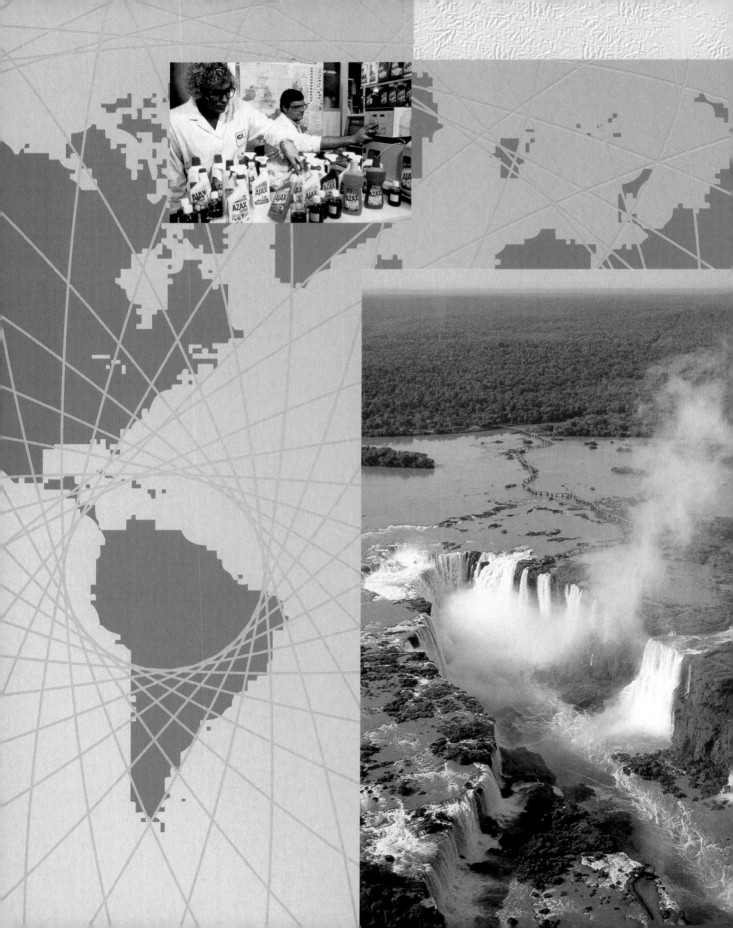

UNIT
5

Marketing in a Global Economy

CHAPTER
18

Global Marketing and Consumer Behavior

After studying this chapter and completing the end-of-chapter activities, you will be able to

- Discuss basic international marketing activities.
- Identify trends that influence global marketing opportunities.
- List the four elements of the marketing mix.
- Describe a marketing plan and its use in global marketing activities.
- Explain the international marketing environment.
- Identify factors that influence consumer behavior in different countries.
- Describe methods used to segment markets and identify a target market.

Breakfast in Britain

In recent years, the population growth rate and the demand for food products in the United States slowed. This decline caused cereal producers to look for new places to sell their products. International marketing promotes Kellogg's Rice Krispies, Kellogg's Frosted Flakes, Cheerios, Wheaties, and other cereals among the British and Europeans. Traditionally, Europeans have eaten less cereal per person than people in the United States. However, these areas were selected because their breakfast habits are similar to those in the United States.

Although the Kellogg Company has sold cereal in London since 1924, it recently modernized and expanded its foreign factories. Kellogg achieves about 40 percent of its sales outside of the United States. The company expects sales to increase. Advertising and selling of cereals in a global marketplace will continue to be a challenge for Tony the Tiger and his buddies.

Niacina	16.0 mg.
Thiamina (B₁)	1.0 mg.
Riboflavina (B₂)	1.5 mg
Vitamina B₆	1.8 mg
Vitamina D	2.8 µg
Hierro	6.7 mg

Una ración de 30 gramos de Frostis proporciona por lo menos una cuarta parte de estas vitaminas para un adulto (o una tercera parte para un niño), y aproximadamente una sexta parte del hierro que se recomienda para la toma diaria.

INGREDIENTES:

Maíz, Azúcar, Sal, Malta, Niacina, Hierro reducido, Vitamina B₆, Riboflavina, Thiamina, y Vitamina D₃.

Kellogg's® y Kellogg's Frostis® son marcas registradas por Kellogg Co., Battle Creek, Michigan, U.S.A.

Fabricado por Kellogg-Figueras España, S.A. en Valls (Tarragona).

사 용 법
1. 켈로그 씨리얼 30g 당 우유 120ml 의 비율로 씨리얼위에 우유를 부어 주세요.
2. 찬 우유를 넣어 드시면 바삭바삭 하고 고소한 맛이 한층 진해집니다.
3. 구미에 따라 설탕을 넣어 드시면 훨씬 맛이 있습니다.

전 세계적으로 인정받는 신용의 상표
켈로그의 빨간색 상표는 널리 알려져 있습니다.
이 상표는 켈로그회사의 설립자

Survival for every company depends on creating and delivering items that consumers will buy. Distribution of products along with developing consumer awareness are major tasks of marketing. Marketing does not always involve a specific good or service. Places such as Bermuda, Jamaica, Mexico, and Puerto Rico advertise on television and in magazines to attract visitors. This type of marketing can stimulate consumer interest in a variety of goods and services in those geographic areas.

Some businesses sell carpeting in one city, while others sell global telecommunications systems throughout the world. Both companies, however, must get the product or service from the producer to the consumer. Customers must be made aware of a product. Then, the item must be delivered at a cost acceptable to both the buyer and the seller.

Marketing involves activities necessary to get goods and services from the producer to the consumer. Marketing includes shipping, packaging, pricing, advertising, selling, and many other tasks. **International marketing** involves marketing activities between sellers and buyers in different countries. Japanese automobile manufacturers perform marketing activities in more than 100 countries. Overnight delivery services are also involved in international marketing as they move packages among countries and continents.

The main focus of marketing is to define and sell to a specific group. A **market** refers to the likely customers for a good or service. Markets could be teenagers in France or retired people in Mexico. Markets are commonly divided into two categories—consumer markets and commercial markets.

Consumer Markets

A **consumer market** consists of individuals and households who are end users of goods and services. You are part of the consumer market when you buy food, clothing, transportation, health care, and recreational products. Consumer markets exist in every country of the world. However, buying habits vary because of factors such as climate, culture, political environment, values, tradition, and religious beliefs.

Commercial Markets

Not all goods and services are sold to end users. **Commercial markets**, also called *organizational markets*, consist of buyers who purchase items for resale or additional production. These buyers include manufacturers, stores, schools, hotels, hospitals, and governments. Items commonly purchased in commercial markets are raw materials, machines, machine parts, warehouses, office equipment, office space, and office supplies.

Commercial markets are important in countries with developing economies. As nations create more factories and start companies, jobs are created. The income earned by these employees contributes to increased consumer spending, which results in an expanded economy.

Global Business Example: Fast Food Goes Global

In recent years, fast-food companies have expanded their international marketing activities into new areas. Burger King, Arby's, Taco Bell, and Wendy's became new competition for McDonald's and Kentucky Fried Chicken (KFC) in Mexico. At about the same time, KFC opened its first restaurant in Paris to compete against McDonald's and Burger King. This was the second of 125 KFC restaurants planned for France by 1996.

GLOBAL MARKETING OPPORTUNITIES

Most businesses need to develop new markets in order to maintain and expand profits. More and more, new customers are found in other countries. For example when sales for electronic products leveled off for Asian companies in their home region, these firms expanded to customers in South America and Europe.

Opportunities for international marketing are influenced by five global trends: expanded communications, technology, changing political situations, increased competition, and changing demographics.

Expanded Communications

Computer networks make it possible to communicate quickly with customers all over the world (see Figure 18-1). Fax machines, electronic mail, and interactive television allow companies to respond to requests from customers within minutes.

Technology

Automated production systems have made it easier for companies to set up manufacturing plants in other countries. Technology has also improved product distribution. Companies are able to ship goods from one location to destinations around the world within a matter of days or, perhaps, within hours.

Changing Political Situations

Countries that desire economic growth are cooperating with new trading partners. Several nations that were formerly governed by communism now have a more cooperative economic attitude toward international business. Many global companies now do business in various eastern European countries in which trade was previously restricted.

Increased Competition

As more companies get involved in exporting, business firms look for new markets in other countries. As discussed in Chapter 5, a more competitive environment requires companies to be more creative and more efficient.

Changing Demographics

Demographics are the traits of a country's population, such as birthrate, age distribution, marriage rate, gender distribution, income distribution, education level, and housing situation. Demographic trends create different marketing opportunities. A lower birthrate in a country could

Figure 18-1
Expanded communication networks increase the speed of international marketing transactions.

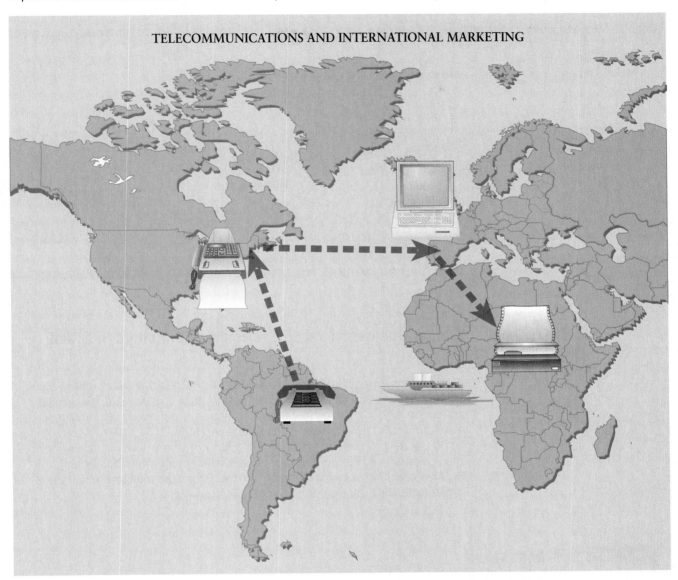

TELECOMMUNICATIONS AND INTERNATIONAL MARKETING

mean a baby-food company must market in other nations or create other types of products. Or, as more parents work, the demand for child care and convenience foods increases.

As shown in Figure 18-2 on page 384, identifying business opportunities is the start of the marketing process. When a business finds a new use for its products or finds a new group of customers, an opportunity for expanded marketing exists. The Disney Company, for example, built amusement parks in Japan and France. The company saw opportunities for foreign expansion of its entertainment services.

Figure 18-2

This process can help a company plan and execute its global marketing activities.

THE MARKETING PROCESS

Identify Business Opportunities → Evaluate Potential Demand and Consumer Behavior Patterns → Plan the Marketing Strategy for the Marketing Mix Based on Marketing Research → Carry Out the Marketing Plan

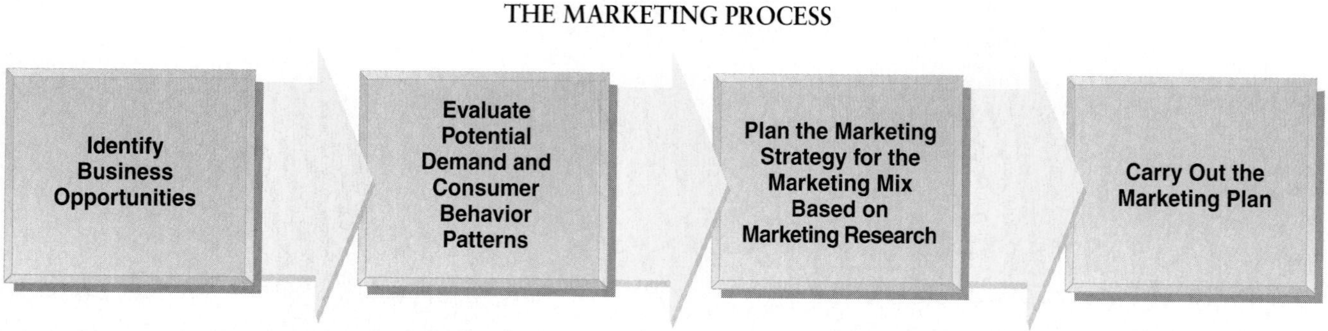

Global Business Example: Banking Customers in Brazil

Eighty percent of Brazilians earn only $60 to $120 a month. However, some banks have aimed their marketing activities toward the smaller group of higher income customers. Citibank increased its advertising toward the 800,000 people in Brazil earning at least $2,500 a month. The bank wanted to provide savings, checking, and credit card business to these Brazilians. Banco Itau created advertisements to highlight its banking by telephone service. Crefisul, a local bank, also increased its marketing activities targeted at upper income customers.

THE MARKETING MIX

As a company plans and organizes its global marketing activities, several questions must be considered. What will be sold? How much will be charged? How will the item get to the consumer? How will consumers become informed about the product? These questions address the four major elements of the **marketing mix**: product, price, distribution, and promotion.

The marketing mix is important whether you are selling clothing in a small community or expanding credit card services throughout South

Unit 5 Marketing in a Global Economy

America. Figure 18-3 illustrates the four elements of the marketing mix: product, price, distribution, and promotion.

Product

Before people will buy anything, the items must satisfy a need or want. **Product** refers to an item (good or service) being offered for sale that satisfies consumer demand. The term *product* refers to everything from automobiles and green beans to life insurance and cable television

Figure 18-3

Businesses coordinate the four elements of the marketing mix to reach their customers.

THE MARKETING MIX

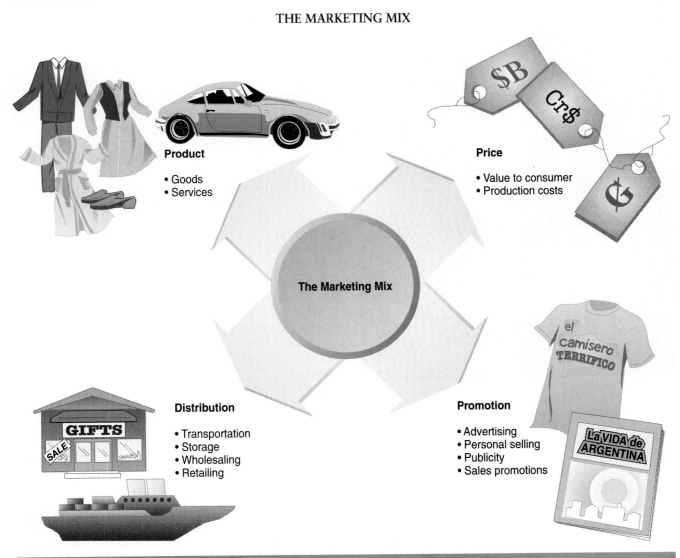

Product
• Goods
• Services

Price
• Value to consumer
• Production costs

The Marketing Mix

Distribution
• Transportation
• Storage
• Wholesaling
• Retailing

Promotion
• Advertising
• Personal selling
• Publicity
• Sales promotions

Global Highlight: The Rain Forest

Rain forests are located in 33 countries in Africa, Asia, and Central and South America. The largest rain forest covers areas in Brazil, French Guiana, Suriname, Guyana, Venezuela, Colombia, Ecuador, Peru, Bolivia, and Chile.

Many food products we commonly eat originated in rain forests. These include avocados, bananas, black pepper, cashews, chocolate, cinnamon, coconuts, coffee, cola, lemons, oranges, sugarcane, and vanilla.

More than 5 million different plant and animal species live in rain forests. Tens of thousands of other species may still be undiscovered. In the Amazon River region of Brazil, every few miles you will find hundreds of different insects, mammals, birds, reptiles, and amphibians making their homes in trees and other plant life.

Many plants from these jungles are used to treat various diseases, including cancer. Aspirin was originally made from a tropical willow tree. Cures for some diseases may lie in uncharted rain forest regions.

In recent years farmers, loggers, cattle ranchers, and highway builders have used many rain forest areas. Their activities have resulted in a changed environment. Many plants and animals are lost forever. It is estimated that rain forests are being destroyed at the rate of a football field a second (55,000 square miles a year). Much of the Pacific rain forests in Guatemala, for example, are now used for coffee, cotton, and sugar farming. Attempts are being made to plant over 50 million new trees in that country to improve the ecology.

Throughout the world, environmental groups are working to save the rain forests. Actions recommended for those concerned about the situation include recycling, using reusable containers, and avoiding products that come from destroyed rain forest areas.

channels. Not all products are offered by businesses. Nonprofit organizations, such as museums and symphony orchestras, offer educational and cultural experiences as their *products*.

The acceptance of a product or service in a foreign market can be affected by many things—such as culture, weather, and economic development. For example, instant foods may not sell in cultures where careful preparation of the family meal is important.

Price

The monetary value of a product agreed on between a buyer and a seller is the **price**. What if you agree to purchase 100 stereo systems at a price of £86 per stereo from a United Kingdom firm? Do you know how much you are paying? As you know, different nations use different money systems. Prices may be stated in terms of deutsche marks, yen, or other currency.

Distribution

Distribution involves the activities to physically move and transfer ownership of goods and services from producer to consumer. Transporting, storing, sorting, ordering, and retailing are examples of distribution activities. Distribution activities vary from country to country. For example, some countries do not have refrigeration systems in stores. Therefore, products like milk are distributed differently than in the United States.

Promotion

The final component of the marketing mix is promotion. **Promotion** involves the marketing efforts that inform and persuade customers. Different languages and customs influence promotional decisions. Many companies have used inappropriate wording when advertising in another country. In Germany, Pepsi's advertising slogan "Come alive with Pepsi" was translated as "Come alive out of the grave with Pepsi."

Marketing of Services

Demand for health care, financial services, and information systems has increased in recent years. This demand has resulted in expanded marketing opportunities for these and other services. Consumer services include those provided by lawyers, doctors, dentists, hairstylists, day-care centers, repair shops, travel agencies, and music teachers. Commercial services include advertising, data processing, delivery, custodial, security, and equipment rental. All types of services continue to grow in importance for companies involved in international business.

When a business markets services, it must adapt the marketing mix for a nonphysical item. Many of the advertising and pricing activities used for goods also apply to services. Distribution of services, however, is quite different. The service is most often produced at the time of consumption. For example, a haircut or dental checkup is produced and consumed at one time.

Global Business Exercise: The Latin American Marketing Mix

Describe each component of the marketing mix that the following businesses might use. For each situation: (1) identify the product or service, (2) give one factor that might affect price, (3) describe a possible distribution method, and (4) explain a possible promotion.

   a. A timber company in Chile,

   b. A shoe store in Panama,

   c. A fruit farmer in Guatemala, and

   d. A restaurant in Brazil.

THE MARKETING PLAN

As previously discussed, a *marketing plan* is a document that describes the marketing activities of an organization. A marketing plan usually consists of the sections shown in Figure 18-4.

The first item of the marketing plan presents what the company wants to accomplish. Common marketing goals may be "to increase consumer awareness for our new personal computer," "to reduce selling costs among regular customers," or "to increase sales in the South American region."

The second part describes the company's customers. What are their needs? What types of television programs do they watch? How often do they go to the store? This information helps the company meet consumer needs.

Parts three and four of the marketing plan provide *external* information to make wise selling decisions. Part five presents *internal* information about the people and funds available within the organization. Every company has limited resources.

The final two parts of the marketing plan help to schedule the marketing activities and measure the success of the actions taken. Measurement of success can be done by comparing results with the goals. How many new customers were obtained? How does this compare to the number we wanted to obtain?

Figure 18-4

A marketing plan provides a business with details for promoting, selling, and distributing a product or service.

THE PARTS OF A MARKETING PLAN

1. Company Goals	2. A Description of Customers and Their Needs	3. Information about Competitors

4. Information about Economic, Social, Legal, and Technological Trends	5. Financial and Human Resources Available	6. A Time Line of Actions to Be Taken	7. Methods for Measuring Success

THE MARKETING ENVIRONMENT

Factors external to companies affect all marketing decisions. As food companies expand into foreign markets, they may have to adapt their recipes to meet the tastes of other cultures. A different seasoning for existing food items may be necessary. Or, they may sell foods not usually sold in their home country. All business activities are affected by economic, social, political, technological, and legal influences.

A company must consider the tastes, habits, and customs that influence consumer behavior in a foreign business environment. Economic conditions such as high inflation may discourage a company from entering a foreign market. Marketers must also be sensitive to social customs and religious beliefs. A message in a Pepsi advertisement in Israel had a caption referring to "Ten Million Years Before the Choice," which contradicts the Orthodox Jewish belief that the universe was created a little more than 5,750 years ago.

Political and legal factors also affect marketing decisions. For example as political differences resulted in the division of Yugoslavia into different countries, companies had to deal with different government regulations in various regions.

Global Business Exercise: Welcome to the United States

Find a product made in another country and sold in the United States. Be careful! Many products that appear to have a foreign origin are actually from U.S.-based companies. Then, complete the following activities:

1. What are some probable reasons that the company decided to market its product in the United States?

2. What are some difficulties that the company may have encountered when introducing the product to this market?

3. Identify each element of the marketing mix for the product (product description, price, stores at which it is sold, and types of advertising and other promotions).

4. What economic and social factors may contribute to the success or failure of the product in the United States?

CONSUMER BEHAVIOR

Think about why you made a recent purchase. The item may have been something you needed for school. Or, it could have been something that you enjoy using. Most consumer purchases involve several factors. Multiply this by the many buying decisions made in the world each day, and you can see that consumer behavior is quite complex. Figure 18-5 provides an overview of the items that can influence consumer behavior.

Physical and Emotional Needs

Every person requires air, water, food, shelter, clothing, and health care. But these basic needs of life can differ for people in different countries. Consumers in industrialized countries demand easy-to-prepare food products, current-fashion clothing, and homes with many appliances and comforts. People in less developed economies may have home-grown food, homemade clothing, and modest housing. In both situations, however, physical needs influence consumer decisions.

Another level of consumer needs involves human emotions. People in many cultures want to feel good about themselves and want to be accepted by others. Products may be offered that appeal to these emotional needs. Personal care products, cosmetics, clothing, and even automobiles are presented to appeal to a need for social acceptance and personal satisfaction.

Geographic and Demographic Factors

Where you live influences buying habits. A person in a warm area will require different housing, clothing, and may prefer different foods than someone living in a cold climate. Another geographic factor influencing consumer buying habits is terrain. Living in mountain areas requires different types of transportation and consumer products than living in prairie regions.

Demographic traits such as your age, gender, and family situation influence how you spend your money. Information on the birthrate, age, marriage, income, education level, and housing situation differ

Figure 18-5
Consumer buying decisions are influenced by many factors.

FACTORS AFFECTING CONSUMER BEHAVIOR

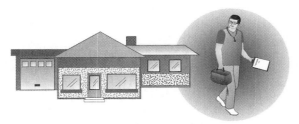

Physical and Emotional Needs

Food, clothing, shelter, health care, transportation, approval of others, personal satisfaction

Geographic and Demographic Factors

Location, climate, population trends, age, gender, income, education

Personality and Psychographic Factors

Attitudes, beliefs, opinions, personality traits, activities, interests

Social and Cultural Factors

Business organizations, community activities, religious or political affiliation, family, friends

from country to country and have a strong effect on a company's marketing plans. For example as the people of a nation live longer, elderly consumers will demand health, travel, and recreational services.

Data show that people in New Zealand, Canada, the United States, and Australia move more often than people in other countries. This information may help moving companies and relocation-related services plan business activities. These businesses will find more marketing opportunities in countries with high mobility rates.

Personality and Psychographic Factors

Attitudes are another influence on consumer behavior. Each day our attitudes and beliefs are shaped by experiences and information. These inputs, in turn, create the personality that determines our buying decisions. Personality traits include your attitudes toward risk, change, convenience, and competition. Marketers use this information to attract customers to certain goods and services.

Attempts to better understand personality traits resulted in the study of psychographics. **Psychographics** are buying factors related to lifestyle and psychological influences, such as activities, interests, and opinions. A person's *psychographic profile* may include hobbies, family activities, work interests, and political and social opinions. As you would probably guess, cultural experiences make the psychographic characteristics of U.S. consumers different from those of Argentineans, Indians, or Moroccans.

Social and Cultural Factors

How we relate to others is another consumer buying factor. Families, friends, business organizations, community activities, and religious affiliation can affect buying behavior. An understanding of such things as social structure and religion in a culture is critical to successful international marketing decisions.

Global Business Example: Fast Food in South Korea

South Korea has become the second largest consumer market in Asia for fast food, after Japan. The main market is young people, especially high school and college females. This group makes up about 70 percent of the market. They spend many hours at these restaurants, which have become afternoon gathering places. U.S. fast-food companies find it easy to do business in South Korea since their menus require minimal adaptation.

Marketers use consumer buying factors to divide customers into subsets that have similar needs. After segmenting the market, marketers must determine which subgroup to serve.

Market Segments

A **market segment** is a distinct subgroup of customers that share certain personal or behavioral characteristics. High-income individuals, for example, purchase certain items that lower income people would not be able to afford. Market segments can be based on characteristics such as demographics, psychographics, buying behavior, or product benefits (see Figure 18-6 on page 394).

Social and economic factors cause changes in market segments. In recent years, more women began working in Japan. This trend resulted in new market segments that demanded more child care services and convenience foods.

Market segments are commonly given names that describe the attitudes and behaviors of those in the group. *Achievers* may be used to refer to successful, upper income people. *Strivers* could describe young, hard-working people. *Traditionals* would be the consumers who resist

Figure 18-6

Consumer markets are divided into market segments based on personal characteristics, attitudes, activities, and buying preferences.

MARKET SEGMENTATION

Demographics

People of different gender, income, age, and family situations require different products. Households with a newborn child will buy diapers or use a diaper service; whereas, single people may be interested in travel services.

Psychographics

Different opinions and attitudes can affect buying; people concerned about nutrition select different food items than other consumers.

Buying Behavior

Actions and shopping preferences differ; some shoppers use mail-order buying, while others go to shopping malls or stores.

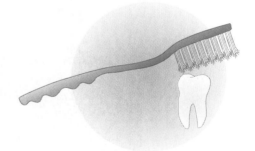

Product Benefits

People require different advantages from their buying choices; some people prefer a toothpaste with good taste, while others want one that fights cavities.

change and prefer the familiar. Since each market segment has different attitudes and buying habits, marketing actions aimed at each group must be different.

Market segments usually differ from country to country. Dividing potential customers into subgroups based on type of employment would not be practical in a nation in which most people work in agricultural jobs.

394

Target Market

A **target market** is the particular market segment that a company plans to serve. After identifying the target market, a company attempts to meet the specific needs of those customers. As shown in Figure 18-7, target markets for international business are commonly selected on the basis of geography.

Figure 18-7
A company involved in international marketing commonly selects one or more countries as its target market.

A GEOGRAPHIC TARGET MARKET IN CENTRAL AND SOUTH AMERICA

To better understand consumers and to segment and target markets effectively, companies analyze buyer behavior through marketing research. Marketing research may be conducted to determine the television viewing habits of Japanese college students or the potential sales among older consumers for an Italian soft drink in the United States.

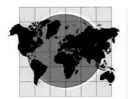

Global Business Example: Market Segments for the Russian Consumer

As foreign companies increased their marketing and selling activities in Russia, researchers took a closer look at Russian customers. Five market segments were created to describe the buying habits of Russian consumers based on their attitudes and beliefs:

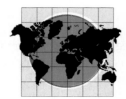

1. *Kuptsi* (or merchants) were found to be practical and seek value in their buying.
2. *Cossacks* were determined to be independent and ambitious status seekers.
3. *Students* tended to be passive and idealistic.
4. *Business executives* were busy, ambitious, and receptive to products and ideas from industrialized countries.
5. *Russian souls* were found to be passive, fearful of new ideas, and followers of others.

This market research information can be used to target the selling of various products and services to the best potential customers.

Sources: Adapted from "Figuring Out the Russian Consumer," by Stuart Elliott, *The New York Times,* April 1, 1992, pp. C1, C19 and *The Russian Consumer: A New Perspective and a Marketing Approach,* DMB&B Worldwide Communications, New York.

Back to the Beginning: Breakfast in Britain

Reread the case at the beginning of this chapter and answer the following questions:

1. What factors influenced cereal companies to expand their marketing in foreign countries?
2. What problems might a cereal company face when planning to sell its products in a new foreign market?
3. What actions might a cereal company take when adapting its marketing mix to new customers?

KNOWING GLOBAL BUSINESS TERMS

The following terms should become part of your business vocabulary. For each numbered item find the term that has the same meaning.

- commercial markets
- consumer market
- demographics
- distribution
- international marketing
- market
- marketing mix

- market segment
- price
- product
- promotion
- psychographics
- target market

1. The monetary value of the product agreed upon between a buyer and a seller.
2. Buying factors related to lifestyle and psychological influences, such as activities, interests, and opinions.
3. Marketing activities to inform and persuade customers.
4. Likely customers for a good or service.
5. Product, price, distribution, and promotion activities among buyers and sellers in different countries.
6. The activities needed to physically move and transfer ownership of goods and services from producer to consumer.
7. The division of a market into distinct subgroups.
8. The traits of a country's population, such as gender distribution, birthrate, marriage rate, age distribution, income distribution, and educational level.
9. An item (good or service) offered for sale that satisfies consumer demand.
10. Individuals and households who are end users of goods and services.
11. The four major elements (product, price, distribution, and promotion) of marketing.
12. Buyers who purchase items for resale or additional production.
13. The group of customers, the country, or the geographic region that a company plans to serve.

REVIEWING YOUR READING

Answer these questions to reinforce your knowledge of the main ideas of this chapter.

1. What business activities are included in marketing?
2. How do consumer markets and commercial markets differ?
3. What is a global marketing opportunity and what influences it?
4. What are the four elements of the marketing mix?
5. How does a marketing plan serve the needs of an organization?
6. What factors affect the marketing environment of a company?
7. What factors influence consumer behavior?
8. Give an example of how a person's needs might affect consumer behavior.
9. What is the difference between demographics and psychographics?
10. What is meant by the target market of a company?
11. What types of consumer characteristics are used to segment markets?

EXPANDING YOUR HORIZONS

You will not find the complete answers to the following questions in your textbook. You will need to use your critical-thinking skills. Think about these questions, gather information from other sources, analyze possible responses, and discuss them with others. Then, develop your own oral or written response as instructed by your teacher.

1. How can marketing be important to both businesses and consumers?

2. How does demand for *consumer* goods and services affect demand in *commercial* markets?

3. What are some examples of global marketing opportunities created by technology or changing demographics?

4. Which element of the marketing mix needs to be adapted the most when conducting business in another country?

5. How would the marketing plan for services of a nonprofit organization differ from the marketing activities for a tangible product?

6. What social and economic factors might affect how a society defines its basic consumer needs?

7. Why do you think many marketing managers believe that demographic information has limited value for defining a company's target market?

8. List some psychographic factors that could affect a person's buying habits.

9. What do you believe to be the most influential social institutions in our country affecting buying decisions?

10. Explain how companies could use age, interests, or attitudes to target their marketing messages to different market segments.

BUILDING RESEARCH SKILLS

The ability to find information from various sources is an important international business skill. The following activities will help you investigate various topics. You will also learn to apply class ideas to situations outside of the classroom.

1. Prepare a bulletin board or poster showing goods and services from other countries that are sold in the United States.

2. Conduct library research and prepare a two-page written report on the four elements of the marketing mix for a good or service

sold in more than one country. Compare the marketing activities in different cultures.

3. Survey several friends to determine the factors that affect their buying habits for food, clothing, or another commonly purchased item. Ask them to explain why they buy certain items. Prepare a list of common reasons that influence consumer buying decisions.

4. Select a product that is aimed at different types of customers. Examples include cereals, toothpaste, or shoes. Find advertisements that show the product aimed at different target markets. Prepare a short oral or written report telling how the selling messages are different for the different market segments.

5. *Global Career Activity.* Prepare a letter of application for a job with an international marketing company. Explain how your global marketing knowledge could be useful to the company. List examples of methods that the company might consider to enhance its international marketing plan.

Continuing Enrichment Project: An International Marketing Plan

Create a marketing plan for a company that is expanding its selling activities into another geographic region. Use information from magazine articles, almanacs, company materials, and other library sources.

Your written summary should include the following:

1. Company goals: Clearly state the objectives that the business wants to achieve, including the target country or region.

2. Description of customers and their needs: Provide details of the buying behaviors of potential customers.

3. Information about competitors: Describe other companies that are aiming their marketing activities at the same customers.

4. Information about economic, social, legal, and technological trends: Describe unique factors that will affect the company's marketing activities.

5. Financial and human resources available: List estimated costs and the skills employees will need to achieve the company's goals.

6. Time line of actions to be taken: Estimate the amount of time that will be needed to implement the marketing plan.

7. Methods for measuring success: Describe how the company will know if it has achieved its goals.

Regional Profile

Central and South America

As your four-wheel drive truck struggles up the bank of yet another river crossing, your guide gestures through the dust and shouts that Bocay is just around the next bend in the narrow road. The daylong drive from Managua, Nicaragua, has brought you to the mountain village of Bocay. From here you will begin the 70-mile canoe trip down the Río de Bocay to the Sumu village.

Your truck passes under a small waterfall where villagers are washing clothes on the rocks. Then, as you crest a small rise, you see the village stretching along the bank of a muddy river. Your eyes confirm what your earlier research told you of this town. Its 2,000 people live in two-room, box-like houses along the road; the walls are wooden, the roofs are tin, and the floors are dirt. There is no plumbing, but there is talk of having electricity in a few months. A family shares some of its rice and beans with you and offers you a place to sleep on the floor, next to a few chickens. Your studies in anthropology did not prepare you emotionally for this culture that is so different from your own.

The next morning, you are standing on the river bank as four Sumus prepare the dugout (canoe). They speak Sumo, your guide speaks Spanish, and you speak English and very little Spanish; this will be interesting. The river trip takes you through miles of natural beauty. The canoe passes through steep walls of rock and roaring rapids. You see alligators and red macaws on the shore. White-faced monkeys scream through the vines; you are in a rain forest.

The 1,800 Sumus that live in five villages along the Río de Bocay are having a difficult time surviving. Their bamboo huts contain just a few pots and, maybe, some rice and beans. They wear clothes that are secondhand: dresses, jeans, and T-shirts from North America. However, the Sumus are in the process of setting up a cooperative business in each village. The Sumu will make crafts from the wood found in the forest, and the villagers will cooperatively sell these products in markets like Bocay.

The Mayan Empire extended over much of Central America between 250 and 900 A.D. Mayan culture centered around religion and ceremony. Mayan cities contained great temple-pyramids which attracted large crowds during festivals. The study of astronomy and mathematics was essential to Mayan religion.

Another of the great empires of Latin America was the Inca Empire whose ruins of Machu Picchu in the Andes Mountains of Peru attract visitors from all over the world. The Inca Empire extended from the northern border of modern Ecuador to central Chile. Its 10-12 million inhabitants enjoyed the benefits of the strong central government in return for helping with the construction of public buildings and roads. The important buildings were plated in gold. In 1532 the Spanish, led by the conquistador Francisco Pizarro, captured the Incan Emperor Atahuallpa. Atahuallpa was murdered by the Spanish in 1533, leaving the Inca without a leader.

The colonization of Central and South America was based on an economic system known as mercantilism—in which a nation's power depended on its accumulation of wealth. Portuguese and Spanish ships carried away great quantities of gold, silver, and other raw materials to the parent countries. In turn, the colonies served as markets for manufactured exports. The Native Americans were forced to work the mines and plantations. Later when European diseases significantly reduced the Inca population, Africans were enslaved and imported.

During the colonial period, approximately 5,400 Spanish and Portuguese immigrated to Latin America each year. These immigrants developed a society based on their European heritage, but infused with cultural aspects of their new environment. They brought Roman Catholicism to the colonies and it remains today the dominant religion.

In the early 1800s, the nationalist leaders Simón Bolívar, José de San Martín, and Bernardo O'Higgins led wars of independence from Spanish rule. Brazilian independence from Portugal, however, was fostered by the liberal Portuguese King João VI, who fled to Brazil after Napoléon invaded his country.

Traditionally, Latin American governments since the European conquest have been controlled by wealthy landowners, merchants, and the military. Governments were frequently overthrown by the army in an attempt to gain power or to protect the wealth and power of the ruling class. Those that spoke up for the poor were often assassinated. In 1991 and 1992 coup attempts occurred in Guatemala, Haiti, Venezuela, and Peru.

The Andes Mountains and their snowcapped peaks extend almost 4,500 miles from Venezuela to the tip of South America, dominating the topography of the western part of the continent. Inland plains spread from Venezuela south through Brazil, Paraguay, Uruguay, and Argentina. A vast desert region in Peru and Chile is one of the driest areas in the world. Rain forests are common along the east coast of Central America; the Amazon basin rain forest takes up one-third of South America. The longest river in the Western Hemisphere is the Amazon. It flows 4,000 miles across the continent before pouring its vital nutrients into the ocean, enriching sea life as far away as the Grand Banks of Newfoundland.

The ethnic groups of Central and South America are as diverse as the land. African, Asian, European, Native American, Mestizo (Native American-European), and Mulatto (European-African) all live together in this region.

Farming and mining continue to be the most important industries in Latin America. Coffee, sugar, bananas, wheat, cotton, and cacao are exported. However, the region still has difficulty feeding its people because of a growing population and primitive farming methods. A few countries produce oil and natural gas. Most countries mine mineral resources, such as, iron, tin, copper, silver, lead, and gold. Brazil ranks in the top ten countries for world gold production.

Future economic growth will depend on industrial development. Many governments are looking to their sparsely populated interiors for hydroelectric power to run factories and offices. The interiors are also rich in timber and could provide farms for the millions of hungry, landless peasants. However, rain forests are essential to the global environment and must be preserved. The wild rivers attract tourists and the rain forest is home to many indigenous people. The forests also contain an abundance of animal species and plants, which are possible sources of medicines.

Latin American nations are under pressure to protect the environment at the expense of industrial development. Yet, it is the Northern countries that continue to consume and pollute. The population of Latin America could double in the next 25 years. Governments will be hard-pressed to fill basic food, housing, health, and education needs for their people. These social, economic, and health problems are all interrelated, and their solutions will be found by those regional and global problem-solvers who comprehend just how interdependent we are.

CHAPTER 9

Developing Goods and Services for Global Markets

After studying this chapter and completing the end-of-chapter activities, you will be able to

- Describe sources of product opportunities for international marketing.
- Identify categories of consumer products and the importance of product lines.
- Explain how services are marketed.
- Discuss the steps in the new-product development process.
- Name the steps in the marketing research process.
- Describe data collection methods used in international marketing research.
- Describe branding and packaging techniques used by global business organizations.
- Explain actions related to a global product strategy.

Barbie Goes Global

The Barbie doll was introduced in the United States in 1959, when 351,000 were sold at $3 each. Since then, more than 500 million Barbies have been sold. While Mattel is assured of new young U.S. consumers each year, the company also looks to markets in other countries for Barbie sales.

The first Barbie dolls were manufactured in Japan in the late 1950s. In the late 1970s, Mattel started distributing the dolls in Japan by creating a limited joint venture with the Bandai Company. The first Barbies sold in Japan had dark eyes. Later the company began marketing its blue-eyed Barbie that is sold everywhere else in the world.

When Barbie was introduced in the Czech Republic (formerly part of Czechoslovakia) she wore traditional Czech clothing of red tights under a yellow and black skirt and black vest. When first available, more than 1,000 dolls were sold a day. People in Prague stood in line for hours to pay from $5 to $20 for dolls and accessories. The average monthly salary of a skilled worker was about $130.

Mattel's global marketing efforts have been a success. Today, Barbie dolls and related items are sold in about 100 countries. As of the early 1990s, more than 60 percent of Mattel's sales were outside of the United States.

Every day you see advertisements for clothing, food, motor vehicles, banks, and other consumer goods and services. It sometimes seems as though everyone has something to sell. When you apply for a job, you are selling your talents and abilities. The product offerings of global companies are the foundation of international business and foreign trade.

PRODUCT OPPORTUNITIES FOR INTERNATIONAL MARKETING

A *product* is a marketplace offering (good or service) that satisfies a need or want. Marketing's major goal is to satisfy unmet needs. This can be accomplished in one of four ways.

A New Product

An organization's marketing activities may start with a marketplace offering that did not previously exist. For example before Apple introduced the personal computer in the late 1970s, this product was almost unknown. Federal Express pioneered overnight delivery services. Now, several companies are involved in this industry.

An Improved Product

Sometimes a product is on the market for several years; however, it is no longer as popular among consumers. When this happens a company may introduce variations, such as new flavors of a food product. Or, technology may result in improved versions of an item.

An Existing Product with a New Use

When a company wants to expand its sales, attempts may be made to find new uses for a product that has been on the market for years. Various kitchen storage containers have been adapted to store tools and supplies for a home workshop or office.

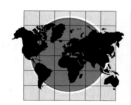

Global Business Example: Skippy in Hungary

Peanut butter is not as popular in other countries as it is in the United States and Canada. In an attempt to expand sales of Skippy peanut butter, CPC International obtained assistance from Dove Frucht, a trading company in Budapest, Hungary. Most young Hungarians liked the taste of the product. Parents, however, had concerns since the $4 price for a 12-ounce jar is quite expensive for consumers in that country. The average monthly wage in Hungary is about $150. The company only had a limited number of Hungarian households that could afford the product.

An Existing Product Sold in a New Market

In the late 1970s and early 1980s when fewer babies were born, Johnson Baby Shampoo was advertised as being mild for adults who want to shampoo every day. Existing products sold in new markets are a significant part of international business. Soft drinks, fast foods, and hundreds of other products that originated in one country are now sold in the global marketplace.

MARKETING PRODUCTS AROUND THE WORLD

Each day, people around the world buy and use thousands of different products. A student in Brazil buys a home computer, while a person in Egypt purchases a bottled soft drink.

Consumer Product Categories

The many items available in the global marketplace can be classified as convenience goods, shopping goods, or specialty goods. Figure 19-1 provides examples for each of these groups.

Figure 19-1
The items bought by people around the world can be classified as convenience goods, shopping goods, or specialty goods.

TYPES OF CONSUMER PRODUCTS

Convenience Goods

Shopping Goods

Specialty Goods

Convenience Goods.   You probably regularly buy low-cost items without thinking much about them. **Convenience goods** are inexpensive items that require little shopping effort. Examples of convenience goods include snacks, soft drinks, personal care products, and school supplies. Marketing for convenience goods involves offering an item in many locations. For example, candy bars are sold in food stores, movie theaters, gas stations, and vending machines.

Shopping Goods.   Some products, such as clothing, furniture, cameras, televisions, and home appliances, are purchased only after consumers take some time to compare buying alternatives. **Shopping goods** are products purchased after consumers compare brands and stores. Shopping goods require a marketing effort that communicates differences in price, quality, and features of various brands.

Stores selling shopping goods may offer several brands and models of the same item to prevent a customer from going to another store to compare products. You will commonly see stores with many makes and models of video recorders or cameras.

Products that are convenience goods in one culture may be shopping goods in another. Toothpaste for U.S. consumers is usually bought quickly without much thought. This same purchase in some South American nations may require much comparison shopping and thought. Consumers in these countries may not be familiar with the item or the toothpaste may be an expensive purchase compared to their income.

Specialty Goods.   When buying certain products, you would probably take a lot of time and effort. **Specialty goods** are unique products that consumers make a special effort to obtain. Buyers of these items refuse to accept substitutes. Marketing of specialty goods requires high brand recognition. In Europe for example, various types of designer clothing, jewelry from well-known firms, and customized automobiles would only be available at selected stores.

The Product Line

Manufacturing companies and stores usually produce and offer a variety of items. A **product line** is an assortment of closely related products to meet the varied needs of target customers. Shoe stores commonly include socks, shoelaces, and shoe polish in their product lines. Procter and Gamble makes different shampoos for people with different wants and needs. One shampoo is for people with a dandruff problem; another one is for easy-to-manage hair.

Organizational Products

Organizational products are items used to produce other goods and services. Factories, machinery, office equipment, component parts, and raw materials are used by companies in their daily business activities.

Most organizational products require less adaptation than do consumer goods before they are sold in different countries. This is a result of the fact that production activities are less influenced by cultural factors and personal taste than consumer purchases. A variety of services are also used by organizations. *Commercial services* may include security systems, information processing, maintenance of equipment, and overnight package delivery.

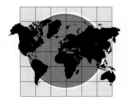

Global Business Example: "Please Turn Down That Refrigerator!"

When refrigerators produced by manufacturers in Western nations were first sold in Japan, they were considered too noisy by Japanese consumers. The motors needed to operate the cooling unit could easily be heard through the very thin walls of most Japanese homes and apartments. This situation resulted in companies developing a quieter refrigerator designed specifically to meet market needs.

CONSUMER SERVICES

How does buying a haircut differ from buying a can of green beans? One is a service, and one is a good. Services are intangible while goods are tangible.

Characteristics of Services

Services cannot be touched like a physical item. In other words, services are *intangible*. Most purchases are a combination of both tangible and intangible items. While you can touch the reel from which a movie is shown, the movie you have seen becomes a memory that is intangible. Since services are intangible, it is more difficult to judge the quality of these purchases. Common measures of service quality are company reputation, comments from customers, and training qualifications of employees.

Increased use of computers and technology for services is contributing to more consistent quality. Automatic teller machines, when operating properly, will make fewer errors than do humans.

Services are consumed as they are produced. Mass production of services is often not possible. Each haircut, oil change, or income tax preparation is produced separately.

Services have no inventory. Empty airline seats, for example, cannot be saved and sold later; they are simply lost revenue.

Types of Services

Services available to consumers may be viewed in three categories:

1. *Rented-goods services* involve a payment for temporary use of items, such as an automobile, apartment, video, or cleaning equipment.

2. *Owned-goods services* are fees for service to the consumer's property, such as auto repair, dry cleaning, or landscaping.

3. *Nongoods services* are personal or professional services for a fee, such as health care, overnight delivery, tax return preparation, real estate sales, legal assistance, and baby-sitting.

Marketing of Services

Services require special marketing efforts. Since the consumer must often be where the service is produced, convenience of location is important. Many service businesses set up stores in shopping malls to be available to many customers. Some hospitals have created urgent care facilities in several locations. Banks bring the service to customers, such as an ATMobile or a temporary cash machine at a sporting event or concert.

The packaging of services is done through the image created by the business. Furniture, decorations, and appearance of employees can create a reputation of quality.

Services are also personalized. Each transaction for a hairstylist, tax accountant, or health-care worker will be slightly different. An organization's ability to meet the individual needs of customers is vital for success.

Services and International Trade

In recent years, services have played an important role for the United States in its foreign trade activities. While our nation has a total trade deficit, exported services far exceed imported services. Companies in other countries provide strong demand for health care, delivery services, information processing, management consulting, and financial services.

As in most industrialized countries, services in the United States are becoming a greater economic influence. As of the early 1990s, for the first time in our history, more people worked in service industries than in manufacturing companies.

Global Business Exercise: Global Marketing of Services

For each of the following situations, list a possible problem that could be encountered if a company planned to sell its service in other countries.

1. Child-care centers aimed at households with two working parents.
2. Repair service for home and office computers.
3. Carpet cleaning service for homes and businesses.
4. Trash collection and recycling service.

CREATING NEW PRODUCTS

Each year between 20,000 and 30,000 new products are introduced in the United States. However, within a year about 75 percent of them are no longer on the market. Why do most new products fail? Some say it is because too many new products are introduced into an already saturated marketplace. Others believe it is because of poor planning. Either way, new products are a high risk for companies.

The Need for New Products

Companies introduce new products for two reasons. First, as old products are no longer popular with customers, sales revenue must come from other sources. Second, competitors take actions that result in lower sales revenue. New products must match or exceed the marketplace offerings of other companies.

Sources of New Products

The needs of customers is one of the main sources of new product ideas. For example, *call waiting* was the answer for people who didn't want to miss a phone call while talking to someone else. *Caller ID* allows customers to display the telephone number of incoming calls and select which calls to answer. These services were created in direct response to customer needs. Other products that were developed to fill customer needs include carbon monoxide detectors for in-home use and wireless fences for pet containment.

Technology is another major source of new products. Fax machines, cellular phones, and computer games would never have been possible without technological breakthroughs.

New-Product Development Process

Companies try to create successful new products with the use of a logical procedure. As Figure 19-2 shows, the new product development process involves four steps. This procedure is used to help a business select products that will be likely to succeed.

Figure 19-2
Four main steps are used by companies to create and market new products.

NEW-PRODUCT DEVELOPMENT PROCESS

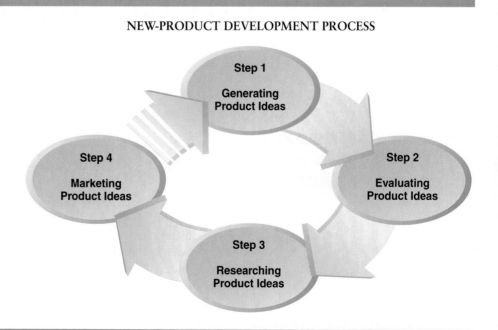

In the first stage, ideas for possible products are obtained based on comments from customers, watching other companies, and using new technology. At this stage, products planned for international markets are viewed from a global perspective.

Global Highlight: The Gauchos of Argentina

Cattle production is one of the major industries of Argentina. A gaucho, similar to a U.S. cowboy, helps to make beef and related products available for consumers in South America and around the world.

Between 1600 and 1750 early settlers in Argentina hunted wild cattle and horses for the hides. These were used to make clothing and other products. Over the next 100 years, herds of cattle were raised in the *estancia* system—large ranches in the fertile plains of the Pampas region of east and central Argentina that were worked by gauchos. Also during this time, the fat and salted meat of the cattle were processed making new products available to Argentinean consumers. This period was followed by the creation of far-reaching sheep ranches between 1830 and 1900.

Today, gauchos continue to contribute to the economic production of Argentina—as the country is one of the world's largest producers of livestock. Nearly 60 percent of Argentina's land is used for grazing and agriculture.

Next, ideas are evaluated based on cost, production possibility, and marketplace acceptance. Can the new item be offered to potential customers at an acceptable price? Are the facilities available to produce the item in needed quantities? Can the product be adapted to meet the cultural and economic needs of customers in various countries?

In the third stage, research is conducted on the proposed product to measure customer attitudes and potential sales. The research phase is covered in detail in the next section of this chapter.

The final phase of the new-product development process involves putting the item on the market. After research shows a strong probability of success, the item is produced, distributed, and sold in one or more countries.

Adapting Products to Foreign Markets

Products must be adapted to various political, social, and cultural factors. The appetite of the Japanese people for pizza is not as great as that of people in the United States. As a result, Dominos offers 10- and 12-inch pizzas in Japan instead of the 14- and 16-inch ones sold in the United States. Tang, for example, is sold in some South American countries as a "fun beverage" rather than a breakfast drink.

Global Business Example: A Japanese Approach to New Product Development

The Kao Corporation of Tokyo makes use of five principles when planning new products:

1. The new product should be useful to society now and in the future.
2. The product should be based on Kao's creative technology.
3. The item should be superior, in both cost and performance, to the new products of competitors.
4. The new product should be able to survive exhaustive product testing at all stages before going on the market.
5. The item should be able to deliver its own message of usefulness and quality at every level of distribution.

Source: Masashi Kuga, "Kao's Marketing Strategy and Marketing Intelligence System," *Journal of Advertising Research,* April-May, 1990, p. 21.

THE MARKETING RESEARCH PROCESS

When developing and marketing new products, companies must find out what consumers need, want, and are willing to buy. **Marketing research** is the orderly collecting and analyzing of data to obtain information about a specific marketing concern. While companies have investigated consumer buying patterns in over 100 countries, marketing research is done regularly in only about 30 or 40 nations.

Marketing research may be conducted to determine the television viewing habits of Australian college students. Or, a company may measure the potential sales for a Brazilian soft drink company in the United States. Figure 19-3 provides an overview of the marketing research process with an international example.

As shown in phase one of Figure 19-3, every research study starts with a research problem. The word *problem* does not necessarily mean that something is wrong—such as declining sales. A research problem provides the basis for studying some aspect of a company's marketing mix. For example, a personal computer company may conduct a marketing research study to determine the information needs of manufacturing companies in Chile. Or, a soup company may study consumer taste preferences in Jamaica. In each situation, the business seeks information to better plan and carry out its marketing activities.

Figure 19-3

The steps of the marketing research process are designed to help a company collect consumer behavior data.

THE MARKETING RESEARCH PROCESS

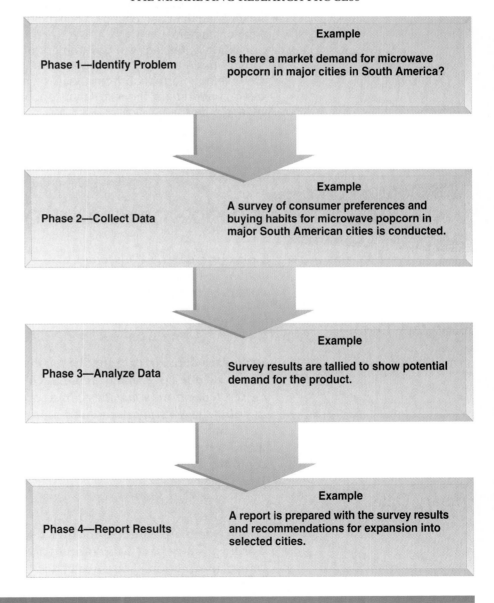

Phase 1—Identify Problem

Example

Is there a market demand for microwave popcorn in major cities in South America?

Phase 2—Collect Data

Example

A survey of consumer preferences and buying habits for microwave popcorn in major South American cities is conducted.

Phase 3—Analyze Data

Example

Survey results are tallied to show potential demand for the product.

Phase 4—Report Results

Example

A report is prepared with the survey results and recommendations for expansion into selected cities.

Global Business Example: Collecting Marketing Research Data in Venezuela

How can marketing information be obtained in countries without extensive computer systems? While visiting Caracas, a researcher may watch to see what items consumers commonly buy. These observations can help managers decide if a certain product might be successful in Venezuela.

Next, researchers may interview selected business owners about their product line. Questions may request information about what items have sold well in the past, changing consumer tastes, and common complaints from customers.

Finally, talking with government officials can provide details about foreign trade barriers and regulations in Venezuela affecting business. Combining information from these several sources can help managers better understand the marketing opportunities in nations with limited research data.

DATA COLLECTION METHODS FOR GLOBAL MARKETING RESEARCH

Collecting data is the second major phase of marketing research. As shown in Figure 19-4, data can be put into two major categories—secondary data and primary data.

Secondary Data

Secondary data are data that have already been collected and published. These include government reports, company documents, library indexes, reference books, business directories, and computerized databases. In countries with modern computerized information systems, such as the United States, secondary data sources can be very helpful. In contrast, access to secondary data may be limited in countries with few computer systems.

Primary Data

Primary data are collected to solve a specific research problem. In other words, primary data collection involves a study to obtain specific marketing information. The three major types of primary data are surveys, observations, and experiments.

Surveys.　Surveys collect data about opinions, behaviors, and knowledge of consumers. Large-scale surveys that collect numeric data, called **quantitative research**, are often used to study consumers. Companies such as A. C. Nielsen conduct surveys in various countries. The Nielsen organization measures television viewing patterns and shopping habits.

In most countries, however, collection of quantitative data is difficult. A country with few telephones makes a phone survey almost impossible and the results questionable. If a nation has a low literacy rate the use of mail surveys will have little value. These situations require that other types of research be used.

Qualitative research, using open-ended interview questions, allows researchers to obtain comments from consumers about their attitudes and behaviors. An example of qualitative research is the focus group, or group-depth interview. A **focus group** is a directed discussion with 8 to 12 people. This group interview obtains opinions, buying habits, and knowledge about a product, a package, or advertisement.

Focus groups can offer insight into planned marketing activities. This information, however, is based only on the opinions of a small group of consumers. In addition, focus groups and personal interviews are not appropriate in cultures in which people do not talk openly to strangers.

Observations.　What people say they do is often different from what they actually do. Observation is the best way to measure consumer behavior. **Observational research** involves data collection by watching

Figure 19-4
Secondary data and primary data help marketing managers make international business decisions.

SOURCES OF MARKETING RESEARCH DATA

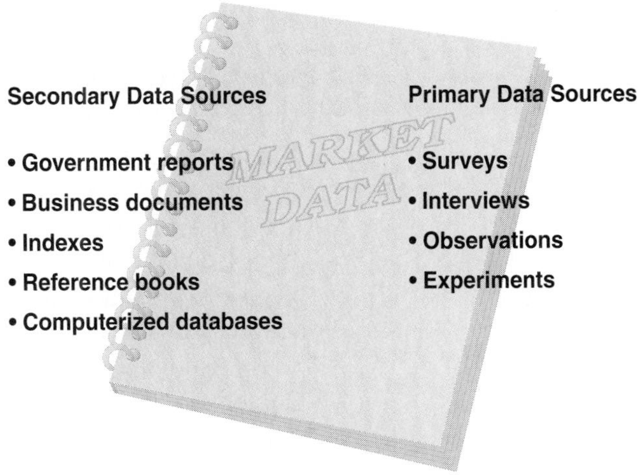

Secondary Data Sources

- Government reports
- Business documents
- Indexes
- Reference books
- Computerized databases

Primary Data Sources

- Surveys
- Interviews
- Observations
- Experiments

and recording shopping behaviors. Common observations involve watching shoppers in stores or counting customers during certain hours. Computerized cash registers with scanners allow companies to observe easily the purchases of customers.

In some research settings, such as with children, observations are necessary. These young consumers may not be able to express themselves well verbally. Observational research has one major weakness. It cannot provide information about the attitudes, opinions, or motivations of consumers.

Experiments.   The most complex type of data collection is the **experiment** involving a statistical comparison of two or more very similar situations. For example, a company may introduce a package with a photograph in one city and a package with a drawing in another city. The firm wants to know how the different packages affect consumer preference and sales. Experiments are expensive to conduct and are most helpful in industrialized countries with access to computerized data collection methods.

Experiments can also predict the success of a product before mass distribution. A **test market** is an experimental research study that measures the likely success of a new good or service. Companies often use one or two cities to try out a new item. U.S. companies usually use cities in the United States. Some firms, however, use foreign cities as test markets. Kentucky Fried Chicken tested its grilled chicken in Regina, Saskatchewan, Canada. Carewell Industries, a New Jersey company, first sold its Dentax toothbrush in Malaysia and Singapore.

Global Business Exercise: Selecting a Data Collection Method

For each of the following research situations, tell which data collection method might be most appropriate:

1. A package food company wants to know the breakfast eating habits in Chile.

2. A manufacturing company wants to determine computer needs among small businesses in Panama City, Panama.

3. A bank needs information about the satisfaction of checking account customers in Argentina.

4. A company needs information on the number of companies in Guatemala that use refrigerated food-storage areas.

5. A travel company is interested in knowing the attitudes and needs of Brazilians who travel regularly on business.

ANALYZING AND USING RESEARCH DATA

After collection, data are analyzed to make them useful for planning marketing activities. Statistical tests are commonly used with quantitative data. The results help managers make marketing decisions. By knowing which consumers watch certain television programs or read certain magazines, a manager can plan a company's advertising. Information about customer opinions and habits can help plan domestic and international marketing activities.

BRANDING AND PACKAGING

You are probably familiar with the names Coca-Cola, McDonald's, Kodak, and Disney. Millions of people around the world also know these names.

Branding and Marketing

A **brand** is a name, symbol, or design that identifies a product. This marketing technique helps consumers remember and regularly buy a company's products. Common brand names which are well known, such as Kellogg's, Kraft, Ivory soap, and Crest toothpaste, may appear on several products or on a single product.

Brands may need to be revised for foreign sales. For example, Coca-Cola had to change *Diet Coke* to *Coke Light* in Japan. The consumers in Japan did not want to be reminded that it was a diet soft drink.

Types of Brands

Brands range from ones known worldwide to those only known in a small region. A *global brand* is used worldwide and is recognized by people in many geographic areas. The Gerber Products Company uses a "superbrand" approach for global marketing activities with the company's famous name appearing on baby food, child-care products, and children's clothing.

A *national brand* is one that is well known within one country. For example, before expanding to overseas markets, Nike and Frito-Lay were considered national brands.

Regional brands are used on products sold only in one geographic region. Certain snack chips or soft drinks may only be available in a few states or regions of countries.

Stores and producers will sometimes put their own name on products. *Store* or *manufacturer brands* are used on products sold only at certain stores or distributed through certain sellers. Venture has a line of health and personal care products with its own name on them. Store and manufacturer brands are also called *private brands*.

Generics are non-name brand, plain wrapper products that can provide a bargain in certain situations. As with store brands, many generics can provide low-cost alternatives for consumers. Certain generics, such as aspirin, bleach, and sugar, are almost exactly the same as higher priced brands.

Packaging

Have you ever noticed a new product because of the color, design, and shape of its package? Companies spent millions of dollars to get the right package. When Diet Coke was introduced, the company tested more than 30 combinations of colors, lettering, and designs for its new soft drink can.

Packaging serves three major purposes for companies and consumers. First, a package protects the product from spoilage or damage during shipping and storage. Second, a package attempts to capture the attention of both new and regular users of the product. Third, the packaging should make the product easy to use. Easy-to-pour containers and resealable boxes add to consumer convenience.

In recent years, packaging has increased in importance as a result of environmental concerns. Many companies now offer packages that are either reusable, refillable, or recyclable.

In some countries, certain packaging regulations influence marketing activities. Food labeling laws in the United States require that certain ingredient and nutrition information be presented in a clear format. While Coca Cola uses the English version of its name in most countries, Korea and Thailand require the name be presented in the national languages of those countries.

Global Business Exercise: Conversions to Metric Measures for Consumer Product Packages

Most products sold in the United States and almost all in other countries use the metric system for weights and liquid measurements. The following is an approximate reference for converting to metric measurements:

When you know:	Multiply by:	To find:
ounces (oz)	28.35	grams (g)
pounds (lb)	.45	kilograms (kg)
fluid ounces (fl oz)	29.57	milliliters (ml)
pints (pt)	.47	liters (l)
quarts (qt)	.95	liters (l)
gallons (gal)	3.79	liters (l)

1. A 14-ounce package of spaghetti would weigh about _____ grams.
2. Six pounds of cheese would weigh about _____ kilograms.
3. Eight pints of fruit juice is equal to about _____ liters.
4. Three quart bottles of soft drinks contain about _____ liters.
5. A gallon of milk is equal to about _____ liters.

Every company must make decisions about what it will sell. These choices are influenced by the popularity of its product offerings and the ability of the business to serve consumer needs throughout the world.

The Product Life Cycle

The stages a good or service goes through from the time it is introduced until it is taken off the market is the **product life cycle (PLC)**. As you get older, you act differently and have different needs. The same thing is true for products. After an item has been on the market for awhile, the company will have a different marketing approach. As shown in Figure 19-5, the PLC has four stages.

Figure 19-5
All goods and services go through stages as they increase and decrease in popularity.

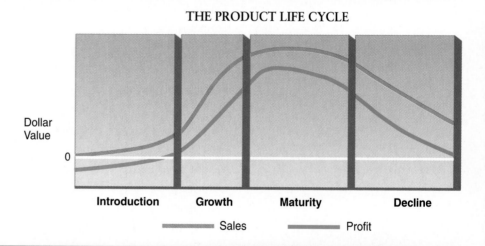

THE PRODUCT LIFE CYCLE

The first stage of the product life cycle is *introduction,* when the product is new and few competitors exist. Marketing activities should emphasize creation of awareness of the item among potential customers. Sales are low and a profit has not been realized.

Next, the *growth* stage of the PLC finds increasing sales and profits starting. New competitors with similar or substitute products enter the market.

Then, in the *maturity* stage sales start to level off as the market is saturated, more competitors appear, and new products compete for the dollars of consumers.

Finally, in the *decline* stage, sales and profits start to decline. The company must decide whether to attempt to revive the product or stop production of it.

Competition and technology determine the speed at which a product moves through the product life cycle. Years ago, radios and televisions would take years to move through the PLC as new models and features were introduced. Today, movement through the product life cycle is measured in months for electronic equipment—such as video players, computers, and cellular phones.

Expanding Global Market Activities

A major marketing decision a company must usually make involves whether to keep its products the same or adapt them to foreign customers. A **global product** is a standardized item offered in the same form in all countries in which it is sold. Common examples of global products are cameras, film, and many home appliances. Food products are usually difficult to market as global products because of differences in tastes. Unilever, however, sells tea, ice cream, and pasta in nearly identical forms worldwide.

In contrast to a global product, an **international product** is customized or adapted to the culture, tastes, and social trends of a country. As a result of different laws and customs, health and personal care products must be adapted to different settings. Food companies often add different seasonings to products sold in various cultures.

Ceasing Foreign Market Activities

Can you think of a product, such as a breakfast cereal based on a cartoon character, that is no longer on the market? As the character declined in popularity, sales of the product probably also declined.

When sales of an item continue to decline, a company will probably decide to stop making and selling it. Gerber no longer operates day-care services and has eliminated its toy and furniture divisions. Such decisions allow the company to concentrate on more profitable products.

Back to the Beginning: Barbie Goes Global

Reread the case at the beginning of this chapter and answer the following questions:

1. What factors may have influenced Mattel's decision to sell Barbie dolls in other countries?
2. What may have influenced Mattel's decision to introduce a different style of Barbie doll in Japan initially?
3. In what ways does Mattel use both a *global product* approach and an *international product* approach?

KNOWING GLOBAL BUSINESS TERMS

The following terms should become part of your business vocabulary. For each numbered item find the term that has the same meaning.

- brand
- convenience goods
- experiment
- focus group
- global product
- international product
- marketing research
- observational research
- primary data

- product life cycle (PLC)
- product line
- qualitative research
- quantitative research
- secondary data
- shopping goods
- specialty goods
- test market

1. Data collection by watching and recording shopping behaviors.
2. Surveys used to collect numeric data.
3. Products purchased after consumers compare brands and stores.
4. Standardized item that is offered in the same form in all countries in which it is sold.
5. Data that are already collected and published.
6. An assortment of closely related products that meet the varied needs of target customers.
7. A directed discussion with 8 to 12 people.
8. The stages a good or service goes through from the time it is introduced until it is taken off the market.
9. Inexpensive items that require little shopping effort.
10. A customized product adapted to the culture, tastes, and social trends of a country.
11. A statistical comparison of two or more very similar situations.
12. Using open-ended interview questions to obtain comments from consumers about their attitudes and behaviors.
13. The name, symbol, or design that identifies a product.
14. Data that are collected to solve a specific research problem.
15. Unique products that consumers make a special effort to obtain.
16. An experimental research study that measures the likely success of a new product.
17. Collecting and analyzing data in order to obtain specific marketing information.

REVIEWING YOUR READING

Answer these questions to reinforce your knowledge of the main ideas of this chapter.

1. How can marketing satisfy an unmet need?
2. How does a shopping good differ from a specialty good?
3. In what ways are services different from goods?
4. What causes a need for new products?
5. What are the steps of the new-product development process?
6. What factors need to be considered when adapting products to foreign markets?
7. What are the phases of the marketing research process?
8. What is the difference between secondary data and primary data?
9. How could observational research help a company with its marketing activities?
10. What is a test market?
11. What is a brand?
12. What purposes does packaging serve?
13. What are the stages of the product life cycle?
14. How does a global product differ from an international product?

EXPANDING YOUR HORIZONS

You will not find the complete answers to the following questions in your textbook. You will need to use your critical-thinking skills. Think about these questions, gather information from other sources, analyze possible responses, and discuss them with others. Then, develop your own oral or written response as instructed by your teacher.

1. Why do stores and manufacturers have larger product lines than in the past?
2. Name some services that have increased in importance for our economy in recent years.
3. List some ideas that could be the basis for new products in our society.
4. Create some examples of topics for international marketing research studies that would be interesting to investigate.
5. When may qualitative research be preferred to quantitative research for a marketing research study?

6. What makes certain brands popular and easy to remember?

7. Does packaging cost too much for certain products? Find examples of products with packaging that could be made less expensive.

8. Why do some items go through the stages of the product life cycle faster than others?

9. Create a list of products that may be sold anywhere in the world without making major changes. What determines if an item is a global product or an international product?

BUILDING RESEARCH SKILLS

The ability to find information from various sources is an important international business skill. The following activities will help you investigate various topics. You will also learn to apply class ideas to situations outside of the classroom.

1. Conduct a survey of the products people buy without comparison shopping. How important is place of purchase, price, and brand for these items?

2. Analyze advertisements for services. Report to the class how these companies attempt to communicate quality to potential customers.

3. Collect advertisements, labels, and packages from products made in other countries. How would you describe the marketing approach for these items?

4. Find examples of secondary data in the library that could help a company with its international marketing activities. These data sources could include an index, business directory, reference book, or computerized database. Describe how the information could be of value to a global marketing plan.

5. Prepare a poster or bulletin board display with examples of products or services in the various stages of the product life cycle. Suggest marketing activities that would be appropriate for one item in each stage of the cycle.

6. *Global Career Activity.* Select a good or service. Describe the jobs that would be required to make the product available to consumers in another country.

Continuing Enrichment Project: Planning a Product for International Marketing

Select a product (good or service) of your firm that would be appropriate to market in a Central or South American country. Based on your research, develop a product strategy that includes the following:

1. A description of the product (good or service) including characteristics and benefits of the item.
2. A description of the target market. Who would be the main buyers and users of the product? What are their demographic characteristics? What are their social attitudes and cultural behaviors?
3. How might the product need to be adapted to accommodate social, cultural, or legal differences?
4. What research activities could the company do to better understand its potential customers and the marketplace?
5. Describe branding and packaging ideas that could be used for this item.

CHAPTER 20

Global Pricing and Distribution Strategies

After studying this chapter and completing the end-of-chapter activities, you will be able to

- Identify the factors that must be considered by businesses when setting prices.
- Describe pricing methods used by businesses.
- Discuss some pricing factors that are unique to global markets.
- Outline direct and indirect channels of distribution.
- Describe the activities of agents, wholesalers, and retailers.
- Explain the role played by global intermediaries.
- Summarize the shipping requirements for international distribution.
- Compare transportation modes available to international distributors.

Toys "Я" Us in Japan

After becoming the largest U.S. toy seller, in 1984 Toys "Я" Us started its international expansion into Canada, Europe, Hong Kong, and Singapore. The company was then attracted by the over $6 billion annual toy sales market in Japan. However, Toys "Я" Us faced several barriers when entering the world's second-largest toy market.

Japan's Large-Scale Retail Store Law attempts to protect smaller businesses. For any store that will be larger than 5,382 square feet (approximately 500 square meters), owners must obtain approval from government agencies to build the facility. This process could take as long as 10 years. Pressure from United States trade representatives and price-conscious Japanese consumers reduced the time needed for Toys "Я" Us to gain approval for a store. The first Toys "Я" Us store in Japan was 44,000 square feet and stocked nearly 15,000 products.

Toys "Я" Us depends on buying in large quantities, which allows it to sell at discounted prices. Instead of buying through wholesalers, Toys "Я" Us attempts to deal directly with manufacturers. However, many toy producers hesitated to participate in the beginning since they did not want to upset their long-term relationships with wholesalers and retailers. For Toys "Я" Us stores to gain acceptance among business people and consumers in Japan, McDonald's Company of Japan owns 20 percent of the Toys "Я" Us stores in that country. Since both enterprises have similar target markets—families with children—plans call for building toy stores and restaurants in the same locations.

As a part of its marketing plan, every business must decide what amount to charge and how to get goods and services to customers. Pricing and distribution for international marketing are influenced by factors such as export costs, values of foreign currencies, and the availability of transportation systems.

PRICE PLANNING FOR INTERNATIONAL MARKETING

Everything has a price. Interest is paid on loans. Fares are paid for airline transportation. Fees are paid for medical and legal services. *Price* is the monetary value of a good or service. Figure 20-1 summarizes the three main factors that influence the price a company charges for goods and services: costs, consumer demand, and competition.

Figure 20-1
Costs, consumer demand, and competition are the main factors that influence the price of goods and services.

FACTORS AFFECTING PRICE

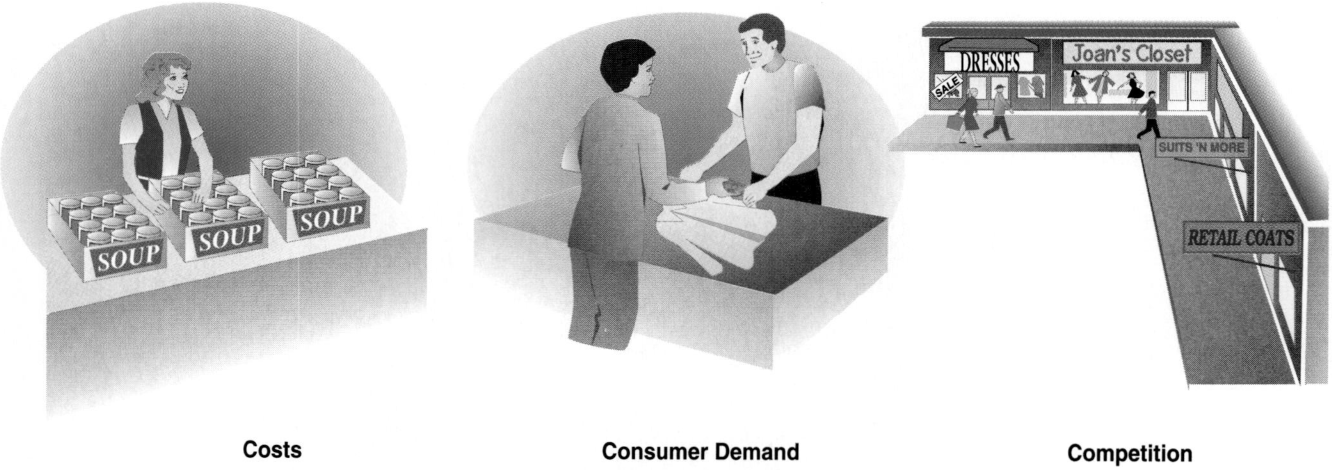

| Costs | Consumer Demand | Competition |

Costs

A company cannot sell an item for less than it costs to make or for the company to buy. Production and other operating costs must be covered by the price of an item. Besides incurring ordinary business expenses, organizations involved in international marketing will incur other costs, such as

- the cost of modifying a product to meet cultural or legal restrictions,
- tariffs and other taxes that must be paid when selling to customers in another country,
- fees to acquire export or import licenses,
- expenses for the preparation of export documents,
- changes in the exchange rate for a nation's currency, and
- transportation costs due to selling to buyers at a greater distance.

Consumer Demand

When prices are high, consumers tend to buy less of an item than when prices are low. The basics of demand operate in all buying situations. Lower incomes, higher prices, and needs for other items result in reduced demand for a good or service. The economic conditions, cultural preferences, and legal restrictions in a foreign market are also likely to affect potential demand and the price that can be charged.

Competition

If many companies are selling an identical or similar product, consumers have more choices than if only one or a few companies are selling the item. Competition tends to keep prices lower. For example if many stores in Bogotá are selling similar products, the consumers will purchase at the store with the lowest price. This competition will force companies to offer special prices to attract customers. As a company starts selling in another country, it faces competition from domestic companies in the other country and from other exporting companies around the world.

Global Business Example: Exchange Rates, Competition, and Prices for Mercedes-Benz

The recession in the early 1980s in the United States had little effect on demand for Mercedes-Benz automobiles. However, the economic downturn in 1991 was a different story for the German auto manufacturer. Because of a weak dollar (compared with the deutsche mark) and a newly imposed U.S. luxury tax, sales of Mercedes dropped 24 percent in the United States. The company also faced rivalry from new competitors from Japan—Lexus and Infiniti.

International marketing managers use a variety of methods to determine appropriate prices. Markup pricing, new product pricing, psychological pricing, and discount pricing can be effective price determination methods.

Markup Pricing

Most stores set prices based on an addition to the cost of an item. **Markup** is an amount added to the cost of a product to determine the selling price. The markup includes operating costs and a profit on the item.

Markups are commonly stated in percentages. A company may use a 40 percent markup on its products, for example. This would result in a $70 selling price for an item that cost $50 [$50 + (.40 × $50)]. If a company uses a markup of 80 percent for a product that cost $100, what would be the selling price?

Markup, like many marketing decisions, is affected by competition. Products in competitive markets with constant demand, such as food products, tend to have low markups. In contrast, products with inconsistent demand—such as high-fashion clothing items and jewelry—will usually have higher markups to cover the carrying costs of these items.

New Product Pricing

When a company decides to sell a new product, managers face the problem of deciding what price to charge. The pricing strategy used for a new product is affected by the product image desired, the amount of competition, and sales goals. Three commonly used methods for pricing new products are competitive pricing, skim pricing, and penetration pricing.

Competitive Pricing. If the new product has competition already on the market, a company may decide to sell its new product at a comparable price. Certain products and services always seem to be priced about the same at all selling locations. Gasoline, pizza, and basic groceries have competitive prices in a given geographic area. Any price differences can usually be attributed to more service or special product features.

Skim Pricing.   When a new product is introduced, managers may decide to charge as much as possible. This approach, called **skim pricing**, sets a relatively high introductory price. Skim pricing attempts to attract buyers who are not concerned with price, while also quickly covering the research and development costs of the new product. This approach was used when VCRs and personal computers were first introduced.

With skim pricing a company faces two potential problems. First, the high price may quickly attract competitors to the market. Second, the company faces the risk of setting the price too high and selling very few items.

Penetration Pricing.   In contrast to skim pricing, **penetration pricing** is the setting of a relatively low introductory price for a new product. This approach attempts to gain strong acceptance in the market. This low-pricing strategy can help a company take sales from competitors as the law of demand suggests people will buy more at lower prices than at higher prices. Penetration pricing can be effective when competing against established companies in other countries and when selling in nations with low economic development.

Psychological Pricing

In an attempt to persuade consumers to purchase a product or service, companies may use pricing to create an image. For example, certain prices can communicate that an item for sale is a bargain. Or, another item may be priced to portray an image of high quality. Common psychological pricing approaches include promotional pricing, odd-even pricing, prestige pricing, and price lining.

Promotional Pricing.   Advertised specials are a common marketing activity, especially in supermarkets and discount stores. Special-event low prices may be offered as "back-to-school" or "end-of-the-season" sales. A **loss leader**, which is a very low-priced item used to attract customers to a store, is used with the hope that shoppers will make other purchases while there.

Odd-Even Pricing.   Have you ever noticed that many items are priced at 59¢, $1.79, $8.95, and $79.99. Over the years companies have found that prices ending in 5 or 9 (odd numbers) present a bargain image. A price ending in an even number or rounded to the nearest dollar amount, such as $175 or $49.50, generally gives an impression of quality. Bargain-oriented restaurants will price meals at $6.95 and $8.99 while quality-conscious restaurants may use $17.50 and $22.

Prestige Pricing. Extensive research has revealed that people believe higher priced items have greater quality than the exact item at a lower price. French manufacturers, such as Yves Saint Laurent, Limoges, and Christofle, set prices to project an image of status, influence, and power.

Price Lining. To make shopping easier for customers and salesclerks, a store may offer all merchandise in a category at the same price. All suits offered by a store may be sold at $150, $225, and $300. Within each category are a variety of styles and colors from which customers in that price range can choose.

Discount Pricing

Price reductions are one of the most common actions taken by companies to attract and keep customers. Four common types of discounts are seasonal, cash, quantity, and trade.

Seasonal Discounts. At various times of the year, companies may reduce prices to sell the remaining items in stock. Seasonal discounts include price reductions of summer clothing in August and reductions on Christmas cards and decorations the first business day after Christmas.

Cash Discounts. Companies may reduce the price charged for items in an effort to encourage customers to pay their bills quickly. For example, customers may be offered a 2 percent discount if their bill is paid within 10 days. If a customer decides not to take advantage of the discount, the full invoice amount is due within 30 days. This discount is expresses as 2/10, net/30.

Quantity Discounts. In an effort to encourage customers to purchase larger amounts of an item, businesses may offer a quantity discount. For example, a garden shop may sell bags of planting soil using the following pricing schedule:

1 to 4 bags	$3.79 per bag
5 to 9 bags	$3.39 per bag
10 or more bags	$3.09 per bag

What are the benefits of quantity discounts for sellers and buyers?

Trade Discounts. Manufacturers commonly sell to distributors and stores based on a percentage of the *list price*, also called the *suggested retail price*. An electronics producer, for example, may sell televisions to stores at a 50 percent trade discount. In other words, a television set that sells to consumers for $450 would cost stores $225.

Global Business Exercise: Computing Markups, Discounts, and Prices

For each of the following, calculate the markup, discount, cost, or price as requested:

1. A French store marks up its prices 70 percent. What would be the selling price for a jacket that cost the store Fr 50?

2. A British company offers a 3 percent discount to a customer to pay for a £600 purchase within 10 days. What amount would the customer pay if paying within 10 days?

3. A Brazilian store sells blank videocassettes for Cr$63,000 each if less than five are purchased, or Cr$58,000 each if a customer buys five or more. What would be the cost of six tapes?

4. A Mexican appliance manufacturer sells to retailers with a trade discount of 35 percent. If a washing machine has a list price to consumers of $900 (pesos), what would be the cost of the item to a store?

PRICING IN GLOBAL MARKETS

Managers setting prices for domestic markets are aware of the pricing actions of competitors, consumer demand, and currency values. However when businesses are setting prices for trade across borders, the process is not as easy and information is not as readily available.

Fluctuations in exchange rates for currencies can result in receiving less money than expected. One way to minimize the effect of fluctuating currency rates is to set prices high enough to cover these changes. *Countertrade*, which is the direct exchange of products or services among companies in different countries, can also minimize this risk.

Sometimes a company intentionally may set prices extremely low for foreign trade. **Dumping** is the practice of selling exported products at a lower price than that asked in the company's home country. While this can benefit consumers, others will suffer. The lower price drives out competition causing workers to lose jobs.

Businesses often pressure governments to prevent dumping. Countries may adopt *antidumping laws* or *antidumping tariffs*. These trade barriers prohibit importers from selling products at artificially low prices.

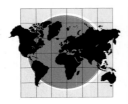

DISTRIBUTION CHANNELS

For a product to be useful it must get from the producer to the user. A **distribution channel** is the path taken by a good or service to get from the producer to the final user.

When would a company sell directly to the user of a product and when would a business use wholesalers and retailers? The answer to this question is influenced by the type of product and consumers involved. For example, a small company that wants to distribute its products in

many stores probably will use a distribution channel with many retailers. Figure 20-2 presents the common distribution channels used.

Distribution Channel A in Figure 20-2 shows only a producer and a consumer. In a **direct distribution channel,** producers sell goods or services directly to the final user. Some examples of direct distribution include farmers selling produce at a roadside stand, sales representatives for a cosmetic company calling on consumers in their homes, and clothing companies selling through the mail with the use of catalogs.

More common than direct distribution is the use of agents, wholesalers, and retailers (see channels B, C, and D in Figure 20-2). An **indirect distribution channel** occurs when goods or services are sold with the use of one or more intermediaries between the producer and the consumer. Channel B is a common distribution method for automobiles and other motor vehicles. Channel C is used to distribute packaged food products and other items sold in supermarkets and discount stores. Finally, Channel D may be used for foreign trade in which an import-export agent is involved.

Figure 20-2
Products can be distributed to final consumers through various channels of distribution.

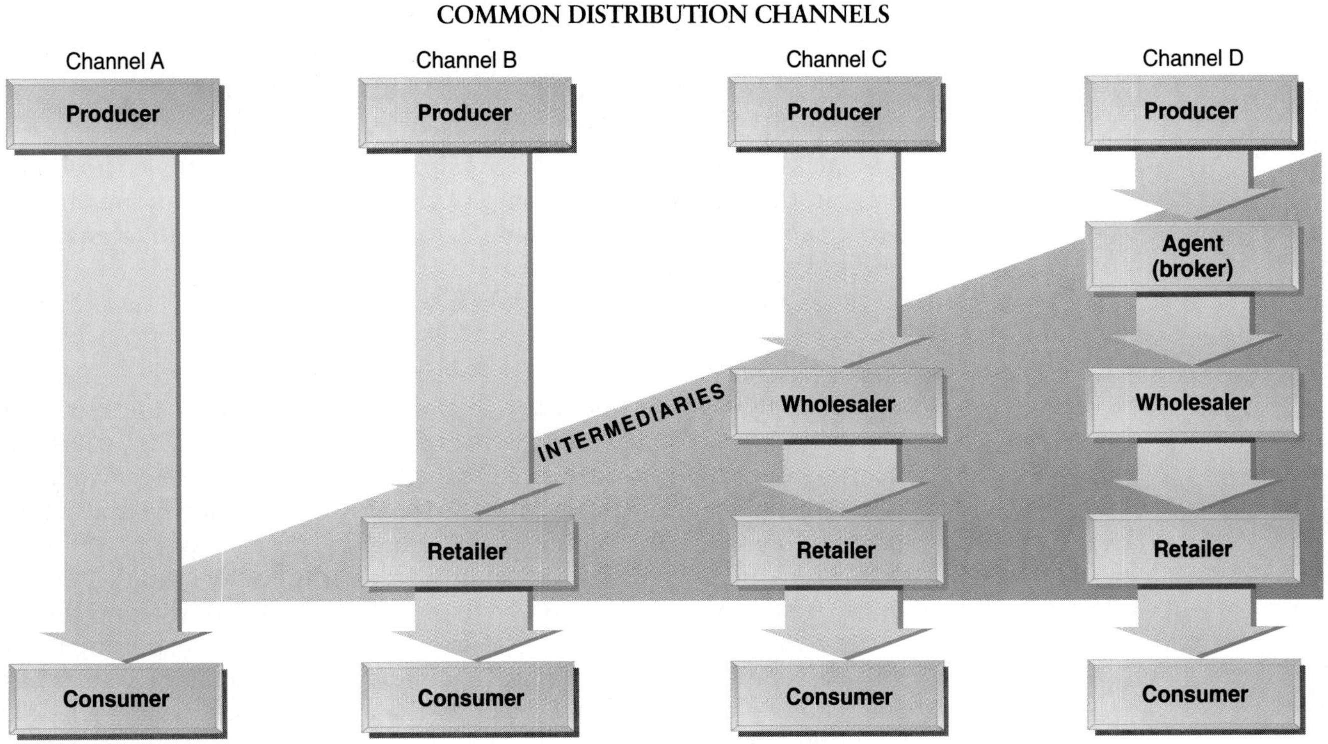

COMMON DISTRIBUTION CHANNELS

Channel A	Channel B	Channel C	Channel D
Producer	Producer	Producer	Producer
			Agent (broker)
		Wholesaler	Wholesaler
	Retailer	Retailer	Retailer
Consumer	Consumer	Consumer	Consumer

INTERMEDIARIES

DISTRIBUTION CHANNEL MEMBERS

Several parties are usually involved when selling goods across borders. An **intermediary** is any person or organization in the distribution channel that moves goods and services from the producer to the consumer. The most common intermediaries are agents, wholesalers, and retailers.

Agents

An **agent,** also referred to as a *broker,* brings together buyers and sellers, but does not take ownership of the products. International agents serve export companies by being knowledgeable about global markets and international trade barriers.

Wholesalers

A **wholesaler** is a business that buys large quantities of an item and resells them to a retailer. Wholesalers do not usually sell directly to final users of a product. As shown in Figure 20-3, wholesalers have five main functions: providing information, processing orders, storing and transporting, financing and taking possession, and promoting.

Many people believe that eliminating wholesalers would reduce marketing costs. While wholesalers may be eliminated, the duties performed cannot be eliminated. Transporting, storing, and ordering must still be done. These duties must be done by either the manufacturer or the retailer—probably less efficiently than by wholesalers who specialize in those tasks.

Figure 20-3
Wholesalers perform important duties that assist with international marketing activities.

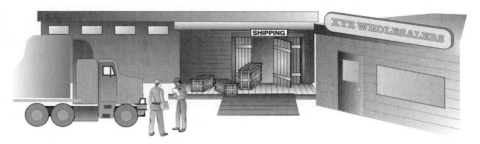

FUNCTIONS OF WHOLESALERS

PROVIDING INFORMATION: Communicating between manufacturers and retailers.

PROCESSING ORDERS: Providing needed products for retailers to sell.

STORING AND TRANSPORTATION: Maintaining warehouses and shipping capabilities.

FINANCING AND TAKING POSSESSION: Accepting ownership of finished goods and extending credit to customers.

PROMOTING: Advertising and selling to retailers and helping retailers promote to their consumers.

Retailers

A **retailer** is a store or other business that sells directly to the final user. Each day hundreds of millions of shoppers make purchases from retailing businesses. In Cairo, Egypt, many people buy needed goods at an open market, while in Paris most people make their purchases at small shops or large retail stores. As shown in Figure 20-4 on page 438, retailers attempt to serve customers in five main ways: product selection, convenience, product quality, sales staff assistance, and special services.

Global Business Example: Bringing the Store to the Customer

Fast-food and snack-food companies selling pizza, hamburgers, fried chicken, yogurt, and ice cream are taking to the road. Vehicles converted into mini-restaurants allow companies to serve customers at temporary locations. Popular locations for these rolling restaurants are sporting events, amusement parks, state fairs, concerts, and zoos. Banks and other financial institutions are taking a similar distribution approach with ATMobiles (portable cash machines).

Figure 20-4
Retailers provide a variety of
services to attract customers.

SERVICES PROVIDED BY RETAILERS

A VARIETY OF STYLES TO CHOOSE FROM FOR EVERYONE!

PRODUCT SELECTION: Variety of sizes, styles, and brands

CONVENIENCE: Location, hours of operation, parking availability, and ease of making purchases

PRODUCT QUALITY: Product excellence and reputation

SALES STAFF ASSISTANCE: Information about product features, uses, and store policies

SPECIAL SERVICES: Delivery, ease of exchanging or returning items, and special sales

Retailers in the United States may be viewed in five major categories: convenience stores, general merchandise stores, specialty stores, direct sellers, and electronic retailers.

Convenience Stores. A family needs milk and bread, or a student needs a report cover. These buying situations may result in consumers shopping at the stores closest to their homes. Convenience stores usually locate near other shopping or near the homes of potential customers. Easy parking, easy-to-find items, and fast service are common among convenience stores.

General Merchandise Retailers. Some retailers offer a larger variety of product types and offer more service than convenience stores. General merchandise retailers include supermarkets, department stores, discount stores, warehouse club stores, and outlet stores.

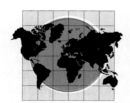

Global Business Example: The Hypermarket

In recent years, several major retailing companies have created super-stores, also called *hypermarkets*. These giant, one-stop shopping facilities offer a wide variety of grocery items and department-store merchandise. While the typical supermarket has about 40,000 to 50,000 square feet, superstores may have 200,000 square feet or more. The first hypermarket was started in France in 1963. Today, these superstores are likely to include a bakery, restaurant, pharmacy, and banking facilities.

Specialty Stores. Shoes, furniture, clothing, sporting goods, home repair products, computer software, or baked goods are commonly sold in stores that specialize in a limited product line. Specialty stores offer a variety of styles and brands of one item along with knowledgeable sales personnel.

Direct Sellers. Mail order, telephone contacts, and door-to-door marketing are called direct selling. This retailing method involves direct contact between the seller and the buyer. Personal care products, vacuum cleaners, and encyclopedias are commonly sold through in-home parties or sales demonstrations.

Direct selling varies in success from country to country. In cultures where personal contacts are important when doing business, direct selling thrives. In other societies, direct selling will have limited success.

Electronic Retailers. Most television viewers have seen a television home-shopping channel. Customers are asked to place orders by telephone for products presented and demonstrated. Interactive computer systems allow consumers to preview products and obtain descriptions for potential purchases from their homes. Vending machines are used to purchase soft drinks, snacks, and newspapers. Technology has expanded vending machine use to also sell books, videos, computer time, clothing, and cooked-to-order foods.

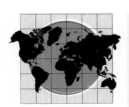

Global Business Example: Discount Stores Invade Mexico

Sidewalk merchants and street vendors in Mexico City are giving way to U.S. discount stores. After the Mexican government reduced import restrictions, Sam's Club, a division of Wal-Mart, opened in a vacant factory. The Price Club, another retailer, also started selling clothing, appliances, personal care products, and packaged and frozen foods in that country. Mexican consumers are attracted to the quality, spare parts, service, and warranties offered by these retailers.

Source: *The New York Times*, March 12, 1993, pp. C1, C2.

GLOBAL INTERMEDIARIES

The distribution channels used for international trade are often different than those used for domestic trade. Common international intermediaries include export management companies, export trading companies, freight forwarders, and customs brokers.

Export Management Company

An **export management company** (**EMC**) provides complete distribution services for businesses that desire to sell in foreign markets. EMCs make it easier to sell in other countries since they have immediate access to established buyers. Most EMCs are small firms that specialize in specific products or in a certain foreign market. EMCs provide exporters with reliable global distribution channels.

Export Trading Company

An **export trading company** (**ETC**) is a full-service global distribution intermediary. An ETC buys and sells products; conducts market research; and packages, ships, and distributes goods abroad. An export trading company may also be involved in banking, financing, and production activities. Japanese trading companies, called *sogo shoshas*, have been in operation since the late 1800s. Today, these companies handle more than half of Japan's imports and exports.

Freight Forwarder

A **freight forwarder** ships goods to customers in other countries. Like a travel agent for cargo, these companies get an exporter's merchandise to the required destination. Often, a freight forwarder will accumulate several small export shipments and combine them into one larger shipment in order to get lower freight rates.

Customs Broker

A **customs broker,** also called a *custom house broker*, is an intermediary that specializes in moving goods through the customs process. This process involves inspection of imported products and payment of duties. Customs brokers are licensed in countries in which they work and must know the import rules and fees.

Global Business Example: Coke vs. Pepsi at the Berlin Wall

When the Berlin Wall fell in 1989, many businesses were ready to enter the previously closed East German market. Pepsi presented dramatic television commercials celebrating the end of the cold war. While Pepsi sales grew, the company continued to ship products from existing bottling plants in western European nations.

Coca-Cola used a different distribution strategy. Coca-Cola invested $400 million to buy five bottling plants, 13 distribution centers, 370 trucks, 900 cars and vans, 170 forklifts, and 20,000 vending machines. This commitment to distribution in eastern Europe by Coca-Cola resulted in the company outselling Pepsi in the German market by 1991.

Source: *Brandweek*, January 18, 1993, pp. 23-26.

Global Highlight: The Panama Canal

The Panama Canal shortens water travel between the Atlantic and Pacific Oceans by 7,000 miles (11,270 kilometers). This 40-mile (64 kilometer) waterway connects the Caribbean Sea with the Pacific Ocean at the Isthmus of Panama, the neck of land connecting North and South America.

The idea of a canal connecting the Atlantic and Pacific was first considered in the early sixteenth century. A project was finally started in 1881; however, work ceased after six years due to the treacherous terrain and diseases such as malaria and yellow fever. After Panama gained its independence from Colombia in 1903, work again started on the canal. Construction was completed in 1914 at a cost of $336 million.

Six pairs of locks raise or lower a ship to the next water level along the length of the Panama Canal. The trip takes between seven and eight hours, with more than 12,000 ships traveling through the canal each year.

As exports are prepared for international distribution, goods must be packed and labeled and various documents may be required.

Packing and Labeling

When preparing for international shipping, an item should be packed to

- avoid breakage,
- maintain the lowest possible weight and volume,
- provide moisture-proof surroundings, and
- minimize theft.

Shipments going by land or sea require strong containers. In contrast, air shipments do not require such heavy packing; the faster movement means less handling. Shippers recommend that exporters avoid mention of brand names or contents on the package. This reduces the potential for theft.

The shipping label for exported goods should include (a) the name and address of the shipper, (b) country of origin, (c) container's weight, (d) size of the container, (e) number of packages per container, (f) destination, and (g) labels for hazardous material. As shown in Figure 20-5, certain symbols are commonly used to inform package handlers of warnings and contents.

Documentation

Various export forms are normally required when shipping merchandise to other countries. These documents include the bill of lading, certificate of origin, export declaration, destination control statement, and insurance certificate.

Bill of Lading. A *bill of lading* is a contract between the exporter and the transporter. This form describes the weight, number, and value of goods along with the names and addresses of the seller and buyer. A bill of lading serves as a receipt for the exported items.

Certificate of Origin. A *certificate of origin* documents the country in which the goods being shipped were produced. This document may be required to determine the amount of any import tax.

Export Declaration. The *export declaration* is required by the U.S. Department of Commerce for shipments with a value of more than $500. This form lists the same information that is on the bill of lading along with the name of the carrier and exporting vessel.

Destination Control Statement. The *destination control statement* verifies the country to which goods are being shipped. This document notifies the carrier and all other handlers that the shipment may only go to certain destinations.

Figure 20-5
Universal package symbols communicate important information that can be understood around the world.

UNIVERSAL PACKING SYMBOLS

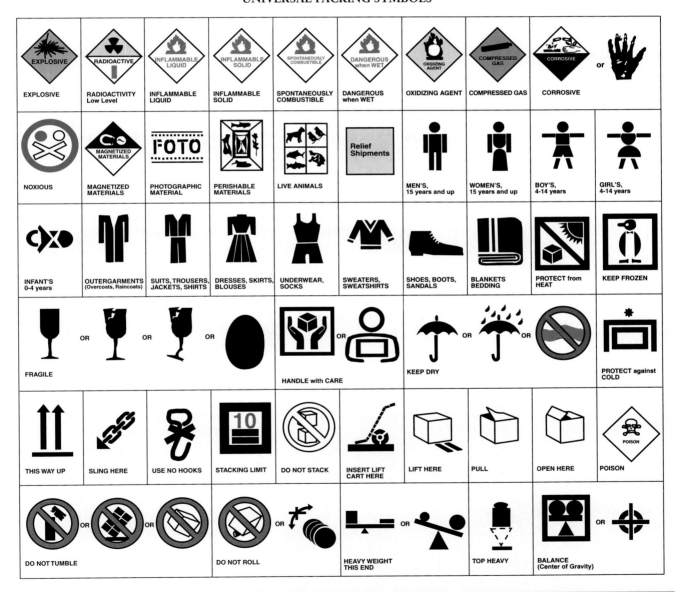

Insurance Certificate.   An *insurance certificate* explains the amount of insurance coverage for fire, theft, water, or other damage that may occur to goods in shipment. This certificate also lists the names of the insurance company and the exporter.

TRANSPORTATION IN THE GLOBAL MARKET

A critical ingredient of distribution is the shipping and delivery of a product. *Physical distribution* refers to the process of transporting, storing, and handling goods in transit between the producer and consumer. As shown in Figure 20-6, the physical movement of goods can be done in one of the following five ways.

Motor Carrier

The trucking industry is an important distribution link in almost every country. Motor carriers can quickly and consistently deliver large and small shipments nearly anywhere. Trucks are commonly used for shipping food products, clothing, furniture, lumber, plastic products, and machinery.

Railroad

Within the United States and many other countries, railroads continue to be a major transportation mode. The products most commonly shipped by rail are automobiles, grain, chemicals, coal, lumber, iron, and steel.

To add flexibility to rail shipping services, truck trailers and containers are transported on flat cars across country. Once near the destination, motor carriers make the local deliveries. These *piggyback* operations combine the long-haul capability of railroads with door-to-door delivery of trucking.

Waterway

Inland water carriers, such as barges, can efficiently transport bulky commodities. Oceangoing ships are slower than other transportation modes; however, they are very cost effective for shipping items overseas. These container-carrying vessels allow exporters to transport items such as coal, steel, lumber, grain, oil, and sand.

Pipeline

More than 200,000 miles of pipelines are in operation in the United States alone. Pipelines provide a dependable, low-cost method for transporting natural gas and oil products. The limitation of this transportation method is speed. Liquids travel at a speed of only three or four miles per hour. In addition, few products can be transported by this method and international pipelines can only be used when a geographic link exists between two countries.

Figure 20-6

International marketers use a variety of transportation modes to move goods and services from the producer to the consumer.

TRANSPORTATION MODES FOR INTERNATIONAL MARKETING

Air Carrier

The use of air transportation for international business activities continues to expand. As global demand for products increases, companies use the quick service offered by air carriers. Items commonly shipped by air include high-priced specialty products, specialized equipment parts, and perishable items (such as fresh flowers).

Back to the Beginning: Toys "Я" Us in Japan

Reread the case at the beginning of this chapter and answer the following questions:

1. What factors may have affected the decision of Toys "Я" Us to first expand into Canada, Europe, Hong Kong, and Singapore?
2. How did the Large-Scale Retail Store Law in Japan protect small stores?
3. How do you think increased competition affected prices for toys in Japan?
4. Do you think the entrance of Toys "Я" Us into the Japanese market served the best interests of Japanese consumers and workers?

KNOWING GLOBAL BUSINESS TERMS

The following terms should become part of your business vocabulary. For each numbered item find the term that has the same meaning.

- agent
- customs broker
- direct distribution channel
- distribution channel
- dumping
- export management company (EMC)
- export trading company (ETC)
- freight forwarder
- indirect distribution channel
- intermediary
- loss leader
- markup
- penetration pricing
- retailer
- skim pricing
- wholesaler

1. When goods or services are distributed with the use of one or more intermediaries between the producer and the consumer.
2. Setting a relatively low introductory price for a new product.
3. A very low-priced item used to attract customers into a store.
4. A full-service global distribution intermediary.

5. An amount added to the cost of a product to determine the selling price.

6. The path taken for a good or service to get from the producer to the final user.

7. A business that buys large quantities of an item and resells them to a retailer.

8. A company, with immediate access to established buyers, that provides complete distribution services for businesses that desire to sell in foreign markets.

9. Setting a relatively high introductory price for a new product.

10. A person or organization in the distribution channel that moves goods and services between the producer and the consumer.

11. A business that ships goods to customers in other countries.

12. When goods or services are sold directly from the producer to the final user of the item.

13. The practice of selling exported products at a lower price than that asked in the company's home country.

14. An intermediary that specializes in moving goods through the customs process.

15. A store or other business that sells directly to the final user.

16. An intermediary that brings together the buyers and sellers; also referred to as a broker.

REVIEWING YOUR READING

Answer these questions to reinforce your knowledge of the main ideas of this chapter.

1. What are the three main factors that affect the price of a product?

2. Other than ordinary business expenses, what types of costs are incurred by companies involved in international marketing?

3. What affect does competition usually have on price?

4. What is a *markup?*

5. How does skim pricing differ from penetration pricing?

6. What is *prestige pricing?*

7. How are trade discounts used to determine the cost that a store is charged for a product?

8. What is *dumping?*

9. How does direct distribution differ from indirect distribution?

10. What are three common intermediaries in the distribution channel?

Chapter 20 Global Pricing and Distribution Strategies

11. What are the common services provided by wholesalers?

12. What services do retailers commonly provide?

13. What are examples of electronic retailing?

14. How do distance and documentation affect international distribution activities?

15. What services does an export trading company provide?

16. What documents are commonly required when shipping goods to other countries?

17. What are the five main transportation systems used for shipping goods?

EXPANDING YOUR HORIZONS

You will not find the complete answers to the following questions in your textbook. You will need to use your critical-thinking skills. Think about these questions, gather information from other sources, analyze possible responses, and discuss them with others. Then, develop your own oral or written response as instructed by your teacher.

1. If companies involved in international marketing usually encounter higher operating costs than do domestic marketers, what benefits are associated with global marketing?

2. What types of products have a high percentage markup?

3. Give examples of discounts used by stores to attract customers.

4. How can dumping have a negative effect on a nation's economy?

5. Explain how wholesaling serves the needs of consumers throughout the world.

6. Describe how different types of retailers in your community attract different types of customers.

7. How might the success of retailers in different countries be affected by cultural, economic, and political factors?

8. Suggest an appropriate transportation method for the following international marketing situations:

   a. A company in Argentina is shipping oil to other countries in South America.

   b. A British company is shipping machines for use in factories in various African countries.

   c. A company in Hawaii is shipping fresh flowers to Japan and California.

   d. A mining company is shipping iron ore to steel factories within the same country.

The ability to find information from various sources is an important international business skill. The following activities will help you investigate various topics. You will also learn to apply class ideas to situations outside of the classroom.

1. Prepare a list of common goods and ask people of various ages for their best guess of the price of each item. Which consumers are most knowledgeable about prices?

2. Collect advertisements that are examples of odd-even prices used at different stores. What types of retailers use this pricing method most often?

3. Interview the manager or an employee of a retail store. Obtain information about the company's operating procedures, product line, and job opportunities.

4. Conduct library research about nonstore retailing. What types of home shopping systems and computerized retailing are expected to increase in popularity over the next few years?

5. Prepare a bulletin board or poster display showing how various products are shipped within and between countries.

6. *Global Career Activity.* If you were the manager of a distribution center that ships products to over 50 different countries, what types of workers would you need to hire? What skills would you need to have to be a global distribution manager?

Continuing Enrichment Project: Creating an International Pricing and Distribution Plan

Based on the company you have researched in previous chapters, choose several main goods or services and conduct research to answer the following questions:

1. How do operating costs and competition affect the prices charged by the company?

2. What factors affect the demand for the company's goods and services in different countries?

3. Describe the distribution channel that is used to get one of the company's main goods or services to consumers.

4. Describe the types of retail stores in which the company's main goods or services are found.

5. What types of shipping methods are used by the company to get its main products to foreign markets?

Global Promotional Strategies

After studying this chapter and completing the end-of-chapter activities, you will be able to

- Draw a diagram that illustrates the communication process.

- Describe the elements of the promotional mix.

- Explain the activities involved in planning advertising for global markets.

- Summarize the personal selling process used in international business.

- Discuss the use of public relations and sales promotion by multinational companies.

Unilever: An Advertising Giant

Unilever sells products known around the world. The company owns brands such as Lipton tea, Good Humor ice cream, Promise margarine, Mrs. Butterworth's syrup, Dove soap, Wisk detergent, and Pepsodent toothpaste. As of the early 1990s, Unilever was the largest advertiser in many countries, including India, Austria, Britain, Greece, Italy, the Netherlands, Turkey, Argentina, Brazil, and Chile.

Despite its success in many nations, Unilever has had to take a back seat to Procter & Gamble in the United States and a few other markets. In 1992, Unilever introduced Omo laundry detergent in the Persian Gulf in an effort to take away some of Procter & Gamble's control in that region. Omo was adapted for use in washing machines from the formula used in Egypt, where most people wash clothes by hand.

Instead of running its operations from London, the company created Unilever Arabia to administer marketing, research, sales, and advertising activities. This division of the company also expanded its product offerings in the Persian Gulf by selling Vaseline petroleum jelly, Vaseline Intensive Care lotion, and Lux soap.

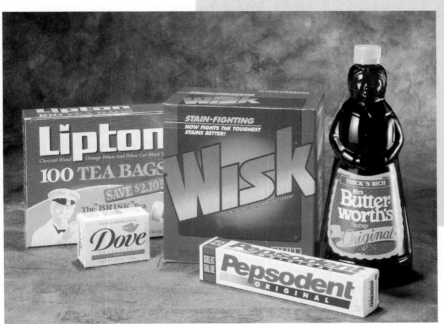

Every business needs to communicate with potential buyers. A company's ability to inform and persuade consumers with promotional efforts is a basic business activity.

THE COMMUNICATION PROCESS

Each day the average person sends and receives thousands of communications. Many of these messages involve television commercials, magazine advertisements, and other marketing promotions. Figure 21-1 on page 452 shows the participants and activities involved in communication.

Figure 21-1
The communication process is the system used to send and receive
marketing messages.

THE COMMUNICATION PROCESS

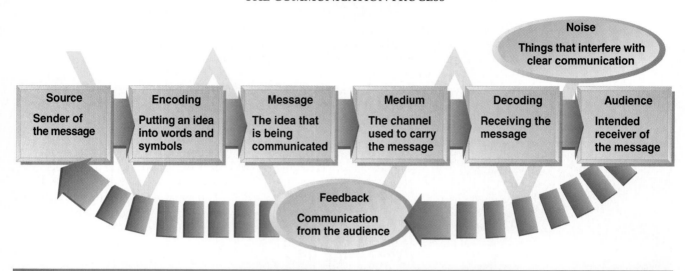

Noise
Things that interfere with clear communication

Source	Encoding	Message	Medium	Decoding	Audience
Sender of the message	Putting an idea into words and symbols	The idea that is being communicated	The channel used to carry the message	Receiving the message	Intended receiver of the message

Feedback
Communication from the audience

Have you ever said something to someone and the other person didn't hear you? Or, have you ever said one thing and a listener interpreted it to mean something completely different from what you intended? In the communication process, the message is sent from a *source* (the sender) to the *audience* (the receiver). You may be the source, and a friend may be the audience. In marketing, a company is commonly the source and consumers are the audience.

The source puts the message in a form that the audience will hopefully understand. This is known as *encoding*. The *message* travels to the audience over a *medium*—such as a television, a telephone, a magazine, or a salesperson talking in a store. *Decoding* is the process of the audience making meaning out of the message.

While communication may seem easy, *noise* can disrupt the process. Noise refers to anything that interferes with the communication process. Things that can obstruct international business communication include language differences, varied cultural meanings for words and gestures, and the setting in which communication takes place.

Finally, *feedback* is communication from the audience back to the sender. A common example of consumer feedback is the availability of 800-numbers that allow people to ask questions, obtain information, or make complaints. These toll-free telephone lines often appear on packages and in advertisements. Or, you can obtain the telephone numbers of companies that have these lines by calling 1-800-555-1212.

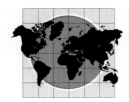

Global Business Example: Cross-Cultural Communication Problems

While companies make extensive efforts to avoid misunderstandings, problems still occur. Here are some examples of communication problems in international business:

- In Spanish-speaking countries, if Chevrolet had used Nova, which in Spanish sounded like *no va,* meaning "it doesn't go" few would have purchased that automobile!

- An owl was used by a company in advertisements in India, a nation in which some view the bird as a symbol of bad luck.

- An outdoor advertisement used by another company had dirty clothes on left, laundry detergent in center, and clean clothes on the right. However in societies where people read from right to left, the ad communicated that the laundry soap takes clean clothes and makes them dirty.

INTERNATIONAL PROMOTIONAL ACTIVITIES

Communication is the basis of promotional activities. Companies attempt to convey product information to potential customers. As defined in Chapter 18, *promotion* involves marketing efforts that inform, remind, and persuade customers. As shown in Figure 21-2 on page 454, the four main promotional activities available to companies are advertising, personal selling, publicity, and sales promotion.

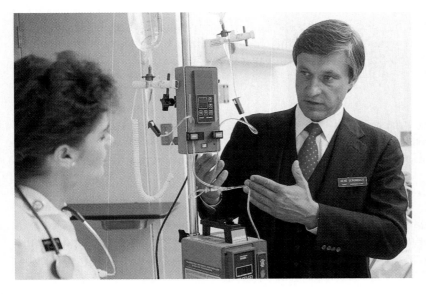

Advertising

Advertising is any form of paid, non-personal sales communication. Advertising is also called *mass selling* since many people are addressed at one time. Millions of people may see a television commercial, or thousands may see an advertisement in a magazine.

Personal Selling

In contrast to the nonpersonal, mass selling used in advertising, **personal selling** is direct spoken communication between sellers and potential customers.

Figure 21-2

Multinational companies use promotional activities to inform, remind, and persuade potential customers.

PROMOTIONAL ACTIVITIES

Advertising

Personal Selling

Publicity

Sales Promotion

This may happen in a face-to-face setting or over the telephone. Personal selling provides the opportunity for immediate feedback directly from the customer to the sales representative.

Publicity

Business organizations benefit from favorable news coverage about their products and business activities. **Publicity** is any form of unpaid promotion, such as newspaper articles or television news coverage.

Sales Promotion

The final element of promotion includes a variety of activities. **Sales promotion** comprises all of the promotional activities other than advertising, personal selling, and publicity. Sales promotions include coupons, contests, free samples, and in-store displays.

The International Promotional Mix

A **promotional mix** is the particular combination of advertising, personal selling, publicity, and sales promotions used by an organization. Which of the four promotional elements should be used most often? Managers must consider a nation's social, legal, and economic environments when answering this question. Cultural factors will influence the promotional mix decision for international marketers. Radio is very popular in Mexico, and advertising would probably be a major component of the promotional mix. In countries with poorly developed postal systems, mail advertising would not be as effective as personal selling or sales promotions.

Marketers must also choose between aiming promotions at end-users of an item or at distributors. **Pull promotions** are marketing efforts directed at the final users of an item. In this promotional approach, companies want consumers to "pull" the product through the distribution channel by demanding the item at stores. Pull promotions include television commercials, advertisements in consumer magazines, coupons, and other selling efforts aimed at consumers.

In contrast to pull promotions, **push promotions** are marketing efforts directed at members of the distribution channel. These promotional activities attempt to get wholesalers and retailers to "push" a product to their customers. Push promotions may include discounts to retailers, special displays in stores, or contests for salespeople.

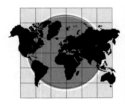

Global Business Example: Colgate's Promotional Efforts in Thailand

To become the largest selling toothpaste in Thailand, Colgate used a variety of promotional activities. First the company used the *Nok Lae* Children in its television commercials. This popular singing group was well known among young consumers and families and emphasized Thai heritage in the advertising.

After the commercials attracted much attention for Colgate, the company distributed printed information about proper dental hygiene. Colgate then made available drinking cups, notebooks, posters, and audiocassettes highlighting both the singing group and the company's product. This led to the creation of the Colgate New Generation Kid's Club with members receiving a free dental checkup, bumper sticker, button, and other items.

During the 1992 Winter Olympics, the Coca-Cola Company broadcast television commercials in 12 languages with a potential of being seen by 3.8 billion viewers in 131 countries. Since soft drinks are not significantly affected by cultural differences, Coca-Cola was able to use the same basic commercial in every country. However, this is not always possible. Multinational companies often adapt advertising to fit social and political differences. Figure 21-3 shows the four steps for planning advertising.

Figure 21-3

Multinational companies must plan advertising effectively to reach consumers in different countries.

THE ADVERTISING PLANNING PROCESS

Analyze Target Market → Create Advertising Message → Select Media → Execute and Evaluate

Analyze Target Market

The advertising process starts by identifying potential users of a good or service. This *target market* should be defined in terms of geographic area, demographic characteristics, buying habits, and media usage. For example, young, male consumers in Brazil will require a different advertising message than older, female shoppers in France.

Create Advertising Message

The traits of the target market influence the advertising message a company uses. For example, jeans in Brazil are sold with an emphasis on fashion. However, in Australia customers are more concerned about product benefits, such as quality and price. An advertising message should do one of the following:

- Get the customer's attention,
- Increase interest in the good or service,

- Improve a company's image in the minds of consumers,
- Boost potential customers' desire to buy, or
- Motivate customers into action.

Figure 21-4 describes some common advertising techniques used by companies to create unique messages for specific target markets.

Figure 21-4

Advertisers use a variety of techniques to communicate with consumers.

COMMON ADVERTISING TECHNIQUES

PRODUCT QUALITY ADS present the quality, brand, price, or features of a product.

COMPARATIVE ADS contrast the features of competing brands.

EMOTIONAL ADS attempt to obtain a response from consumers by appealing to feelings or needs and desires, such as fear, guilt, love, beauty, pleasure, convenience, safety, power, status, or security.

HUMOROUS ADS use comedy to draw attention to a product or service.

LIFESTYLE ADS present a product or service in a situation to which people can relate, such as at home, at work, or in recreational settings.

ENDORSEMENT ADS make use of famous or ordinary people as spokespersons for a product, service, or company. These are also called testimonial advertising.

If customers for a product are similar from one nation to another, a company may use a common advertising message. **Standardized advertising** is the use of one promotional approach in all geographic regions. For example, Tony the Tiger promotes Kellogg's Frosted Flakes in more than 20 countries.

In contrast to standardized advertising, cultural factors and social customs may require a company to adapt advertising messages in different nations. **Localized advertising** is the use of promotions that are customized for various target markets. Yogurt, for example, is promoted in some countries as a breakfast food, as a lunch item in other nations, and as a snack in still others. Because of social customs, a multinational company must customize its yogurt advertisements in different societies.

Global Business Example: Regulation of Advertising

Besides language differences, government regulations also limit the use of global advertising approaches. For example:

- Québec prohibits television commercials aimed at children. However, English-speaking residents of the Canadian province can still see ads for toys, cereals, and snacks on television programs broadcast from Ontario or the United States.

- In Great Britain, viewers must be informed of the cost of toys advertised on television if these items cost £15 or more.

- The (South) Korean Broadcasting Commission requires standard amounts be used in laundry detergent commercials.

- In the Netherlands, children may not appear in ads for candy and companies must put a little toothbrush symbol at the end of the commercial as a reminder for people to brush their teeth.

Select Media

Marketers must decide what media to use to deliver the advertising message. The major advertising media include newspaper, television, radio, magazine, direct mail, and outdoor (see Figure 21-5).

The availability of advertising media varies considerably among the nations of the world. For example, Turkey has over 350 newspapers with varied political positions, while other countries have less than 20. Cinema (theater) advertising is important in countries with limited commercial television, such as India and Nigeria.

Newspaper Advertising. Most people do not realize that more money is spent on advertising in newspapers than in any other medium. Think about the classified ads in which thousands of people pay to promote jobs, used cars, garage sales, and pets for sale. As international business expands, some newspapers have created regional editions for different geographic areas. *The Wall Street Journal*, for example, has European and Asian editions.

Television Advertising. Television commercials can have a strong effect on potential customers. Nonetheless, some nations limit the time available for television advertising. However, expansion of cable and satellite television systems makes it easier for advertisers. Channels such as CNN, ESPN, and MTV are available to billions of viewers.

Radio Advertising.   Radio advertising can be adapted to changing marketplace needs faster than any other medium. Radio is frequently more available than other communication methods. Nations with few television sets or with people who can't read are still likely to have radio stations.

Magazine Advertising.   Magazines, like newspapers, encourage international advertising by creating regional editions. *Business Week* has editions in Europe, Asia, and Latin America. *National Geographic* also covers these regions along with separate editions for Africa and the Middle East. *Reader's Digest* publishes over 40 different editions in 17 languages, including its Russian version started in the early 1990s.

Direct Mail.   Each day hundreds of millions of ads and catalogs fill the mailboxes of the world. Technology fosters increased use and reduced

Figure 21-5
Advertising media are used to communicate with potential customers.

ADVERTISING MEDIA

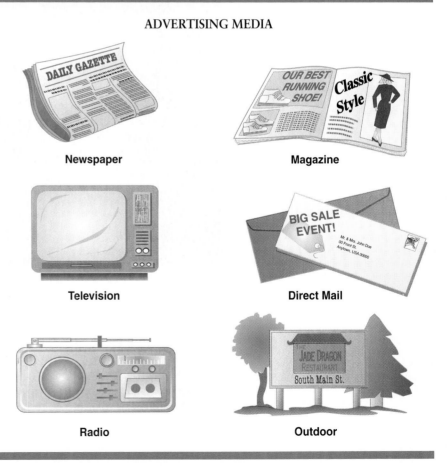

Newspaper

Magazine

Television

Direct Mail

Radio

Outdoor

costs of direct mail advertising. **Database marketing** is the use of computerized information systems to identify customers with specific demographic traits and buying habits. With a database, direct mail marketers can target potential customers to receive appropriate advertisements. For example, families in a database who have computers in their homes might receive mailings selling software for children to learn a foreign language.

Outdoor Advertising.   Billboards and transit ads on buses and trains are common in most countries. The use of this advertising medium, however, is usually limited to high-traffic and urban areas. In recent years creativity and technology have expanded outdoor advertising to include mechanical characters and three-dimensional displays.

Using an Advertising Agency

Some companies have their own advertising department to do promotional activities. However, most multinational companies use the services of an advertising agency. An **advertising agency** is a company that specializes in planning and implementing advertisements.

Most of the largest advertising agencies in the world are located in the United States, Tokyo, and Europe. These organizations usually have four main divisions:

1. The research department studies the target market and measures the effectiveness of advertisements.
2. The creative department develops the message and the artistic features to deliver the message.
3. The media department selects where and when the advertising will be presented.
4. Account services are the link between the agency and the client (the company selling the product).

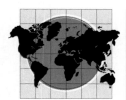

Global Business Example: The Infomercial Goes Global

"We have with us today several people who have quit their jobs and are now earning more with an amazing investment opportunity."

Statements like this are commonly heard on late-night, program-length commercials, known as *infomercials*. This promotional device sells cosmetics, health-care products, home appliances, investment opportunities, and personal improvement products. Although these advertisements look like television talk shows, audience members and other participants are often professional performers. Started in the United States as a result of expanded television cable and satellite channels, infomercials are gaining popularity in Canada, Europe, Asia, and Latin America.

PERSONAL SELLING

Consumers encounter salespeople in stores, on the phone, at their doors, and at their places of work. As defined earlier, *personal selling* is direct spoken communication between sellers and potential customers.

Personal Selling Activities

Personal selling involves activities to promote and sell goods and services. These duties include locating customers, taking orders, processing orders, providing information, and offering customer assistance.

In the past, most personal selling took place in face-to-face settings. Today, however, telemarketing has increased in importance. **Telemarketing** involves the selling of products during telephone calls to prospective customers. Personal selling over the telephone provides fast, low-cost contacts for business organizations. This selling method is most commonly used for insurance, investments, credit cards, magazine subscriptions, books, videos, and home improvements.

The Personal Selling Process

The ability to plan and execute a sales presentation is important in many career fields. As shown in Figure 21-6, the personal selling process may be viewed in five steps.

Figure 21-6
Personal selling involves an ability to plan and make a sales presentation.

THE PERSONAL SELLING PROCESS

Step 1. Identifying Potential Customers

Step 2. Preparing and Making the Sales Presentation

Step 3. Handling Objections

Step 4. Closing the Sale

Step 5. Providing Follow-up Service

Step 1.   In step one of the personal selling process, potential customers are identified. Names of prospects may come from computer databases, current customer lists, telephone calls, referrals from employees, mail-in coupons, and many other sources.

This first step, *prospecting,* is the foundation of successful personal selling. Qualified prospects are usually identified based on age, income, occupation, or interests. A company selling golf equipment would attempt to contact people who regularly participate in that sport.

Step 2. Step two of the personal selling process involves preparing and making the sales presentation. In this stage, a creative and effective product description and demonstration must be prepared. The sales presentation should highlight a product's main features, positive traits, and marketplace acceptance. For instance, one hotel chain demonstrated its room features by presenting a simulated room inside a truck trailer for viewing by potential customers.

In the sales presentation, specific information is provided to address the needs and wants of customers. For example, some automobile buyers are interested in the performance of a vehicle, while others identify style as the most desired product attribute.

Step 3. The third phase of the personal selling process involves obtaining feedback. A salesperson is looking for objections, or opposition, to the product. Awareness of objections allows the salesperson to provide additional information to overcome perceived negative aspects of the product.

Objections may be addressed by either clarifying some aspect of the sales presentation or by changing the conditions of the sale. If a customer likes everything about a product except the color and style, a reduced price may eliminate these objections.

Step 4. Once major objections are overcome, the closing of the sale should occur. In step four, the salesperson asks the customer to commit to the purchase. Questions, such as the following, are commonly used to close a sale:

Global Highlight: Promotional Efforts Expand Soccer's Popularity

By most estimates, soccer is the most popular sport in the world. Each year, 20 million organized soccer matches are played. Tournaments are held on three continents. The European Cup is the goal of European soccer players; while in South America, teams compete for the Liberator's Cup. The Cup of Nations and the Cup of Champion Clubs are the ambition of African nations. In 1990, 1.4 billion television viewers watched the World Cup Final.

In most countries, the game is referred to as football. Soccer was introduced to the United States in the late 1800s. However, it was not until 1959 that the National Collegiate Athletic Association (NCAA) recognized it as an official collegiate sport. Today, more than 12 million people in the United States under the age of 19 are involved in organized soccer programs.

Global popularity of soccer continues to expand. In 1993, Japan started its first professional soccer league. Teams are sponsored by companies such as Mitsubishi, Mazda, Nissan, Toyota, Ford Japan, WordPerfect Japan, and Coca-Cola Japan. Promotional efforts are expected to result in extensive ticket sales for games. Television advertising, soccer magazine subscriptions, and sales of products featuring players and team logos are a major promotional feature of Japanese soccer activities.

- Is this the style you were thinking about buying?
- If we can deliver it in three days, would you be interested?
- Would you like the item in blue?
- If we include the extended warranty, would this meet your needs?

Favorable responses to questions of this type can result in the completion of the sale.

Step 5. Finally, personal selling should not end when the sale is closed. Customer needs continue with operating instructions, repairs, and additional products. Follow-up activities can ensure continued sales and referrals from satisfied customers.

Personal Selling in International Markets

Global managers need salespeople with product knowledge and who are able to work in the social and cultural context of a country. International companies have three choices when selecting sales staff members—expatriates, local nationals, and third-country nationals.

Expatriates are employees living and working in a country other than their home nation. Multinational companies use expatriates when the available number of host country salespeople is limited. Expatriate salespeople are probably very familiar with their companies and products. However, they may not be acquainted with a nation's culture and social customs. Getting right down to business may be accepted in some societies. In other cultures, business associates are expected to get to know each other on a personal level before conducting business.

As the demand for international business employees increases, companies must expand the pool of workers. Organizations are increasingly using people from within the targeted country to sell products and services in that country. **Local nationals** are employees based in their home country. Because local nationals are familiar with the culture, their training usually emphasizes product knowledge.

A third source of international salespeople involves those with a broad global viewpoint. **Third-country nationals** are citizens of one country, employed by a company from another country, who work in a third country. These salespeople frequently are able to speak several languages and possess a highly developed sense of cultural sensitivity. An example of a third-country national would be a German working in Chile for an Italian company.

Global Business Example: Training Managers for Assignments Abroad

Sales managers and other executives of Samsung, South Korea's largest company, attend a month-long training camp before starting an assignment in another country. This culturally sensitive instruction covers language, eating habits, leisure activities, clothing styles, and cultural values. The program has helped Samsung managers who work in more than 50 countries to avoid social blunders.

OTHER PROMOTIONAL ACTIVITIES FOR INTERNATIONAL BUSINESS

Advertising and personal selling account for a large portion of an organization's promotional efforts. However, other types of promotions address various marketing objectives.

Public Relations

Companies are continually concerned about communicating a favorable public image. Companies can gain publicity with press releases, company newsletters, and by sponsoring sporting and entertainment events. To improve or keep its image, a company may take actions such as the following:

- Hewlett-Packard Company donated computers to the University of Prague,
- H. J. Heinz funded infant nutrition studies in China and Thailand, and
- DuPont sent water-jug filters to African nations to remove dangerous impurities from drinking water.

Global Sales Promotions

As noted earlier, sales promotions comprise all promotional activities other than advertising, personal selling, and publicity. These communication efforts attract attention and stimulate demand for a company's products.

Coupons.   Nearly 280 billion coupons are distributed each year in the United States. The use of money-off coupons is also expanding around the world. In one year in the early 1990s, 5.1 billion coupons were distributed in the United Kingdom.

In Italy and Spain, most coupons are right on the package rather than distributed through newspapers, magazines, or the mail. In Belgium, door-to-door distribution is most common. The use of coupons as a promotion was legalized in Denmark in recent years.

Premiums.   For more than 50 years consumers have bought Cracker Jack looking forward to the toy surprise inside. Food packages commonly include baseball cards, toys, or other items to attract buyers.

Contests and Sweepstakes.   "You may already be a winner" is a common slogan. Everything from trips around the world to a free bottle of ketchup are offered as prizes when companies want to attract attention to their products. Many contests are used to create a database of customer information.

Point-of-Purchase Promotions. The use of in-store advertising continues to increase. Electronic exhibits, television monitors, and display screens on shopping carts attempt to get customers to select a product or brand at the point of purchase.

Specialty Advertising. Look around home or school and you will see the names of organizations almost everywhere. You will see pens, key chains, calendars, notepads, briefcases, ice-cream scoops, drinking cups, towels, T-shirts, baseball caps, and golf balls with advertising messages. These promotional items keep a company's name and products in the eyes and minds of consumers.

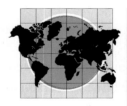

Global Business Example: Pepsi's Wrong Number Contest

Pepsi-Cola used a contest promotion to attract attention to its soft drink in Chile. The results were not the type the company expected. Chileans could win from $14 to $30,000 depending on the amount next to the prize number under the bottle cap. Pepsi expected to award 40 prizes over an eight-week period. However, when 688 was announced as the winning number instead of the correct 588, more than 100 people demanded prizes.

Many of the people who thought they were winners had already started spending their prize money. Two brothers who came to claim $17,000 did not have money for the 40-mile trip home. Pepsi and its advertising agency planned to work out some arrangement with all winners.

Source: *Advertising Age,* May 25, 1992, pp. I-3, I-29.

Back to the Beginning: Unilever: An Advertising Giant

Reread the case at the beginning of this chapter and answer the following questions:

1. What promotional efforts contribute to the success of Unilever in global markets?
2. What strategy did Unilever take in the Persian Gulf?
3. How might changes in its organizational structure strengthen the marketing efforts of Unilever?

KNOWING GLOBAL BUSINESS TERMS

The following terms should become part of your business vocabulary. For each numbered item find the term that has the same meaning.

- advertising
- advertising agency
- database marketing
- expatriates
- localized advertising
- local nationals
- personal selling
- promotional mix
- publicity
- pull promotions
- push promotions
- sales promotion
- standardized advertising
- telemarketing
- third-country nationals

1. Employees based in their home country.
2. Direct spoken communication between sellers and potential customers.
3. Promotional efforts directed at the final user of an item.
4. Promotional activities other than advertising, personal selling, and publicity.
5. A company specializing in planning and implementing advertisements.
6. Any form of paid, nonpersonal sales communication.
7. Employees living and working in a country other than their home nation.
8. The use of one promotional approach in all geographic regions.
9. The use of computerized information systems to identify customers with specific demographic traits and buying habits.
10. Any form of unpaid promotion, such as newspaper articles or television news coverage.

11. Employees who are citizens of one country, employed by a company from another country, who work in a third country.

12. Promotional efforts directed at members of the distribution channel other than consumers.

13. The particular combination of advertising, personal selling, publicity, and sales promotions used by an organization.

14. The use of promotions that are customized for various target markets.

15. The selling of products during telephone calls to prospective customers.

REVIEWING YOUR READING

Answer these questions to reinforce your knowledge of the main ideas of this chapter.

1. How is the communication process used in marketing?
2. What causes noise in the communication process?
3. What are the four promotional activities?
4. What is a promotional mix?
5. How do pull promotions differ from push promotions?
6. What things should an advertising message do?
7. How does standardized advertising differ from localized advertising?
8. What are the six main media used by advertisers?
9. What are the main divisions of an advertising agency?
10. What duties are involved in personal selling?
11. What are the five steps of the personal selling process?
12. How do salespeople who are expatriates differ from local nationals?
13. What are common sales promotions used by companies?

EXPANDING YOUR HORIZONS

You will not find the complete answers to the following questions in your textbook. You will need to use your critical-thinking skills. Think about these questions, gather information from other sources, analyze possible responses, and discuss them with others. Then, develop your own oral or written response as instructed by your teacher.

1. List examples of noise that can reduce the effectiveness of communication in your classroom, home, and in stores.

2. Describe marketing situations in other nations in which sales promotions or publicity would be used more effectively than advertising or personal selling.

3. Why would a company use push promotions instead of pull promotions?

4. Describe examples of advertisements that use the endorsement method (see Figure 21-4).

5. Name some products that could be best promoted using standardized advertising. What types of products would require localized advertising?

6. What qualifications would a salesperson look for in prospective customers when selling

    a. vacation homes in the Caribbean?

    b. computer software for teaching children at home?

    c. men's and women's business suits?

7. What advantages could third-country nationals have over expatriates and local nationals when applying as sales manager for a multinational company?

8. How important is publicity to the success of a company?

9. List examples of sales promotions you see in your home, school, and community.

BUILDING RESEARCH SKILLS

The ability to find information from various sources is an important international business skill. The following activities will help you investigate various topics. You will also learn to apply class ideas to situations outside of the classroom.

1. Prepare a poster or bulletin board that shows the four elements of promotion.

2. Collect examples of advertisements that use each of the techniques presented in Figure 21-4. Describe the type of customer targeted by each ad.

3. Conduct library research about the availability of television, radio, newspaper, and other advertising media in selected Central and South American countries.

4. Analyze television commercials with the sound off to determine how much of the information presented is visual.

5. Interview a person who does personal selling. What skills are most important for success in this career field?

6. Prepare a sales presentation for a good or service that is sold in a country in Central or South America.

7. *Global Career Activity.* Find an advertisement from a company that sells its goods or services around the world. Prepare a poster or bulletin board display that identifies the various careers involved in planning and executing the ad.

Continuing Enrichment Project: Creating a Global Promotional Mix

Select a good or service that would be sold in several Central and South American countries. Based on your research, develop a promotional strategy that includes the following:

1. A description of the product's target market.

2. Examples of advertisements that would be appropriate for the company.

3. An explanation of the different advertising media used by the company.

4. A description of personal selling activities that the company could use to promote its good or service.

5. An explanation of how publicity could help the company or product's image.

6. Types of sales promotions that would be most appropriate for this situation.

Global
Financial
Management

Global Financial Activities

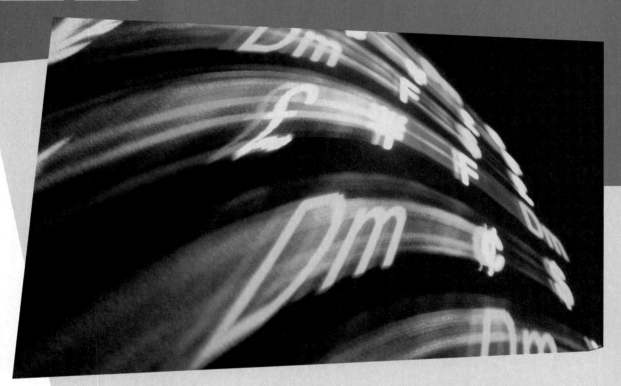

After studying this chapter and completing the end-of-chapter activities, you will be able to

- Describe the flow of funds for international businesses.
- Identify types of global financial institutions.
- Discuss the activities of global stock markets.
- Explain the purpose and operation of the bond market.
- Describe the role of other global financial markets.

Koor Industries, Ltd.

Koor Industries, based in Tel Aviv, is a diversified company involved in electronics, building supplies, metals, chemicals, food processing, and foreign trade. The company is a significant part of Israel's economy, accounting for nearly 10 percent of its industrial output.

From its creation, Koor Industries' primary goal was to provide employment. The company was never very profitable; and when economic conditions declined, the situation went from fair to poor. Sales revenue and profits declined and Koor was unable to pay off loans when they were due.

In order to pay off debt, the company started to cut costs by closing some factories and cutting staff. These cost reductions resulted in a 50 percent smaller work force at Koor Industries.

When Koor was faced with bankruptcy, the Israeli government approved a Is 275 million ($100 million) loan guarantee to help Koor out of its financial difficulties. In addition, the company decided to sell part ownership in some of its subsidiaries. The company is offering stock listed on the New York Stock Exchange (NYSE). The funds raised in this way can also help reduce its debt.

A global clothing manufacturer plans to update its equipment. A computer company plans to expand into Egypt, Saudi Arabia, Israel, Turkey, and Iran. These plans, like every international business activity, require funding. International financing activities are necessary for a company to operate in the global business market.

INTERNATIONAL FLOW OF FUNDS

In your daily life you are probably aware of the fact that you and your family must have money coming in to cover living expenses (the money going out). The same is true for businesses. Financial operations involve two major activities—the receipt of money and the payment of money.

Sources of Funds

Every company must have money to operate. Employees must be paid, operating expenses are incurred, and equipment must be purchased. As shown in Figure 22-1, organizations have two main sources of funds: equity and debt.

Figure 22-1
Every organization has money coming in and money going out.

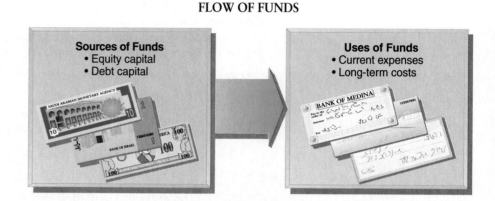

FLOW OF FUNDS

Equity Capital. The owners of a business are the initial source of financial resources. **Equity capital** consists of funds provided by a company's owners. Equity capital comes from several sources: investments from owners, reinvested profits, sale of stock, and liquidation of company assets. The stock market, discussed later in this chapter, is a major source of equity capital funds in the global economy.

Debt Capital. When a company has limited equity capital sources, it must turn to outsiders. **Debt capital** involves funds obtained by borrowing. Bank loans, bonds, and mortgages are examples of debt. The bond market, discussed later in this chapter, is the main source of international debt capital.

The use of debt has advantages. First, debt allows a company to expand when equity funds are not available. Second, debt has tax benefits. The interest on loans is a business expense. Like other business expenses, interest payments reduce a company's net income and lower the amount paid in taxes. Third, debt doesn't affect the control of a company. Lenders do not have ownership in a company.

Despite advantages, debt also has risks. If a company cannot make its interest payments on what is borrowed or is unable to repay a loan, creditors can take control of the company.

Borrowing is often used by companies that have most of their sales during one part of the year. For example, a company that manufactures summer clothing will have most of its sales concentrated in late winter and spring. Borrowing may be necessary in the summer, fall, and early winter months. The loans are then repaid during the main selling season.

Uses of Funds

The daily operations of a business also involve making payments for various business costs and other expenses. As Figure 22-1 shows, current expenses and long-term costs are the two main uses of funds. Current expenses include rent, materials, wages and salaries, utilities, repairs, advertising, supplies, and other items that keep a business operating from day-to-day. These expenses usually cover a period of one month to one year.

Some business costs cover longer periods of time. For example, a new building, heavy machinery, or computer system will probably be paid for and used over several years. These long-term costs, also called *capital projects,* are necessary for companies to produce, store, and deliver goods and services.

Global Business Example: Egypt's Use of Debt

Nations, as well as individuals and businesses, use debt. These funds are used to make up for the country's reduced income. During the Persian Gulf War in the early 1990s, tourism to Egypt declined and Suez Canal receipts fell, which resulted in a lower national income for the country. Egypt had to borrow from financial institutions and other countries. As repayment for Egypt's involvement in the war, some of its foreign debts were canceled. However, a weakened economy has made it difficult for Egypt to keep up with payments on other loans.

GLOBAL FINANCIAL INSTITUTIONS

Each day millions of financial transactions occur. These business activities use cash, checks, letters of credit, credit cards, countertrade, and other financial services. Various organizations serve the financial needs of consumers and businesses. Figure 22-2 on page 478 provides an overview of the main institutions in the global financial market.

Figure 22-2

Several financial institutions exist to serve the needs of consumers and businesses.

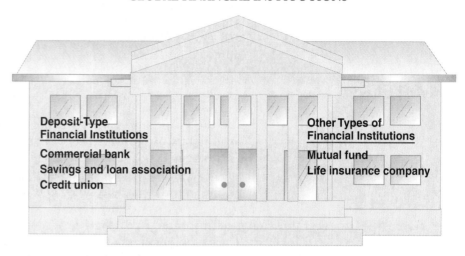

GLOBAL FINANCIAL INSTITUTIONS

Deposit-Type
Financial Institutions

Commercial bank
Savings and loan association
Credit union

Other Types of
Financial Institutions

Mutual fund
Life insurance company

OSTERREICHISCHE LÄNDERBANK

Deposit-Type Financial Institutions

Most consumers are familiar with companies that are in business to receive money for deposit and then make that money available for personal and business purchases. These organizations are called deposit-type financial institutions.

Commercial Banks. The financial institution with the most international business visibility is the commercial bank. A **commercial bank** is a business organized to accept deposits and to make loans. Traditionally, commercial banks offer the widest range of services of any financial institution. Figure 22-3 lists the main services offered by commercial banks.

Services provided by banks differ throughout the world. In the United States, stock investments are usually made using a stock broker. However, most British stock purchases are made through banks.

As of the early 1990s, eight of the ten largest commercial banks in the world were based in Japan; the other two were in France. Other major banks are located in Britain, Germany, Switzerland, China, and the Netherlands. Large commercial banks based in the United States include Citicorp, Chemical Bank, BankAmerica, and Chase Manhattan.

Savings and Loan Associations. A **savings and loan association** traditionally specialized in savings accounts and home mortgages. As laws regulating financial institutions changed, savings and loan associations expanded the services they offered. Today, these organizations provide checking accounts, auto loans, financial planning advice, and electronic banking.

In the United Kingdom, a financial institution comparable to the savings and loan association is the Building Society. As the name implies, this financial institution actively provides funds to finance buildings for businesses and for home purchases by individuals.

Credit Unions. *Cooperatives* are businesses owned by their members and operated for their benefit. A **credit union** is a nonprofit, financial

---

Figure 22-3
Commercial banks offer a wide range of services to meet the needs of consumers and businesses.

FINANCIAL SERVICES OF COMMERCIAL BANKS

Savings	Payment Services	Borrowing	Other Services
Savings accounts	Checking accounts	Personal loans	Trusts
Money market accounts	Electronic funds transfer	Business loans	Investment advice
Certificates of deposit	Letters of credit	Credit cards	Tax assistance
	Traveler's checks	Mortgages	Estate planning
	Currency exchange	Home equity loans	Retirement planning

---

cooperative. Credit unions were originally organized based on various groups in society, such as places of employment, religious organizations, and community organizations.

The services offered by credit unions are comparable to most banks, although they have slightly different names. For example, a regular savings account is called a *share account*. Checking accounts at credit unions are officially called *share draft accounts*.

Because of their nonprofit status, most credit unions offer slightly higher rates on savings and slightly lower rates for loans than do other financial institutions. Since most credit unions are community-based, these organizations commonly provide more personalized service than do other financial institutions.

The World Council of Credit Unions reports that over 80 million people around the world are credit union members. Credit unions operate in more than 60 countries, including Kenya, Ethiopia, Nigeria, Botswana, India, Singapore, Australia, New Zealand, Fiji, and most countries in Central and South America.

Global Business Example: The Techiman Women's Market Credit Union

Most days for the market women of Techiman begin at sunup and continue until after sunset. The women sell multicolored fabrics, produce, dried cassava (a starchy root), soup, furniture, and clothing. As many as 10,000 customers come to the Techiman market in Ghana on a Thursday or Friday.

The vendors in this market need money for stall fees, supplies, school fees, and day care. Before the creation of the Techiman Women's Market Credit Union, moneylenders were the main source of borrowed funds and charged as much as 50–60 percent interest. Now, the more than 200 credit union members can borrow at 18 percent interest.

Other Types of Financial Institutions

The financial needs of consumers and businesses are also served by organizations that specialize in specific financial services.

Mutual Fund.   How would you like to be able to own stock in hundreds of companies while only investing a small amount of money? That's what is possible when you purchase shares in a mutual fund. A **mutual fund** is an investment company that combines funds from many investors.

A major benefit of a mutual fund is *diversification*. By pooling money from many investors, a mutual fund manager is able to invest in

Global Highlight: The Gulf War of 1991

On August 2, 1990, military troops from Iraq invaded the small country of Kuwait. Once a part of Iraq, Kuwait was declared to be Iraq's "19th province." The attack was prompted by a breakdown in talks between the two countries about oil production and debt repayment. Other countries, however, viewed the invasion as an attempt by Iraq to control the region's oil supply.

After five months of unsuccessful negotiations to resolve the situation, the United Nations launched "Operation Desert Storm." This effort started with the most damaging air attack in history against military targets in Iraq and Kuwait. Many Iraqi planes were flown to Iran (neutral in the conflict) to escape destruction.

The ground war started on February 23. As a result of air superiority, it only took four days for the United Nations troops to break through and defeat Iraq's defense. The official cease-fire was accepted and signed on April 6.

The Persian Gulf War effort involved more than 600,000 troops from countries that included the United States, Canada, Britain, France, Saudi Arabia, and Syria. Casualties for the United Nations' forces were fewer than 200 dead and 500 wounded. Iraq's death toll was estimated at between 25,000 and 100,000; more than 80,000 Iraqi soldiers were taken prisoner.

many types of stock and/or bonds. This spreads out the risk for the investors and reduces the danger of losing all of one's money.

Over 4,000 different mutual funds exist in the United States. More than 30 million U.S. citizens own mutual funds. Mutual funds are available to meet a variety of investment goals. For example, an income fund would be selected by someone who wants current earnings from investments.

Global mutual funds allow investors to own the stock of companies in many countries. This method of international investing eliminates the high brokerage commissions and high currency conversion fees of individual investments. Global mutual funds reduce the risk that exchange rate changes may wipe out profits even when stocks increase in value.

Life Insurance Company.   People throughout the world buy life insurance policies to protect family members and others from financial difficulties when a person dies. The money paid for insurance premiums is invested by the insurance companies. Life insurance companies commonly lend these funds to large corporations and invest in commercial real estate. These actions make capital available to companies.

Global Business Example: Scudder Investor Services

Scudder Investor Services combines the funds of many people to invest in various stocks and bonds. As international business expands, Scudder wanted to provide its investors with worldwide investment opportunities. The company created the Scudder Global Fund to buy stocks of large companies that have the potential of profiting in the global economy. Scudder also has a Latin America Fund, which seeks long-term growth of stocks in companies in Central and South America, and a Pacific Opportunities Fund, which invests in Asian companies.

GLOBAL STOCK MARKETS

International companies may borrow from financial institutions; however, they also raise funds by selling *stock*. Stock represents a share of ownership in an organization. Stockholders are the owners of a corporation who elect the board of directors. The board hires the officers who run the company.

Stock Exchanges

A **stock exchange** is a location where stocks are bought and sold. The New York Stock Exchange (NYSE) is the largest in the world. The market value of stocks and bonds sold each year on the NYSE exceeds $1,600 billion. The stock of many multinational companies based in other countries, such as British Airways, Nestle, Royal Dutch/Shell, and Sony Corporation, is bought and sold on the New York Stock Exchange.

In addition to the NYSE, other major stock exchanges around the world include the American (AMEX), Bombay, Copenhagen, Düsseldorf, Istanbul, Milan, Rio de Janeiro, Seoul, Stockholm, Taiwan, Tel Aviv, Toronto, and Zürich stock exchanges. Figure 22-4 lists some major companies traded on four selected stock exchanges.

Figure 22-4
Stock exchanges provide a location where shares of stock are bought and sold.

MAJOR COMPANIES TRADED ON SELECTED GLOBAL STOCK EXCHANGES

London	**Tokyo**	**Frankfurt**	**Paris**
British Aerospace	Industrial Bank of Japan	Allianz Holding	Carrefour
British Gas	Mazda Motor Co.	Daimler-Benz	Credit Lyonnais
Marks and Spencer	Minolta Camera	Deutsche Bank	Euro Disneyland
Rolls-Royce Motors	Nippon Steel	Porsche	Hachette
Unilever		Siemens	Michelin

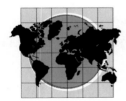

Global Business Example: The Prague Stock Exchange

On January 1, 1993, Czechoslovakia split into two separate countries—the Czech Republic and the Republic of Slovakia. As the countries moved from a central-planned economy, under communist rule, to a free-market economy, citizens were allowed to invest in stocks.

The Prague Stock Exchange (in the Czech Republic) started with only six stocks. By mid-1993 nearly 1,000 companies were offered to investors. Most of these enterprises were previously government-controlled businesses that had been *privatized*. Some of the most popular stocks are companies in the hotel and glass manufacturing industries. With low inflation, low unemployment, low foreign debt, and high political stability, the Prague Stock Exchange may provide some attractive investment alternatives.

The Stock Exchange in Action

Every hour of the day, investors buy and sell stocks. On the trading floor of the stock exchange and through computer systems, representatives of buyers and sellers interact to determine the prices of shares of stock. Figure 22-5 summarizes the main steps involved in a stock transaction.

Figure 22-5
Stocks are bought and sold at a stock exchange with prices determined by supply and demand.

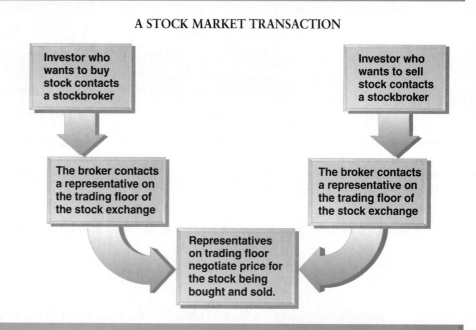

A STOCK MARKET TRANSACTION

The purchase of stock through a stock exchange involves a stockbroker. A **stockbroker** is a person who buys and sells stocks and other investments for customers. Besides handling stock transactions for investors, full-service brokers will provide information about current stock market trends and other types of investments.

Completely computerized stock trading stock exchanges, without trading floor representatives, are becoming common. These high-speed, low-cost automated systems are used by most major stock exchanges in Europe and Canada. London has the world's largest screen-based system for global stocks.

Stocks prices are affected by many factors. The main influence on stock prices is demand for ownership in a company. If people believe a company is a good investment, demand will cause the stock price to rise. In contrast, as fewer investors buy the stock of a company its stock price will decline. In addition, economic conditions, the political situation, and social trends can influence stock prices.

Global Business Exercise: Analyzing the Effect of News on Stock Prices

For each of the following news items, tell what types of companies would be affected and how (higher or lower stock prices):

1. A country announces rigid regulations to protect the environment.
2. A new food-processing system keeps foods fresh without refrigeration for several weeks.
3. Families are spending more time at home rather than going out for food and entertainment.
4. Scientists discover a device that makes an electric car more practical.
5. A telecommunications company develops a system that delivers current news and class presentations to schools.

Stock Market Information

After an agreement on price is reached, this information becomes public. Each day millions of stocks are bought and sold. Information about current stock prices, dividends, volume, and past prices are reported in the newspaper. Figure 22-6 on page 486 presents a sample of the stock market information reported every day.

Global Business Exercise: Changing Stock Prices

Refer to Figure 22-6 on page 486 to answer the following questions: (Convert fractions to decimals for dollar figures.)

1. What was the highest price paid for a share of McDonald's stock during the past year?
2. What was the lowest price paid for a share of American Express stock during the past year?
3. How many shares of WalMart were traded on this business day?
4. What was the highest price paid for a share of Disney stock on this trading day?
5. What was the closing price of General Motors stock on the previous trading day?
6. If a company pays an annual dividend of $2 per share and the stock sells for $50 a share, what is the yield percentage?

Figure 22-6

Current stock prices and other information on stock market activities are reported each business day in newspapers.

REPORTING STOCK INFORMATION

NYSE 52 WEEKS		Stock	Sym.	Divd.	Yld %.	PE	Vol. 100s	Hi	Low	Close	Net Chg.
High	Low										
1	2	3	4	5	6	7	8	9	10	11	12
$34\frac{3}{8}$	20	AmExpress	AXP	1.00	3.0	33	12658	$33\frac{1}{4}$	$32\frac{3}{4}$	$33\frac{1}{8}$	$+\frac{1}{8}$
$47\frac{7}{8}$	$33\frac{1}{4}$	Disney	DIS	.25	.6	22	9301	$39\frac{1}{8}$	$38\frac{3}{8}$	$38\frac{7}{8}$	$-\frac{1}{8}$
$49\frac{3}{4}$	28	GenMotor	GM	.80	1.8	– –	10393	$46\frac{1}{2}$	$45\frac{3}{8}$	$45\frac{1}{2}$	$+1\frac{1}{2}$
$55\frac{1}{4}$	$40\frac{7}{8}$	McDonalds	MCD	.43	.8	20	5807	$54\frac{1}{8}$	54	54	$-\frac{1}{8}$
$34\frac{1}{8}$	$23\frac{3}{8}$	WalMart	WMT	.13	.5	26	60575	$25\frac{3}{4}$	$24\frac{1}{2}$	$34\frac{3}{4}$	$+1$

Column	Explanation
1	Reports the highest price paid for one share of the stock over the past year.
2	Reports the lowest price paid for one share of the stock over the past year.
3	Lists the abbreviated name of the corporation.
4	Identifies the symbol used to report stock prices for the corporations in column 3.
5	Reports the dividends paid per share during the past 12 months.
6	Represents the yield percentage, which is the dividend divided by the current price of the stock.
7	Identifies the price-earnings ratio, which is computed by dividing the current price per share by the company's earnings (profits) per share over the last 12 months.
8	Reports the number of shares traded during the day, based on hundreds of shares.
9	States the highest price paid for one share on the trading day.
10	States the lowest price paid for one share on the trading day.
11	Reports the price paid for a share in the last stock purchase of the day.
12	Represents the difference between the price paid for the last share bought today and the price for the last share bought on the previous trading day.

THE BOND MARKET

A *bond* is a certificate representing money borrowed by a company or other organization to be repaid over a long period of time. The bond market helps organizations raise debt capital.

Corporate Bonds

A **corporate bond** is a debt certificate issued by a multinational company or other corporate enterprise. Most corporate bonds in the United States are sold in amounts of $1,000. This amount is called the *face value* or *maturity value*. In France, the typical corporate bond is issued for Fr 50,000.

The interest rate on a bond is important to investors. For example, a 10 percent bond would pay an investor $100 a year in interest. This is computed as follows:

$$\$1,000 \times .10 \times 1 \text{ year} = \$100$$

The *rate of return* on a bond is computed by dividing the income from the investment by the cost of the investment. For example:

$72 annual income	÷	$1,000 cost of investment	=	.072 (7.2 percent) annual rate of return

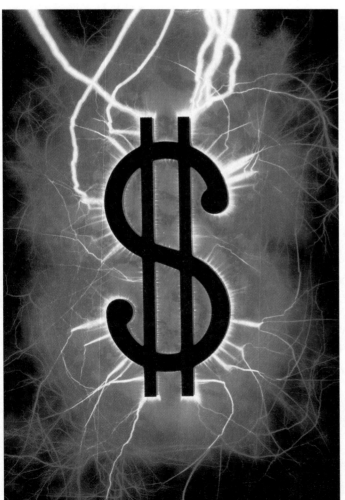

Bond investors should also consider the *maturity date*. This is the point in time when the loan will be repaid. A 20-year bond, for example, means an investor will earn interest each year for 20 years. Then, at the end of the 20 years the investor will be repaid the face value. Remember, when a company issues bonds it is borrowing money that must be repaid.

Government Bonds

Governments also issue bonds. The federal government of the United States, for example, sells treasury bonds to obtain needed funds for its operations. State and local governments in the United States also borrow by issuing municipal bonds.

Federal Government Bonds. The U.S. government sells bonds to finance the national debt and to pay operating expenses. Three common debt instruments of the federal government are treasury bills, treasury notes, and treasury bonds. Treasury bills (T-bills) are short-term borrowing instruments, with maturities ranging from 91 days to 1 year. Treasury notes (T-notes) are intermediate-length borrowing instruments, with maturities from 1 to 10 years. Treasury bonds (T-bonds) are for long-term borrowing, ranging from 10 to 30 years.

Global Business Example: Are All Junk Bonds Garbage?

Risky bonds are commonly called *junk bonds.* This investment can be attractive to people seeking a high return. Remember, however, high risk is associated with junk bonds. During the 1980s, junk bonds had average returns of nearly 14 percent. During that same period, several companies filed for bankruptcy with bondholders receiving nothing.

The debt of many companies in less-developed foreign countries may be rated as "junk bonds." This label results from economic and political uncertainty in their nations. As foreign companies attempt economic expansion, they will issue bonds to fund business activities. While many of these investments are risky, some will provide a high return for those willing to take a chance.

U.S. savings bonds are another type of federal government debt instrument. These bonds are commonly purchased by individuals who want to save for the future. U.S. savings bonds are purchased at one-half of their face value (e.g., a $100 bond costs $50). The time it takes for a savings bond to grow to the maturity value will vary depending on the current interest rate paid by the U.S. Treasury Department.

In recent years, earnings on U.S. savings bonds were not taxed if the funds were used to pay tuition and fees at a college, university, or qualified technical school. For a quick update on U.S. savings bonds rates and other information, call 1-800-US BONDS.

State and Local Government Bonds.   A **municipal bond** is a debt certificate issued by a state or local government agency. Since most countries organize their government structures differently from the United States, municipal bonds are not common in other nations.

The major benefit of municipal bonds for U.S. investors is that the interest earned is excluded from federal income taxes. Such income, not subject to tax, is called **tax-exempt income.** Other types of investments, such as certain types of retirement accounts, earn **tax-deferred income,** which is income that will be taxed at a later date.

OTHER FINANCIAL MARKETS

In addition to stock and bond markets, other financial markets exist to serve companies involved in global business.

The Over-the-Counter Market

Large companies that meet the requirements of a stock exchange and are traded regularly are called *listed* stocks. In contrast, stocks of new and small companies are traded through a system of computers, teletype machines, fax machines, and telephones. The **over-the-counter (OTC) market** is a network of stockbrokers who buy and sell stocks not listed on a stock exchange.

The National Association of Securities Dealers Automated Quotations (NASDAQ) is the major computerized trading system for OTC stocks in the United States. The Unlisted Securities Market is the over-the-counter market for fast-growing companies in England. In addition, the European Union wants to create a similar OTC market to help emerging enterprises raise capital.

Foreign Exchange Market

The foreign exchange market involves the buying and selling of currencies needed to pay for goods and services bought from companies in other countries. A **Eurodollar** is a U.S. dollar deposited in a bank outside of the United States and used in the money markets of Europe. The term *Eurocurrency* has come to mean *any* money deposited in a bank outside the country of its origin and used in the money markets of Europe. These funds are used to make payments among countries for foreign trade.

Futures Market

Farmers want to get a fair price for their grain. Food companies want to avoid paying high prices for grain that will be used to make breakfast cereals. By agreeing to a price now, for delivery in the future (usually three or six months from now), a farmer is protected against receiving a lower price for grain. The cereal company is protected against higher costs.

The **futures market** allows investors and others to buy or sell contracts on the future prices of commodities, metals, and financial instruments. Futures markets involve contracts on corn, oats, soybeans, wheat, cattle, cocoa, sugar, oil, natural gas, gold, silver, treasury bonds, and currencies—yen, pound, deutsche mark, franc, and Eurodollar.

Global Business Example: Computerized Financial Markets

Computer technology allows brokers, investors, and financial managers anywhere in the world to instantly contact any other financial agent. A Chicago Board of Trade broker can conduct automated after-hours transactions with the Marche à Terme International de France futures market in Paris. High-speed, computerized stock trading allows a broker in London to buy and sell stocks of multinational companies listed on stock exchanges in Bombay, Istanbul, Rio de Janeiro, Seoul, or Taiwan. The system allows investors to complete buy and sell orders anytime, day or night.

Back to the Beginning: Koor Industries, Ltd.

Reread the case at the beginning of this chapter and answer the following questions:

1. How did the cost reduction activities of Koor Industries affect the company?
2. What problems can occur during poor economic times for a company with high levels of debt?
3. To what extent should government assist major companies when they face financial difficulties?

KNOWING GLOBAL BUSINESS TERMS

The following terms should become part of your business vocabulary. For each numbered item find the term that has the same meaning.

- commercial bank
- corporate bond
- credit union
- debt capital
- equity capital
- Eurodollar
- futures market
- municipal bond
- mutual fund
- over-the-counter (OTC) market
- savings and loan association
- stockbroker
- stock exchange
- tax-deferred income
- tax-exempt income

1. A financial institution that traditionally specialized in savings accounts and home mortgages.

2. Funds obtained by borrowing.

3. Income that will be taxed at a later date.

4. An investment company that manages a pool of funds contributed by others.

5. A network of stockbrokers who buy and sell stocks not listed on a stock exchange.

6. Funds provided by a company's owners.

7. Income not subject to tax.

8. A debt certificate issued by a state or local government agency.

9. A business organized to accept deposits and to make loans.

10. A location where stocks are bought and sold.

11. A market that allows investors and others to buy or sell contracts on the future prices of commodities, metals, and financial instruments.

12. A U.S. dollar deposited in a bank outside of the United States and used in the money markets of Europe.

13. A debt certificate issued by a multinational company or other corporate business enterprise.

14. A person who buys and sells stocks and other investments for customers.

15. A nonprofit, financial cooperative.

REVIEWING YOUR READING

Answer these questions to reinforce your knowledge of the main ideas of this chapter.

1. How does equity capital differ from debt capital?

2. What are examples of current expenses encountered by most businesses?

3. What are the main deposit-type financial institutions?

4. How do credit unions serve their members?

5. What is a mutual fund?

6. What is a stock exchange?

7. What services does a stock broker provide?

8. What factors affect daily stock prices?

9. How is the rate of return on a bond computed?

10. What three common debt instruments are used by the federal government of the United States?

11. What is a municipal bond?

12. What types of stocks are commonly traded on the over-the-counter market (OTC)?

13. What is a Eurodollar?

EXPANDING YOUR HORIZONS

You will not find the complete answers to the following questions in your textbook, you will need to use your critical-thinking skills. Think about these questions, gather information from other sources, analyze possible responses, and discuss them with others. Then, develop your own oral or written response as instructed by your teacher.

1. Explain reasons why a company uses debt. Also, tell why a company might avoid using debt to finance its operations.

2. Name some benefits of capital projects for a community.

3. Would your needs as a consumer be better served by a large international bank or a small local bank?

4. How does a mutual fund provide small investors with opportunities they might otherwise not have?

5. Why are many international companies traded on the New York Stock Exchange (NYSE) instead of on stock exchanges in their home countries?

6. Why do some people use a "discount" stockbroker instead of a "full-service" broker?

7. What happens when there is no buyer for shares of stock that someone wants to sell?

8. Which type of investment involves more risk for an investor: stocks or bonds? Why?

9. How does the futures market serve the needs of many groups of people in a country?

BUILDING RESEARCH SKILLS

The ability to find information from various sources is an important international business skill. The following activities will help you investigate various topics. You will also learn to apply class ideas to situations outside of the classroom.

1. Collect articles and advertisements that present examples of sources of funds (debt and equity) and uses of funds (current

operating costs and long-term expenses). Prepare a poster or bulletin board display with these materials.

2. Survey people who use different types of financial institutions. Obtain information about their reasons for doing business with a certain bank, savings and loan association, credit union, or other financial institution.

3. Interview a stockbroker about his or her duties and obtain information about the handling of stock market transactions.

4. Select a company and chart the changing price of its stock. Prepare a graph showing the closing price of a share over a three-week period. Conduct library research to locate news about the company and economic conditions. Prepare a short report explaining how this news has affected the company's stock price.

5. Locate bond prices in *The Wall Street Journal* or the business section of a daily newspaper. Report to the class about the information that is included in the daily bond report.

6. *Global Career Activity.* Collect articles and other information about financial institutions in other countries. How do the jobs with these companies differ from finance jobs in the United States?

Continuing Enrichment Project: International Financial Activities

Based on the company you have researched in previous chapters or another company, conduct library research to answer the following questions:

1. To what extent does the company use debt to finance its business activities?

2. What long-term projects is the company currently planning or implementing?

3. If the company is a major corporation, on what stock exchange is the company's stock traded? What is the current price of a share of the company's stock?

4. What economic, social, and political factors have recently affected the company's stock price?

5. What is the current interest rate paid on the company's bonds?

Regional Profile

Middle East

Zainab is a young Iraqi woman who is studying to be an archaeologist at a university in Baghdad. During the 1980–1988 war with Iran and the war with the 28-nation coalition after Iraq invaded Kuwait, Zainab feared for the safety of the ancient ruins. Her recent visit to the site of the Mesopotamian capital of Babylon allayed her fears of large-scale damage to the ruins. The famous Ishtar gate, the remains of the tower of Babel, and the remains of Nebuchadrezzar II's palace had not been affected.

Zainab's study of history has made her deeply aware of this land between the Tigris and Euphrates rivers. Known as the Fertile Crescent, this area gave birth to farming and allowed farmers to produce a surplus of food as early as 4000 B.C. About 500 years later Sumerians moved into the area and established 12 city-states. The Sumerians invented cuneiform (a type of writing), the wagon wheel, the 12-month calendar, and metal plows.

The area known as the Middle East includes countries on three continents. Generally scholars agree that the Middle East consists of Bahrain, Cyprus, Egypt, Iran, Iraq, Israel, Jordan, Kuwait, Lebanon, Oman, Qatar, Saudi Arabia, Sudan, Syria, Turkey, the United Arab Emirates, and Yemen. The Middle East is bordered by several bodies of water: the Mediterranean Sea, the Black Sea, the Caspian Sea, the Persian Gulf, the Arabian Sea, and the Indian Ocean. It is home to about 262 million people; holds 60 percent of the world's supply of oil; and is the site of continuous political, ethnic, and religious conflicts.

Zainab knows that in some nations of the Middle East, the conditions under which women live are extremely restrictive. They must cover their heads and faces, they may not drive a car, and they may not vote. Zainab is aware that women in Iraq have been jailed and tortured for demanding equal rights. However in some countries of the Middle East, women have made progress in their battle to gain equality in society.

Three major monotheistic religions—Judaism, Christianity, and Islam—began in the Middle East. According to the Torah, Judaism can be traced back to Abraham, who led the Hebrews from the Mesopotamian city of Ur west to the land of Canaan. The Hebrews believe that God made a covenant with Abraham: In return for their being faithful to God, they would be protected and made a great nation. The Hebrews migrated to Egypt where they lived for many years before being enslaved by the pharaohs. In the twelfth century B.C., Moses led the Hebrews in an exodus from Egypt into the Sinai Desert, where they believe that God renewed the covenant and gave them the Ten Commandments. At this time they became Jews— Israel, or "God's chosen." Eventually they returned to Canaan and established the kingdom of Israel with its capital at Jerusalem.

By the time Jesus was born, the Roman Empire had control over much of the Middle East. The Jews were treated poorly by the Romans and many of them looked forward to a savior who would restore their kingdom. About A.D. 26 to 30, Jesus preached a new message among the Jews in Palestine. He told them to love one another just as they love themselves. His followers believed that he was the long-awaited messiah or savior, while others thought that he was an imposter and accused him of blasphemy. The Romans believed that Jesus might cause civil strife or even political rebellion. He was arrested as a troublemaker and crucified. After his death, his followers said that he had risen from the dead and called him the Son of God. Those who believed this to be true called themselves Christian, and they began spreading Jesus' teachings and their beliefs throughout the world.

Zainab, like the majority of the people of the Middle East, is a Muslim. Muslims are followers of the religion of Islam. According to the Islam holy book, the Koran, the Islamic religion was founded on the Arabian Peninsula in 622 A.D. The nation of Saudi Arabia accounts for most of the peninsula today; however at that time, the area consisted of many separate Arab tribes. The city of Makkah (Mecca) was a center of trade and worship, and it is where the founder of Islam, Muhammad (the Prophet), claimed God first spoke to him and revealed the Koran.

Beginning in A.D. 613, Muhammad began preaching that there was just one God, Allah, and people had to worship and obey him or else they would be punished. He also said that Allah's followers were equal and that the rich must help the poor. Many among the poor welcomed his message, but the merchants forced him to flee in 622. This year of *Hifrah* (emigration) is considered the first year of the Islamic calendar. Muhammad found success in the city of Madinah (Medina) where he was given authority in religious and political matters. Thus began the Islamic state that is similar to modern Iran. In A.D. 630, Muhammad defeated the Makkans in battle and took control of their city.

After Muhammad's death, Caliphs (successors) were elected to lead the political-religious community and to spread the teachings of Islam. The Caliphs sent armies against the Byzantine and Persian empires to bring converts and wealth to the growing empire. By A.D. 750, the Islamic Empire stretched from the Indus River in Asia across North Africa and into most of Spain.

The complex geopolitical forces that operated in the Middle East following World War II involved the conflicting interests of the Soviet Union and the United States. The ongoing wars between the Arabs and the Israelis—since the creation of the Jewish state of Israel in 1948—were the most obvious problem. Israel received billions of dollars from the United States, and the Soviet Union supplied weapons and advisers to the Arab countries. Other sources of great interest among outsiders are the region's strategic waterways and the abundant oil supplies in the Persian Gulf region.

The Persian Gulf countries continue to enjoy the benefits of their oil industries, but many countries in the Middle East are not so fortunate. Most economies, with the exception of Israel and Turkey, do not have strong industrial bases. The region suffers from an inadequate base of skilled and professional labor, insufficient transportation facilities, religious and ethnic conflicts, and the absence of a reliable supply of fresh water.

In political developments, by 1993, the Israeli government had agreed to a plan of peace with the Palestine Liberation Organization (PLO) and, in return, most Arab countries were acknowledging Israel's right to exist. It seemed that most people were tired of war. To Zainab, these are hopeful signs in a land that has experienced both widespread suffering and great enlightenment since the beginning of recorded Western history.

CHAPTER 23

Managing International Business Risk

After studying this chapter and completing the end-of-chapter activities, you will be able to

- Describe the types of risks related to international business activities.
- Discuss the risk management process.
- Explain the basic elements of insurance coverage.
- Identify the major types of insurance coverages for international business activities.
- Describe strategies that multinational companies use to reduce risk.

Lloyd's of London

The world's most famous insurance organization began in Edward Lloyd's coffeehouse in London. In 1688, shipowners and merchants bought marine insurance from Lloyd's to cover the risks of sending goods to other countries. In the late 1800s, Lloyd's of London expanded into nonmarine insurance. Over the years, this association of insurance underwriters has insured some unusual assets, including the legs of Hollywood dancers and voices of singers.

Lloyd's of London is different from other insurance companies. This insurance society consists of investors called *Names* who pool their money to cover possible financial risks. The Names profit when insurance claims are less than income. However when a peril happens, the Names have to be prepared to pay for the financial losses of the disaster.

In recent years, Lloyd's has experienced lower profits due to natural disasters, environmental problems, and changing tax laws in Britain. These events may force the organization to make changes. Nonetheless, some traditions continue. In Lloyd's headquarters is the bell from the *Lutine* which shipwrecked in 1857. The bell tolls once for good news, twice for bad news.

Risk is the uncertainty of an event or outcome. Every organization faces potential risks, ranging from employee theft to natural disasters. Companies, as well as individuals, must manage risk.

INTERNATIONAL BUSINESS RISKS

If all business ventures were sure things, life would be a lot simpler. However, in reality every business activity has some risk. A war may destroy a factory in another country, or a company may go bankrupt and not be able to repay its debts. As shown in Figure 23-1, the three common risks faced by companies involved in international business are political risk, social risk, and economic risk.

Figure 23-1

Companies involved in international business activities face different risks.

TYPES OF INTERNATIONAL BUSINESS RISKS

Political Risk

• Government instability
• Change in business regulations
• New trade barriers

Social Risk

• Religious beliefs
• Values
• Family-work relationships

Economic Risk

• Consumer spending patterns
• Inflation
• Exchange rate fluctuations

Political Risk

Would a company be safer doing business in a democratic country with a newly formed government or in an autocratic nation which has been ruled by the same dictator for ten years? Political risk is difficult to evaluate. Government instability and political uncertainty are risks global companies must monitor constantly. Political control may change hands during civil unrest or a revolution. The new government may not allow certain companies to continue to operate in the country.

Business regulations vary from country to country. Regulations on business might be very tight in one nation, while great freedom is allowed elsewhere. Food packages in one country may require extensive nutritional information. However, another market may not have any laws regulating food labeling.

Trade barriers also pose a potential political risk. Tariffs, antidumping laws, import quotas, and currency exchange controls are examples of political actions taken to limit imported goods.

Social Risk

As you know, business is conducted differently in different parts of the world. Social and cultural factors such as religious beliefs, values, and family-business ties affect the risk faced by multinational companies.

Companies doing business in other countries must respect the religious beliefs of people in those nations. Failure to do so is likely to result in an unsuccessful endeavor even though all other business actions are proper. In a similar manner, companies that stress individualism would face greater risk when doing business in nations that emphasize collectivism.

The connection between family and business is very important in some cultures, and less important in others. In most areas of Central and South America, much of southern Europe, most of Asia, northern Africa, and the Middle East, family-business ties are strong. Companies must work within this cultural environment to minimize business risk.

Economic Risk

Economic conditions have ups and downs. The demand for a company's goods and services varies based on the income of consumers, interest rates, and levels of employment. When fewer people are working, less money is available for consumer spending.

When a company receives one dollar today, it hopes to be able to buy something worth one dollar in the future. However if inflation erodes the buying power of a currency, the monetary unit will not have as much purchasing power in the future.

Companies that do business in other countries face the risk of receiving payment in a currency that may have less value than expected. With exchange rates changing daily, financial managers must make sure that the payment received is appropriate after the currency conversion.

Monitoring Global Business Risk

Change is the only constant in all aspects of business. Reading current materials, talking with residents, and watching economic data are ways to note changes in a country's business environment. Awareness of factors such as political stability, religious influences, and fluctuating interest rates can help a manager predict changes in business risk. An ability to anticipate and act early can reduce risk and lessen poor business decisions.

Global Business Example: Practicing Unexpected Events

Royal Dutch/Shell is the world's largest petroleum and natural gas company. It continually encounters fluctuating oil prices, environmental concerns, and uncertainty in supplier nations. When the Persian Gulf War started in the early 1990s, Shell was no longer able to obtain oil from Kuwait and Iraq.

How can a company prepare for these types of risks? Royal Dutch/Shell simulates disasters. A couple of times a year, oil shipments are unexpectedly interrupted. Then, employees must put back-up plans into operation. Therefore, during the Gulf War, the company had already arranged to locate and ship oil from alternative sites.

THE RISK MANAGEMENT PROCESS

Multinational companies will face many business risks. Figure 23-2 presents steps that may be taken to manage these international business risks.

Figure 23-2
Companies manage risk by following a step-by-step approach.

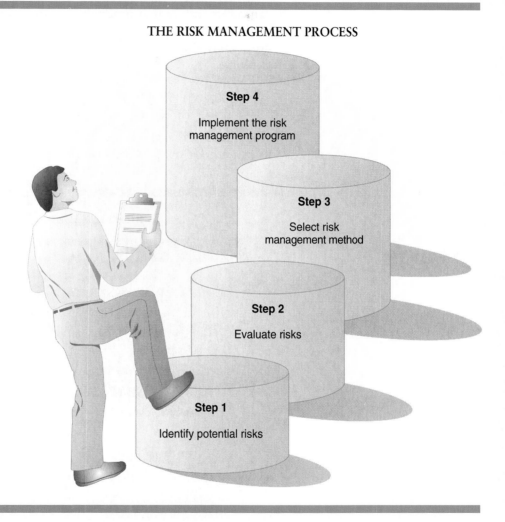

THE RISK MANAGEMENT PROCESS

Step 4
Implement the risk management program

Step 3
Select risk management method

Step 2
Evaluate risks

Step 1
Identify potential risks

Step 1—Identify Potential Risks

In the first step of the risk management process, managers list the factors that might affect a company's operations. Government policies, currency values, and local customs are some examples of risk-causing elements. Managers can use current reports, field interviews, and other data sources to uncover conditions that increase uncertainty.

Step 2—Evaluate Risks

In this step, managers analyze the potential effect of risks for a company. Will a *change* in government mean higher costs to cover new environmental regulations? Or, could the *change* in government result in the company no longer being allowed to operate in the nation? Managers must decide how and to what extent the risks will influence sales and profits.

Be aware that a factor in the international business environment can affect different companies in different ways. A weak economy may hurt a company selling entertainment products. However, the same poor economic conditions may benefit a company selling low-cost clothing.

Step 3—Select Risk Management Method

Next, managers must decide how to handle the identified risks. The four methods used to manage risk are shown in Figure 23-3.

Figure 23-3
Risks are managed by companies in four main ways.

RISK MANAGEMENT METHODS

Risk Avoidance

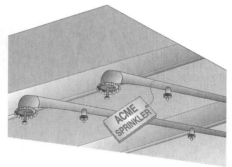

Risk Reduction

Risk Assumption

Risk Sharing

Risk Avoidance. Certain risks can be avoided. A company avoids the risks related to international business by only selling products in its home country. However, this approach to risk management is not always practical. A business limits its potential for expansion by only selling in a domestic market.

Risk Reduction. The risk of an event may be reduced by taking precautionary actions. For example, businesses use security systems and sprinklers to reduce the risk of theft and fire. Multinational companies can reduce business risks by selling products that have been successful in other countries.

Risk Assumption. Sometimes, a company takes responsibility for losses from certain risks. For example, a business may set aside funds for fire damage that may occur to its factories. This action, called **self-insurance,** involves setting aside money to cover a potential financial loss. A company with many stores or factories in different locations may save money by using self-insurance.

Risk Sharing. Sharing risks among many companies that face similar risks is a common practice. Insurance is often purchased for financial protection from property losses, motor vehicle accidents, and other business activities.

Step 4—Implement the Risk Management Program

Finally, managers must execute the risk management plan. This phase involves both taking relevant action and measuring the success of the action. Various factors in the business environment and within the company may change an organization's risk management course in the future.

Global Business Exercise: Managing Risk

For each of the following situations, describe actions that the organization might take to manage its business risk.

1. Stealing by employees and customers.
2. Changes in the value of foreign currencies.
3. Actions of global competitors.
4. Changing clothing styles.
5. Political instability in a foreign country.

Insurance is planned protection for sharing economic losses among many people. Insurance is commonly purchased to reduce or eliminate the financial loss due to risks. A company's place of business is usually covered by property insurance. When driving a car, a traveling salesperson probably has automobile insurance. Most everyone reading this book uses insurance as a method for managing risk.

Insurance is an agreement between one party, called the *insured*, and an insurance company, the *insurer*. A **stock insurance company** is owned by stockholders and is operated for profit. A **mutual insurance company** is owned by its policyholders. This type of organization returns any surplus (after paying claims and operating expenses) to policyholders.

Insurable Interest

A basic requirement of insurance is the presence of an *insurable interest*, something of value that may be lost or destroyed. For example, equipment owned by a company represents an insurable interest. In the case of life insurance, the insurable interest is the financial loss caused by someone's death.

Insurable Risk

Another basic requirement of insurance is an *insurable risk*. An insurable risk is a risk that has the following elements:

- *Common to many people*—The risk must be one that is faced by many people or businesses. This allows many people with the same risk to share the cost of the few who actually suffer a financial loss due to the risk.

- *Definite*—The risk must be something that can be documented. The destruction of a building by fire or the death of a person is something that can be documented.

- *Not excessive in magnitude*—An insurance company would not be able to cover the cost of replacing *all* homes it insures at one time. Hurricanes in Florida caused such extensive damage that some insurance companies can no longer afford to do business in that state.

- *Not trivial*—Insurance on small items would not be worth the time, effort, and expense necessary to provide coverage.
- *Able to be calculated*—The insurer must be able to calculate the probability of the risk occurring. This allows the insurer to plan what amount to charge for insurance.

Insurance Policy Elements

An **insurance policy** is the legal agreement between an insurance company and the insured. This contract states the conditions of protection. Figure 23-4 shows the major elements of an insurance policy.

Figure 23-4
An insurance policy is the contract between an insurance company and the insured.

THE ELEMENTS OF AN INSURANCE POLICY

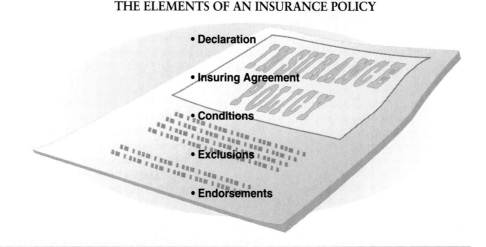

The *declaration* states what is covered and lists the amount of coverage. For example, the declaration for a multinational company's insurance would describe the company's factories in different countries and at what amount they are covered.

The *insuring agreement* explains the coverages of the insurance policy. A company's insurance policy may cover fire and theft losses for property up to $14 million.

The *conditions* of an insurance policy provide information about the cost of insurance, called the **premium.** Also listed are any deductibles. A **deductible** is the portion of an insurance claim paid by the insured. A company, with a $1,000 deductible, for example, may incur $4,500 of wind damage to a building. In this situation the insurance company would pay $3,500. The first $1,000 of the claim is paid by the insured. Deductibles reduce the cost of insurance premiums.

Property or risks not covered by an insurance policy are called *exclusions*. For example, many insurance policies do not cover property losses resulting from war. Why do you think insurance companies exclude financial loss of wars from policies?

An **endorsement** is a certificate that adds to or changes the coverage of an insurance policy. For example, if a company sells a factory, an endorsement would delete the building from its insurance coverage.

Exports should be insured against loss or damage occurring while in transit. An **insurance certificate** provides evidence of insurance to protect goods from loss or damage while in transit. Sales terms determine if insurance costs are paid by the importer or exporter.

Global Business Example: The Russian Insurance Industry

When the former Soviet Union evolved from communism to capitalism, many insurance companies were started. Russia's first insurance law, effective January, 1993, allowed an applicant to become a licensed insurance seller with only 2 million rubles in capital—about $1,100. This has allowed many inexperienced entrepreneurs to enter the market.

Foreign ownership of Russian insurance companies is restricted to 49 percent. One company, Giva, received financial support from RBS Holding, a communications and food service firm from Bloomfield Hills, Michigan. In 1993, Giva earned 80 million rubles (about $65,000) on over one billion rubles ($820,000) in insurance premiums.

Vera (Russian for *trust*) is an insurance company with the Christian Russian Bank as one of its largest shareholders. Vera specializes in insuring the real estate of the Russian Orthodox Church. The company also provides insurance coverage for the church's art and other priceless treasures made from gold and diamonds.

(Source: *Financial World,* June 7, 1994, pp. 20–22, 24.)

GLOBAL INSURANCE COVERAGES

Companies involved in international business can share certain risks with insurance. Commonly used coverages of multinational companies are marine insurance, property insurance, coverage for political risk through the Overseas Private Investment Corporation, and credit risk insurance.

Marine Insurance

Overseas transporters usually assume no responsibility for the merchandise they carry unless the loss is caused by their carelessness. Marine insurance provides protection from loss during shipment of products. This insurance has two types of coverage.

Ocean marine insurance protects goods while shipped overseas and while temporarily in port. In contrast, **inland marine insurance** covers the risk of shipping goods on inland waterways, railroad lines, truck lines, and airlines.

Marine insurance is usually sold in three forms, with varied coverages:

1. *Basic coverage* provides protection from hazards such as sea damage, fires, jettisons, explosions, and hurricanes.
2. *Broad coverage* includes basic coverage plus theft, pilferage, nondelivery, breakage, and leakage.
3. *All-risk coverage* consists of any physical loss or damage due to an external cause, excluding risks associated with war. As expected, an all-risk policy is the most expensive of the three types since the most coverage is provided.

The amount charged for marine insurance is affected by a variety of factors. Premium factors include the value of the goods, the destination, the age of the ship, the storage location (on deck or under deck), the packaging, and the size of the shipment (volume discounts are common).

Property Insurance

Crimes such as burglary, theft, and arson disturb business activities throughout the world. Companies face three main risks as property owners:

1. Loss of real property.
2. Loss of personal property.
3. Financial responsibility for injuries or damage.

Loss of Real Property.   *Real property* refers to structures permanently attached to land, such as factories, stores, garages, or office buildings. A company's building and land represent a significant financial investment. Property insurance provides protection for damage or loss of real property. Buildings and structures are insured for loss or damage from fire, lightning, wind, hail, explosion, smoke, vandalism, and crashes of aircraft and motor vehicles.

Loss of Personal Property.   *Personal property* refers to property not attached to the land. Loss or damage of office furniture, machinery, equipment, and supplies can also be covered by property insurance.

Financial Responsibility for Injuries or Damage.   **Liability** is legal responsibility for the financial cost of someone else's losses or injuries. Customers, company guests, employees, and others may be injured while on the premises of a business. Or, a company representative may accidentally damage the property of others. When any of these occur, the company may be responsible for the financial loss that results from the incident.

Quite often legal responsibility is the result of **negligence;** that is, failure to take ordinary or reasonable care. An employer may also be held financially responsible for the actions of an employee. Liability insurance protects a company from financial losses due to the actions of its employees.

The Overseas Private Investment Corporation

To encourage investment in less-developed countries, the U.S. government created the Overseas Private Investment Corporation (OPIC). This agency protects U.S. companies from various hazards. OPIC covers financial losses resulting from three major types of risk:

1. Inconvertibility—This is an inability to convert foreign currency into U.S. dollars. Most refusals by a host government to convert a currency to dollars are covered under this insurance program.
2. Expropriation—This refers to the seizure of assets by a host government. OPIC provides protection against political actions by host governments resulting in the loss of control of an investment located in that country.
3. Political unrest—This includes financial losses of assets and property resulting from war, revolution, or civil conflicts.

A U.S. company is eligible for OPIC coverage if 50 percent or more of the corporation is owned by U.S. citizens. A foreign corporation may be eligible for the program if it is at least 95 percent owned by U.S. citizens.

Credit Risk Insurance

One hazard of conducting business in other countries is not receiving payment. **Credit risk insurance** provides coverage for loss from nonpayment for delivered goods. This protection helps reduce the risk of international business activities.

Credit risk insurance is available through the Foreign Credit Insurance Association (FCIA), a private association that insures U.S. exporters. FCIA enables exporters to extend credit to overseas buyers.

Credit insurance covers 100 percent of losses for political reasons (e.g., war, asset seizure, and currency inconvertibility). This insurance covers up to 95 percent of commercial losses, such as nonpayment due to insolvency or default.

About 200 banks in the United States have purchased master policies from FCIA and can insure loans made to U.S. exporters. Banks typically charge about 1 percent of the amount insured for the coverage.

Global Business Example: AIG in China

Small business owners in Shanghai are the newest customers of American International Group (AIG), one of the first insurance companies to sell directly to Chinese citizens. The People's Insurance Company of China, a state-owned monopoly, fought to keep AIG out of the country. However,

political leaders ruled in favor of AIG. If this business relationship is satisfactory for both sides, the Chinese market may open for other service companies. Accountants, airlines, banks, freight forwarders, and stockbrokers are hoping to sell in a country with one-fifth of the world's population.

Source: *The Wall Street Journal,* July 21, 1993, pp. A1, A5.

RISK REDUCTION STRATEGIES FOR MULTINATIONAL COMPANIES

Risk is something every company will face in every business situation. However, as shown in Figure 23-5, management experts recommend four strategies to help reduce international business risk.

Conduct Business in Many Countries

By operating businesses in several countries or regions, an organization reduces the risk faced in only one country or region. When a company depends on a variety of nations for its sales and profits, it will not be greatly affected by turmoil in one of its markets. U.S. companies doing business in Cuba when Castro gained power in 1959 lost their business assets. Luckily, most of these multinational companies were also operating in many other nations.

MULTINATIONAL RISK REDUCTION STRATEGIES

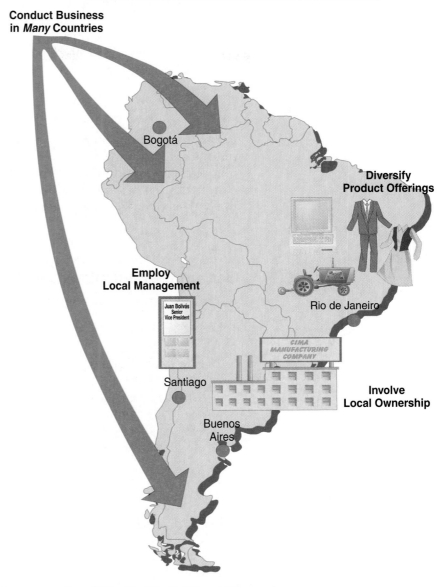

Diversify Product Offerings

Just as a company should operate in several nations, it should not be dependent on one or a few products. By having a varied portfolio of goods and services, an organization reduces its risk when one product is no longer desired by consumers. By seeking new uses for products and by creating new products, a company reduces its international business risk.

Involve Local Ownership

Local ownership of multinational firms usually is viewed favorably by local governments. A company that is completely owned by citizens of another country faces the greatest risks. A host nation feels threatened when its economic existence is controlled by people who may have different political and social beliefs. Joint ventures with local private partners are less risky.

Employ Local Management

Hiring local managers allows a company to maintain a good working relationship with the host government. Administrators who are native to a country or region understand local customs and cultural norms. A comfortable working relationship among all involved will be more likely when local managers are employed.

Back to the Beginning: Lloyd's of London

Reread the case at the beginning of this chapter and answer the following questions:

1. How does Lloyd's of London serve the needs of global business organizations?
2. What are the similarities and differences between Lloyd's and other insurance companies?
3. What factors have reduced profits for Lloyd's?

KNOWING GLOBAL BUSINESS TERMS

The following terms should become part of your business vocabulary. For each numbered item find the term that has the same meaning.

- credit risk insurance
- deductible
- endorsement
- inland marine insurance
- insurance
- insurance certificate
- insurance policy
- liability
- mutual insurance company
- negligence
- ocean marine insurance
- premium
- risk
- self-insurance
- stock insurance company

1. Legal responsibility for the financial cost of someone else's losses or injuries.
2. The portion of an insurance claim paid by the insured.
3. Coverage for loss from nonpayment for delivered goods.
4. An insurance company owned by stockholders and operated for profit.
5. Setting aside money to cover a potential financial loss.
6. The uncertainty of an event or outcome.
7. Protection from loss while goods are being shipped overseas and while temporarily in port.
8. Planned protection for sharing economic losses among many people.
9. A certificate that adds to or changes the coverage of an insurance policy.
10. The cost of insurance.
11. Failure to take ordinary or reasonable care.
12. An insurance company owned by its policyholders.
13. Covers the risk of shipping goods on inland waterways, railroad lines, truck lines, and airlines.
14. A document that provides evidence of insurance to protect goods from loss or damage while in transit.
15. The legal agreement between an insurance company and the insured.

REVIEWING YOUR READING

Answer these questions to reinforce your knowledge of the main ideas of this chapter.

1. What are the three main categories of risk faced by multinational companies?
2. How can managers monitor international business risk?
3. What are the steps of the risk management process?
4. What are the four methods that may be used to manage risk?
5. What is *self-insurance?* Give an example.
6. How does a stock insurance company differ from a mutual insurance company?
7. What is an insurable interest?
8. What is the purpose of an endorsement?
9. What is marine insurance? What are the types?
10. How does real property differ from personal property?

11. What is the Overseas Private Investment Corporation? What does it do?
12. What is the purpose of credit risk insurance?
13. What actions can companies take to reduce risks associated with international business activities?

EXPANDING YOUR HORIZONS

You will not find the complete answers to the following questions in your textbook, you will need to use your critical-thinking skills. Think about these questions, gather information from other sources, analyze possible responses, and discuss them with others. Then, develop your own oral or written response as instructed by your teacher.

1. Name some risks that could be faced by exporters that might not be present when a company sells within its own country.
2. Describe ways you could reduce risks in your home and at your school.
3. *Speculative* risks include such things as starting a new business or introducing a new product. These cannot be covered by insurance. Why will insurance companies not cover speculative risks? List other examples of speculative risks.
4. Explain why deductibles reduce the premium paid for insurance.
5. An exporter might not make a marine insurance claim, even if it is valid. Many small claims can increase the cost of insurance in the future. Why might an exporter decide not to make a claim?
6. Liability insurance coverage is considered vital by most people who own or operate a business. Why?
7. You are the regional manager in Saudi Arabia for a multinational company that manufactures and distributes plastic products. What actions would you take to reduce risk for your company?

BUILDING RESEARCH SKILLS

The ability to find information from various sources is an important international business skill. The following activities will help you investigate various topics. You will also learn to apply class ideas to situations outside of the classroom.

1. Prepare a poster illustrating methods that companies could use to reduce business risk.

2. Obtain a sample insurance policy from your parents or a local insurance agent. What coverages are included in this policy?

3. Conduct library research about marine insurance. Prepare a report that explains risks and hazards of this international business insurance.

4. Talk to someone with homeowner's or renter's insurance. Report to the class about the types of risks that are covered by property insurance.

5. *Global Career Activity.* Interview a person who works in an insurance career. What training and skills are required for jobs in the insurance industry?

Continuing Enrichment Project: Global Risk Management

Using the international company you used in previous chapters, or another organization, conduct research to answer the following questions:

1. What are the company's main international business risks?

2. Is self-insurance practical for the company?

3. Describe situations for which the company might make use of marine insurance.

4. What types of property does the company own that needs to be insured?

5. Why might liability coverage be important to the company?

6. What types of insurance might the company provide as an employee benefit for its workers?

Appendix A

Analyzing International Investments

Changing currency rates, environmental concerns, and political instability are typical in the international business environment. Just as companies attempt to make the right global business decisions, individuals want to make investments that will achieve their personal financial goals.

INVESTMENT GOALS

The long-term financial security of a person or family results from an ability to save and invest for the future. *Saving* is the storage of money for future use. In contrast, *investing* involves putting money to work in a business venture. The risks associated with investing are higher than the risks associated with saving. However, the potential returns from investing are also greater. Investing has two common goals: current income or long-term growth.

Current Income

Some people depend on investment income for current living expenses. Retired people and others may need investments that provide income. These earnings may be in the form of dividends (from stocks), interest (from bonds), or rent (from real estate).

Long-Term Growth

In contrast to current income, many people invest for long-term financial security. They want funds for retirement or for the college education of their children. Investors who desire long-term growth of their funds will choose investments that will increase in value over time.

The earnings obtained over the long term can provide substantial wealth. A **capital gain** is the profit made from the resale of investments—such as stocks, bonds, or real estate. For example, land purchased in 1989 for $12,000 and sold in 1996 for $31,000 represents a capital gain of $19,000.

The growth in value of an investment can be projected with the use of future value calculations. *Future value* involves computations for determining the expected worth of an investment in the future. Future value is calculated as follows:

$$\text{Future value} = \text{Amount invested} \times (1 + \text{annual rate earned})^n$$

The n represents the number of years the investment will be earning the yield. For example, the future value of $1,000 invested at 7 percent for two years would be calculated as follows:

$$\$1,000 \times (1.07)^2 = \$1,000 \times 1.1449 = \$1,144.90$$

Figure A-1 lists some of the common investments used to meet the two main investment goals: current income and long-term growth.

Figure A-1
People with different investment goals select different types of investments.

REACHING YOUR INVESTMENT GOALS

Current Income

• Stocks paying dividends

• Savings certificates

• Corporate bonds

• Rental property

Long-Term Growth

• Growth stocks

• Raw land

• Gold, silver

• Coins, stamps

• Art, antiques

Global Business Exercise: Future Value Calculations

Calculate the future value of the following investments:

1. The expected value of a stock in 3 years that grows at 4 percent a year and that has a current value of £100.
2. The future value of land, costing Cr$3,000 today, in 5 years with an expected growth rate of 7 percent per year.
3. The future value of an antique automobile, with a current value of $12,000, in 8 years with an expected growth rate of 6 percent per year.

INVESTMENT OPPORTUNITIES

Should a person invest in a gold mine in South America, real estate in the Middle East, or a computer company in Nevada? When planning to invest, people must identify potential investments and evaluate those investment opportunities.

Identifying Potential Investments

Successful investments can result from a variety of activities around the world. For example as the demand for health care increases because of illness or an aging population, companies involved in medicines, medical supplies, and hospital equipment may become more profitable.

As illustrated in Figure A-2, news stories can be used to identify good investment opportunities. When hearing a news report, ask yourself what types of companies might be affected by this news. Next, decide what type of investment would be appropriate. Investors may buy stock in the company or even start their own company. Finally, investors must select an action to take—buy, sell, or keep holding certain investments.

Heinz Hockmann of Commerz International Capital Management, Frankfurt, Germany, recommends selecting a country before choosing specific companies when investing. A nation's economic conditions and political environment strongly influence business success. Companies in the same industry—such as automobiles, chemicals, or electrical equipment—tend to perform differently depending on the country. For example, auto stocks in Britain may decline during a period in which German auto stocks rise.

Figure A-2

Local, national, and world news provide information about investment opportunities every day.

FINDING GOOD INVESTMENT OPPORTUNITIES

1. Monitor news reports

2. Determine industry and specific companies affected

3. Select investment type and action (buy, sell, or hold)

Evaluating Investment Opportunities

When choosing among various investments, usually four major factors are considered—rate of return, liquidity, taxes, and safety (see Figure A-3 on page 520).

Rate of Return. The annual earnings for an investment are measured by the *annual rate of return* or *yield*. This rate is the percentage of the investment cost that is earned in a year. The annual rate of return for an investment is calculated as follows:

$$\text{Rate of return} = \frac{\text{Annual income}}{\text{Cost of investment}}$$

For example, an investment that costs $5,000 and produces an annual income of $450 has an annual rate of return of 9 percent, calculated as follows:

$$\frac{\$450}{\$5,000} = 0.09 = 9\%$$

Liquidity. Many people want to be able to obtain and use their money quickly. **Liquidity** refers to the ability to easily convert an asset into cash without a loss in value. Certain types of assets are highly liquid, such as stocks, bonds, and mutual funds. These investments have a continuing market of buyers and sellers.

Figure A-3
Investors weigh various factors when selecting an investment.

Rate of Return

Liquidity

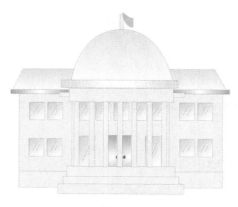

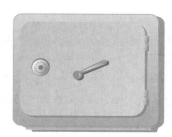

Taxes

Safety

In contrast, real estate, rare coins, and other collectibles have low liquidity. These assets may be difficult to sell quickly. Buyers for these investments are not always available.

A trade-off between liquidity and rate of return is common for investments. In general, assets with high liquidity have a lower return over time. Low liquidity can give you a higher rate of return over the long run.

Taxes. The amount earned on an investment is frequently affected by taxes. If an investor has to pay taxes on earnings, that lowers the annual rate of return. As presented in Chapter 22, a *tax-exempt investment* earns income that is not subject to tax. In contrast, a *tax-deferred investment* earns income that will be taxed at a later date.

Safety. When making an investment, people expect their money to be available in the future. Most people want investments that minimize their chance of losing money.

INVESTMENT INFORMATION SOURCES

Wise investing, as with any business decision, requires reliable, up-to-date information. The main sources of investment information are the news media, financial experts, investment information services, and computer software.

News Media

Business periodicals and the business section of the daily newspaper provide a readily available source of investment news. Investors find *The Wall Street Journal, Business Week, Fortune,* and *Forbes* helpful. Besides domestic and international business, economic, and financial information, these publications feature articles on companies and product trends.

Financial Experts

A stockbroker advises customers and sells investments. Other financial experts who provide investment recommendations and assist with purchases are bankers, personal financial planners, insurance agents, and real estate brokers.

Before acting on the advice of any investment advisor, do the following:

- Research the investment and company using several sources.
- Talk to others who have this type of investment.
- Contact state and federal government agencies for information about the investment and the seller of the investment. and
- Compare costs of the investment broker with others who provide this service.

In one year in the early 1990s, U.S. citizens lost more than $1 billion in phoney investments. Common investment scams in recent years included fake low-cost stocks, wireless cable television partnerships, and false medical "cures."

Investment Information Services

Information on the current performance and the future of stocks and bonds is published in *Value Line, Moody's Investors Service,* and *Standard & Poor's Reports*. These investment services provide financial data, current stock prices, recent company developments, and recommendations for buying and selling. Investors can find these information sources at libraries.

On-line databases are another investment information source. The Dow Jones Information Retrieval, CompuServe, and Prodigy instantly provide information on company performance and current market values.

Computer Software

Value Line, the *Business Week Mutual Fund Scorecard*, and other investment information services are available for personal computers. This software offers quick access to the data discussed in the previous section.

Investors may also use personal computers to analyze, select, and monitor stocks and other investments. Software such as *Managing Your Money, Wealth Builder,* and *Portfolio Manager* are available for planning and managing an investment portfolio.

Appendix B
Maps

WORLD

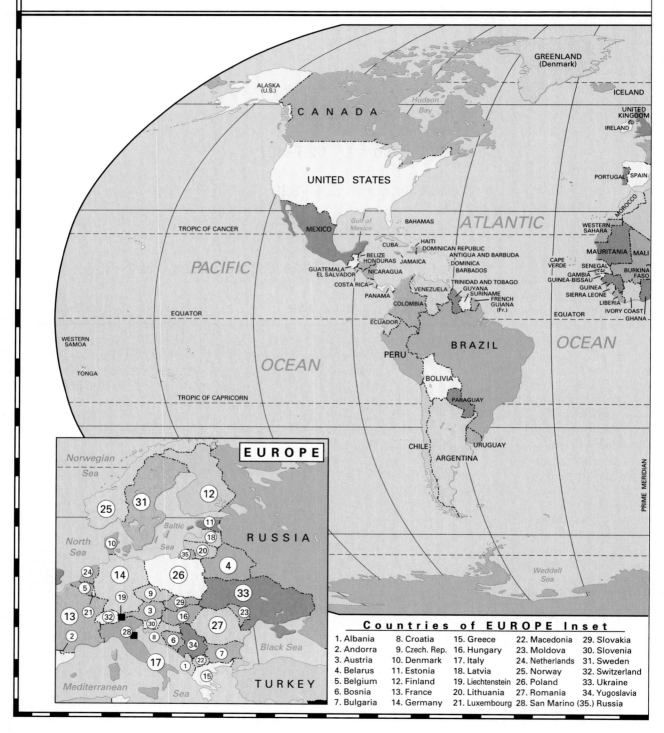

GREENLAND (Denmark)

ICELAND

ALASKA (U.S.)

C A N A D A

Hudson Bay

UNITED KINGDOM

IRELAND

UNITED STATES

PORTUGAL SPAIN

MOROCCO

TROPIC OF CANCER

MEXICO

Gulf of Mexico

BAHAMAS

ATLANTIC

WESTERN SAHARA

CUBA
HAITI
DOMINICAN REPUBLIC
ANTIGUA AND BARBUDA
DOMINICA
BARBADOS

BELIZE
HONDURAS JAMAICA

GUATEMALA
EL SALVADOR

NICARAGUA

COSTA RICA

PANAMA

VENEZUELA

COLOMBIA

TRINIDAD AND TOBAGO
GUYANA
SURINAME
FRENCH GUIANA (Fr.)

MAURITANIA MALI

CAPE VERDE
SENEGAL
GAMBIA
GUINEA-BISSAU
GUINEA
SIERRA LEONE
LIBERIA
IVORY COAST
GHANA

BURKINA FASO

PACIFIC

EQUATOR

ECUADOR

PERU

B R A Z I L

EQUATOR

OCEAN

WESTERN SAMOA

OCEAN

BOLIVIA

PARAGUAY

TONGA

TROPIC OF CAPRICORN

CHILE

URUGUAY

ARGENTINA

PRIME MERIDIAN

Weddell Sea

EUROPE

Norwegian Sea

(12)

(25) (31)

Baltic Sea

(11)

(18)

RUSSIA

North Sea

(10)

(35)

(20)

(24)

(14)

(26)

(4)

(5)

(19)

(9)

(29)

(33)

(13)

(21)

(32)

(3)

(16)

(23)

(2)

(30)

(8)

(6)

(27)

(28)

(34)

(7)

Black Sea

(17)

(22)

(1)

(15)

Mediterranean Sea

TURKEY

Countries of EUROPE Inset

1. Albania	8. Croatia	15. Greece	22. Macedonia	29. Slovakia
2. Andorra	9. Czech. Rep.	16. Hungary	23. Moldova	30. Slovenia
3. Austria	10. Denmark	17. Italy	24. Netherlands	31. Sweden
4. Belarus	11. Estonia	18. Latvia	25. Norway	32. Switzerland
5. Belgium	12. Finland	19. Liechtenstein	26. Poland	33. Ukraine
6. Bosnia	13. France	20. Lithuania	27. Romania	34. Yugoslavia
7. Bulgaria	14. Germany	21. Luxembourg	28. San Marino	(35.) Russia

POLITICAL

Projection: Robinson

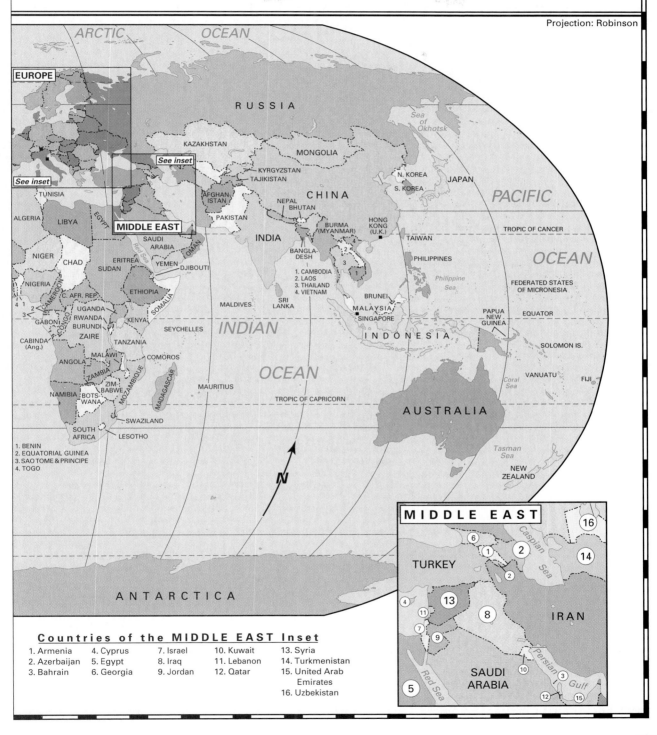

ARCTIC OCEAN

EUROPE

See inset

RUSSIA

Sea of Okhotsk

See inset

KAZAKHSTAN

MONGOLIA

TUNISIA

KYRGYZSTAN

TAJIKISTAN

N. KOREA

S. KOREA

JAPAN

PACIFIC

ALGERIA

LIBYA

EGYPT

AFGHAN-ISTAN

CHINA

HONG KONG (U.K.)

MIDDLE EAST

SAUDI ARABIA

OMAN

PAKISTAN

NEPAL

BHUTAN

TROPIC OF CANCER

NIGER

CHAD

SUDAN

ERITREA

YEMEN

DJIBOUTI

INDIA

BANGLA-DESH

BURMA (MYANMAR)

TAIWAN

OCEAN

NIGERIA

CAMEROON

C. AFR. REP.

ETHIOPIA

SOMALIA

1. CAMBODIA
2. LAOS
3. THAILAND
4. VIETNAM

PHILIPPINES

FEDERATED STATES OF MICRONESIA

4 1
2
3

GABON

CONGO

UGANDA

RWANDA

BURUNDI

ZAIRE

KENYA

TANZANIA

SRI LANKA

MALDIVES

BRUNEI

MALAYSIA

SINGAPORE

INDONESIA

PAPUA NEW GUINEA

EQUATOR

CABINDA (Ang.)

SEYCHELLES

INDIAN

SOLOMON IS.

ANGOLA

ZAMBIA

MALAWI

COMOROS

OCEAN

VANUATU

FIJI

ZIM-BABWE

MOZAMBIQUE

MADAGASCAR

MAURITIUS

TROPIC OF CAPRICORN

Coral Sea

NAMIBIA

BOTS-WANA

SOUTH AFRICA

SWAZILAND

LESOTHO

AUSTRALIA

Tasman Sea

NEW ZEALAND

1. BENIN
2. EQUATORIAL GUINEA
3. SAO TOME & PRINCIPE
4. TOGO

N

ANTARCTICA

Countries of the MIDDLE EAST Inset

1. Armenia	4. Cyprus	7. Israel	10. Kuwait	13. Syria
2. Azerbaijan	5. Egypt	8. Iraq	11. Lebanon	14. Turkmenistan
3. Bahrain	6. Georgia	9. Jordan	12. Qatar	15. United Arab Emirates
				16. Uzbekistan

MIDDLE EAST

TURKEY

6

1

2

16

14

2

4

13

8

IRAN

11

7

9

10

3

SAUDI ARABIA

Red Sea

Caspian Sea

Persian Gulf

5

12

15

WORLD

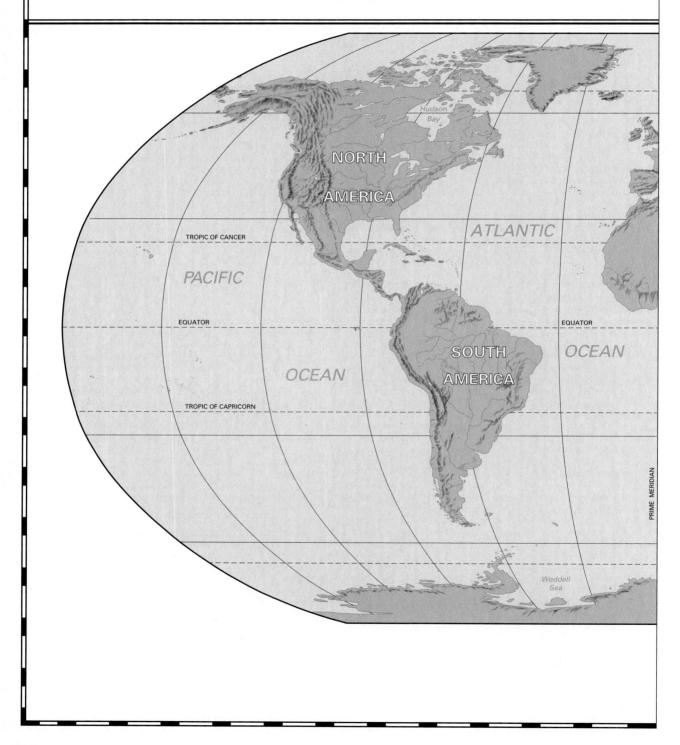

NORTH
AMERICA

Hudson
Bay

ATLANTIC

TROPIC OF CANCER

PACIFIC

EQUATOR

EQUATOR

OCEAN

OCEAN

SOUTH
AMERICA

TROPIC OF CAPRICORN

PRIME MERIDIAN

Weddell
Sea

LANDFORMS

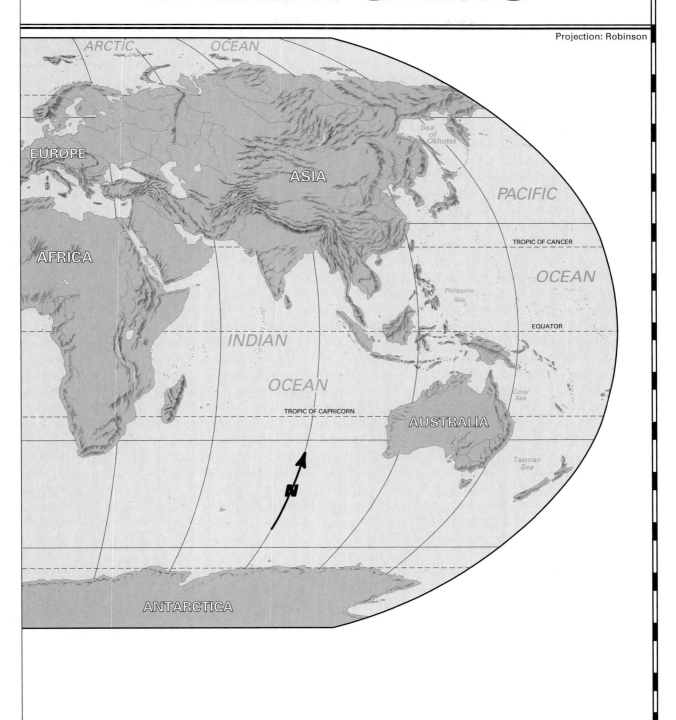

Projection: Robinson

ARCTIC OCEAN

EUROPE

ASIA

PACIFIC

AFRICA

Sea of Okhotsk

TROPIC OF CANCER

OCEAN

Philippine Sea

Red Sea

INDIAN

EQUATOR

OCEAN

Coral Sea

TROPIC OF CAPRICORN

AUSTRALIA

Tasman Sea

N

ANTARCTICA

World Landforms

WORLD

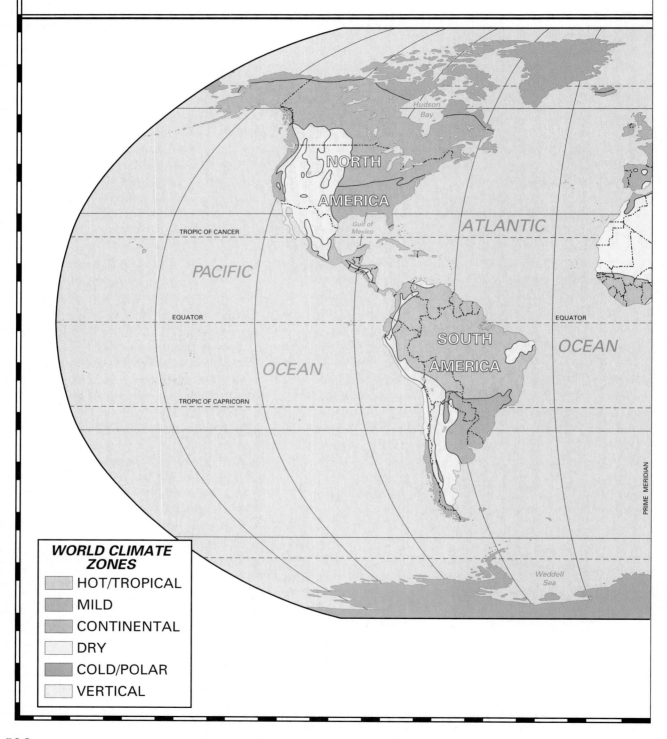

Hudson Bay

NORTH AMERICA

TROPIC OF CANCER

Gulf of Mexico

ATLANTIC

PACIFIC

EQUATOR

EQUATOR

OCEAN

OCEAN

SOUTH AMERICA

TROPIC OF CAPRICORN

PRIME MERIDIAN

Weddell Sea

WORLD CLIMATE ZONES

- HOT/TROPICAL
- MILD
- CONTINENTAL
- DRY
- COLD/POLAR
- VERTICAL

CLIMATES

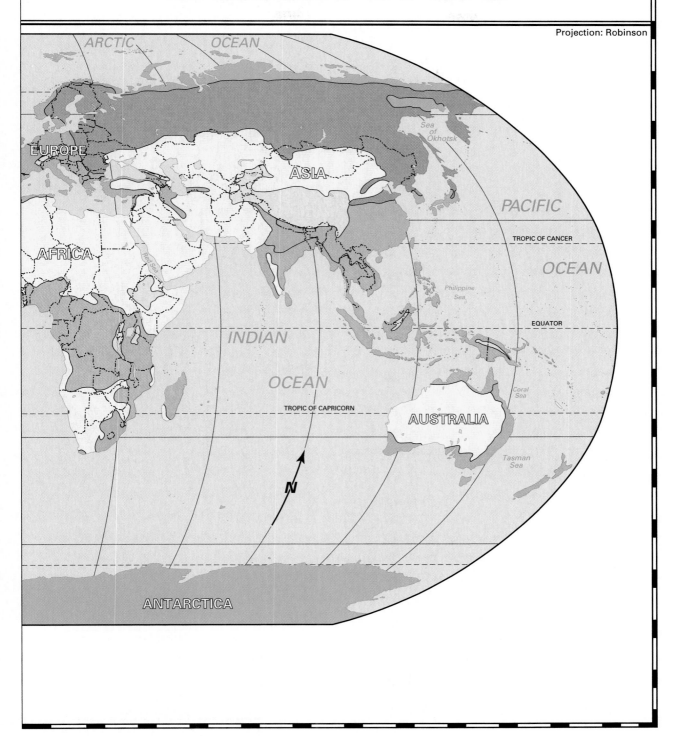

Projection: Robinson

ARCTIC OCEAN

EUROPE

ASIA

Sea of Okhotsk

PACIFIC

TROPIC OF CANCER

OCEAN

AFRICA

Red Sea

Philippine Sea

INDIAN

EQUATOR

OCEAN

TROPIC OF CAPRICORN

Coral Sea

AUSTRALIA

Tasman Sea

N

ANTARCTICA

World Climates

WORLD

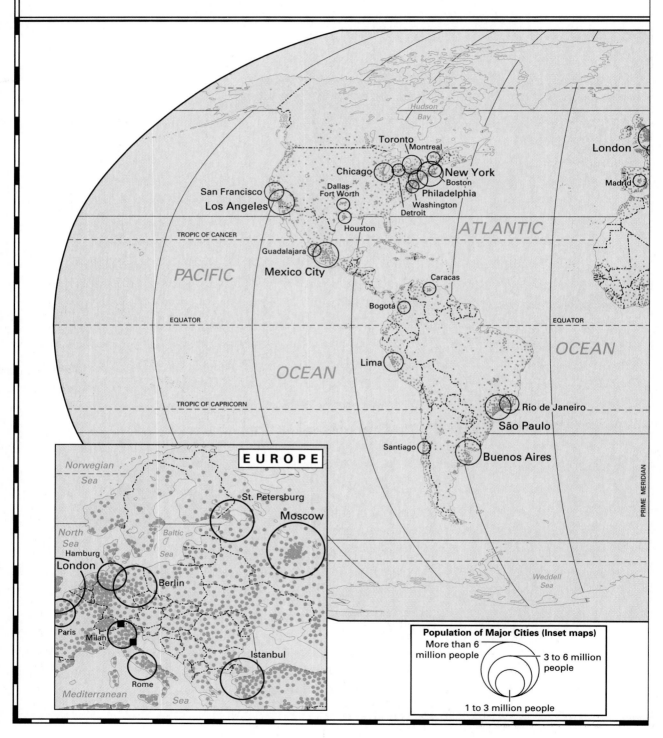

London

Toronto
Montreal
Chicago
New York
Boston
Dallas-
Fort Worth
Philadelphia
San Francisco
Los Angeles
Washington
Detroit
Madrid

Houston

TROPIC OF CANCER

ATLANTIC

PACIFIC

Guadalajara

Mexico City

Caracas

Bogotá

EQUATOR

EQUATOR

OCEAN

Lima

OCEAN

OCEAN

TROPIC OF CAPRICORN

Rio de Janeiro

São Paulo

Santiago

Buenos Aires

PRIME MERIDIAN

Weddell
Sea

EUROPE

Norwegian
Sea

St. Petersburg

Moscow

North
Sea

Baltic
Sea

Hamburg

London
Berlin

Paris

Milan

Istanbul

Rome

Mediterranean   Sea

Population of Major Cities (Inset maps)

More than 6
million people

3 to 6 million
people

1 to 3 million people

POPULATION

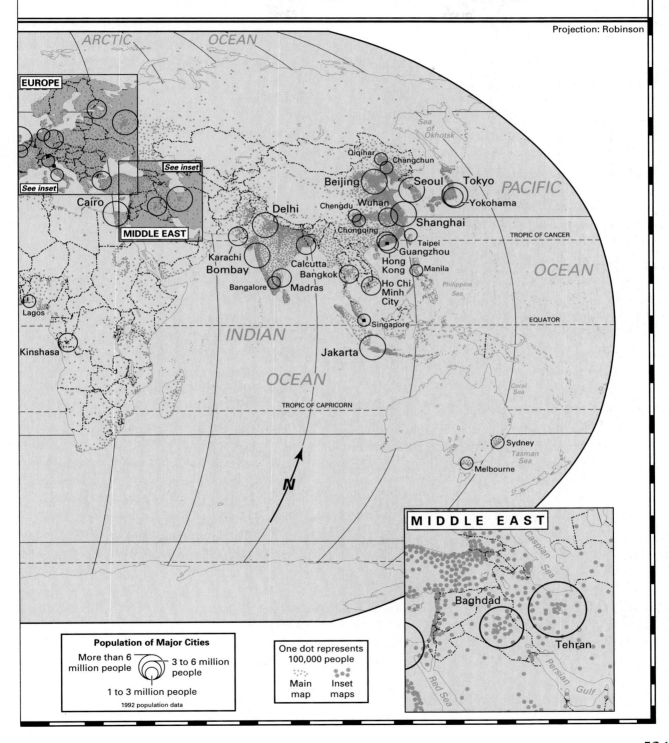

Projection: Robinson

ARCTIC OCEAN

EUROPE

See inset

Cairo

MIDDLE EAST

Sea of Okhotsk

Qiqihar
Changchun
Beijing
Seoul
Tokyo
PACIFIC
Chengdu
Wuhan
Yokohama
Delhi
Shanghai
Chongqing
TROPIC OF CANCER
Taipei
Guangzhou
Karachi
Hong Kong
Manila
OCEAN
Bombay
Calcutta
Bangkok
Bangalore
Madras
Ho Chi Minh City
Philippine Sea
Lagos
Singapore
EQUATOR
Kinshasa
Jakarta

INDIAN

OCEAN

TROPIC OF CAPRICORN

Coral Sea

N

Sydney
Tasman Sea
Melbourne

MIDDLE EAST

Caspian Sea

Baghdad
Tehran

Red Sea
Persian Gulf

Population of Major Cities

More than 6 million people
3 to 6 million people
1 to 3 million people

1992 population data

One dot represents 100,000 people

Main map   Inset maps

World Population

MAJOR INTERNATIONAL TRADE ORGANIZATIONS

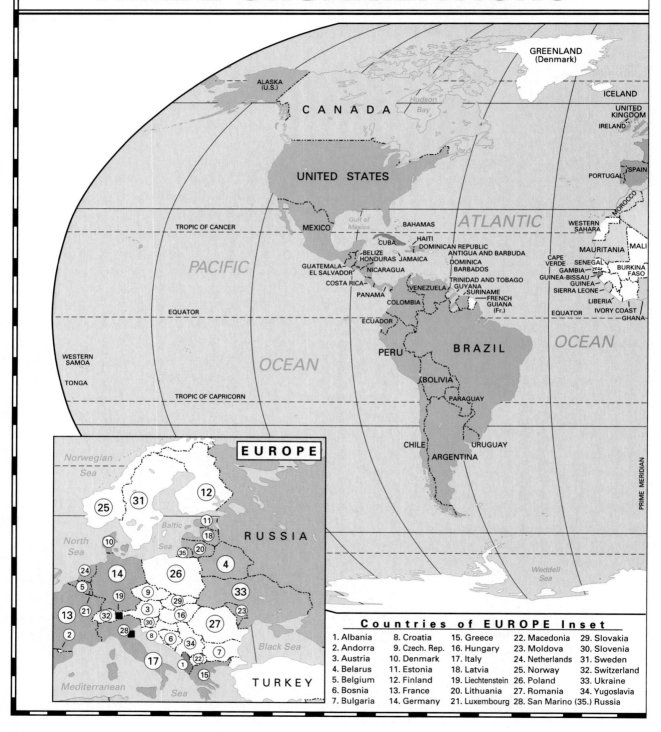

GREENLAND (Denmark)

ALASKA (U.S.)

CANADA

Hudson Bay

ICELAND

UNITED KINGDOM

IRELAND

UNITED STATES

PORTUGAL SPAIN

MOROCCO

TROPIC OF CANCER

MEXICO

Gulf of Mexico

BAHAMAS

ATLANTIC

WESTERN SAHARA

MAURITANIA MALI

CUBA

HAITI

DOMINICAN REPUBLIC

ANTIGUA AND BARBUDA

BELIZE

HONDURAS JAMAICA

DOMINICA

BARBADOS

CAPE VERDE

SENEGAL

GAMBIA

BURKINA FASO

GUATEMALA-

EL SALVADOR NICARAGUA

PACIFIC

TRINIDAD AND TOBAGO

GUINEA-BISSAU GUINEA

COSTA RICA

VENEZUELA GUYANA

SURINAME

SIERRA LEONE

PANAMA

COLOMBIA

FRENCH GUIANA (Fr.)

LIBERIA

IVORY COAST

EQUATOR

ECUADOR

EQUATOR

GHANA

PERU

BRAZIL

OCEAN

WESTERN SAMOA

OCEAN

BOLIVIA

TONGA

TROPIC OF CAPRICORN

PARAGUAY

CHILE URUGUAY

ARGENTINA

Weddell Sea

PRIME MERIDIAN

EUROPE

Norwegian Sea

RUSSIA

Baltic Sea

North Sea

TURKEY

Black Sea

Mediterranean Sea

Countries of EUROPE Inset

1. Albania	8. Croatia	15. Greece	22. Macedonia	29. Slovakia
2. Andorra	9. Czech. Rep.	16. Hungary	23. Moldova	30. Slovenia
3. Austria	10. Denmark	17. Italy	24. Netherlands	31. Sweden
4. Belarus	11. Estonia	18. Latvia	25. Norway	32. Switzerland
5. Belgium	12. Finland	19. Liechtenstein	26. Poland	33. Ukraine
6. Bosnia	13. France	20. Lithuania	27. Romania	34. Yugoslavia
7. Bulgaria	14. Germany	21. Luxembourg	28. San Marino	(35.) Russia

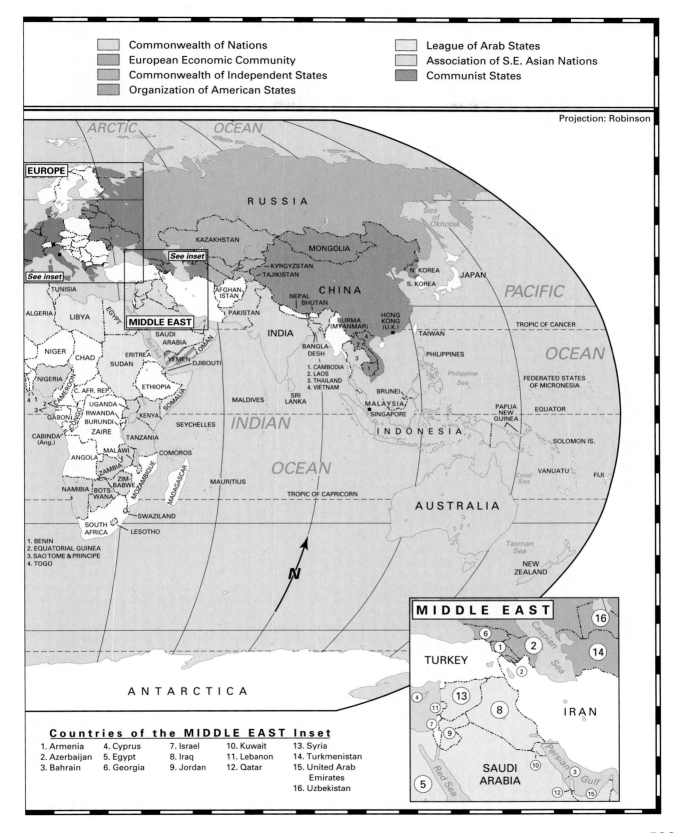

Legend

- Commonwealth of Nations
- European Economic Community
- Commonwealth of Independent States
- Organization of American States
- League of Arab States
- Association of S.E. Asian Nations
- Communist States

Projection: Robinson

ARCTIC OCEAN

EUROPE

See inset

See inset

RUSSIA

KAZAKHSTAN

TUNISIA

ALGERIA   LIBYA   EGYPT

MIDDLE EAST

SAUDI ARABIA

NIGER   CHAD   SUDAN   ERITREA   YEMEN   DJIBOUTI   OMAN

NIGERIA   C. AFR. REP.   ETHIOPIA   SOMALIA

CAMEROON   UGANDA   RWANDA   KENYA

GABON   CONGO   BURUNDI   ZAIRE

CABINDA (Ang.)   TANZANIA   SEYCHELLES

ANGOLA   MALAWI   COMOROS

ZAMBIA   ZIM-BABWE   MOZAMBIQUE   MADAGASCAR

NAMIBIA   BOTS-WANA

SOUTH AFRICA   SWAZILAND   LESOTHO

1. BENIN
2. EQUATORIAL GUINEA
3. SAO TOME & PRINCIPE
4. TOGO

Red Sea

MONGOLIA

KYRGYZSTAN
TAJIKISTAN

AFGHAN-ISTAN

PAKISTAN

CHINA

NEPAL
BHUTAN

INDIA

BANGLA-DESH

BURMA (MYANMAR)

1. CAMBODIA
2. LAOS
3. THAILAND
4. VIETNAM

MALDIVES   SRI LANKA

N. KOREA   JAPAN
S. KOREA

Sea of Okhotsk

HONG KONG (U.K.)

TAIWAN

PHILIPPINES

BRUNEI

MALAYSIA
SINGAPORE

INDONESIA

Philippine Sea

FEDERATED STATES OF MICRONESIA

PAPUA NEW GUINEA

SOLOMON IS.

VANUATU   FIJI

INDIAN OCEAN

SEYCHELLES

MAURITIUS

TROPIC OF CAPRICORN

AUSTRALIA

Coral Sea

Tasman Sea

NEW ZEALAND

PACIFIC

TROPIC OF CANCER

OCEAN

EQUATOR

N

ANTARCTICA

Countries of the MIDDLE EAST Inset

1. Armenia	4. Cyprus	7. Israel	10. Kuwait	13. Syria
2. Azerbaijan	5. Egypt	8. Iraq	11. Lebanon	14. Turkmenistan
3. Bahrain	6. Georgia	9. Jordan	12. Qatar	15. United Arab Emirates
				16. Uzbekistan

MIDDLE EAST

16

6
1   2
TURKEY
2

Caspian Sea

14

4   13
11   8
7
9

IRAN

SAUDI ARABIA

10

Persian Gulf

5   Red Sea

12   15   3

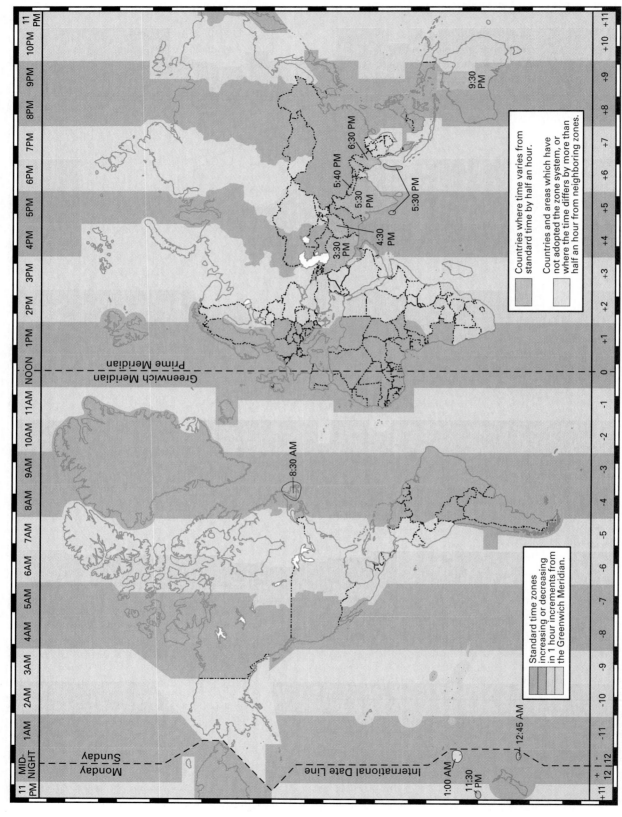

WORLD TIME ZONES

Glossary

A

absolute advantage: the ability of one country to produce a good or service at a lower cost than other countries.

account payable: an amount owed to a supplier.

account receivable: an amount owed by a customer to a company that sells on credit.

advertising: any form of paid, nonpersonal sales communication; also called *mass selling*.

advertising agency: a company that specializes in planning and implementing advertisements.

AFL-CIO: an umbrella union that has smaller unions as members; created by a merging of the American Federation of Labor (AFL) and the Congress of Industrial Organizations (CIO).

agent: intermediary who brings together buyers and sellers, but does not take ownership of the products.

application letter: communicates one's interest in a specific employment position; also called *cover letter.*

arbitration: a dispute alternative method that makes use of a neutral third party to make a binding decision.

arbitrator: an unbiased third party brought in to settle employer-union grievances; decision is usually final and binding.

artificial intelligence (AI): a branch of computer science that deals with designing computer systems that use deductive reasoning.

autocratic manager: manager who centralizes power and tells employees what to do.

automated production: the process of using machines as the means of transforming resources into goods and services.

B

balance of payments: the total flow of money coming into a country minus the total flow going out.

balance of trade: the difference between a country's exports and imports.

balance sheet: document that reports a company's assets (items of value), liabilities (amounts owed to others), and owner's equity (net worth).

ban: a restriction on the import of certain products from certain countries.

bill of exchange: a written order by an exporter to an importer to make payment.

bill of lading: records the agreement between the exporter (seller) and the transportation company and serves as a receipt for the exported (transported) items.

body language: nonverbal communication involving facial expressions, body movements, and gestures.

bond: a certificate representing money borrowed by a company over a long period of time, usually between 5 and 30 years.

boycott: regularly avoid the purchase of certain goods and/or services as a form of protest.

brand: a name, symbol, or design that identifies a product.

breakeven point: the production level at which profit is zero.

budget: a financial tool that estimates a company's funds and its plan for spending those funds.

business plan: a guide used to start and operate a business.

C

capital gain: the profit made from the resale of investments.

capitalism: a market economy comprised of private property, profit motive, and a free competitive marketplace.

capital project: an expensive, long-term financial activity.

capital resources: the funds and materials necessary to produce a good or service.

career: a commitment to a profession that requires continued training and has a clear path for advancement.

cash flow: the inflow and outflow of cash in a business.

central processing unit (CPU): a hardware device in which electronic circuits process the data input in a computer.

certificate of origin: states the name of the country in which the shipped goods were produced; may be used to determine the amount of any import tax.

charter: the document granted by the federal or state government that allows a company to organize as a corporation.

chief executive officer (CEO): the top-ranking manager within a company.

civil law: a complete set of rules that are enacted as a single, written system or code; also called code law.

class system: a means of dividing the members of a society into various levels.

closed shop: an arrangement in which all workers at a union-represented workplace are required to join the union before they are hired; generally illegal, today.

codetermination: the policy of having union members serve on the board of directors of a company.

collective bargaining: negotiation between union workers and their employers on issues of wages, benefits, and working conditions.

collectivism: belief that the group is more important than individuals.

command economy: a system in which the government regulates the amount, distribution, and price of everything produced.

commercial bank: a business organized to accept deposits and to make loans, as well as to provide a wide range of service.

commercial invoice: a description of the merchandise and terms of the sale prepared by the exporter.

commercial markets: markets consisting of buyers who purchase items for resale or additional production; also called *organizational markets*.

common law: the establishment of law on a case-by-case basis, also called case law.

common market: an arrangement in which member countries eliminate duties and other trade barriers, allowing companies to invest freely in each member's country, and allowing workers to move freely across borders.

comparative advantage: a country specializes in the production of a good or service at which it is relatively more efficient.

computer: an electronic device that processes and stores data.

computer-aided design (CAD): equipment used by designers to develop a detailed design and key it to computer-assisted manufacturing (CAM) specifications.

computer-assisted manufacturing (CAM): the use of computers to run production equipment.

computer-integrated manufacturing (CIM): a manufacturing process guided entirely by computers.

computerized production: the use of computers to control the machines used in automated production; computers also do some of the work in this process.

computer network: a collection of individual computers that are connected by communication channels, such as telephone lines, and share data and information.

consulate: an office located in a foreign country that represents the home country and serves the interests and businesses of citizens of the country it represents.

consumer market: market consisting of individuals and households who are end-users of goods and services.

consumer price index (CPI): a monthly report produced by the U.S. government that measures inflation based on price levels of various products and services in different regions of the country.

contract: a legally enforceable agreement between two or more persons either to do or not do a certain thing or things.

convenience goods: inexpensive items that require little shopping effort.

cooperative: a business owned by its members and operated solely for their benefit.

copyright: legal protection of the original works of authors, composers, playwrights, artists, publishers, and software programmers.

corporate bond: a debt certificate issued by a multinational company or other corporate business enterprise.

corporation: a business that operates as a legal entity separate from any of the owners.

cost and freight: a shipping term that means the cost of the goods and freight are included in the price; buyers must pay insurance separately.

cost, insurance, and freight (CIF): a shipping term that means that the cost of the goods, insurance, and freight are included in the price.

countertrade: the exchange of goods and services among companies in different countries with the possibility of limited currency involved in the transaction.

credit risk insurance: provides coverage for loss from nonpayment for delivered goods.

credit terms: a description of the time required for payment and other conditions of a sale on account.

credit union: a nonprofit, financial cooperative.

culture: a system of learned, shared, unifying, and interrelated beliefs, values, and assumptions.

currency futures: contracts to purchase for a fee a foreign currency at today's rate with payment and delivery at a later date.

customs broker: international intermediary that specializes in moving goods through the customs process; also called *custom house broker.*

customs official: government official who is authorized to collect the duties levied on imports.

D

data: facts—expressed as numbers, symbols, or words—that are used as the basis for reasoning, discussions, or calculation.

database: a body of data, or information, stored in a systematic way so that users can manipulate, retrieve, and update the information.

database marketing: the use of computerized information

systems to identify customers with specific demographic traits and buying habits.

debt capital: funds obtained for a company by borrowing.

debt funds: business funds obtained by borrowing.

decision support system (DSS): a computer-based system that helps companies make decisions by summarizing and comparing data from internal and external sources.

deductible: the portion of an insurance claim paid by the insured.

degree of centralization: a measurement of the amount of authority and responsibility that is delegated to employees or to organizational units.

demand: the amount of a good or service that consumers are willing and able to purchase at a certain price.

democracy: a political system in which all citizens take part in making the rules that govern them.

demographics: the traits of a specific population—such as birthrate, age distribution, marriage rate, income distribution, educational level, and housing situation.

desktop publishing: the use of a computer to produce documents containing text and graphics in an original layout.

developing country: country evolving from less developed to industrialized.

direct barter: the exchange of goods and services between two parties with no money involved.

direct distribution channel: producers sell goods or services directly to the final user.

direct exporting: a company actively seeking and conducting exporting.

distribution: the activities necessary to physically move goods and services from producer to consumer.

distribution channel: the path taken by a good or service to get from the producer to the final user.

dividend: a share of a corporation's profits.

domestic business: the making, buying, and selling of goods and services within a country.

dumping: selling exported goods at a lower price than that asked in the company's home country.

duty: an import tax on products sold internationally; also called a *tariff*.

E

economic community: an organization of countries that bond together to allow a free flow of products; the group acts as a single country for business activities with other regions of the world.

economic nationalism: the trend to restrict foreign ownership of companies and to establish laws that protect against foreign imports.

economics: the study of how people choose to use limited resources to satisfy their unlimited needs and wants.

economic system: the method a country uses to decide what, how, and for whom goods and services are to be produced.

electronic funds transfer (EFT): a system that moves payments through computerized banking systems.

employment forecasting: estimating in advance the types and numbers of employees needed.

endorsement: a certificate that adds to or changes the coverage of an insurance policy.

entrepreneur: a risk taker who operates a business; the person who brings together the resources of land, labor, and capital for a company to get started and operate successfully.

equity capital: funds provided by a company's owners.

equity funds: business funds obtained from the owners of the business.

ethical standards: rules that govern the acceptability of actions.

ethnocentric approach: a human resources approach that uses natives of the parent country of a business to fill key positions at home and abroad.

ethnocentrism: belief that one's culture is better than other cultures.

Eurodollar: U.S. dollar deposited in a bank outside of the United States and used in the money markets of Europe.

exchange control: government restriction to regulate the amount and value of a nation's currency.

expatriate: person who lives and works outside her or his native country.

experiment: a comparison of two or more very similar research situations.

expert system: a software system with artificial intelligence that compares past information to current information in order to reach a conclusion; it uses a knowledge base and inference rules.

export management company (EMC): international intermediary that provides complete distribution services for business that desire to sell in foreign markets.

exports: products sold to a company or government in another country.

export trading company (ETC): international intermediary that provides full-service global distribution.

expropriation: when a government takes control and ownership of foreign-owned assets and companies.

extended family: parents, children, and other relatives living together.

external data sources: sources outside an organization that provide input.

F

facsimile machine (fax): a machine that digitizes text and graphic images and sends the digitiz- ed images over phone lines to a receiving fax that translates the data back into the original image.

factors of production: the elements necessary to make a product or service: natural resources, human resources, and capital resources.

file server: a minicomputer that houses the software and data that all computers on a network need to share.

fixed cost: business expense that does not change as the level of production changes.

floating exchange rates: a system in which currency values are based on supply and demand.

focus group: a directed discussion with 8 to 12 people to obtain opinions, buying habits, and knowledge about a product, package, or advertisement.

foreign debt: the amount a country owes to other countries.

foreign direct investment: a company purchases land and other resources in a foreign country.

foreign exchange: the process of converting the currency of one country into the currency of another country.

foreign exchange market: banks and other financial institutions that buy and sell different currencies.

foreign exchange rate: the value of one country's money in relation to the value of another country's money.

franchise: the right to use a company name or business process in a specific way.

free on board (FOB): a shipping term that means the selling price of the product includes the cost of loading the exported goods into transport vessels at the specified place.

free-rein manager: manager who avoids the use of power; lets employees establish their

Glossary

539

own goals and monitor their own progress.

free-trade agreement: an arrangement by which member countries agree to eliminate duties and trade barriers on products traded among themselves.

free- (foreign-) trade zone: a designated area, usually around a seaport or airport, where products can be imported duty-free, and then stored, assembled, and/or used in manufacturing.

freight forwarder: intermediary who arranges for the shipping of goods to customers in other countries.

front-line manager: supervisor who oversees the day-to-day operations in specific departments of a business.

futures market: a market in which investors and others may buy or sell contracts on the future prices of commodities, metals, and financial instruments.

G

geocentric approach: a human resources approach that uses the best available managers for a business without regard for their country of origin.

global dependency: a situation in which many of the items consumers need and want are created in other countries.

global product: a standardized item offered in the same form in all countries in which it is sold.

grievance procedure: a clause in most collective bargaining contracts that provides for a number of steps if an employee of the union or the employer has a complaint.

gross domestic product (GDP): measures the total value of all goods and services produced by the resources within a country's borders, including items produced with foreign resources.

gross national product (GNP): measures the total value of all goods and services produced by the resources of a country, both within its borders and outside of its borders.

H

hard currency: a monetary unit that is freely convertible into other currencies.

hardware: the physical parts—electronic devices and plastic housing—that make up a computer system.

home country: the country in which a multinational enterprise is headquartered.

home-country national: expatriate from the country where the company for which he or she works is headquartered.

host country: a country in which a multinational enterprise is a guest.

host-country national: native of the country in which she or he works, especially someone working for a foreign company.

human resources: people and their physical and intellectual abilities.

I

imports: products bought by a company or government from a business in another country.

income statement: document that summarizes a company's revenue from sales and its expenses over a period of time, such as a year.

indirect distribution channel: goods or services are sold with the use of one or more intermediaries between the producer and consumer.

indirect exporting: a company selling its products in a foreign market without any special activity for that purpose.

individualism: belief in the individual and her or his ability to function relatively independently.

industrialized country: a country with strong business activity usually resulting from advanced technology and a highly educated population.

industry: companies involved in the same type of business.

540 *Glossary*

inference rules: the processes of comparing the knowledge base to new circumstances.

inflation: an increase in the average prices of goods and services in a country.

information: data that have been processed and organized into a usable format.

informational interview: a meeting with another person to gather information about a career or organization.

infrastructure: a nation's transportation and communications systems.

injunction: a court order that immediately stops a party from carrying out a specific action until the court has heard both sides of the issue.

inland marine insurance: covers the risk of shipping goods on inland waterways, railroad lines, truck lines, and airlines.

insurance: planned protection for sharing economic losses among many people.

insurance certificate: a document that explains the amount of insurance coverage for fire, theft, water, or other damage that may occur to goods in shipment.

insurance policy: the legal agreement between an insurance company and the insured.

intellectual property: the technical knowledge or creative work developed by a person or business.

interest rate: the cost of using someone else's money.

intermediary: person or organization in the distribution channel that moves goods and services from the producer to the consumer.

internal data sources: sources that provide input from within an organization.

international business: business activities necessary for creating, shipping, and selling goods and services across national borders. Also called *foreign trade.*

International Court of Justice: established by the Charter of the United Nations to settle disputes between nations at the request of both parties; also advises the U.N. on matters of international law.

international marketing: marketing activities between sellers and buyers in different countries.

International Monetary Fund (IMF): a cooperative deposit bank established in 1946; helps to promote economic cooperation by maintaining an orderly system of world trade and exchange rates.

international product: a product that is customized or adapted to the culture, tastes, and social trends of a country.

inventory control: monitoring the amount of raw materials and completed goods on hand.

issue: controversial matter for which there may be no final answer.

J

job: an employment position obtained mainly for money.

job description: a document that includes the job identification, statement, duties and responsibilities, and specifications and requirements.

joint venture: an agreement between two or more companies to share a business project.

just-in-time (JIT): a method of inventory control that ties the manufacturer closely to a material supplier so that raw materials are provided only when the production process needs them.

K

knowledge base: historical data on a subject from which to draw comparisons to current data.

L

labor union: an organization of workers formed for the purpose of improving members' working conditions, wages, and benefits.

less-developed country (LDC): a country with little economic wealth and emphasis on agriculture or mining.

letter of credit: a financial document issued by a bank in which the bank guarantees payment.

liability: a broad legal term referring to almost every kind of responsibility, duty, or obligation; in business law, responsibilities relating to debt, loss, burden, or product liability.

licensing: selling the right to use some intangible property for a fee or royalty.

limited liability: a shareholder's responsibility for debts of the corporation that extends only up to the amount invested by the shareholder.

lines of authority: channels that indicate who is responsible to whom and for what.

liquidity: the ability to easily convert an asset into cash without a loss in value.

litigation: a lawsuit or a contest in a court of law to enforce a person's or an organization's rights or to seek a remedy to the violation of their rights.

local: native of the country in which he or she works.

local area network (LAN): a computer network designed for a limited area (such as an

office); it connects a series of computers and peripheral equipment via a continuous wire.

localized advertising: the use of promotions that are customized for various target markets.

local national: an employee based in her or his home country.

lockout: a right of employers to lock employees out of the workplace if they believe that the union's demands are unreasonable.

loss leader: a very low-priced item used to attract customers to a store with the hope that shoppers will buy other items while there.

M

mainframe computer: a large, fast computer that can handle many tasks at once.

management contract: a situation in which a company sells only its management skills.

management information systems (MIS): a computer-based system that delivers information to all levels of management in a company.

manager: person in charge of organizations and resources.

manual production: the process of using human hands and bodies as the means of

transforming resources into goods and services.

market: the likely customers for a good or service.

market economy: a system of supply and demand in which individual companies and consumers decide what, how, and for whom goods and services are to be produced.

marketing: activities necessary to get goods and services from the producer to the consumer.

marketing mix: the combination of product, price, distribution, and promotion to be considered when marketing a good or service.

marketing plan: a document that details the marketing activities of an organization.

marketing research: the orderly collecting and analyzing of data to obtain information about a specific marketing situation.

market price: the point at which supply equals demand.

market segment: a distinct subgroup of customers that share certain personal and behavioral characteristics.

markup: an amount added to the cost of a product to determine the selling price; includes operating costs and a profit.

mediation: a dispute settlement alternative that makes

use of a neutral third party to reconcile the disputing parties' viewpoints.

microcomputer: a small computer designed to run software applications at home, in schools, and in small businesses; also called a personal computer (PC).

microprocessor: an arrangement of tens of thousands of transistors and other electronic parts on a silicon chip about the size of a fingernail; some can process millions of tasks per second.

middle manager: supervisor who oversees the work and departments of front-line managers.

minicomputer: generally, a desktop-sized computer that has less capacity and operates more slowly than a mainframe computer.

mixed economy: an economic system that blends government and private ownership.

money: anything people will accept for the exchange of goods and services.

monopolistic competition: a market situation with many sellers who each have a slightly different product.

monopoly: a market situation in which one seller controls the entire market (holds the entire supply) for a product or service; usually government regulated.

most favored nation (MFN) status: conferred on a country to allow it to export to the granting country under the lowest customs duty rates.

multinational company or corporation (MNC): an organization that conducts business in several countries.

municipal bond: debt certificate issued by a state or local government agency.

municipal corporation: an incorporated town or city organized to provide services for citizens rather than to make a profit.

mutual fund: an investment company that combines funds from many investors.

mutual insurance company: an insurance company owned by its policyholders.

N

natural resources: the basic elements from the air, water, or earth that can be used to create goods.

negligence: the failure to follow a generally accepted standard of care.

net income or **profit:** the difference between money taken in by a business and payments for expenses by the business.

nonprofit corporation: corporation that is organized to pro-

vide a service and is not concerned with making a profit.

nonverbal communication: communication that does not involve the use of words.

nuclear family: a parent or parents and unmarried children living at home.

O

observational research: data collected by watching and recording shopping behaviors.

ocean marine insurance: protects goods while shipped overseas and while temporarily in port.

oligopoly: a market situation in which a few large sellers, offering slightly different products, control the industry.

open shop: an arrangement in which workers at a union-represented workplace may choose not to join the union and not pay a fee.

operations management: the process of designing and managing a production system.

opportunity cost: resources given up when a choice is made.

organizational chart: a drawing that shows the structure of an organization.

over-the-counter market (OTC): a network of stockbrokers who buy and sell stocks not listed on a stock exchange.

P

parent-country national: expatriate from the country where the company for which she or he works is headquartered.

participative manager: manager who decentralizes power and shares decision making with employees.

partnership: a business that is owned by two or more people, but is not incorporated.

passport: a government document proving the bearer's citizenship in the country that issues it.

patent: the exclusive right of an inventor to make, sell, and use a product or process.

penetration pricing: a management decision to set a relatively low introductory price for a new product in order to gain strong market acceptance or take sales from competitors.

personal selling: direct spoken communication between sellers and potential customers.

political risk: the possibility that government actions or political policies will change in such a way that foreign companies operating in those countries are adversely affected.

political system: the means by which people in any soci-

ety make the rules by which they live.

polycentric approach: a human resources approach that uses natives of the parent country of a business to manage operations within the parent country and uses natives of the host country to manage operations in the host country.

premium: the cost of insurance.

price: the monetary value of a product agreed on between a buyer and a seller.

primary data: data collected to solve a specific research problem.

privatization: the process of selling government-owned companies to private citizens.

product: an item (good or service) offered for sale that satisfies consumer demand.

production process: the means by which a company changes raw materials into finished goods.

productivity: the amount of work that is accomplished in a unit of time.

product liability: the specific responsibility that both manufacturers and sellers have for the safety of a product.

product life cycle (PLC): the stages a product goes through

from the time it is introduced until it is taken off the market.

product line: an assortment of closely related products to meet the varied needs of targeted customers.

promissory note: a document that states a promise to pay a set amount by a certain date.

promotion: marketing efforts that inform and persuade customers.

promotional mix: the particular combination of advertising, personal selling, publicity, and sales promotions used by an organization.

property: everything that can be the subject of ownership—such as land, money, stocks and bonds, buildings, factories, and other goods; also intellectual property (patents, trademarks, and copyrights).

property rights: in democratic countries, the exclusive rights to possess and use property and its profits, to exclude everyone else from interfering with it, and to dispose of it in every legal way.

protectionism: a government policy of protecting local or domestic industries from foreign competition.

psychographics: buying factors related to lifestyle and psychological influences.

publicity: any form of unpaid promotion, such as a newspaper article or television news coverage.

pull promotions: marketing efforts directed at the final users of an item.

pure competition: a market situation with many sellers each offering a nearly identical product.

push promotions: marketing efforts directed at members of the distribution channel.

Q

qualitative research: data collection using open-ended interview questions.

quality circle: small group of employees from different parts of the company who meet to improve the quality of goods, services, and processes within a company.

quality control: the process of measuring goods and services against a product standard.

quantitative research: large-scale surveys that collects numeric data.

quota: a limit on the total number, quantity, or monetary amount of a product that can be imported from a given country.

R

random access memory (RAM): main computer memory storage that is easily accessible and stores the operating system, applications, programs, and data.

read only memory (ROM): computer memory (storage) that is permanently installed in the CPU when the computer is manufactured; can only be read and used, not altered.

references: people who can report to a prospective employer on one's abilities and experiences.

regiocentric approach: a human resources approach that uses managers from various countries within the geographic regions of a business.

repatriation: the process of a worker returning home and getting settled after having worked and lived abroad.

representation election: an election held to find out if the workers in a workplace want to be represented by a union.

résumé: a written summary of a person's education, training, experience, and other job qualifications; personal data sheet.

retailer: store or other business that sells directly to the final user.

risk: the uncertainty of an event or outcome.

robotics: the technology connected with the design, construction, and operation of robots.

robots: computerized output devices that can perform difficult, repetitive, or dangerous work in industrial settings.

S

sales promotion: all promotional activities other than advertising, personal selling, and publicity; includes coupons, contests, free samples, and in-store displays.

savings and loan association: a business that traditionally specialized in savings accounts and home mortgages; today, it also offers checking accounts, auto loans, financial planning advice, and electronic banking.

scarcity: the result of limited resources available to satisfy the unlimited wants and needs of a people.

screening interview: an initial meeting to select finalists from the applicant pool for an employment position.

secondary data: data that have already been collected and published.

selection interview: a post-screening session that involves a series of in-depth questions designed to select the best person for a job.

self-insurance: setting aside money to cover a potential financial loss.

senior manager: supervisor who oversees the work and departments of a number of middle managers.

shopping goods: products purchased after consumers compare brands and stores.

skim pricing: a management decision to charge as much as possible for a new product; attracts buyers not concerned with price and quickly covers research and development costs.

small business: an independently owned and operated business that does not dominate an industry.

socialism: an economic system in which most basic industries are owned by the government.

social responsibility: functioning as a good citizen, sensitive to the surroundings.

soft currency: a currency that is not easy to exchange for other currencies.

software: a computer program that is the instructions used by the computer and CPU.

sole or **single proprietorship:** a business owned by one person.

span of control: the number of employees that a manager supervises.

specialty goods: unique products that consumers make a special effort to obtain.

spreadsheet: a computer program that allows the user to arrange and calculate numeric information in columns and rows.

standardized advertising: the use of one promotional approach in all geographic regions.

statute: law that has been enacted by a body of law makers.

stockbroker: a person who buys and sells stocks and other investment vehicles for customers.

stock certificate: the document that represent ownership in a corporation.

stock exchange: a location where stocks are bought and sold.

stockholders or **shareholders:** the owners of a corporation.

stock insurance company: an insurance company owned by stockholders and operated for profit.

storage access network (SAN): a computer network that can work in connection with a local area network by doing the read/write tasks for the file server and storing the data.

strike: a refusal by employees to work in order to force an employer to agree to certain demands.

subculture: a subset or part of a larger culture; it may have values, beliefs, and assumptions that vary from the larger culture of which it is a part.

supply: the amount of a good or service that businesses are willing and able to make available at a certain price.

supply analysis: determining if there are sufficient types and numbers of employees available.

synchronized manufacturing: evolved from the just-in-time (JIT) inventory system, an approach to productivity in which the work flow is distributed as needed throughout the production cycle.

strict liability: imposes responsibility on a manufacturer or seller for intentionally or unintentionally causing injury.

T

tailored logistics: combining services with a product to better serve consumers.

target market: the particular market segment that a company plans to serve.

tariff: a tax on imported goods; also called a *duty*.

tax-deferred income: income that will be taxed at a later date.

tax-exempt income: income not subject to tax.

tax holiday: an arrangement by which a host country charges no corporate income tax of a foreign corporation in exchange for the foreign corporation investing in the host country.

telecommuting: using a computer and other technology to work at home instead of in a company office or factory.

telemarketing: selling products during telephone calls to prospective customers.

test market: an experimental research study that measures the likely success of a new product.

third-country national: citizen of one country, employed by a company from another country, who works in a third country.

totalitarian system: a political system in which most people are excluded from making the rules by which they live.

total quality control (TQC): a quality control system that requires every employee to take responsibility for high-quality production of a good or service.

trade barriers: restrictions that reduce free trade among countries.

trade embargo: an order imposed against a foreign country to prohibit all import-export trade with that country.

trade credit: buying or selling on account.

trade deficit: the total amount a country owes to other countries as a result of importing more than it exports.

trademark: a distinctive name, symbol, word, picture, or combination of these used by a business to identify its services or products.

transformation: the stage of the production process in which resources are used to create a good or service.

U

union shop: an arrangement in which all workers at a union-represented workplace must pay either union dues or a fee.

unlimited liability: the owner's or owners' personal assets can be used to pay for any of the debts of the business that the business cannot satisfy.

V

variable cost: a business expense that changes as the level of production changes.

visa: a stamp of endorsement issued by a country that allows a passport holder to enter that country and to remain for a specified purpose and period of time.

W

wholesaler: intermediary that is a business that buys large quantities of an item and resells them to a retailer.

wholly owned subsidiary: an independent company owned by a parent company.

wide area network (WAN): a computer network that connects computers and peripherals across large geographic areas via telephone lines, satellites, microwaves, or a combination of these.

word processing: a system of keying, changing, and deleting text in a document.

work permit (work visa): a document that allows a person into a foreign country for the purpose of employment.

World Bank: created in 1944 as the International Bank for Reconstruction and Development; provides economic assistance to less developed countries.

Index

export management company
(EMC), 440
export trading company (ETC), 440
Export-Import Bank of the United
States, 330
exporting, 117
barriers to, 122
company, 221
defined, 9
direct, 104, 120
of ice cream, 117
indirect, 103–104, 120
jobs related to, 262
process, 120–122
software for, 343
of U.S. culture, 125
of U.S. food products, 71
express contract, 171
expropriation, 80
extended family, 50–51
external data sources, 322
external motivation, 214
extracting companies, 186
eye contact, communication through,
58

F

face-saving, 57
facsimile machines (fax), 353, 382
factories, automated, 363–365
factors of production, 30–31
family units, 50–51
family-work relationships, 51–52
FAS (Foreign Agricultural Services),
331
fast food industry, 3, 30, 106, 381,
437
fax machines, 353, 382
FCIA (Foreign Credit Insurance
Association), 509
federal government bonds, 487–488
file servers, 327
film industry, U.S., 207
financial agencies, international,
147–150
financial experts, 521
financial records, small business,
193–194
financing
defined, 151–152
international, 150–153
long-tern, 152
short-term, 152

FinnTrade Inc., 183
fixed costs, 192
floating exchange rates, 145
flow of funds, international,
475–477
FOB (free-on-board), 121
focus group, 415
Food and Drug Administration (FDA),
300
food products, U.S. export of, 71
Ford Motor Co., 365
Foreign Agricultural Services (FAS),
331
Foreign Credit Insurance Association
(FCIA), 509
foreign debt, 40
foreign direct investment, 108
foreign exchange, 141–147
activities, 145–147
balance of payments, effect of,
142
controls, 147
defined, 141
economic conditions, effect of,
143–144
market, 146–147, 489
political stability, effect of, 144
rate, 40
tourism and, 147
foreign government agencies, 332
foreign products, demand for, 5
foreign suppliers, 118
foreign trade
economic effect of, 123–125
economics of, 36–37
payment methods, 151, 153
zones, 77
franchising, 106
free enterprise systems, 32–33
free on board (FOB), 121
free-rein managers, 210
free-trade agreements, 78
free-trade zones, 77, 127–128
freight, 121
freight forwarder, 122, 440
French cuisine, 59
front-line managers, 218, 219
function, organization by, 215–216
funds
for small businesses, 192
sources of, 476–477
uses of, 477
future markets, 489
futures, currency, 146–147

G

GATT. *See* General Agreement on
Tariffs and Trade (GATT)
gauchos (cowboys), 411
GDP (gross domestic product),
37–38
gender roles, 51
General Agreement on Tariffs and
Trade (GATT), 73–74, 125,
172
general merchandise retailers, 438
generics, 418
geocentric approach to human
resources management, 236
geography
consumer behavior and,
391–392
organization by, 217
Germany, 440–441
Ghana, 150, 480
Glaxton company, 300
global advertising, 456–461
global brands, 418
global business risk. *See* international business risk
global business technology,
338–357
global companies. *See* multinational
corporations (MNCs)
global dependency, 5
global financial activities, 150–153,
474–493. *See also* global
financial institutions
bond market, 486–488
computerized markets, 490
flow of funds, 475–477
foreign exchange market, 489
future market, 489
international agencies for,
137–150, 331
investments, 5, 516–522
over-the-counter market, 489
payment methods, 151, 153
sources of financing, 151–152
stock market, 482–486
global financial institutions,
477–482
deposit-type, 478–480
life insurance companies, 481
mutual funds, 480–481, 482
global insurance coverages,
506–510
global management skills, 223

Acknowledgments

COVER
© SuperStock, Inc.

PREFACE
p. iii: © R. Ian Lloyd/Westlight.

TABLE OF CONTENTS
p. vii: top: © Dallas & John Heaton/Westlight; **bottom:** © K. Kummels/SuperStock, Inc.; **p. viii:** © Nicholas DeVore/Tony Stone Images; **p. ix: top:** © Greg Stott/Masterfile; **bottom:** © Steven Rothfeld/Tony Stone Images; **p. x: top:** © S. Vidler/SuperStock, Inc.; **bottom:** © Warren Jacobs/Tony Stone Images; **p. xi: top:** © Dallas & John Heaton/Westlight; **bottom:** © H. Kanus/SuperStock, Inc.; **p. xii: top:** © Nicholas DeVore/Tony Stone Images; **bottom:** © W. Strode/SuperStock, Inc.; **p. xiii:** © Jeff Greenberg.

UNIT 1
p. xiv: top: © Richard Simpson/Tony Stone Images; **bottom:** ® The Procter & Gamble Company. Used with permission.; **p. 1:** © Malak/SuperStock, Inc.

CHAPTER 1
p. 2: Bruce Rowell/Masterfile; **p. 3:** Greg Stott/Masterfile; **p. 5:** © Jed Share/Westlight; **p. 8:** AP/Wide World Photos; **p. 11:** © Howard Grey/Tony Stone Images; **p. 13:** © John Edwards/Tony Stone Images.

UNIT 1 REGIONAL PROFILE
p. 20: © Donovan Reese/Tony Stone Images.

CHAPTER 2
p. 22: © Mark Harwood/Tony Stone Images; **p. 23:** © K. Kummels/SuperStock, Inc.; **p. 26:** © Walter Hodges/Westlight; **p. 30:** Star-Kist Foods, Inc.; **p. 34:** AP/Wide World Photos; **p. 37:** © Xavier Richer/Tony Stone Images.

CHAPTER 3
p. 45: © Lois Ellen Frank/Westlight; **p. 46:** AP/Wide World Photos; **p. 50:** © Walter Hodges/Westlight; **p. 53:** © Nicholas DeVore/Tony Stone Images; **p. 54:** © 1994 by Sidney Harris; **p. 61: top:** © Mike Timo/Tony Stone Images; **bottom:** © Warren Morgan/Westlight; **p. 63:** © Ralph Mercer/Tony Stone Images.

CHAPTER 4
p. 70: © Mark Segal/Tony Stone Images; **p. 71:** © Wendt WorldWide; **p. 73:** © J. DeSelliers/SuperStock, Inc.; **p. 77:** © Paul Chesley/Tony Stone Images; **p. 83:** © Wendt WorldWide.

UNIT 2
p. 90: top: © Dallas & John Heaton/Westlight; **bottom:** Eastman Kodak Company; **p. 91:** © Nicholas DeVore/Tony Stone Images.

CHAPTER 5
p. 92: © Greg Pease/Tony Stone Images; **p. 93:** MC Machinery Systems, Inc., a company of Mitsubishi Corporation; **p. 100:** International Committee of the Red Cross; **p. 104:** © Randy Faris/Westlight.

UNIT 2 REGIONAL PROFILE
p. 114: © Jeff Greenberg.

CHAPTER 6
p. 116: © M. Fife/SuperStock, Inc.; **p. 117:** © J. Amster/SuperStock, Inc.; **p. 121:** Pepsi-Cola International; **p. 125:** AP/Wide World Photos; **p. 129:** adidas Predator soccer shoes; **p. 132:** © Robert Everts/Tony Stone Images.

CHAPTER 7
p. 137: © Jon Bradley/Tony Stone Images; **p. 138:** AP/Wide World Photos; **p. 141:** © Jeff Greenberg; **p. 145:** Photo courtesy of Vic Huber Photography and Mazda Motor of America; **p. 148:** © J. Smoljan/SuperStock, Inc.; **p. 150:** © H. Lanks/SuperStock, Inc.

CHAPTER 8
p. 159: G. Biss/Masterfile; **p. 160:** G. Biss/Masterfile; **p. 163:** © Billy E. Barnes/Tony Stone Images; **p. 168:** Philips CD-i System; **p. 172:** © Mike Yamashita/Westlight; **p. 178:** © SuperStock, Inc.

CHAPTER 9
p. 182: Pier 1 Imports; **p. 183:** FinnTrade, Inc.; **p. 186:** © Jeff Greenberg; **p. 189:** © Jeff Greenberg; **p. 194:** AP/Wide World Photos; **p. 198:** © M. Roessler/SuperStock, Inc.

UNIT 3
p. 204: **top:** © Jeff Greenberg; **bottom:** © John Lawrence/Tony Stone Images; **p. 205:** Photograph by British Petroleum.

CHAPTER 10
p. 206: Mimi Ostendorf/Photonics; **p. 207:** © Don Smetzer/Tony Stone Images; **p. 209:** Larry Williams/Masterfile; **p. 220:** © SuperStock, Inc.; **p. 224:** © Graeme Harris/Tony Stone Images.

UNIT 3 REGIONAL PROFILE
p. 228: AP/Wide World Photos.

CHAPTER 11
p. 230: © Donna Griffith/Westlight; **p. 231:** © Jeff Greenberg; **p. 237:** © W. Cody/Westlight; **p. 241:** © Robert E. Daemmrich/Tony Stone Images; **p. 243:** © Jeff Greenberg; **p. 246:** © Frank Herholdt/Tony Stone Images; **p. 249:** AP/Wide World Photos.

CHAPTER 12
p. 258: © Jim Pickerell/Tony Stone Images; **p. 262:** © Lloyd Sutton/Masterfile; **p. 266:** © Robert E. Daemmrich/Tony Stone Images; **p. 270:** © Robert E. Daemmrich/Tony Stone Images; **p. 275:** © Philip & Karen Smith/Tony Stone Images.

CHAPTER 13
p. 280: © S. Vidler/SuperStock, Inc.; **p. 281:** AP/Wide World Photos; **p. 284:** AP/Wide World Photos; **p. 288:** © Brian Leng/Westlight; **p. 290:** © Mathew Neal McVay/Tony Stone Images; **p. 291:** © Jeff Greenberg.

CHAPTER 14
p. 299: © SuperStock, Inc.; **p. 300:** © Charles Thatcher/Tony Stone Images; **p. 302:** © Barry Rowland/Tony Stone Images; **p. 310:** © Brian Sytnyk/Masterfile.

UNIT 4
p. 318: **top:** © SuperStock, Inc.; **bottom:** © Jacques Jangoux/Tony Stone Images; **p. 319:** © Dallas & John Heaton/Westlight.

CHAPTER 15
p. 320: © Keith Ballinger/Masterfile; **p. 321:** Milt & Joan Mann, Cameramann International, Limited; **p. 324:** Blockbuster Entertainment Corporation; **p. 325:** Picture provided by Ameritech Mobile Communications, Inc.; **p. 330:** Photo by Richard Anderson, M.D.; **p. 332:** © Larry Fisher/Masterfile.

UNIT 4 REGIONAL PROFILE
p. 336: © G. Ricatto/SuperStock, Inc.

CHAPTER 16
p. 338: © Phil Jason/Tony Stone Images; **p. 339:** © Mark Tomalty/Masterfile; **p. 340:** © Hans Blohm/Masterfile; **p. 345:** Photo provided courtesy of Eastman Kodak Company; **p. 351:** © Mike Yamashita/Westlight; **p. 353:** Pitney Bowes Facsimile Systems.

CHAPTER 17
p. 358: © Mike Dobel/Masterfile; **p. 359:** © Kevin & Cat Sweeney/Tony Stone Images; **p. 361:** © G. Vikentiev/SuperStock, Inc.; **p. 364:** © Charles Thatcher/Tony Stone Images; **p. 369:** © W. Jacobs/SuperStock, Inc.; **p. 370:** © Manoj Shah/Tony Stone Images.

UNIT 5
p. 376: **top:** Photo courtesy of Colgate-Palmolive Company; **bottom:** © Donald Nausbaum/Tony Stone Images; **p. 377:** © D. Brown/SuperStock, Inc.

CHAPTER 18
p. 378: © S. Vidler/SuperStock, Inc.; **p. 379:** © Cathlyn Melloan/Tony Stone Images; **p. 381:** Kentucky Fried Chicken (KFC) Corporation, Louisville, KY; **p. 386:** © Norbert Wu/Tony Stone Images; **p. 393:** © Michael S. Yamashita/Westlight.

UNIT 5 REGIONAL PROFILE
p. 400: © Michael Scott/Tony Stone Images.

CHAPTER 19
p. 402: Photo courtesy of Colgate-Palmolive Company; **p. 403:** Photo by Erik Von Fischer/Photonics; **p. 406:** Photo courtesy of Colgate-Palmolive Company; **p. 408:** © Jeff Greenberg; **p. 411:** © Carlos Goldin/Westlight; **p. 417:** © Jeff Greenberg.

CHAPTER 20
p. 426: © David Joel/Tony Stone Images; **p. 427:** Toys "Я" Us, Inc., Kashihara Store, Nara, Japan; **p. 434:** © Jeff Greenberg; **p. 441:** © A. Upitis/SuperStock, Inc.; **p. 444:** © Hans Blohm/Masterfile.

CHAPTER 21
p. 450: © D. Forbert/SuperStock, Inc.; **p. 451:** Photo by Erik Von Fischer/Photonics; **p. 453:** © Wynn Miller/Tony Stone Images; **p. 460:** © S. Vidler/SuperStock, Inc.; **p. 464:** © Dave Cannon/Tony Stone Images.

UNIT 6
p. 472: **top:** Photo by Arthur Meyerson; **bottom:** © James Willis/Tony Stone Images; **p. 473:** © H. Kanus/SuperStock, Inc.

CHAPTER 22
p. 474: © John Lamb/Tony Stone Images; **p. 475:** © Oliver Benn/Tony Stone Images; **p. 478:** © Jim Zuckerman/Westlight; **p. 482:** © Roger Tully/Tony Stone Images; **p. 487:** © Gary A. Bartholomew/Westlight; **p. 489:** © Andy Sacks/Tony Stone Images.

UNIT 6 REGIONAL PROFILE
p. 494: © Nabeel Turner/Tony Stone Images.

CHAPTER 23
p. 496: © Boden/Ledingham/Masterfile; **p. 497:** © Doug Armand/Tony Stone Images; **p. 500:** © Pierre Kopp/Westlight; **p. 504:** © Jeff Greenberg; **p. 507:** © Ron Sherman/Tony Stone Images; **p. 510:** © R. Ian Lloyd/Westlight.